UNDERSTANDING
DIABETES

A handbook for people who are living with diabetes

12TH EDITION

H. Peter Chase, MD
&
David M. Maahs, MD, PhD

BARBARA DAVIS CENTER FOR CHILDHOOD DIABETES
DEPARTMENT OF PEDIATRICS
UNIVERSITY OF COLORADO AT DENVER
AND HEALTH SCIENCES CENTER

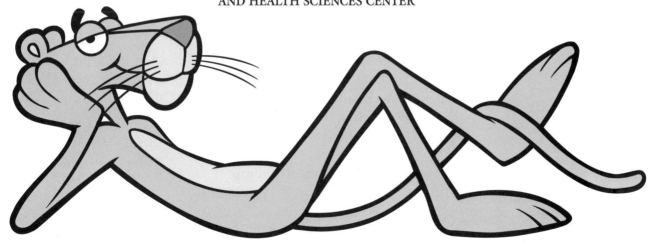

CHILDREN'S DIABETES FOUNDATION
AT DENVER

For information, contact

Children's Diabetes Foundation at Denver
777 Grant Street, Suite 302
Denver, CO 80203

www.childrensdiabetesfdn.org

Chase, H. Peter.
    Understanding diabetes / H. Peter Chase. — 12th ed.
    p. cm.
    Includes bibliographical references and index.
    LCCN 2005935089
    ISBN 978-0-9832650-0-9

    1. Diabetes--Popular works.   I. Title.

RC660.4.C43 2006   616.4'62
                          QBI05-200170

Production Management by
Paros Press
1551 Larimer Street, Suite 1301   Denver, CO 80202
303-893-3331   www.parospress.com

Book Design by Scott Johnson

Printed in the United States of America

1 3 5 7 9 10 8 6 4 2

Dedication

Dedicated to all of
the diabetes educators worldwide.
Their dedication helps the millions of people
with diabetes, and their families,
to learn about the disease so
they can manage it and
lead happy and fulfilling lives.

A big THANK YOU!

Table of Contents

Please note: Many parts of this book have been written at an eighth grade level and may be too complex for younger children. A shorter book, *"A First Book for Understanding Diabetes"* is also available. The book follows the same outline and may be more appropriate for them. A parent working with a child in reading and understanding parts of this book may also be helpful.

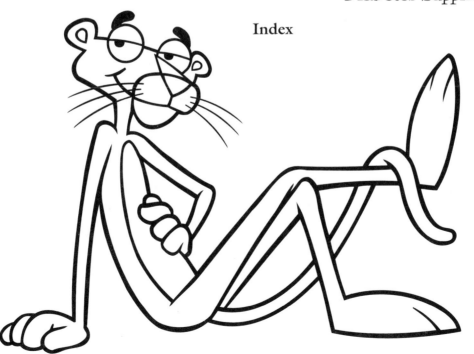

Special Thanks To...

- Editors: Lauren King, BA and Patricia Chase-Hamilton, BA

- Assistant editor, manuscript preparation and typist: Regina Reece

- Proofreaders: Linda Chase, RN, BSN and Jaime Realsen, BS

- Typists: Erica Blum-Barnett, BA and Jaime Realsen, BS

- Scott Johnson for book design, graphics, and illustrations.

- MGM Consumer Products for allowing the use of the Pink Panther™.

    www.pinkpanther.com

Additional copies of this publication may be purchased from the Children's Diabetes Foundation at Denver. See available publications at the end of this book.

Topics for the
Recommended ADA Curriculum

with Their Related Chapters

TOPIC	CHAPTER LOCATION
Diabetes disease process	1-4
Goal setting and problem solving	10, 13, 14 and 18-21
Medications	4, 8, 9, 22 and 28
Monitoring	1, 4, 5, 7, 14, 21-26 and 30
Nutritional management	4, 11 and 12
Physical activity	4, 13 and 27
Preconception care, management during pregnancy and gestational management	19, 23 and 30
Prevent, detect and treat acute complications	4-6, 15, 16, 25, 26 and 30
Prevent, detect and treat chronic complications	4, 14, 23, 24 and 31
Psychosocial adjustment	10, 17-27

TEACHING OBJECTIVES:
These are provided with each chapter to assist the person(s) doing the teaching.

LEARNING OBJECTIVES:
These are provided with each chapter to help the learners (parents, child, relatives or self) know the important points.

Chapter 1
The Importance of Education in Diabetes

TEACHING OBJECTIVES:

1. Design a care plan that reflects the family's lifestyle and the person's educational level/developmental stage (also see Chapters 17-20).

2. Design a care plan that allows the person/family to become skilled in the management of diabetes.

LEARNING OBJECTIVES:

Learners (parents, child, relative or self) will be able to:

1. Identify basic management routines.

2. Assist the healthcare provider in developing a diabetes care plan.

3. Begin the process of understanding management through charting and recording blood sugars or using electronic downloads as directed by the healthcare provider.

4. Communicate blood sugars to healthcare provider.

5. Communicate concerns about high or low blood sugars to healthcare provider.

INTRODUCTION

Families and children need to understand as much as possible about diabetes. A shorter book, *"A First Book for Understanding Diabetes"* is also available. It provides a synopsis of each of the chapters in this book, and may be easier for a family with a newly diagnosed child to read in the first week after diagnosis. The knowledge provided in this book and the skills learned will help people with diabetes and their families feel more secure about managing diabetes. It will help them manage problems when no doctor or nurse is available. It will also help them minimize hospitalizations for diabetes problems. Families who feel they can manage diabetes confidently maintain control, rather than the diabetes controlling them.

This book is written for families when diabetes is a new condition to them. It is also for those who have had the condition for a long time. It may serve as a reference that can be used with the doctor and diabetes team. It may also be used alone as a "refresher" course. Some of the chapters are written to provide very basic information. Other chapters are for readers wanting more in-depth information. Advances are taking place at such a rapid rate that new editions are needed about every three years. Families may choose to bring this book to clinic appointments. It can then be used as a guide for discussion and learning. This is particularly important in the first year after diagnosis.

One of the major changes currently occurring in diabetes management involves the use of continuous glucose monitors (CGM). Thus a new chapter (Chapter 29) on CGM use has been added. In addition, rather than referring only to blood glucose levels, the words blood/CGM glucose levels are now used when appropriate. This notes that the glucose value may be from a blood or a CGM value (or both).

OUTLINE FOR INITIAL EDUCATION (Table 1)

Initial education is variable based on:

- how sick the person is
- the emotional and physical readiness of the person and family to learn
- hospitalization versus outpatient care
- the availability of appropriately trained educators and healthcare team

It is **essential for all parents, guardians** or other care-providers to be present for the initial education. Most families initially come to the clinic for six to eight hours per day for one to two days.

Initial survival skills are required prior to home care:

- ✔ use of the blood glucose meter
- ✔ drawing up insulin
- ✔ giving shots
- ✔ checking ketones
- ✔ handling possible low blood sugar

Topics are covered in the order of importance. How much is covered the first day depends on the family's emotional state and readiness to learn. Additional teaching may require more than one day.

After approximately one week the family returns for group and individual education and care. Families are not expected to remember all the information the first time. Written guidelines are always given to the family at each visit to ensure safety at home. Review and reinforcement of basic concepts occur at each visit. The content of this book should be used for periodic review as needed.

Helpful ways to continue learning are:

- writing down questions and making notes
- websites: www.ChildrenWithDiabetes.com or www.BarbaraDavisCenter.org (please see the back of the book for additional website addresses)

- video tapes and library books
- parent and child educational group meetings

The topics considered important for initial diabetes education by the American Diabetes Association (ADA) are outlined at the beginning of this publication. The chapters where each of these topics is covered are also shown. Please let your diabetes healthcare provider know if there are topics which apply to you/your child that are unclear or ones which you would like to spend more time discussing.

It is essential that families know how to recognize and handle low blood sugar from day one. Anyone who has received insulin has the potential to have low blood sugar. Families must understand the causes, signs and treatment of mild to severe low blood sugar, including treatment with gel or glucagon. The educator will discuss this with you. It is the topic of Chapter 6.

CONTINUING EDUCATION

Following initial education, the family usually returns to the clinic:

- in one week
- after four weeks
- after twelve weeks
- then every three months

This may vary for different families and different clinics. Clinic visits every three months should include an evaluation of the family's current diabetes management. Modifications to care are made with feedback from the person and family. Children who were too young to learn self-care when diagnosed with diabetes will need age-appropriate ongoing education. Clinic visits every three months with the healthcare team can assist in their learning process.

Children who develop diabetes prior to age 10-13 will need to learn specifics about the disease as they are ready. A science project on diabetes is one way to encourage learning and self-discovery. This book can provide information for such a report.

The diabetes nurse educator may start working on chapters in the book with the child alone. This can encourage the child to ask and answer questions. Education from *all* the diabetes team members should continue with the every-three-month clinic visits as needed. We feel a solid educational foundation and the development of good habits will help the person to stay in good diabetes control throughout life. With a supportive family and good habits, the need for later diabetes-related hospitalizations or problems is reduced.

FAMILY RESPONSIBILITIES

Diabetes is a unique disease. It requires ongoing communication and assistance between the person and significant others in all areas of the day-to-day care. **A knowledgeable and supportive family is very important for good diabetes care.** This is discussed in more detail in Chapter 17, Family Concerns.

Families must assume responsibility for:

- consistency in meals, snacks, shots
- doing blood sugar checks as directed
- insulin injections (type 1), oral medicines and/or insulin (type 2)
- blood or urine ketone checks
- ordering and having supplies available
- communication with day care/school or work
- contacting healthcare providers for insulin adjustments between routine visits when blood sugar numbers are out of the desired range
- maintaining knowledge for treating high and low blood sugars and learning about new developments in diabetes treatment

It should be apparent that the family does 95 percent of the diabetes management.

Table 1

Topics Covered After New Diagnosis

Survival Skills in Hospital or Clinic

Different clinics have different schedules for education of newly diagnosed families. Education may be done primarily in the clinic setting (after discharge if hospitalization was necessary). Day one usually involves learning survival skills needed for care in the home setting.

These include:
- ☐ Blood sugar testing on a specific meter (Chapter 7)
- ☐ Learning about insulin (Chapter 8)
- ☐ How to draw up and administer insulin (Chapter 9)
- ☐ Urine or blood ketone measurements (Chapter 5)
- ☐ Recognizing the signs of low blood sugar and how to treat (Chapter 6)

We write specific instructions (see Table 2) for the family. These relate to: meals, snacks, when to test blood sugar or urine ketone levels and how to record results, and when to phone us. The dietitian may discuss ideas for meals and snacks.

Any of the following may be covered:
- ☐ The Importance of Education in Diabetes (Chapter 1)
- ☐ What is Diabetes? (Chapter 2) And how do we know you have it?
- ☐ What Causes Diabetes? (Chapter 3)
- ☐ Blood Sugar Testing (Chapter 7)
- ☐ Insulin (Chapter 8)
- ☐ Insulin Injections (Chapter 9)
- ☐ Practice injection technique
- ☐ Urine or Blood Ketone Testing (Chapter 5)
- ☐ Low Blood Sugar (Chapter 6)

Additional Initial Education

- ☐ Review above concepts and answer questions
- ☐ Review insulin and insulin injection technique
- ☐ Review Low Blood Sugar (Chapter 6)
- ☐ Normal Nutrition (Chapter 11) and meet with dietitian
- ☐ Food Management and Diabetes (Chapter 12)
- ☐ Prescriptions for supplies
- ☐ Communication plan for the next week
- ☐ Grief-Adjustment Issues (Chapter 10) and meet social worker
- ☐ Review of specific routines and recommendations for exercise (Chapter 13)
- ☐ Monitoring Blood Sugar Control (Chapter 14)
- ☐ Complete the care plan for school/daycare
- ☐ Adjusting insulin (Chapter 22; if appropriate)
- ☐ Review the two emergencies of diabetes (Table 3, Chapter 15)

Additional Initial Education (variable with 1 Week Visit)

- ☐ Review above concepts and answer questions
- ☐ Family Concerns (Chapter 17) and reducing fears of shots and pokes
- ☐ The Outpatient Management of Diabetes (Chapter 21)
- ☐ Long-Term Complications of Diabetes - if questions (Chapters 23 and 24)

At One-Week/ 1 Month Visit

- ☐ Research and Diabetes (Chapter 31)
- ☐ Review all of the above
- ☐ Review Ketonuria, Ketones and Acidosis (Ketoacidosis; Chapter 15)
- ☐ Sick-Day Management (Chapter 16)
- ☐ Problem solving and/or quiz
- ☐ Child-sitters and Diabetes (Chapter 26)
- ☐ Vacations and Camp (Chapter 27)
- ☐ Long-Term Complications of Diabetes - if questions (Chapters 23 and 24)
- ☐ Pregnancy and Diabetes if appropriate (Chapter 30)
- ☐ Problem solving and/or quiz

Table 2

This is a general plan. The timing is varied and may change if the person is hospitalized versus when treated only in the clinic. A trend in recent years has been to teach survival skills in the first one to two days, and to make the visit at one week (when stress is lower) a longer and more in-depth visit.

New Patient First-Night Instructions for _____

A. ***The diabetes supplies you will need the first night include*** *(your nurse will mark which you need):*

____ Blood glucose meter	____ Meter test strips	____ Alcohol swabs
____ Ketone check strips	____ Glucose gel & tabs	____ Log book
____ Insulin	____ Syringes	____ Phone contact card

The first night you will either get your insulin injection at our clinic, or you will give the shot at home or where you are staying.

B. ***If the insulin is given while at the clinic:***
   ☐ 1. If rapid-acting insulin (Humalog®, NovoLog® or Apidra®) has been given, eat in 20 minutes if blood sugar is above 120 mg/dL (>6.7 mmol/L) (may need to eat sooner if below this level).

   ☐ 2. If regular insulin has been given, try to eat your meal within 30 minutes – or – have a snack containing carbohydrates on the way home if it will be more than 30 minutes (or if blood sugar is below 80 mg/dL [8.4 mmol/L]).

   ☐ 3. One of the above insulins and a longer-lasting insulin will be given to cover overnight insulin needs.

   4. Allow your child to eat until their appetite is satisfied, avoiding high sugar foods (especially sugar drinks and sweet desserts).

C. ***If the dinner insulin is to be given at home:***
   1. Check your child's blood sugar right before your meal. Enter the result into the log book.

   2. Check for urine ketones if directed. Enter the result into the log book.

   3. Call Dr. _____ at _____ or page at _____ for an insulin dose or if questions.

      Give this dose: _____.

   4. Draw up and give the insulin injection right before your meal (see Chapter 9). If your child is not very hungry or is tired, you can give the shot after they eat and call the physician with any dose questions.

   5. Eat your meal, allowing your child to eat until their appetite is satisfied. Avoid high sugar foods.

D. ***Before Bed:***
   1. Check your child's blood sugar. Enter the result into the log book.

   2. Check for urine ketones if directed. Enter the result into the log book.

   3. Call your physician at the numbers listed above if your child's blood sugar is below _____ or above _____, or if urine ketones are "moderate" or "large" or if blood ketones are >1.0 mmol/L. If urine ketones are "trace" or "small", have your child drink 8-12 oz of water before going to bed.

   4. Give an insulin injection if your physician instructs you to do so. (Dose, if ordered _____.)

   5. Have your child eat a bedtime snack. Some ideas for this snack include: cereal and milk, toast and peanut butter, a slice of pizza, yogurt and graham crackers or cheese and crackers. (See Chapter 12 in this book for other ideas.)

E. ***The morning before coming to the clinic:***
   1. If your physician has instructed you to give the morning insulin at home before coming in, follow the steps listed above (see letter "**C**") and give dose as directed by MD before eating breakfast.

   2. If you have been instructed to wait to give the morning dose until after coming to the clinic, do a blood sugar test and a urine ketone test if directed upon awakening (if blood sugar is less than 70 mg/dL [<3.9 mmol/L], give 4–6 oz of juice promptly).
      Write the blood sugar and urine ketone results in your log book.
      ☐ Eat breakfast at home, and then come to the clinic for your insulin injection.
      ☐ Bring your breakfast to the clinic, and you will eat it after the insulin has been given.

   3. Please bring all blood testing supplies and materials you received the first day back to the clinic (including your log book, Pink Panther book, insulin and supplies).

8

Chapter 2
What Is Diabetes?

TOPIC:
Diabetes Disease Process

TEACHING OBJECTIVES:
Design informational sessions for families in all chapters with consideration for their:

- educational level
- primary language
- culture or ethnicity
- family structure
- learning style
- previous experience with the medical community

LEARNING OBJECTIVES:
Learners (parents, child, relative or self) will be able to:

1. Define the basic disease process of type 1 and type 2 diabetes (also see Chapters 3 and 4).

2. Define normal and abnormal blood sugars along with HbA1c as part of the diagnosis of diabetes.

3. Define symptoms of type 1 or type 2 diabetes and compare with the symptoms experienced by the patient at diagnosis.

TYPE 1 (INSULIN-DEPENDENT) DIABETES

Type 1 (also known as insulin-dependent diabetes mellitus [IDDM] or juvenile or childhood) diabetes is the most common type found in children and young adults. **This condition occurs when the pancreas (see Figure 1) doesn't make enough insulin.** As explained in Chapter 3, type 1 diabetes is in part due to autoimmunity (a "self-allergy"). Thus, most people having type 1 diabetes have islet-cell antibodies, which reflect an allergy against the islet cells (where insulin is made) in the pancreas.

TYPE 2 DIABETES

There is another kind of diabetes that is sometimes found in overweight pre-teens and teenagers, and is also the most common type of diabetes in adults over age 40 years. It is called **type 2 diabetes**, or sometimes adult-onset or non-insulin-dependent diabetes mellitus (NIDDM). In type 2 diabetes, **insulin is still made** in normal or increased amounts (at least initially), but it doesn't work very well in helping the body use sugar. People who develop childhood (type 1) diabetes are insulin dependent for life. They will always have this type of diabetes. They will not convert to type 2 diabetes as they grow older. Likewise, people with type 2 diabetes do not convert to type 1 diabetes.

In type 2 diabetes, ketones (Chapter 5) may still be present at diagnosis as well as high blood sugars (Chapter 7) and an elevated HbA1c level (Chapter 14). If ketones are present, insulin shots may be started. At a later time, if the islet-cell antibodies (Chapter 3) are negative and the blood sugars and HbA1c levels have decreased to near normal, then oral medications may be tried. **Insulin cannot be taken in pill form because the acid in the stomach would break it down.** Type 2 diabetes is discussed in more depth in Chapter 4.

WHY WE NEED INSULIN:

- **Insulin allows sugar to pass into our cells so that it can be "burned" for our energy.** The cells are like a furnace, which burn fuel to make energy. Our bodies constantly need energy for all of our body functions, such as allowing our heart to beat and our lungs to breathe. Sugar comes from two places (see Figure 2 in this chapter). **"Internal"** sugar comes from our body's own production in the liver or from the release of stored sugar from the liver. This sugar is released into the blood stream. **"External"** sugar comes from the food we eat. It enters the stomach and then moves into the intestine where it is absorbed. When people **do not** have diabetes, the pancreas makes insulin to regulate use of both internal and external sugar. This means a person without diabetes can eat sugary foods and their blood sugar will remain in the normal range.

When people have type 1 diabetes, the pancreas does not make enough insulin. The sugar in the blood can't pass into the body's cells to be burned. Instead, the blood sugar rises to a high level and overflows through the kidneys into the urine. When sugar enters the urine, water is pulled from all over the body to go out with the sugar.

*The results are the usual **SYMPTOMS** of diabetes:*

- **Frequent passing of urine:** to carry excess sugar out of the body

- **Frequent drinking of liquids:** to make up for water lost in the urine

- **Frequent eating of food:** because the body can't use the food it takes in and is hungry for the energy it isn't getting. This

Figure 1:
Body Parts

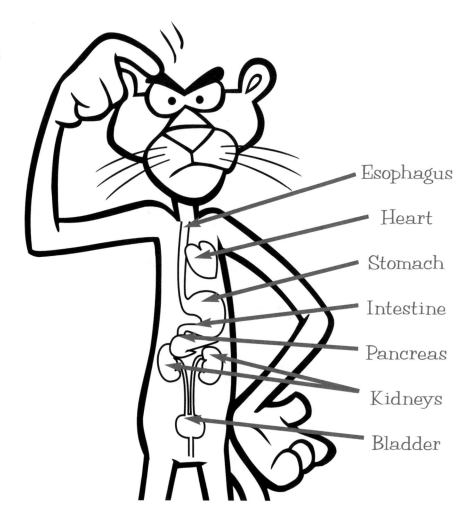

Esophagus

Heart

Stomach

Intestine

Pancreas

Kidneys

Bladder

"Internal" and "External" Sugar Production

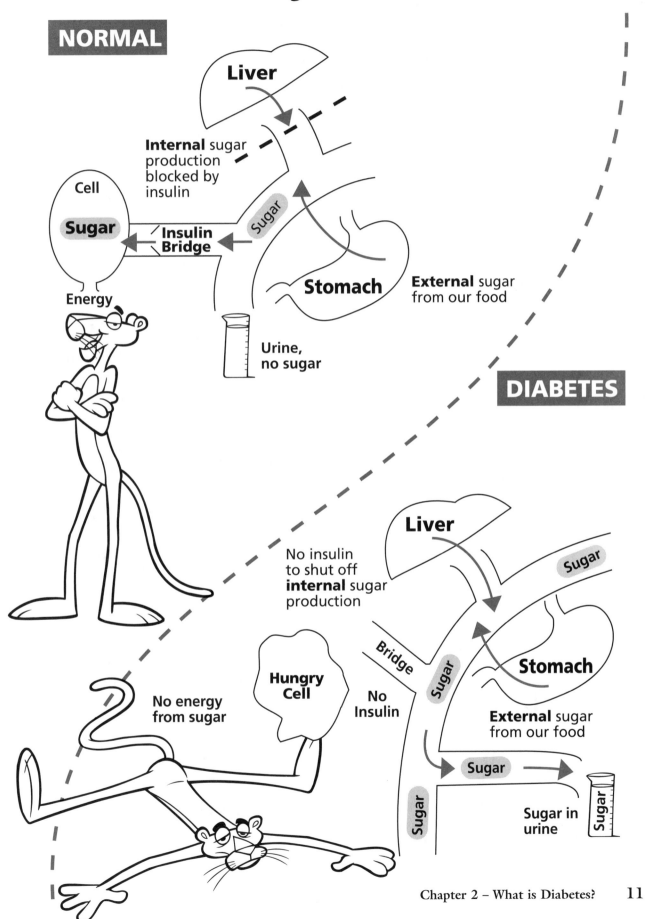

hunger is not always present in children. Sometimes the appetite may even decrease. Ketones (see Chapter 5) can cause an upset stomach and possible vomiting.

🐾 **Weight loss:** when the body can't get sugar into the cells, it burns its own fat and protein for energy. This causes weight loss.

🐾 **Changes in behavior:** if the person is getting up frequently at night to pass urine, sound sleep will not occur. This can result in behavioral changes.

● **A second function of insulin is to shut off the body's internal production of sugar** (Figure 2). This internal sugar mostly comes from the liver. When the insulin level is too low, too much internal sugar is made.

Thus, when there is not enough insulin, the blood sugar level can be high for two reasons:

🐾 Too much internal sugar being made

🐾 The sugar (from internal production and from external food) cannot pass into the cells

HONEYMOON (GRACE) PERIOD

According to what we now know, people with type 1 diabetes will need insulin injections for the rest of their lives. Often, though, there is a honeymoon or grace period that may occur a short time after the onset of diabetes. It commonly starts within two to eight weeks, although not all people have this honeymoon period. During the honeymoon, sugar production is turned off in the liver and a fair bit of insulin is still being made in the pancreas. This is a time when people often think they don't have diabetes. They may be attracted to miracle cures. The honeymoon period may last a few weeks to a few years. During this time, the body may not need much extra insulin. After this period, the body will again need more insulin, although small amounts of insulin may still be made by some. We advise our patients to continue their insulin during the grace period, even though the dose may be small. We know from experience that the body will again need more insulin. Usually with growth, illness or stress there may be a need for more insulin. This need may be evident when the morning blood sugars start to be above the desired range. It is usually hard to begin insulin shots again if the shots were discontinued.

The **MOST IMPORTANT RULE** for the patient with diabetes to remember is: **I MUST TAKE MY INSULIN (OR ORAL MEDICINES) EVERY DAY FROM NOW ON. IF I FORGET MY INSULIN/ORAL MEDICINES, MY DIABETES WILL GET OUT OF CONTROL. THERE IS ABSOLUTELY NO WAY I WILL NOT NEED INSULIN EVERY DAY FROM NOW ON IF I HAVE TYPE 1 DIABETES.** Even if I get sick, I still need insulin. I may need more or less insulin, but I must have it every day. **IMPORTANT:** The only known difference about people who develop type 1 diabetes is that their bodies don't make enough insulin. THE PERSON AND EVERY OTHER PART OF THE BODY ARE OTHERWISE COMPLETELY NORMAL.

DEFINITIONS

Bladder: The organ (sac) that collects the water from the kidneys and holds it until it is passed as urine (see Figure 1).

Bloodstream: The flow of blood within the blood vessels to and from the different parts of the body.

Cells: Very small units of the body. You can only see them with a microscope.

Enzymes: Proteins in liver, muscle and intestine that help make sugar. (There are many enzymes that have other functions.)

Esophagus: The swallowing tube (see Figure 1).

External sugar: The sugar taken in from food. Insulin allows the external sugar to pass into the body's cells to be used for energy.

Insulin: The substance (hormone) made by the pancreas that allows sugar to pass into cells.

Internal sugar: The sugar made by the body (or sugar released from stored sugar in the liver). Insulin shuts off the excess production of internal sugar.

Intestine: The part of the GI tract (gut) below the stomach where most sugar (and other food) is actually absorbed into our blood stream (see Figure 1).

Islet cells (pronounced eye-let): The groups of cells within the pancreas that make insulin.

Islet cell antibody: The material we measure in the person's blood to show that they have had an allergy against the cells in the pancreas (the islet cells) that make insulin. They are usually present in the blood with people with type 1 diabetes, but not of those with type 2 diabetes.

Kidneys: The two organs in the body that remove waste products and water from the bloodstream and make urine (see Figure 1).

Pancreas: The organ where insulin is normally made (see Figure 1). People who have type 1 diabetes cannot make enough insulin and are thus insulin-dependent.

Stomach: Where the food is collected and processed after it is swallowed (see Figure 1).

Type 1 diabetes: (Also called juvenile diabetes or childhood diabetes or insulin-dependent diabetes mellitus [IDDM].) The condition that results when the body cannot make enough insulin. The most common type of diabetes in persons under age 40. Insulin must be taken by shots. Pills do not help. This type of diabetes is discussed in detail in Chapter 3.

Type 2 diabetes: (Also called adult-onset diabetes or non-insulin-dependent diabetes mellitus [NIDDM].) The condition in which the body still makes insulin but is unable to use it. This is the most common type in adults over age 40. It also occurs in overweight preteens and teenagers. Pills may be able to stimulate the pancreas to make more insulin or help the person to use the insulin better. The pills are not insulin. People with type 2 diabetes do not have islet cell antibodies. This type of diabetes is discussed in detail in Chapter 4.

Urine: Water with wastes passed from the body by the kidneys.

QUESTIONS AND ANSWERS FROM NEWSNOTES

 When our son was diagnosed with diabetes, he had been vomiting and had kept no food down for over 24 hours. Yet his blood sugar was over 1,000 mg/dL (55 mmol/L). How could that be when he had not eaten any sugar?

 Insulin has several actions in the body. One is to allow all (or any) sugar to pass from the blood stream into cells where it can be burned for energy. A second function is to shut off the body's own production of sugar (primarily from the liver). When insulin is not available, as in your son at the time of diagnosis, the liver production of sugar can be enormous. This likely accounted for the high blood sugar even though no sugar had been eaten.

Chapter 3
Type 1 Diabetes

TEACHING OBJECTIVES:
Design an educational plan with the family that will ensure an adequate diabetes knowledge foundation on which to build.

LEARNING OBJECTIVES:
Learners (parents, child, relative or self) will be able to:

1. List two causes each for type 1 and type 2 diabetes.
2. State one major difference in the treatment of type 1 and 2 diabetes.

Type 1 diabetes is one of the most common chronic disorders of childhood. Unfortunately, it is increasing in incidence, particularly in young children. The reason for this is unknown, although it is most likely related to the environment (see below). It is also the most common form of diabetes to occur in people under age 40. Type 2 is the most common form after age 40. The list of famous people—sport stars, politicians, movie stars and artists—who have type 1 or type 2 diabetes is long. Following diagnosis, children frequently discover classmates who also have diabetes. Their looks, personalities and activities are no different from those of anyone else.

The rate of development of type 2 diabetes in children has increased in recent years. There is also a worldwide increase in type 2 diabetes in adults. This is due primarily to eating high calorie and high fat foods as well as a lack of exercise resulting in excess weight gain. Type 2 diabetes will be discussed in Chapter 4.

CAUSES

We know that diabetes is not contagious, like a cold. We also know that type 1 diabetes isn't caused from eating too much sugar.

Three risk factors seem to be important in determining why a person develops type 1 diabetes:

1. inherited (or genetic) factors

2. self-allergy (autoimmunity)

3. environmental damage (e.g., from a virus or chemical)

1. Inheritance (genetic)

The first important reason seems to be an inherited or genetic factor, such as the way a person inherits the color of the eyes from a mother, father or other relative.

Facts about inheritance:

🐾 People with type 1 diabetes are more likely to have inherited certain cell types (called **HLA types**). Those who don't have diabetes are less likely to have these HLA types.

🐾 The HLA types are determined by using *white blood cells* (WBCs) for typing. Blood types (A, B, AB and O) are determined using red blood cells.

🐾 Nearly all people with type 1 diabetes have a high-risk HLA type **DR3** or **DR4 gene**. There are also other less frequent genes that have been associated with an increased risk.

🐾 Fifty-three percent of people with type 1 diabetes have one DR3 and one DR4, **with one of these coming from each parent**.

🐾 Only three percent of people without diabetes have this DR3/DR4 combination. This combination makes a person more likely to develop diabetes. This is especially true when they have a relative with diabetes.

🐾 Over half of the families (up to 90 percent in one study) have no close relative with type 1 diabetes. Perhaps a family has a DR3 or a DR4 gene, but no family member has ever married into a family with the other DR gene. If a family member with a DR3 gene then marries into another family carrying the DR4 gene, the child may end up with the DR3/DR4 combination. They may then be at high risk for diabetes.

🐾 It is now known that there are also different genes that help to protect a person from developing diabetes.

🐾 Children from a family who have a child with diabetes have a greater chance of developing it than without a family history. A brother or sister of a child with diabetes has about a 1 in 20 (five percent) chance of developing diabetes.

🐾 The cause is not completely due to heredity. We know this from studies of identical twins. When one identical twin gets diabetes, only in half of the cases does the other twin also develop the disease. If it were entirely due to heredity, both twins would always develop it. We don't completely understand the inheritance factors. We do believe that **both** mother and father transmit the tendency to develop diabetes to their child.

2. Self-allergy (autoimmunity)

The second cause that seems to be important in type 1 diabetes is self-allergy (or autoimmunity). Normally, our immune systems protect our bodies from disease.

Facts about self-allergy (autoimmunity):

🐾 In the case of type 1 diabetes and other autoimmune diseases such as lupus, arthritis and multiple sclerosis, the immune system turns against a body part. The immune system treats that body part like something it is allergic to and damages the body part.

🐾 There can be evidence of this allergic reaction found in the blood. The allergic reaction In type 1 diabetes is against the cells in the pancreas (islet cells) that make insulin. Most Anglo and about half of Hispanic and African-American children show this allergy when they develop diabetes. The evidence in the blood is called an antibody or, more specifically, an **"islet cell antibody" (ICA)**. We now know that some people can have this antibody present in their blood for many years before they need insulin.

🐾 Other diabetes antibodies called biochemical antibodies ("GAD" antibodies, insulin autoantibodies [IAA], ICA 512, and ZnT8 [zinc-transport] antibodies) can now be measured. They are also found in the blood of people who are developing diabetes.

🐾 Identifying these antibodies in the blood has made it possible to screen people who are at risk to develop diabetes. This screening has led to research trials (see Chapter 31) which

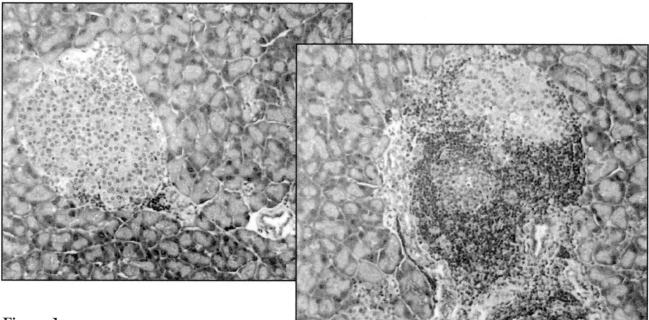

Figure 1:

Microscopic Photograph of Pancreatic Islet:

The photo on the left shows a normal islet (center) surrounded by other pancreatic tissue. This other tissue is responsible for making digestive enzymes. The photo on the right is from a diabetic animal. The white blood cells (WBCs) have invaded and destroyed most of the islet.

are trying to prevent diabetes. We believe it is important for brothers, sisters and other relatives to have this screening.

🐾 The antibodies may gradually disappear from the blood after the onset of type 1 diabetes.

🐾 People who develop type 2 diabetes (previously called adult-onset) do not have these antibodies.

3. Environmental (virus or nutritional?)

A third factor is also believed important. This environmental factor may either be a virus or something in the food we eat or something we do not yet know about. This factor may be the bridge between the genetic (inherited) part and the allergic reaction.

An example of the sequence of events might be:

🐾 A person *inherits* the tendency for diabetes

🐾 This tendency might allow a virus or other particle to injure the islet cells

🐾 Part of the damaged islet cell may then be released into the blood

🐾 The body would then make islet cell antibodies (an allergic or autoimmune reaction)

🐾 The damage can attract white blood cells (WBCs) to the area of the islet cells. These now active WBCs produce chemicals, which further injure the other islet cells (Figure 1).

🐾 Anything that activates the WBCs in the future (viral infections, certain foods, stress, etc.) may result in more of the islet cells being destroyed

We now know that most people who get diabetes don't just suddenly develop it. They have been in the process of developing it for many years, sometimes even from birth. Most likely many viral infections and other factors result in damage and destroy a few more islet cells. As more and more islet cells are destroyed the person moves closer to having diabetes (see Figure 2, where onset of diabetes is represented by the broken line).

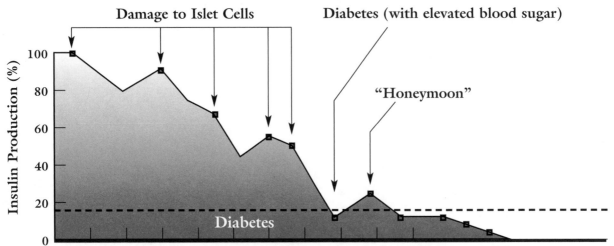

Figure 2:
The Gradual Onset of Type 1 Diabetes

It is now believed that diabetes develops gradually, over many months or many years. It does not just come on suddenly in the week or two before the elevated blood sugars. Many insults (represented by the arrows in this Figure) likely result in further damage until the diagnosis of diabetes is made. The insults may include viral infections, stress, parts of the diet, or other agents. These agents may work by "activating" white blood cells in the islets to make toxic chemicals that cause injury to the insulin-producing cells (beta cells). However, a "genetic-predisposition" (inherited factors) must be present for the process to start.

TYPE 2 (ADULT-ONSET) DIABETES:

Chapter 4 explains type 2 diabetes in more depth.

The three main risk factors for type 2 diabetes are:

1. **Being overweight**
2. **Insulin insensitivity**
3. **Inheritance (genetics)**

1. **Being overweight (obesity):** Being overweight is an important risk factor for type 2 (adult-onset) diabetes. In contrast, it is not the main risk factor for type 1 diabetes.

2. **Insulin insensitivity:** Insulin does not work as effectively in the person with type 2 diabetes. Initially it can still be made in normal or above-normal amounts. This is different from type 1 diabetes, where insulin cannot be made at all or is made in small amounts. Later, people with type 2 diabetes may also have reduced insulin production. They will then need insulin shots.

3. **Inheritance (genetics):** Type 2 diabetes also has a strong inherited (genetic) cause. People with type 2 diabetes do not have the same association with the HLA genes as do people with type 1 diabetes. They also do not make islet cell antibodies. The causes of the two types of diabetes seem to be completely different.

DEFINITIONS

Allergy: A special reaction of the body to some material. This is similar to what happens if you are allergic to something that makes you sneeze.

Antibody: The material we measure in the blood if someone has an allergy (example: milk antibodies might be present if someone has a milk allergy).

Autoimmunity (self-allergy): The process of forming an allergic reaction against one's own tissues. This happens in diseases such as lupus and arthritis. People with type 1 diabetes make an antibody against their islet cells (where the insulin is made).

Genetic (inherited): Features, such as eye color, that are passed from both parents to children.

HLA type: The way to group cell types just as red blood cells are grouped into A, B, AB and O blood types. HLA stands for Human Leukocyte Antigen. A leukocyte is another name for a white blood cell. The white blood cell is the type of cell used in HLA typing.

Identical twins: Twins that come from the same egg. All their features (genetics) are exactly alike.

Islet cell (pronounced eye-let): The groups of cells within the pancreas that make insulin.

Islet cell antibody: The material we measure in the person's blood to show that they have had an allergy against the cells in the pancreas (the islet cells) that make insulin.

QUESTIONS AND ANSWERS FROM NEWSNOTES

Q My daughter was in a car accident the week before the onset of her diabetes. Could that have caused the diabetes?

A It is now accepted that diabetes comes on gradually over many months or many years. It is not just brought about by one event. After initial damage occurs to the islets in the pancreas (where insulin is made), islet cell antibodies may be positive, indicating that some damage has occurred. We have followed many people with positive islet cell antibodies. Some have not needed to start insulin treatment for as long as ten years.

After the initial damage, many factors may cause activation of white blood cells (WBCs) in the islets. These factors may include some viral infections, content of the diet or even stress. When the WBCs in the islets are activated by these factors, they produce toxic chemicals that destroy a few more islets each time. Gradually, a person gets closer to having full-blown diabetes. Thus, the stress of the automobile accident may have been the final precipitating event, but it was most likely only one of several insults over many years.

"Think
Pink!"

Chapter 4

Type 2 Diabetes

(previously referred to as
adult onset diabetes or
non-insulin dependent diabetes)

H. Peter Chase, MD
Cindy Cain, NP-C, CDE
David Maahs, MD, PhD
Philip Zeitler, MD

INTRODUCTION

Type 2 diabetes is the most common type of diabetes in adults over the age of 40. While it used to be uncommon in children and adolescents, type 2 is now appearing more often in overweight pre-teens and teenagers. The disorder occurs in all ethnic groups, but more frequently in people of Hispanic, American Indian, Asian, and African-American heritages.

Type 2 diabetes is often referred to as a **"disease of lifestyles."** For thousands of years in the past, people by necessity were very active. However, we now live in a world of automobile travel, television, computers and video games. The main exercise many adults and children receive is walking from their car or bus into work or school. In many households and neighborhoods, children do not have access to routine activity or time outside. Some schools do not offer physical education on a daily basis, further limiting children's physical activity. In addition, high-calorie convenience foods, fast foods, and sugar-containing drinks have become a major part of our meals and snacks. The net result of these changes in diet and activity levels has been an increase in the incidence of being overweight and of type 2 diabetes in the U.S. and worldwide. The prevention of type 2 diabetes in people at high risk is discussed in this chapter and Chapters 13 and 30.

TOPICS:
Diabetes Disease Process (type 2)
Medications (type 2 diabetes)
Nutritional Management (also see Chapters 11 and 12)
Physical Activity (also see Chapter 13)
Monitoring (checking blood sugars and ketones; also see Chapters 5 and 7)
Prevent, Detect and Treat Acute and Chronic Complications (also see Chapter 23)

TEACHING OBJECTIVES:

1. Present the basic concepts of type 2 diabetes and management.
2. Introduce the medications to be used including dosing and side effects.
3. Assess current dietary habits and develop an individual nutritional management program.
4. Assess current activity level and develop an individualized exercise program.
5. Discuss monitoring blood sugars, ketones and laboratory tests.
6. Introduce acute and chronic complications.

LEARNING OBJECTIVES:

Learner (parents, child, relative or self) will be able to:

1. State two differences between type 1 and type 2 diabetes.
2. Identify the name, dose, schedule and side effects of medication(s) to be used.
3. Identify the individualized nutritional management program (see Chapter 12).
4. Work with healthcare provider to develop an exercise program (see Chapter 13).
5. Identify time frames for monitoring blood sugars, ketones and laboratory tests.
6. List two possible acute and two possible chronic complications.

21

DIFFERENCES BETWEEN TYPE 2 AND TYPE 1 DIABETES

- In type 2 diabetes, the primary disorder is a problem with the action of insulin, which is no longer effective in controlling metabolism. This is called "insulin resistance" and is usually related to being overweight and inactive. Insulin resistance means that insulin cannot act normally to keep blood sugars in the desired range. Type 2 diabetes is a progressive disease that will require the eventual use of insulin.

- In response to insulin resistance, increased amounts of insulin are made initially. This is the opposite of type 1 diabetes, where the insulin levels are low or absent. Over time, the amount of insulin produced by individuals with type 2 diabetes decreases. This happens as the pancreas fails to keep up with the body's higher demands for insulin. Even though there is less insulin being produced by the pancreas and the patient may need to take insulin injections, the individual still has insulin resistance and type 2 diabetes. One type does not turn into the other type.

- Laboratory measurements sometimes help in deciding if someone has type 1 or type 2 diabetes. **ISLET CELL ANTIBODIES** (ICA: see Chapter 3) **ARE NOT PRESENT IN TYPE 2 DIABETES.** In type 1 diabetes, ICA antibodies are usually present. Measurements of C-peptide, an insulin-related protein, may be normal or elevated in type 2 diabetes, but are generally low in type 1. However, sometimes it takes monitoring the individual with diabetes for a while to differentiate between the two types.

CAUSES

🐾 Inheritance (genetics)

Type 2 diabetes has a stronger risk for inheritance than type 1 diabetes. In almost all cases, a parent and/or grandparent will also have the disease. In the case of identical twins, if one twin develops type 2 diabetes, the other twin has an 80 percent chance of also developing the disease. In type 1 diabetes, an identical twin has a 35-50 percent chance of developing the disease.

In type 2 diabetes, there are many different potentially-inherited (genetic) defects, which vary between families. There is not just one common defect in all families.

Children who are born to mothers with type 2 diabetes, or mothers with gestational diabetes, have an increased risk of developing type 2 diabetes in childhood. Children born with a low birth weight for length ("small for date") are also at an increased risk for developing type 2 diabetes.

🐾 Lifestyle

Most (but not all) people with type 2 diabetes are overweight and do not lead active lives. According to a study of a sample of U.S. children, the obesity prevalence has increased from around 5% in 1963 to 17% in 2003 to 2004. In the past two decades, the obesity-related cost of illnesses during childhood increased from 35 million to 127 million US dollars. Factors that can play a role in obesity include genetics, certain medications, eating on the run, recreational eating, eating foods higher in fat, increased portion size, increased TV and video time, and decreased physical activity.

Insulin resistance usually occurs with excessive weight and decreased physical fitness. Insulin resistance means that the body loses its sensitivity to insulin. The insulin doesn't work as well to allow sugar to pass into the cells. In some cases, the increased insulin that the body makes to try to overcome the resistance causes darkening of the skin (called acanthosis nigricans). The most common areas for this darkening are the neck, armpits and/or the elbows. By losing weight (eating fewer calories and exercising more), the sensitivity to insulin may return again and the dark skin coloring may lessen or disappear.

Table 1
OGTT Blood Sugar Values (mg/dL and mmol/L)

	NORMAL		BORDERLINE		DIABETIC	
	mg/dL	mmol/L	mg/dL	mmol/L	mg/dL	mmol/L
FASTING	< 100	< 5.5	100-126	5.5-7.0	> 126	> 7.0
TWO HOURS AFTER DRINKING THE GLUCOLA	< 140	< 7.8	140-200	7.8-11.1	> 200	> 11.1

DIAGNOSIS

Adults with type 2 diabetes can go several years with high blood sugar levels without other signs of diabetes. Then, with an illness or stress and less effective function of the pancreas, symptoms begin. In young people, this long period of time with high blood sugars before the appearance of symptoms does not seem to occur. Instead, type 2 diabetes in young people is usually diagnosed around the time of late puberty. This is because insulin resistance normally increases at this time.

How it can be discovered

✔ Sometimes sugar is found in the urine during a routine check-up. There may not be any other signs or symptoms.

✔ The increased urination and drinking of fluids may be absent or mild with type 2 diabetes

✔ Weight loss can occur (though variable)

✔ Increasing fatigue may be present

✔ During an illness, blood sugar levels (and/or ketones) may become very high. The illness may be a deep skin infection (abscess) or yeast infection.

✔ Trouble with vision (blurry/frequent change of glasses) may occur due to swelling of the lens of the eye from high blood sugars

🐾 *Laboratory testing for diabetes:*

● If a blood sugar value is very high (e.g.,>200 mg/dL or 11.1 mmol/L), the glucose tolerance test (Table 1) may not be needed

● If the hemoglobin A1c (HbA1c) level is elevated (two values >6.5%, Chapter 14), it is considered diagnostic

● The 2-hour oral glucose tolerance test (**OGTT**) is a test done after fasting (no food for 10 hours). After a fasting blood sugar is drawn, the person then drinks all of a high sugar drink (Glucola) within five minutes. A second blood sample is drawn after two hours. See Table 1 for normal, borderline and diabetic blood sugar values.

TREATMENT

As in type 1 diabetes, the family must learn as much as they can, as diabetes is a family disease. In children with type 2 diabetes, there is typically a family member with this disease. However, the family member may have never received any education regarding their diabetes when they were diagnosed.

The family may need to initially learn how to give insulin shots (Chapter 8 and 9) if:

● ketones are present (Chapter 5)

● symptoms of increased urination, thirst or severe weight loss are present

● there is uncertainty about the diabetes type

● if the HbA1c is >10%

❧ Lifestyle Changes are IMPORTANT

Dietary changes are very important in type 2 diabetes, since weight loss and changes in the nutrients of the diet can make a very important difference in the insulin resistance. It is important to understand your family's attitude toward food, eating habits, and activities associated with eating (e. g. eating when stressed, rewarding good behavior with food). Binge eating in the afternoon and evening is common in children/teens with type 2 diabetes. The individual in the family who does the grocery shopping and meal planning will be a key factor in dietary change. It will be important for this individual to know how to read food labels and to purchase and prepare healthy foods/meals.

Lowering calorie, fat, and carbohydrate intake through control of **portion sizes** and learning how to make **healthier food choices** are essential to losing weight and improving blood sugar control. Usually, the most effective approach at the beginning is to keep dietary changes simple and achievable. Some simple changes include the elimination of sugary beverages and junk foods, reducing portion sizes, and limiting the consumption of convenience foods, fast food, and restaurant food.

The plate method is another method for families to follow for meal planning (see Chapter 11). In this method, the plate is divided into 3 sections. One-fourth of the plate is devoted to starches (pastas, rice, potatoes, etc), another fourth is devoted to protein (meat, fish, chicken, etc), and other half of the plate is devoted to non-starch vegetables (carrots, broccoli, green beans, etc). One serving of milk, fruit and any free foods (e.g., lettuce) are on the side (see figure in Chapter 11). Purchasing plates that are divided into sections for each can be a helpful tool. For some families, carbohydrate counting may be useful, but takes practice.

The overweight individual may have trouble knowing what hunger feels like and/or what it feels like to be full. Reviewing these feelings can help with better food regulation. Behavioral habits such as putting the fork down between bites, chewing food twenty times, use smaller plates/bowls, and drinking a glass of water before eating can be simple and helpful tools in weight regulation. Food management is discussed in more detail in Chapters 11 and 12. Most important, the family **must** work with a knowledgeable dietitian. The dietitian will help to individualize the meal plan to fit personal preferences.

Exercise is **equally important** for managing type 2 diabetes (Chapter 13). Most children with type 2 diabetes are not active and do not enjoy being active. It is important to identify some activities that the child/adolescent might enjoy. Make physical activity fun, such as going on a family bike ride or playing basketball as a family. Then work on small achievable weekly exercise goals, such as "I will walk with my dog for 10 minutes, three days this week". The person will need to feel successful in order to stay active. Increase the physical activity and set new goals weekly. It is also helpful to establish rules to promote activity, such as restricting video games until after completion of the activity for the day. In order to motivate the child/adolescent to become more active, give them a choice between doing a household chore such as vacuuming, or going outside and riding a bike for 20 minutes. While most physical activity experts suggest 60 minutes of activity per day, starting out slowly is more realistic and will reduce muscle soreness that will hinder daily exercise. In addition, it is important to reduce sedentary activity such as television, computer, and video game time. Finally, increasing general activity levels by walking (pacing) while talking on a phone or playing video games, taking the stairs instead of elevators, and parking further from the store can make surprising differences in weight and blood sugar control.

It is important that the **entire family** make the same lifestyle changes. If family members are active along with the child/adolescent with diabetes, success will be more likely. Similarly, if foods with little nutritional value (e.g., sugary beverages, chips) are brought into the home by other family members, it will be more difficult for the person with diabetes to make healthy choices. It is important to **praise** all individuals in the family who have made healthy changes.

🐾 Blood Sugar (Glucose) Testing

This is covered in detail in Chapter 7. The blood sugar target range in an individual with type 2 diabetes is 70 - 140 mg/dL (3.9 - 7.8 mmol/L). In general, doing blood sugars for a person with type 2 diabetes who is on insulin is no different from a person with type 1 diabetes. Insulin may be started initially to lower the HbA1c (Chapter 14). If there is success in weight loss and returning the HbA1c level to normal, monitoring blood sugars is still important, but may be done less frequently. In people who are not taking insulin, the frequency of measuring blood sugars is often decreased to two times per day, approximately 3 days a week. The aim would be to maintain the morning fasting sugar between 80 to 120 mg/dL (4.5 - 6.7 mmol/L). The value two hours after any meal should be below 160 mg/dL (<8.9 mmol/L). More frequent values are essential during illness.

🐾 Insulin Shots

Some people with type 2 diabetes will always need to take insulin shots. Others will be able to take oral medications for several years. Eventually, those taking oral medications may need to take insulin shots. People with type 2 diabetes who have ketones or an HbA1c >10% when their diabetes is diagnosed may need to be treated with insulin shots at the beginning. A once a day shot of Levemir/Lantus insulin along with oral medicines is often very effective in improving blood sugars even when they are very high. People who are able to lose weight and become more active may be able to come off insulin shots and just take their oral medicine. However, they often need to return to insulin shots in later years due to the progressive nature of type 2 diabetes.

It is important to remember that during times of illness, especially if ketones return, insulin shots may need to be given.

🐾 Oral Tablets

Oral tablets are **NOT** insulin. If taken orally, insulin would be destroyed by the stomach acid. The tablets used for diabetes are medicines that make the person more sensitive to their own insulin. Some of the medicines also make the pancreas release extra amounts of insulin (Table 2 also lists some of these medications).

1. Metformin (Glucophage): the medication that is the most common for children/teens with type 2 diabetes and the only oral medication that is FDA-approved for use in children. Metformin is usually very effective in bringing down the HbA1c in young people with type 2 diabetes. In addition to helping to control blood sugar levels, it may help with weight loss.

- Main side effect: upset stomach, diarrhea, nausea, and bloating. These side effects can be reduced by always taking the medicine with food and increasing the dose slowly.

- Vitamin B12 levels may be reduced and could require supplements.

- Lactic acidosis is a very rare side effect which can occur if metformin is not stopped when a person has the stomach flu or severe illness. It can also happen during an x-ray procedure using dyes and during episodes of vomiting, diarrhea, pneumonia or with lung diseases.

♦ Dosing

- Start low with 500 mg (0.5 g) once a day with breakfast or dinner. Take metformin with some food, usually at breakfast or dinner.

- After one week, try this dose twice a day (with breakfast and dinner).

- After the third week, try one tablet (0.5g) in the morning with breakfast and two tablets (1g) with dinner.

- The fourth week, if stomach upset is not a problem, try two tablets (1g) with breakfast and with dinner.

- Some people can use the long-acting form

of this medication. This can be taken in the morning with the dosage gradually increased. As noted above, it is important to know if a person is taking metformin if they become ill. Metformin needs to be stopped during times of severe illness or with vomiting or diarrhea. It is often best to take insulin shots during an illness. Consult your health care provider.

2. Other Oral Medications

The sulfonylureas (Table 2) have been around the longest and are the most common tablets used in adults with type 2 diabetes. They act to make the person's own pancreas secrete more insulin and can lower the HbA1c, though not as well as metformin. Low blood sugar (Chapter 6) is a possible side effect, particularly in young patients. These medications are not commonly used in young people with type 2 diabetes and none have been approved by the FDA for use in children.

Two agents, Actos and Avandia (Table 2), belong to a class of medicine, called thiazolidinediones that act to increase the body's sensitivity to insulin. They have been commonly used in adults with type 2 diabetes and can lower the HbA1c almost as much as metformin. There is limited experience with these medications in children/adolescents, and concerns have been raised about their safety because of rare but important effects on liver, heart, and bone. Neither of these medications has been approved by the FDA for use in children.

Glucagon-like peptide (GLP-1) and related medications:

GLP-1 is another hormone that is made in response to food. It works closely with insulin to regulate blood sugar. In recent years, the importance of GLP-1 in keeping the blood sugar normal has been recognized, and a number of new medications are related to this important hormone. None of these has been approved by the FDA for use in children.

There are two groups of GLP-1 medications: 1) medications that directly increase the amount of GLP-1, and 2) medications that prevent the breakdown of GLP-1 so more remains in the body.

Table 2
Commonly Used Oral Hypoglycemic Medications

Name	Action	Initial Dose	Maximum Dose	Side-effects
1. Metformin (Glucophage)	Reduces liver secretion of glucose; may help reduce weight	0.5g	2g	Stomach upset, diarrhea, nausea, bloating; acidosis with illness (rare)
Metformin XR (Glucophage XR)	a long acting form of Metformin	(dose same as above)		

2. Insulin sensitizers: help cells respond to insulin better.

a. Pioglitazone (ACTOS)		15 mg	45 mg	Stuffy nose, headache,
b. Rosiglitazone (Avandia)		4 mg	8 mg	liver problems, weight gain

For Both: **Must follow liver function tests initially and after 2-3 months.**

3. Sulfonylureas stimulate the pancreas to make more insulin.

a. Chlorpropamide (Diabinese)		125-250 mg	500 mg	Low blood sugar, dizziness
b. Gliburide (Diabeta) (Micronase)		2.5-5.0 mg	20 mg	Skin rashes, headache and stomach upset
c. Glipizide (Glucotrol)		5 mg	40 mg	" "
d. Glucotrol XL (extended release)		5 mg	20 mg	" "
e. Glimeperide[a 24 hour product], (Amaryl)		0.4 mg	0.8 mg	" "

Others include: Glynase, Orinase and Tolinase.

4. Meglitinides: stimulate early insulin release with meals.

a. Nateglinide (Starlix)		60 mg (30 minutes before each meal)	120 mg	Diarrhea, nausea, low blood sugar
b. Repaglinide (Prandin)		0.5 mg (30 minutes before each meal)	16 mg	Stuffy nose, low blood sugar, chest pain

Successful treatment of type 2 diabetes may require the use of combinations of agents.
Some of these combinations are available as single tablets. Examples are:
a. A sulfonylurea and metformin (e.g., Glucovance: combination of glyburide and metformin; Metaglip: combination of glipizide and metformin)
b. Metformin and a thiazolindinedione (e.g., Avandamet: combination of metformin and rosiglitazone)
c. A sulfonylurea and a thiazolindinedione
d. A meglitinide and metformin
e. Insulin and any of the oral agents (e.g., Lantus and metformin)

NOTE: There are many other oral agents which are preferred by some physicians, but were not included on this listing due to space.

1. In the first GLP-1 group are Symlin (pramlintide), Byetta (exenatide), and Victoza (liraglutide), proteins that are similar to GLP-1 and may be particularly helpful in lowering blood sugars after meals and promoting weight loss. They do this by:

   • increasing insulin production

   • reducing the production of glucagon, a hormone that raises blood sugar

   • delaying stomach emptying

   • decreasing appetite

   All of these medications are taken by injection. Symlin is taken immediately prior to each major meal. Byetta is taken 60 minutes before breakfast and dinner. Victoza is taken once a day. These medications cannot be taken in the same syringe as insulin. Side effects include headache and nausea. Some cases of pancreatitis (inflammation of the pancreas) have been reported in Byetta users.

2. The second group is called DPP-4 inhibitors because they inhibit the enzyme that breaks down the body's own GLP-1. This group currently includes sitagliptan (Januvia) and saxagliptin (Onglyza) in the U.S, but other medications will likely be approved soon. These are oral medications taken once a day and have many of the same effects as the GLP-1 agents in the first group, but do not cause weight loss. Some cases of pancreatitis have been reported with DPP-4 inhibitors.

Monitoring for Complications

Acute:

1. Low blood sugars are less frequent with type 2 diabetes than with type 1 diabetes. However, they can occur. They are most frequently associated with use of insulin, sulfonylurea, and meglitinide medications (Table 2). Treatment of low blood sugars is explained in Chapter 6.

2. Diabetic ketoacidosis can be present in some children at diagnosis. Ketone production is less frequent with type 2 than with type 1

diabetes. However, it can occur during times of illness. If a person is receiving oral medications, they usually need to return to using insulin shots when ketones are present.

3. Hyperglycemic hyperosmolar state is a situation in which the blood sugars rise to dangerously high levels, leading to severe dehydration and changes in mental function. It can be caused by infections, medications, non-compliance with diabetes therapies, substance abuse, undiagnosed diabetes, and other illnesses. This is a life-threatening emergency that requires immediate treatment.

Chronic:

1. High Blood Pressure (Hypertension): High blood pressure is a common finding in children/adolescents with type 2 diabetes. Blood pressure should be assessed using the correct cuff size and using blood pressure standards that are based on gender, age, and height. When hypertension is diagnosed in children, a type of blood pressure medicine called an ACE-inhibitor (Chapters 22 and 30) is commonly used. They may also have a positive effect on preventing diabetic kidney disease. Blood pressure should be monitored at each clinic visit.

2. Abnormal lipids: Children/adolescents with type 2 diabetes may have decreased HDL (good cholesterol) and increased LDL (bad cholesterol) and triglycerides (blood fat). Lifestyle changes with improved glycemic control will improve the lipids. Medications are used when lifestyle changes cannot be maintained. Yearly screening is recommended.

3. Obstructive sleep apnea: Most often found with overweight individuals. Symptoms include snoring with long breathing pauses when sleeping, frequent arousal during sleep, restless sleep, morning headaches, and daytime sleepiness. A sleep study should be performed if you suspect this condition.

4. Polycystic Ovarian Syndrome: This condition is often associated with menstrual irregularity, increased hair on the face, and acne. Metformin may be very effective in reversing these symptoms, though sometimes an oral contraceptive is added for better effect. Metformin may improve irregular menses as well as fertility. There may be an increased risk of pregnancy in sexually active teens. The need for birth control is important to consider.

5. Microalbuminuria: This refers to protein in the urine, which can be seen at diagnosis. When found, ACE-inhibitors (see Hypertension above) are used because they can prevent worsening of kidney problems. Yearly screening for microalbuminuria is recommended.

6. Non-alcoholic fatty liver disease: This consists of fatty deposits in the liver. This is diagnosed through laboratory testing, ultrasound, or CT scan. In this disease, the progression of chronic inflammation can lead to cirrhosis and liver failure. Weight loss, good glucose control, and reduction in carbohydrates can help this condition in most individuals.

7. Retinopathy: A dilated eye exam is recommended at onset and yearly to identify early diabetic eye disease.

8. Social and psychological issues: Overweight children are at risk for being teased about their weight by both their peers and family members. When children are teased about their weight it can lead to unhealthy eating habits and binge eating behaviors. Overweight children/teens are also at risk for depression and low self-esteem.

🐾 Two references for those wanting more information specifically on type 2 diabetes in youth are:

1. American Diabetes Association. *"Diabetes Care"* 28 (Suppl 1) S4-536, 2005

2. ISPAD Clinical Practice Consensus Guidelines, Type 2 Diabetes Mellitus In the Child and Adolescent. Pediatr Diabetes. 9, 512, 2008.

DEFINITIONS

C-peptide: An insulin-related protein. It is split off from proinsulin when the active insulin is formed. It is easier to measure than insulin in the laboratory and is often used as a measure of insulin production.

FDA: Food and Drug Association. The agency responsible for approving the use of new medicines in the US, and thus for our safety.

Glucagon-like peptide (GLP-1) and Byetta, Symlin, & Victoza: These agents have been approved by the FDA for use in adults with type 2 diabetes. When injected prior to meals, they reduce glucagon, increase insulin, and delay stomach emptying.

Lifestyle changes: In this chapter, exchanging sedentary (little exercise) habits for daily exercise, and decreasing high calorie, high fat and high carbohydrate food intake (particularly fast foods).

Oral glucose tolerance test (OGTT): Blood sugar levels before and after drinking a highly sugared drink. It may be used to diagnose diabetes when the diagnosis is uncertain. Normal values are in Table 1 in this chapter.

Oral hypoglycemic agents: These are pills which help to make the body more sensitive to insulin or cause it to release more insulin. However, they are NOT insulin. Table 2 gives the names of a few of these agents.

Type 2 diabetes: The condition in which the body still makes insulin, but is unable to use it effectively to metabolize sugar. This is the most common type of diabetes in adults over age 40. It is also becoming increasingly more common in overweight teenagers.

Exercise is important

Chapter 5
Ketone Testing

KETONES

Ketones are chemicals which appear in the urine and blood when body fat is used for energy. Ketones are a side product of fat breakdown (see Chapter 15).

Body fat is used for energy under the following circumstances:

- when there is not enough insulin to allow sugar to be burned as energy in the body.

- when not enough food has been eaten to provide energy.

Ketone testing is **VERY** important. A method of testing for ketones must be kept in the home and taken on trips at all times.

We usually teach families how to do the urine ketone test on the first day of diagnosis of diabetes. Frequent urine ketone tests are important in the first few days after diagnosis to determine if enough insulin is being given to turn off ketone production. **Turning off ketone production is one of the first goals in the treatment of newly diagnosed diabetes.** This often takes one or two days after starting insulin.

Another goal is to lower blood sugar levels (done primarily by giving insulin to turn off internal sugar production in the liver). This can take one or two weeks after starting insulin. Giving insulin helps to accomplish both goals.

TEACHING OBJECTIVES:

1. Discuss when ketone measurement should be done.
2. Introduce method to be used for measuring ketones.
3. Present the appropriate time to call the healthcare provider.

LEARNING OBJECTIVES:

Learner (parents, child, relative or self) will be able to:

1. Define ketones and the importance of measuring ketones
2. Identify and demonstrate when and how to measure for ketones.
3. State the appropriate time to call the healthcare provider.

Table 1
Comparison of Blood Beta Ketone and Urine Ketone Readings *

Blood (mmol/L)		Urine
< 0.6		negative
0.6 to 1.5		small to moderate
1.6 to 3.0		usually large
≥ 3.0	←→ go directly to the E.R. ←→	very large

* The blood and urine ketone values do NOT always agree. The urine may have been in the bladder for several hours. The blood levels tell what the ketones are at the moment the test is done. (Also read the second Q and A at the back of this chapter.)

The healthcare provider should be called for all values > 1.0 mmol/L in the blood or if the urine ketones are moderate or large.

REASONS FOR MEASURING KETONES

It is important to test for urine or blood ketones because they can build up in the body. This can result in one of the two emergencies of diabetes, acidosis (also called diabetic ketoacidosis or DKA) (see Chapter 15). In the past, it was only possible to test for urine ketones. The Precision Xtra™ meter is now available to do a home fingerstick test for blood ketones. The diabetes care provider should be notified when the urine ketone test shows moderate or large ketones or if the blood ketone test is above 1.0 mmol/L.

Usually extra insulin is taken to help make the ketones go away. If the ketones are not detected early, they will build up in the body and ketoacidosis (DKA - Chapter 15) may result. This is particularly true during illnesses. Early detection of ketones and the treatment with rapid-acting insulin (Humalog/NovoLog/Apidra) can help prevent hospitalizations for ketoacidosis (see Chapter 15). Hospitalizations for ketoacidosis are still listed as the number one reason for hospitalizing children in the U.S. with known diabetes. **It is our belief that these hospitalizations for ketoacidosis are completely preventable. To accomplish this, the ketone testing must be done, the diabetes care provider called when indicated, the fluid intake** increased, and extra shots of insulin given. As more youth use continuous glucose monitors (CGM), the alarms will alert people of the high glucose level (and the need to check ketones).

WHEN TO MEASURE KETONES

Ketones must always be checked if the blood/CGM glucose value is high (above 240 mg/dL [13.3 mmol/L] fasting, or above 300 mg/dL [16.7 mmol/L]) during the day. They must also be checked ANY TIME THE PERSON FEELS SICK OR NAUSEATED (especially if he/she vomits, even once). **If the person is sick, ketones can be present even when the glucose level is not high.**

CALL YOUR DIABETES CARE PROVIDER NIGHT OR DAY IF MODERATE OR LARGE URINE KETONES ARE PRESENT OR FOR BLOOD KETONES ≥ 1.0 MMOL/L. TELL THE PERSON ANSWERING THE PHONE THAT THE CALL IS URGENT.

People who have been recently diagnosed with diabetes may need to check ketones twice daily (or more often if they are positive). After the first few days, if all ketone checks have been negative, daily measurement of ketones is not needed.

WHAT TEST MATERIALS ARE AVAILABLE?

Testing for Urine Ketones

The two strips that are most frequently used in checking for urine ketones are the Ketostix® and the Chemstrip K®. If a child is not yet toilet trained, it is usually best to press a test strip (see section on Ketostix) firmly against the wet diaper. It is also possible to place cotton balls in the diaper where the diaper is wettest. Drops of urine can then be squeezed from the cotton ball.

❖ Ketostix

Ketone strips are reliable for urine testing IF THEY ARE CAREFULLY TIMED WITH A SECOND HAND ON A CLOCK. The Ketostix are cheaper than the Ketodiastix (also measuring urine sugar) and it is not necessary to do the urine sugar, as a blood/CGM glucose level is more accurate. There is a place on the side of the bottle to write the date the bottle is opened. The strips are then good for six months. Individually foil-wrapped Ketostix will not expire for two or three years. This gets around the problem of having to throw any unused Ketostix away once the bottle has been open for six months. Ask your pharmacist to order them if he/she does not have them. The Bayer product number for ordering is 2640 (20 foiled strips).

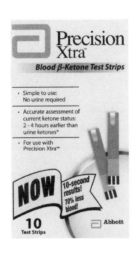

The following procedure must be followed exactly:

1. Completely cover the colored square on the end of the strip by dipping into FRESH urine. Then immediately remove the strip from the urine. We suggest that the urine be collected in a cup and that the strip then be timed and read by two people. This prevents errors due to color blindness or psychological factors. A supply of small paper cups might be kept in the bathroom medicine cabinet for this purpose.

2. Gently tap the edge of the strip against the side of the urine container to remove excess urine.

3. Compare the test area closely with the corresponding color chart. The timing is very important. READ KETONES AT **EXACTLY** 15 SECONDS AFTER DIPPING THE STRIP. HOLD THE STRIP CLOSE TO THE COLOR BLOCK AND MATCH THE COLORS CAREFULLY. These tests must always be timed with the second hand of a clock. Counting is NOT accurate enough.

4. Immediately record the result of the ketone test as negative, small (15), moderate (40), large (80) or extra large (160) in the notebook so that it is not forgotten.

❖ Chemstrip K

The Chemstrip K (or Chemstrip uGK® with the urine glucose check) is the second method that can be used to check for urine ketones. The only difference from the instructions for the Ketostix is in the timing. Chemstrip K must be timed for one minute. Read as negative, small, moderate or large at exactly one minute.

❖ Testing for Blood Ketones

The Precision Xtra™ Meter is the only meter which allows testing for blood beta ketones. The test strips can be purchased in boxes of ten foil-wrapped beta ketone strips (see scan of box). Although the blood ketone strips are more expensive, they do not have to be replaced (like Ketostix) every six months. Thus, the cost is not all that different. When insurance will not cover the cost of the blood strips, some people screen with the urine strip and just do the blood test when the urine test is moderate or large. As discussed in Chapter 15, the blood ketone gives the ketone level at that minute. In contrast, the urine level may be hours behind (depending on how long urine has been in the bladder).

Steps:

1. The purple control strip must first be inserted to calibrate for beta ketones. Make sure the calibration code on the calibration strip matches the code on the ketone strip.

2. Open a strip and place it into the meter with the three black bars going first into the meter. Push the strip completely into the test port of the meter until it stops.

3. After washing and drying the hand, lance the finger.

4. Place a drop of blood into the white target area at the end of the strip.

5. The result is then displayed on the meter in 10 seconds.

We suggest interpreting the readings as follows (in mmol/L):

     < 0.6 = normal

0.6 – 1.0 = slightly elevated. Drink extra fluids.

1.0 – 3.0 = serious, call healthcare provider and state the call is urgent. Take extra rapid-acting insulin and drink extra fluids.

    > 3.0 = **Go directly to the Emergency Room. Have someone take you!**

A doctor in Boston (Dr. Lori Laeffel) showed that youth who were sick were 53 percent likely to check urine ketones and 93 percent likely to check blood ketones. The saving of one hospitalization from treating ketones earlier would save 5,000 - 10,000 US dollars.

DEFINITIONS

Chemstrip K: Strips for measuring urine ketones (acetone). They are also available as Chemstrip uGK (for urine ketones and sugar).

Ketoacidosis (Acidosis; DKA): What happens in the body when not enough insulin is available. Blood/CGM glucose levels are usually high at this time. Moderate or large urine ketones and blood ketones > 3.0 mmol/L are usually present. This is the subject of Chapter 15.

Ketostix: Strips for measuring urine ketones (acetone). They are also available as Ketodiastix (for urine ketones and sugar).

Ketones (Acetone): The chemicals that appear when not enough insulin is present and fat is broken down. AcuTest tablets, Ketostix or Chemstrip K measure urine ketones. The Precision Xtra measures blood beta ketones.

mg/dL and mmol/L: Milligrams of material in a measured amount (100cc). Blood sugar (glucose) levels are expressed in mg/dL in the U.S., but they are usually expressed as mmol/L in Europe. It is possible to convert mg/dL to mmol/L by dividing by 18 (or multiplying by 0.0555). The opposite is done to go from mmol/L to mg/dL. A conversion table for glucose values is in the Appendix.

Void: Passage of urine.

QUESTIONS AND ANSWERS FROM NEWSNOTES

Q Why are you now advising that we buy the foil-wrapped rather than the bottles of Ketostix for measuring urine ketones?

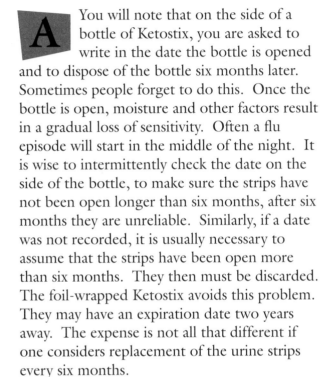

A You will note that on the side of a bottle of Ketostix, you are asked to write in the date the bottle is opened and to dispose of the bottle six months later. Sometimes people forget to do this. Once the bottle is open, moisture and other factors result in a gradual loss of sensitivity. Often a flu episode will start in the middle of the night. It is wise to intermittently check the date on the side of the bottle, to make sure the strips have not been open longer than six months, after six months they are unreliable. Similarly, if a date was not recorded, it is usually necessary to assume that the strips have been open more than six months. They then must be discarded. The foil-wrapped Ketostix avoids this problem. They may have an expiration date two years away. The expense is not all that different if one considers replacement of the urine strips every six months.

Ketone measurements are **VERY** important. A method for ketone testing **MUST** be in the home at all times and be taken along on trips away from home. It is **ONLY** by measuring the ketones that one can know if moderate or large urine ketones or high levels of ketones in the blood are present. If present, the physician must be called immediately. This may prevent a life-threatening episode of ketoacidosis (Chapter 15).

Q We recently obtained a Precision Xtra meter that measures the blood ketones as well as the blood sugars. How do the blood ketone measurements compare with the urine ketone measurements? When do we need to call our doctor or nurse?

A Like a blood sugar measured on a meter, the blood (serum) ketone value gives the ketone level at the time the test is done. The urine ketone measurement, like a urine sugar, can be hours behind. (The urine collected is since the last void.) The blood ketone value thus has the potential to be more representative of the current situation than the urine ketone measurement.

The blood test is particularly helpful when a person cannot void frequently due to dehydration, or when a person has not voided for several hours, so that it is not possible to tell if the urine ketone measurement represents the current level.

Blood ketone testing can be especially helpful for younger children. It would be wise to routinely call the diabetes care provider when blood ketone values above 1.0 are obtained.

It has been shown that youth are more likely to check blood ketones with an illness (93 percent did) than to check urine ketones (only 53 percent did). Finding ketones earlier could save a hospitalization OR A LIFE!

Who
is low?

Chapter 6
Low Blood Sugar
(Hypoglycemia or Insulin Reaction)

There are two emergency problems in blood sugar control for people with diabetes. The first, discussed in this chapter, is low blood sugar or hypoglycemia. (The second, discussed in Chapters 5 and 15, is high blood sugar or ketoacidosis.) Low blood sugar can come on quickly and must be treated by the person, family or friends. Early treatment helps prevent a more severe reaction and possible hospitalization.

Any time a person has received a shot or bolus of insulin, or an oral diabetes medicine, there is a chance of a low blood sugar reaction. The family of a person with newly diagnosed diabetes must know the signs and symptoms of hypoglycemia before going home the first night.

A normal (non-diabetic) random blood/CGM glucose level is usually between 70-140 mg/dL (3.9-7.8 mmol/L). Normal fasting values are usually between 70 and 100 mg/dL (3.9-5.5 mmol/L). For purposes of this book, **we define a true low blood sugar as < 60 mg/dL (< 3.2 mmol/L).** The American Diabetes Association (ADA) defines a low blood sugar level as **any level < 70 mg/dL (< 3.9 mmol/L).** This is the level at which the symptoms of hypoglycemia commonly occur. However, it is not uncommon for people who do **NOT** have diabetes to have values between 60 and 70 mg/dL (3.2 to 3.9 mmol/L).

TEACHING OBJECTIVES:

1. Present the symptoms, causes, and treatment of mild, moderate and severe hypoglycemia.

2. Identify the appropriate time to contact the healthcare provider.

LEARNING OBJECTIVES:

1. Define mild, moderate and severe low sugar symptoms, causes and treatment.

2. State the appropriate time to contact a healthcare provider.

CAUSES OF LOW BLOOD SUGAR

Hypoglycemia (low blood sugar) occurs because the body doesn't have enough sugar to burn for energy. The level of sugar in the blood falls too low. Sometimes it is called an **insulin reaction,** a **reaction** or a **low**.

Frequent causes are listed below:

- Meals and snacks that are late or missed

- Exercise (extra sugar may be burned during or after intense exercise, which may cause a low blood sugar)

- An insulin or oral medicine dose that is too high

- An insulin dose peaking at a different time than usual

- Giving a shot into muscle instead of under the skin, which results in rapid absorption of insulin

- Making a mistake in the drawing up and giving of an insulin dose

- Taking a bath or shower (or hot tub) soon after taking a shot/bolus of insulin. (The blood vessels in the skin dilate from the hot water and cause insulin to be rapidly absorbed.) It is always wise to wait at least 90 minutes to take a shower, bath or hot tub after an insulin shot/bolus. It is only necessary to wait a short time (10-15 minutes) after being in hot water to then do the shot.

Prevention of low blood sugars (lows) is much wiser than having to treat the lows. One of the advantages of using a continuous glucose monitor (CGM) is that it has formulas to help predict low glucose levels and alarms to warn the person when a low sugar is about to happen or is happening (Chapter 29).

SYMPTOMS OF LOW BLOOD SUGAR

Usually the body gives a warning when low blood sugar or an insulin reaction is developing. DIFFERENT PEOPLE GET DIFFERENT WARNINGS.

These signs are the most common warnings of an insulin reaction:

- **Hunger:** the person may either feel hungry or have an upset stomach (nausea)

- **Shakiness:** the person's hands or body may feel shaky

- **Sweatiness:** the person may sweat more than usual (often a cold sweat)

- **Color:** the face may become pale, gray or red

- **Headache**

- **Confusion:** the person may feel or look spacey or may appear dazed

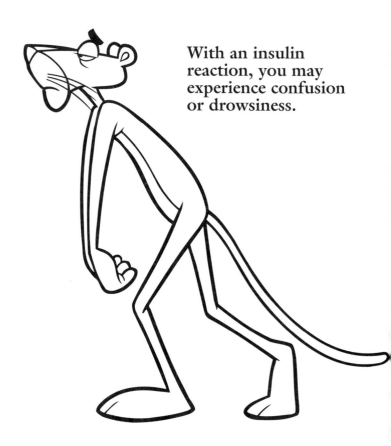

With an insulin reaction, you may experience confusion or drowsiness.

- **Drowsiness:** the person may yawn, feel sleepy or may have trouble thinking clearly; preschoolers frequently get sleepy

- **Behavioral changes:** changes in behavior are quite common; often the person may cry, act intoxicated, or act angry; they also may feel weak or anxious

- **Double vision:** the person may see double or the pupils of the eyes may get bigger; the eyes may appear glassy; the whites of the eyes may look blood shot

- **Loss of consciousness**

- **Seizure or convulsion:** both loss of consciousness and convulsion occur late in the reaction. They are usually the result of not treating a reaction quickly enough.

The first four initial symptoms (hunger, shakiness, sweatiness and color) are due to the output of the "fight or flight" hormone, adrenaline (epinephrine is another name). The latter symptoms are more related to the lack of sugar to the brain. Sugar is the main source of fuel for the brain. If the low sugar continues too long, the brain can be harmed. **It is particularly important to prevent severe low blood sugar in young children.** The brain grows very rapidly in the first four years of life.

NIGHTTIME LOWS

People may wake up with symptoms (infants may just cry) when lows occur during the night. *The symptoms may be the same as during the daytime although there are sometimes special clues:*

- **Inability to sleep or waking up alert, hungry, restless, moaning, etc.**

- **Waking up sweating**

- **Waking up with a fast heart rate**

- **Waking up with a headache**

- **Sleep walking**

- **Waking up feeling foggy-headed or with memory loss**

DELAYED HYPOGLYCEMIA

Delayed hypoglycemia is also discussed in Chapter 13 on exercise. It usually occurs from 4-12 hours after exercise. However, it can occur up to 24 hours after the exercise. For some people, blood/CGM glucose levels can be high during or after exercise. This is due to the normal response of releasing adrenaline during exercise (or from the extra snacks). Adrenaline causes sugar to come out of the liver and raise the blood sugar. At some point after the exercise, the adrenaline levels go back down (sometimes not until the time of sleep), and the sugar moves back into the muscle and liver. The result can be a low blood sugar or **"delayed hypoglycemia."** The symptoms are similar to those discussed above.

Prevention involves lowering the insulin dose (discussed in detail in Chapter 13). This must be done after heavy exercise even though the blood sugar may be high. Taking extra carbohydrates at bedtime (even with high blood sugar) may also be helpful. Exercise is essential for the heart and cardiovascular system. Therefore, it is important to always be thinking about how to best prevent post-exercise lows.

RECOGNIZING A LOW BLOOD SUGAR

It is important to recognize a low blood sugar at the earliest possible time. By doing this, the reaction will not progress to a severe reaction. The common symptoms are listed above, but they can vary from person to person. The early warning signs of a reaction are due to the release of a hormone called adrenaline. Most people make it when they are excited or scared. Another name for this "fight or flight" hormone is epinephrine. It causes shakiness, sweating, dilated pupils, a rapid heart rate and other symptoms. During the day, it is released when the blood/CGM glucose level falls below 70 mg/dL (3.9 mmol/L). People who have had diabetes for a longer period of time often make less of the protective hormones with low blood sugar, particularly at night. Some people tend to have only mild reactions and can easily detect symptoms. This seems to be more common in the first few years after diagnosis. Others may have more difficulty detecting symptoms. This seems to happen to people who have had diabetes longer or whose blood/CGM glucose values run at more normal levels. A term, **"hypoglycemic unawareness"** is sometimes applied to this condition, and it is discussed later in this chapter. Sometimes this is due to less adrenaline being available. In other cases, the lack of symptoms may be due to a slow or less dramatic fall in blood/CGM glucose levels, such as from 70 to 50 mg/dL (3.9 to 2.7 mmol/L) rather than from 170 to 50 mg/dL (9.5 to 2.7 mmol/L). Symptoms are more likely to occur with a greater and faster fall of a blood sugar level. Some people are less likely to detect low blood sugar in the morning because the sugar has fallen gradually during the night. Thus, adrenaline release and its symptoms did not occur. The use of CGM with alarms for a set low glucose level can be very helpful. Different children learn to tell if they have low blood sugar at different ages (see Chapter 18). It may be possible to train young children (or older people who have difficulty detecting low blood sugars) to recognize certain signs, and also to teach them words to express how they are feeling.

Parents may frequently need to remind a young child as below:

"Remember how you felt shaky and you came and told me there was a tiger in your tummy? You did a great job! Remember to tell a grown up if you feel that way again."

Ask the child how he/she feels when a low is found. This will reinforce their awareness of the symptoms. For very young children, the parent can often tell when the child has low blood sugar by the type of cry or fussiness he/she presents. Young children may be unaware of lows because they are busy playing. It is critical for adults to be aware of the need for snacks. A snack is especially important when a child discontinues naps during the day. It can be compared with an adult adding a new exercise program.

PREVENTING INSULIN REACTIONS (THINKING AHEAD)

It is important to prevent lows. This may allow the stores of epinephrine, glucagon, and other "protective" hormones to build up so they are available when needed.

Considerations in preventing insulin reactions:

🐾 **Snacks can be important when:**

✔ heavy physical exercise or all day exercise is planned, such as hiking or skiing

✔ the bedtime blood/CGM glucose level is below 130 mg/dL (<7.3 mmol/L)

✔ a person has a low (but be careful not to eat in excess - see the "Rule of 15" below)

🐾 **Giving insulin:**

✔ Reduce the dose of insulin which will be acting during and/or after the exercise period (see Chapter 13)

✔ Take the insulin injection AFTER a hot shower, bath or hot tub

✔ For some people, with careful insulin dose adjustments, or using Lantus/Levemir insulin or an insulin pump, extra bedtime snacks may not be needed unless the glucose level is < 130 mg/dL (< 7.3 mmol/L)

✔ If doing corrections for high blood sugars at bedtime or during the night, use half the usual dose and recheck blood/CGM glucose level in 2 hours

🐾 **Blood/CGM glucose levels:**

✔ Doing blood/CGM glucose levels before, during (hourly) and after periods of exercise will help to prevent lows and plan for future activity

✔ Knowing a blood/CGM glucose level can help decide the amount of treatment needed

✔ Do a blood/CGM glucose check during the night if it was a heavy exercise day

✔ **Always** do a recheck if the value was low (in approximately 15 minutes), especially if it was prior to the bedtime snack or during the night, to be certain it came back up

TREATMENT FOR A LOW BLOOD SUGAR (see Tables 1 and 2)

The general rule is to **GIVE SUGAR IN SOME FORM AS FAST AS POSSIBLE.** If the reaction is not severe, do a blood sugar first. If unable to do a blood sugar, then just give juice or sugar pop. A person with diabetes won't get sick from excess sugar. It will just cause high blood sugar and then be passed in the urine. Insulin reactions come quickly and should be treated at once by the person, parent, friend or teacher.

Different forms of sugar can be carried to treat low blood sugar. **PEOPLE WITH DIABETES SHOULD CARRY SUGAR PACKETS, GLUCOSE TABLETS, OR ANOTHER SOURCE OF SUGAR IN THEIR POCKETS AT ALL TIMES FOR EMERGENCIES.** Candy is sometimes too tempting. It also may be taken by other children. A special pocket for sugar packets can be sewn inside of gym shorts. Some people

carry them in a jogger wallet attached to a shoe. Others slip packets in high stockings. It is often best to wrap the packet in foil or a plastic bag in case of leaks. Insta-Glucose™ comes in a tube and looks like toothpaste. It is available in most pharmacies. Walgreens has the GLUCOSHOT ($10 US for 3), although if the taste is too desirable, they may be eaten when not low. A tube of clear cake gel or honey tube from the grocery store will also work. **The initial sugar will be absorbed more quickly if the person waits before eating the solid food.** After the blood sugar is back up, the person can eat some other longer-lasting solid food, like crackers or half of a sandwich. Gradually, each person will become familiar with the type of reactions that occur. The person will learn how severe the reactions tend to be, when they are most likely to occur and how best to treat them.

Eventually, as a person becomes more familiar with diabetes, it may be possible to treat the various reactions differently. Remember, when possible, it is always wise to do a blood sugar if the reaction is not severe. As CGM values are least accurate at low glucose levels, it is wise to use blood sugar determinations to evaluate possible lows. If the level is above 70 mg/dL (3.9 mmol/L), it is usually possible to treat the reaction with fresh fruit and solid food rather than juice or sugar pop. **ALSO, REMEMBER THAT IT TAKES 10 TO 20 MINUTES FOR THE BLOOD SUGAR LEVEL TO RISE, AND IT IS WISE TO WAIT UNTIL THE VALUE IS BACK UP TO RETURN TO NORMAL ACTIVITY. IT IS IMPORTANT TO REPEAT THE BLOOD SUGAR AFTER THE LOW TO MAKE SURE IT HAS RETURNED TO NORMAL.**

SOME PEOPLE USE THE "RULE OF 15": take 15g of carbohydrate and check again in 15 minutes. Then if the blood sugar is still below 70 mg/dL (<3.9 mmol/L), have another 15 g of carbohydrate. Some sources of quick-acting sugar with appropriate amounts for people of different ages are given in Table 1.

Table 1
Sources of Quick-Acting Sugar (Glucose) for Hypoglycemia

FOOD (Measured in grams of carbohydrae)	AGE		
	5 years or less (10g)	6-10 years (10-15g)	over 10 years (15-20g)
Glucose Tabs (4g each - check label; some = 5g)	2	3-4	4-5
Instant Glucose (1 tube = 31g)	⅓ tube	⅓-½ tube	½-⅔ tube
GLUCOSHOT/GLUCOGEL (15g – Walgreens)	⅓ tube	½ tube	1 tube
Cake gel (1 small tube = 12g)	1 tube	1 tube	1-2 tubes
Apple juice (½ cup = 15g)	⅓ cup	⅓-½ cup	½-⅔ cup
Orange juice (½ cup = 15g)	¼-½ cup	½-¾ cup	¾-1 cup
Sugar (1 tsp = 4g)	2 tsp	3-4 tsp	4-5 tsp
Honey (1 tsp = 5g; do not use if child is less than two years old)	2 tsp	2-3 tsp	3-4 tsp
Regular pop (soda) (1 oz = 3g)	3 oz	4-5 oz	5-6 oz
Milk (12g/cup)	¾ cup	1 cup	1½ cup
LIFE-SAVERS® (2.5g each)	4	4-6	6-8
Skittles® (1g each)	10 pieces	10-15 pieces	15-20 pieces
Sweet Tarts® (1.7g each)	6 pieces	6-8 pieces	8-12 pieces
Raisins (1 Tbsp = 7½g)	1-2 Tbsp	2 Tbsp	2½ Tbsp

g = gram; tsp = teaspoon; Tbsp = Tablespoon

TREATMENT BY SEVERITY OF REACTION (see summary, Table 2):

🐾 **Mild Reaction** (such as hunger at an unusual time, pale face, shakiness or irritability): If possible, do a blood sugar. If below 70 mg/dL (<3.9 mmol/L), give a small glass (4 oz) of juice or sugar pop (soda) or other quick acting sugar. Wait 10-15 minutes for absorption of the sugar and then give solid food (crackers, sandwich, fresh fruit, etc.). If the blood sugar is above 70 mg/dL (<3.9 mmol/L), give just solid food, without the juice or soda.

🐾 **Moderate Reaction** (very confused or spacey, very pale or very shaky): Give Insta-Glucose, Reactose™, Monojel™ or any source of simple sugar, such as sugar pop or juice. One-half tube of the Insta-Glucose can be placed between the cheeks and gums, and the person should be told to swallow. Always check for the risk of choking. Do a blood sugar as soon as possible. Repeat the blood sugar after 10-15 minutes to make sure it is above 70 mg/dL (>3.9 mmol/L). If not, repeat the initial treatment and wait another 10-15 minutes. Once the blood sugar has risen above 70 mg/dL (3.9 mmol/L) give solid food.

🐾 **Severe Reaction:** If the person is completely unconscious, it is risky to put the concentrated sugar around the gums. It could get into the airway. It is better to just give glucagon as instructed in Table 3 in this chapter. Remember to do the blood sugar level as soon as possible. If the person does not improve after 10-20 minutes, it may be necessary to call 911 to get extra help. A second dose (same amount) of glucagon (from the same vial) can also be given. In the preliminary part of the Diabetes Control and Complications Trial (DCCT; Chapter 14), one of every 10 people (10 percent) receiving standard treatment had a severe reaction each year. One of four people (25 percent) on intensive treatment (including insulin pumps) had a severe insulin reaction each year. Every family must have glucagon available and know how to use it (see Table 3). Our hypoglycemia video may be helpful in understanding how to use glucagon. Adjustments in the next insulin dose will be necessary. We recommend aiming for slightly higher blood sugars for several days after a severe reaction. Call your diabetes care provider if you need help making this adjustment. Remember, it is always okay to call 911 for a severe reaction, if you do not feel comfortable treating it yourself. Knowing how to administer glucagon, however, may help avoid emergency services.

We are concerned about any blood sugar below 60 mg/dL (<3.3 mmol/L). When these are obtained frequently, the insulin dose or snacks should be changed so that further low values do not occur. In a child under five years old, we are concerned about values below 70 mg/dL (3.9 mmol/L). When values are below these levels at the time of an insulin injection, we usually recommend not giving the usual amount of rapid-acting insulin (at least until after eating). If two or three values below 60 mg/dL (<3.3 mmol/L) are present at the same time of day in the same week, a decrease in insulin dose is probably needed. CALL THE DIABETES CARE PROVIDER IF HELP IS NEEDED.

🐾 **Hypoglycemic Unawareness:** Sometimes low blood sugars will be found during routine testing, and the person will not have had symptoms. This may be due to a very gradual fall in the blood sugar, or in young children, because they have not learned to recognize the symptoms. Some adults with very strict sugar control do not release adrenaline and may have the problem medically referred to as **"HYPOGLYCEMIC UNAWARENESS."** In this case, they must not aim for such strict blood sugar control. Sometimes the insulin dose can be lowered. Use of a CGM to warn

Table 2

Hypoglycemia: Treatment of Low Blood Sugar (B.S.)

Always check blood sugar level!

Low Blood Sugar Category	MILD	MODERATE	SEVERE
Alertness	<u>ALERT</u>	<u>NOT ALERT</u> **Unable to drink safely (choking risk)** Needs help from another person	<u>UNRESPONSIVE</u> Loss of consciousness Seizure **Needs constant adult help (position of safety)** ***Give nothing by mouth*** *(extreme choking risk)*
Symptoms	Mood Changes Shaky, Sweaty Hungry Fatigue, Weak Pale	Lack of Focus Headache Confused Disoriented 'Out of Control' (bite, kick) *Can't* Self-treat	Loss of Consciousness Seizure
Actions to take	✔ Check B.S. ✔ Give 2-8 oz sugary fluid (amount age dependent) ✔ Recheck B.S. in 10-15 min. ✔ B.S. < 70, repeat sugary fluid and recheck in 10-20 min. ✔ B.S. > 70, (give a solid snack)	✔ *Place in position of safety* ✔ Check B.S. ✔ If on insulin pump, may disconnect or suspend until fully recovered from low blood sugar (**awake and alert**) ✔ Give Insta-Glucose or cake decorating gel - put between gums and cheek and rub in. ✔ Look for person to 'wake up' ✔ Recheck B.S. in 10-20 min. ✔ *Once alert* – follow "actions" under 'Mild' column	✔ *Place in position of safety* ✔ Check B.S. ✔ If on insulin pump, disconnect or suspend until fully recovered from low blood sugar (**awake and alert**) ✔ Glucagon: *can be given with an insulin syringe* like insulin Below 6 years : **30 units (3/10 cc)** 6-16 years: **50 units (1/2 cc)** Over 16 years: **100 units (all of dose or 1 cc)** ✔ If giving 50 or 100 unit doses, may use syringe in box & inject through clothing. ✔ **Check B.S. every 10-15 min. until > 80** ✔ <u>**If no response, may need to call 911**</u> ✔ **Check B.S. every hour x 4-5 hours** ✔ High risk for more lows x 24 hours *(need to ↑ food intake and ↓ insulin doses)*
Recovery time	10-20 minutes	20-45 minutes	→ Call RN / MD ← and report the episode Effects can last 2-12 hours

about low glucose values may help to reverse this condition. After blood/CGM glucose levels have been higher for two or three weeks, it may be possible to again recognize low blood sugars.

🐾 **One-sided Weakness (paralysis):** It is not known why, but on rare occasions some people experience weakness (or paralysis) on one side of the body with a severe insulin reaction. This can last for one to 12 hours, but eventually clears. It is particularly worrisome to doctors in emergency rooms. They often insist on a very expensive evaluation to prove that a stroke has not occurred.

🐾 **PREVENTING SEVERE LOWS:**
A parent's greatest fear is a severe hypoglycemic reaction. This is often the biggest factor in not achieving optimal sugar control (a low HbA1c level, Chapter 14). Unfortunately, the most common time for severe lows to occur is during the sleeping hours. This is because the adrenaline response to hypoglycemia is lower when sleeping and the person is not awakened when the blood sugar falls. The good news is that the incidence of nighttime severe lows is now decreasing. This is due to several factors:

1. Probably the main reason for the decrease in severe lows is the recent use of basal/bolus insulin therapy using insulin analogs. An important contributor to this decrease is the non-peaking Lantus/Levemir basal insulin, rather than the large peaks of NPH insulin working during the night (see Chapter 8, Figure 1). The rapid-acting analogs (Humalog, NovoLog, and Apidra) also act during the post meal-time rises in blood sugar, particularly when given 20 minutes prior to the meal. In contrast, regular insulin acts after the rise in blood sugar has already occurred. The basal insulin from insulin-pump therapy also avoids the peaks during the night and helps to prevent lows.

2. The routine use of home blood glucose measurements (and of CGM) has helped to reduce the severe night-time lows. It has been shown that the risk of lows is greater when the pre-bedtime glucose level is below 130 mg/dL (<7.3 mmol/L) or following a heavy exercise day. Extra snacks obviously help if the value is low at bedtime. If the value is low, it is important to do a repeat check later to make sure it has come back up. Approximately 10 percent of blood/CGM glucose levels are not back up within 30 minutes.

3. Education is also a big factor. Families can "think-ahead' and reduce the insulin acting during the night if there has been unusual exercise that day. Parents will often get up at night and do a blood sugar or observe the CGM value on those nights.

4. The use of CGM has increased in recent years, with the alarms for predicted lows or actual lows helping to reduce the likelihood of severe hypoglycemic episodes.

GLUCAGON

Glucagon is a hormone made in the pancreas, like insulin. However, it has the opposite effect of insulin and raises the blood sugar level. Glucagon injections are rarely needed, but we ask families to keep it on hand and to be prepared to use it if necessary. The expiration date on the box should be checked regularly and, if outdated, a new bottle should be obtained. If a very severe reaction occurs and the person loses consciousness, glucagon should be given promptly. It can be stored at room temperature. It should not reach a temperature above 90° or below freezing. It can be taken in a cooler with the insulin and blood sugar strips for trips away from home.

Table 3
Glucagon Injections – When To and How To

🐾 Use when a person is unconscious or having a seizure.

🐾 Keep in a convenient and known place. Store in a refrigerator during hot weather. Protect from freezing.

🐾 Keep a 3cc syringe available or use the fluid-filled syringe in the emergency kit. An insulin syringe and needle can also be used (preferably a 1.0cc syringe). Some people tape the syringe to the kit so they have this readily available (see video on hypoglycemia).

🐾 If you have the emergency kit, the fluid does not need to be withdrawn from bottle 1 (diagram at right) as it is already in the syringe. Put the liquid into the glucagon vial and swirl gently to mix. The large syringe that the liquid was in can also be used to give the glucagon injection. Draw up the dose indicated below. Clear the air pointing the needle upward.

🐾 Withdraw from the mixed glucagon bottle:
If using an insulin syringe, put needle into center of stopper.

(Estimate dose if using the emergency kit syringe.)

0.3cc (30 units) for a child less than six years old

0.5cc (50 units) for a child 6-16 years of age

1.0cc (100 units) for a person over 16 years of age

🐾 If using the syringe that comes in the emergency kit, inject into deep muscle (in front of leg or upper, outer arm) though it is OK to inject into the subcutaneous fat. Inject through clothing if needed. If the glucagon is drawn into an insulin syringe then give it just as you would an insulin shot. If a blood sugar has not yet been done, it can be done now.

🐾 Wait 10 minutes. Check blood sugar. If still unconscious and blood sugar is still below 60 mg/dL (3.3 mmol/L), inject second dose of glucagon (same amount as first dose).

🐾 If there is no response to the glucagon, or if there is any difficulty breathing, call paramedics (or 911).

🐾 As soon as he/she awakens, give sips of juice, sugar pop or sugar in water initially. Honey may help to raise the blood sugar for children over the age of 1 year. After 10 minutes, encourage solid food (crackers and peanut butter or cheese, sandwich, etc.).

🐾 Notify diabetes care team of severe reaction prior to next insulin injection (so dose can be changed if needed). Complete recovery may take 1-6 hours.

Please copy this page as often as you wish. Tape a copy to the box of glucagon.

1.
Insert 1/2 cc of air into fluid bottle (1cc won't fit). Rotate to mix.

2.
Draw out 1cc of fluid from bottle.

3.
Inject the 1cc of fluid into bottle with powder. Mix.

Use of Glucagon

1. Severe Low Blood Sugar

Glucagon comes in a bottle containing 1 mg as a tablet or powder. There is a syringe containing diluting solution in the emergency kit. The method for giving glucagon is shown in Table 3. **This table may be copied and attached to the glucagon kit.** Our hypoglycemia video (see Ordering Materials in the back) demonstrates the methods for glucagon administration. In addition a video from Eli Lilly and Co giving instructions for glucagon use is also available as a link on our website, www.barbaradaviscenter.org. Novo Nordisk also provides a "Hypokit"™ to instruct people on glucagon usage.

Sometimes vomiting will occur after a severe reaction. This may be from the person's own glucagon output or from the glucagon that was injected. It usually does not last very long, and if the blood sugar is above 150 mg/dL (8.3 mmol/L), it is not a big problem. If the person is lying down, the head should be turned to the side to avoid choking. Urine or blood ketones should be checked (see Chapter 5) as they can sometimes also form. If the family is concerned about the ketones, or if the blood sugar did not rise, or if the vomiting continues, the diabetes care provider should be called.

2. Low Dose Glucagon

Sometimes the blood sugar can be low (< 70 mg/dL [< 3.9 mmol/L]) and the person cannot keep any food down (such as with vomiting or diarrhea). In this case, a very low dose of Glucagon can be mixed (Table 3) and given just like insulin – using an insulin syringe. The dose is one unit per year of age up to age 15 years. Older people can just use the 15 units.

For example: a five-year-old would get five units or a 10-year-old would get 10 units.

If the blood sugar is not higher in 20-30 minutes, the same dose can be repeated. This treatment has saved many ER visits.

RECORD ALL INSULIN REACTIONS

Record insulin reactions in your record book. Many families circle all values < 60 mg/dL (< 3.3 mmol/L). Try to identify and record the cause of any low or high blood sugars (Table 4). If more than two mild insulin reactions occur in a short time period, adjust the amount of insulin or call the diabetes care provider. It is usually possible to call during office hours, but if a severe reaction occurs, call the care provider prior to giving the next regularly scheduled insulin shot.

MEDICAL IDENTIFICATION

In case of a severe insulin reaction, EVERYONE needs to know that the person has diabetes. This includes teachers, strangers, police, co-workers, friends and medical personnel. The person with diabetes should wear a bracelet or necklace with this information. A card in the wallet is not enough; this may not be found by paramedics. A diabetes ID card can also be stapled to the registration of the car in the glove compartment. Bracelets or necklaces can be found at most pharmacies or medical supply houses.

The MedicAlert Foundation
(provides MedicAlert tags)
2323 Colorado Avenue
Turlock, California 95382
888-633-4298
www.medicalert.org

The MedicAlert tag includes a number that can be called 24 hours a day for information concerning both the person and the doctor. The minimum charge for the bracelet or necklace and keeping the information readily available 24 hours per day is $35. Then the annual membership renewal after the first year is $20.

A bracelet, necklace or medallion with your personal medical information (name, condition and medications) can be engraved and ordered through American Medical Identifications, Inc.

The prices for an identification tag start at $21.95.

American Medical Identifications, Inc.
P.O. Box 925617
Houston, Texas 77292
800-363-5985
www.americanmedical-id.com

Colorful sports bracelets are sometimes preferred and can be ordered from FIFTY 50 PHARMACY. The cost per bracelet ranges from $9.95 to $14.95 plus $4.50 for shipping. Mail your order with payment to:

FIFTY 50
1420 Valwood Parkway, Suite 120
Carrollton, Texas 75006
Phone: 800-746-7505
www.fifty50.com

Medical charms are also popular. These work well for attaching to the toddler shoe laces. The addresses are:

Miss Brooke's Company
P.O. Box 558
Bryant, Arkansas 72089
Phone: 888-417-7591
www.missbrooke.com

For those who desire additional choices, see www.tah-handcrafted-jewelry.com or http://childrenwithdiabetes.com/d_06_700.htm. For people who will not wear a necklace or bracelet, a watch or shoe tag may be the next best choice. There are medallions that stick to the front of a wallet, cell phone, insulin pump, etc. These can be purchased from LIFETAG, Inc., 888-LIFETAG or www.lifetag.com.

Toddlers should not wear a neck chain (too risky), but they often do well with ankle bracelets, charms or a medallion laced in the shoe. The sports bracelet described above works quite well around the ankle.

Rubber bracelets can be purchased at http://coolmedid.com.

Table 4
Some Factors That Change the Blood Sugar

Lowers:

- Insulin

- Hot bath, showers or hot tubs may increase insulin absorption and cause a low blood sugar

- Exercise, although for some people, the values may be higher immediately following exercise

- Less food or eating late

Raises:

- Sugar intake

- Glucagon

- Hormones such as glucagon, adrenaline, growth hormone and cortisol (prednisone); their action is opposite to that of insulin

- Illness (which may cause ketones)

- Rapid growth; teenagers usually require more insulin with increased growth

- Menstrual periods (may cause ketones)

- Emotions such as anger and excitement; some younger children can have lower blood sugars with extra excitement

- Inhalers given for asthma which have epinephrine derivatives in them

DEFINITIONS

Adrenaline (used collectively to include epinephrine and non-epinephrine): The excitatory hormone. This is released with a low blood sugar or a rapid fall in blood sugar, which then causes the symptoms of low blood sugar (shaking, sweating and pounding heart).

Glucagon: A hormone also made in the pancreas (like insulin) that causes the blood sugar to rise. It is available to inject into people who are unconscious from a severe insulin reaction.

Hypoglycemia: The term used for a low blood sugar (insulin reaction).

Hypoglycemic unawareness: The term used to describe low blood sugars without the person having any warning signs or symptoms.

Insta-Glucose, Monojel, or Reactose: Sources of concentrated sugar that can be purchased. It can be given to a person in case of low blood sugar.

Ketoacidosis (Acidosis): What happens in the body when not enough insulin is available. The blood sugar is usually high at this time. Moderate or large ketones (acetone) are present in the urine (see Chapter 15).

Seizure (convulsion): Loss of consciousness with jerking of muscles. This can occur with a very severe low blood sugar (insulin reaction).

QUESTIONS AND ANSWERS FROM NEWSNOTES

Q **Do we still need to keep glucagon?**

A YES!

The current statistic (from three studies) is that four to 13 percent of standard insulin-treated patients have one or more severe episodes of hypoglycemia each year. With intensive insulin therapy in the DCCT, 25 percent (one in four) of subjects had a severe reaction each year. Glucagon should be given anytime there is loss of consciousness without being able to arouse the person. If paramedics are to be called, it is still wise to give the glucagon before they arrive.

The biggest change in giving glucagon is that two studies have shown it will work just as fast when given subcutaneously (the same place as insulin) as when given into muscle. People used to think it always had to be given into muscle.

The Eli Lilly Company Glucagon Emergency Kit comes with the diluting solution already in the syringe ready to be injected into the bottle with the powdered glucagon for mixing. The syringe and needle they provide can then also be used for the subcutaneous or intra-muscular injection (either is fine).

Some people have rebounding, a high blood sugar and even ketones after glucagon. Vomiting can also occur, but these side effects can be handled.

Q **Since I have changed to three or more injections of insulin per day, and my Hemoglobin A1c has come down, I don't seem to feel low blood sugar reactions. Is this common?**

A Unfortunately, this is not unusual. It is called hypoglycemic unawareness. People on intensive insulin therapy often do not make the counter-regulatory hormones as effectively as they did previously. Adrenaline (epinephrine) output is sometimes reduced in people with very tight sugar control. This is probably the most important hormone involved, which normally increases with low blood sugar and then causes the symptoms (shakiness, sweatiness, rapid heart beat, etc.). Sometimes it is possible to reduce the insulin dose to let the blood sugars run a bit higher for two or three weeks in order to regain the ability to feel low blood sugars.

Other hormones which normally help to raise the blood sugar may also have reduced output following intensive insulin therapy. Production of the hormone glucagon, normally made in the pancreas like insulin, is reduced in most people who have had diabetes for longer than one year. Therefore, it also may not be available to help raise the blood sugar. It is important to let your diabetes care provider know if you are having low blood sugars without symptoms.

Q **We were recently told at a clinic visit that our child should not be given insulin just prior to a hot bath, shower or hot tub. Would you please explain the reason for this?**

A The hot bath, shower or hot tub increases blood flow to the skin. As more blood flows to this area, more insulin is rapidly taken up by the blood (probably primarily Humalog, NovoLog, Apidra or Regular insulins). This can then result in a severe low blood sugar. The answer is to **always take the insulin after the hot shower or bath.** The shower or bath should not be taken in the 10-15 minutes after Humalog/NovoLog/Apidra or in the four hours after taking Regular insulin. This may help to prevent a severe low blood sugar.

Wait to take your shot after a bath or shower.

Chapter 7
Blood Sugar (Glucose) Monitoring

TEACHING OBJECTIVES:

1. Present blood sugar (glucose) concepts: rationale, times, frequency and desired ranges for the individual.

2. Provide instruction for the meter of choice.

3. Discuss how to troubleshoot problems with the meter.

4. Introduce the concept of following blood sugars and observing trends.

LEARNING OBJECTIVES:

Learners (parents, child, relative or self) will be able to:

1. Describe rationale for doing blood sugars and list times, frequency and desired ranges.

2. Demonstrate use of meter including setting time and code when necessary.

3. Locate and state the 1-800 number listed on the meter to call for problems.

4. Choose and apply a method for following blood sugar results and recognizing trends.

MEASURING BLOOD SUGARS

The ability of people (or families) with diabetes to check blood sugar levels quickly and accurately changed diabetes management more than anything else in the past 30 years. Prior to this, diabetes was primarily managed by measuring urine sugars, which were very unreliable. The people in the intensive treatment group of the Diabetes Control and Complications Trial (DCCT) did at least four blood sugars every day (see Chapter 14). They were able to achieve excellent diabetes control as a result of frequent blood sugar testing, more frequent dosages of insulin and following a dietary plan. The improved glucose control was shown to significantly reduce the risk for eye,

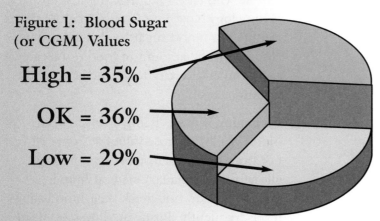

Figure 1: Blood Sugar (or CGM) Values

High = 35%

OK = 36%

Low = 29%

Graphs can be obtained from some of the blood sugar meters when they are brought to the clinic. This young man had a HbA1c (see Chapter 14) of 7.1 percent, but was having too many lows. We like no more than 10 percent of values to be low and for at least 50 percent of values to be in the target range (see suggested ranges for different ages in Table 4).

kidney, nerve and cardiovascular complications of diabetes. Clearly, for people who are able to check blood sugars more frequently, or to consistently use a continuous glucose monitor (CGM), improved sugar control is now possible. The Standards of Diabetes Care (see Chapter 21) recommends "frequent blood-glucose monitoring" (at least 3-4 times per day). However, fewer values may be needed if a CGM is worn (discussed in Chapter 29).

WHY DO BLOOD/CGM GLUCOSE MONITORING?

There are many reasons why measuring blood sugars or using CGM at home has become a "cornerstone" of diabetes care. Blood sugar measurements are usually used initially in diabetes management. Then, when the subject/family is ready, CGM use can be initiated. CGM measures subcutaneous glucose levels rather than blood sugar levels. Although Chapter 29 is devoted to CGM, reference to CGM will also be included in this chapter when applicable. A few of the reasons why measuring sugar (glucose) levels is important will be discussed. They are listed in Table 1:

- **Safety:** A big reason for the use of blood/CGM glucose checking relates to safety. Almost no one feels all the low blood sugars that occur and very young children may not report feeling any lows. Checking the blood sugar level (or CGM value) before the bedtime snack may help in choosing ways to prevent low blood sugars during the night.

- **Improving sugar control:** Studies have clearly shown that doing a minimum of four blood sugars daily (or consistently using a CGM) and using the results wisely can result in overall improved sugar control. This results in a reduced risk for diabetic complications.

- **Adjusting the insulin dosage:** If blood (or CGM) glucose values are checked regularly, and the results are analyzed to look for patterns of lows or highs, the insulin dosage can be adjusted as needed. Chapter 22

Table 1
Reasons for Blood/CGM Glucose Levels

- Safety
- Improve sugar control
- Adjust the insulin dosage
- Manage illnesses
- Understand the effects of various foods, insulin doses, exercise or stress
- Discriminate a rapid fall in blood sugar from a truly low blood sugar value
- Know the blood sugar level immediately
- Sense of control
- Indicate a need to test for urine or blood ketones

provides examples of insulin adjustments. People who take a rapid-acting insulin (Humalog/NovoLog/Apidra) before meals can use the blood sugar level/CGM values along with the amount of food to be eaten and planned exercise to decide how much insulin to take.

- **Managing illness:** Being able to check blood/CGM glucose values at home when a person is sick or before or after surgery allows for safe management at home. People who do not check their blood sugar levels frequently during an illness are more likely to become seriously ill and to be admitted to the hospital.

- **To understand the effects of various foods, exercise or stress:** By checking blood/CGM glucose values two hours after eating a certain food or doing a certain amount of exercise, one can better plan the insulin dose the next time. Pizza, for example, tends to raise blood sugars higher and longer than other foods for some people. If this is found to be true, extra rapid-acting insulin can be considered for the next time it is to be eaten. Similarly, some people lower or raise their blood sugar with a certain exercise, whereas others do not. Knowing the blood sugar value after doing the exercise a few times will help in future planning.

🐾 **To discriminate a rapid fall in blood/CGM glucose values from a truly low blood sugar value:** Some people report frequent symptoms of an insulin reaction when the blood sugar is still above 70 mg/dL (3.9 mmol/L). This may occur when the blood sugar falls rapidly (for example from 300 to 150 mg/dL [16.7 to 8.3 mmol/L]) or when a low blood sugar truly occurs. Doing a blood sugar at the time of a reaction will help determine whether the symptoms are due to a rapid fall (**false reaction**) or a truly low blood sugar. We consider a truly low blood sugar to be below **60 mg/dL (< 3.3 mmol/L)** or in a preschooler, **below 70 mg/dL (< 3.9 mmol/L).** Sugar can be given if the level is low, but it is not needed if the symptoms are just due to a rapid fall in sugar. If the level is between 70 and 100 mg/dL (3.9 and 5.5 mmol/L), it is often helpful to eat food that is not high in sugar. These differences will not be known unless a blood/CGM glucose level is available at the time of the insulin reaction.

🐾 **To know the blood sugar level immediately:** A blood/CGM glucose value will give immediate results. For example, a child may be irritable and the cause may be unknown. The blood sugar value will quickly help the parent decide if the irritability is due to a low blood sugar level or another cause. Another person may have an important event and just want to know the blood/CGM glucose value prior to starting the event.

🐾 **To give people a "sense of control" over their diabetes:** Many people feel better knowing how their blood/CGM glucose values are running. However, it is important to remember that there may not always be an exact relationship between the blood sugar level and what one expects it to be. There are always unknown factors that result in occasional high or low levels. This can be very upsetting for the person who expects blood/CGM glucose values to always be in the target range. It is important not to become discouraged when values do not always match the expected results. We emphasize that sugars are "in target" or "high" or "low," but not "good" or "bad." Questions or concerns about the blood sugar values should be discussed with the diabetes team.

🐾 **As an indicator to check the urine or blood ketone level:** A fasting blood/CGM glucose value above 240 mg/dL (13.3 mmol/L) or a value above 300 mg/dL (16.7 mmol/L) during the rest of the day should indicate a need to check the blood or urine ketone level. (Some meters now even flash this advice.) Checking for blood or urine ketones when the glucose level is high may help to prevent an episode of ketoacidosis (see Chapter 15).

HOW TO DO SELF-BLOOD SUGAR LEVELS

🐾 **Finger-poking**

A finger-poking (lancing) device is used to get the drop of blood. There are many good devices on the market, and these can now often be set at different depths for different people. The adjustable pokers are particularly helpful for young children who have tender skin and may not need much lancing depth.

The hands should be washed with warm water (to increase blood flow and to make sure they are clean). Any trace of sugar on the finger may give a false elevated reading. We do not

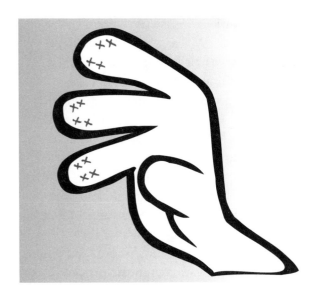

base of the thumb, the upper arm and the thigh and calf. The main problem has been that the blood flow through the arm is slower than through the fingertips. The slower blood flow means the blood sugar value from the arm may be 10 minutes or more **behind** the fingertip. It is important to rub the site to be used on the arm prior to doing the stick. The rubbing will increase the blood flow in the area. The person may feel low or have a low value from a fingerstick, but the arm level will not be low. We advise families **to use the fingertip if the child is feeling low.** Also, people who do not feel their lows (hypoglycemic unawareness; Chapter 6) should always use their fingertips for

recommend routinely wiping with alcohol because any trace of alcohol left on the skin will interfere with the chemical reaction for the blood sugar determination (Table 2). Alcohol also dries and toughens the skin. Occasionally, when away from home (e.g., camping, picnics), it is necessary to use alcohol-free travel wipes to cleanse the finger. Air dry the finger before doing the blood sugar check.

It is often helpful to place the finger to be used on a table top. This prevents the natural reflex of withdrawing the finger and not getting an adequate poke. The side of the finger should be used rather than the fleshy pad on the fingertip, which is more painful. If the drop is not coming easily, hold the hand down to the side of the body to increase the blood in the finger. IT IS IMPORTANT TO ROTATE FINGERS SO THAT ONE FINGER DOES NOT BECOME TOO "ABUSED." If the fingers become sore, the toes or the ball at the base of the thumb may be used.

🐾 Alternate Sites for Blood Sugars

Many people are now poking sites other than the fingers or toes. These sites are used because they may not hurt as much. The poker may need to be "dialed" to the maximum depth to get enough blood. The most common site is the forearm. Meters approved for the arm include The FreeStyle™, The FreeStyle Flash™ and the One Touch Ultra®. The FreeStyle is also approved for use on the fleshy pad at the

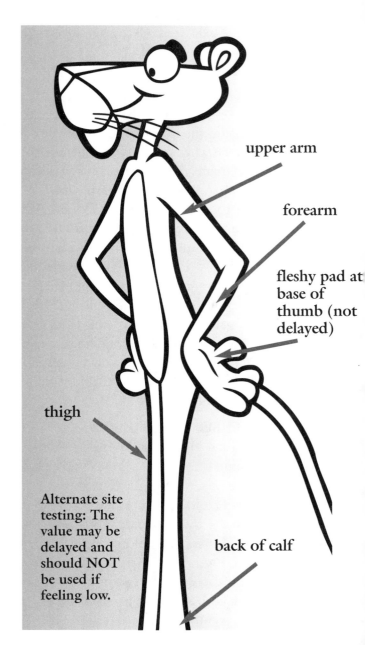

upper arm

forearm

fleshy pad at base of thumb (not delayed)

thigh

back of calf

Alternate site testing: The value may be delayed and should NOT be used if feeling low.

Table 2
Common Problems Causing Inaccurate Blood Sugar Results

🐾 Finger is not clean and dry (sugar on finger will raise result; alcohol or water will interfere)

🐾 Adding more blood after the first drop has been put on pad (now ok for some meters)

🐾 Meter parts are dirty (e.g., with dried blood)

🐾 Too small a drop of blood on pad

🐾 Strips have expired

🐾 Strips have been exposed to heat (> 90°, e.g., left in hot car) or frozen (e.g., left in cold car)

blood sugars. **Remember** to change the lancet everyday. A sharp lancet will lessen injury to the site and help prevent an infection.

🐾 **Blood Sugar (Glucose) Meters**

Some of the desirable features in selecting a meter are listed in Table 3. The meter chosen should meet the person's needs. Some people leave a meter at school or at work. If using more than one meter, try to use no more than two different brands. Families tend to prefer small meters that are easy to slip into a pocket. They also prefer meters that take a short time for the glucose determination. Particularly for younger children, the need for only a small amount of blood is helpful. Most of the strips now have a capillary action to pull the blood into the strip. This may be helpful for a small child who has difficulty holding still. For some people, accuracy in cold, heat, high humidity or high altitude is important. If a strip has been in a cooler or refrigerator (most strips spoil at above 90° or if they freeze), they should always be brought to room temperature before using.

Often the main reason one meter is selected over another in the U.S. is that the family's health insurance will pay for that meter and its strips. The glucose strips usually add up to a cost of $3-4 (U.S.) per day, and so insurance coverage is important. The cost of strips is usually a more important factor than the cost of the meter.

It is important with most meters to check a control strip or solution at regular intervals to

Table 3
Desired Features of Blood Glucose Meters

🐾 Accurate (in environment where it is to be used)

🐾 Storage of at least the last 100 values

🐾 Able to be downloaded at clinic and/or at home

🐾 Small in size

🐾 Short determination time

🐾 Small drop of blood (capillary action of strip)

🐾 Blood is applied to the end of the strip and does not get into the meter

🐾 Cleaning is easy or not necessary

🐾 A control solution or strip can be used to check for accuracy

🐾 Strips are paid for by the family's insurance

make sure reliable results are being obtained. Some clinics with a more accurate meter may wish to intermittently check the family's meter with the clinic's meter. Some common problems causing inaccurate blood sugar results are shown in Table 2.

We do request that families choose a meter with a memory for at least the last 100 glucose values. **The meter(s) must always be brought to the clinic visit** so that it can be downloaded. The values as well as graphs, such as the pie-chart (Figure 1), can be printed. Some families like to download their blood glucose results in their homes. Research from our Center showed that if at least half of the blood/CGM glucose values are within range for the person's age (see Figure 2 and Table 4), the HbA1c values will usually be in the desired range for the age (Chapter 14). During the "honeymoon" phase (Chapter 2), or when the body still makes much of its own insulin, most of the blood/CGM glucose values will be in the desired range for age. For other people with diabetes, it is a reasonable goal to try to get half of the values at any time of day within range for that person's age.

WHEN TO DO BLOOD/CGM GLUCOSE LEVELS

We encourage people to do at least four blood sugar values every day or to use CGM.

When four blood sugars are done each day, they are often scheduled before breakfast, before lunch, before the afternoon snack or before dinner, and before the bedtime snack. Occasional values should also be done two hours after meals and during the night. The blood/CGM glucose goals for before meals and two hours after meals are shown in Figure 2 and Table 4. Suggested bedtime and nighttime values are also given in Table 4. Blood/CGM glucose goals are further discussed in Chapter 14.

1. Pre-breakfast

The morning blood/CGM glucose value reflects the levels during the night and is probably the most important value related to diabetes control. For example, it directly reflects the dose of Lantus insulin no matter when it's given during the day. This is because there is no food or rapid-acting insulin affecting the glucose level in the morning. As shown in the figure at the beginning of Chapter 2, this value reflects the "turning off" of internal sugar production by the liver. It is not usually elevated due to the bedtime snack or eating during the night. The rapid-acting insulin dose

Table 4
Suggested Blood Sugar/CGM Levels (See also Chapter 14)

Age (years)	Fasting (a.m.) or no food for 2 hours		Bedtime (before bedtime snack or during the night)	
	mg/dL	mmol/L	mg/dL	mmol/L
Below 5	80-200	4.5-11.1	Above 150* [80**]	above 8.3* [4.5**]
5-11	70-180	3.9-10.0	Above 130* [70**]	above 7.3* [3.9**]
12 and above	70-150	3.9-8.3	Above 130* [60**]	above 7.3* [3.3**]

*If values are below these levels, milk or other food might be added to the solid protein and carbohydrate bedtime snack.

**If values are below these levels, the level should be rechecked 10-30 minutees later to make certain it has come back up. If this happens more than once within a week, either reduce the dinner rapid-acting or Regular insulin or call the diabetes care provider for advice.

Note: The ADA recommended sugar levels for children of different ages vary somewhat from our suggestions. The levels for before meals and during the night recommended by the ADA can be found in Table 1 of Chapter 14.

at breakfast is also usually based, at least in part, on the morning blood/CGM glucose result. Using Lantus/Levemir insulin or an insulin pump, it is now usually possible to get the majority of fasting glucose values "in range" (see Table 4).

2. Pre-lunch

A blood/CGM glucose value before lunch helps to decide if the morning rapid-acting insulin and/or Regular insulin dosage is correct. For people using morning NPH insulin, it may also be having an effect at this time. Families of school children should routinely request that a value be done prior to eating lunch. For most children (and schools), this is not a problem and can be done without interfering with the child's normal school life.

3. Pre-dinner

The blood/CGM glucose value before dinner reflects the dose of morning NPH insulin (if taken) and/or the dose of rapid-acting insulin given at lunch. It may also reflect afternoon sports activities and the food eaten for an afternoon snack. Youth who eat a large afternoon snack should use Humalog/NovoLog/Apidra to cover the food to be eaten. The pre-dinner value will then tell if the dose given was correct.

4. Bedtime

The blood/CGM glucose value prior to the bedtime snack is important for all people with diabetes. It is particularly important for:

🐾 people who tend to have low sugars during the night

🐾 children who play outside after dinner or who have had heavy exercise that day

🐾 anyone who did not eat well at dinner

🐾 knowing if the rapid-acting insulin dose given at dinner is correct

As can be seen in Table 4, suggested bedtime blood/CGM glucose values are given for the different ages. **If the values are below the values in brackets (two stars), doing a follow-up blood sugar check during the**

night is wise. These values may be different for each person.

5. After meals

In recent years, more emphasis has been placed on doing blood/CGM glucose values two hours after eating a meal. The highest blood sugars of the day occur after meals and these values add to the HbA1c value (Chapter 14). More people are now using carbohydrate counting. They may inject insulin 20 minutes prior to meals based on their expected carbohydrate intake (Chapter 12). The blood/CGM glucose values two hours after the meal confirm if the **I**nsulin to **C**arbohydrate ratio (**I/C** ratio – Chapter 12) and the estimated carbohydrates were correct. **The blood/CGM glucose values listed in Table 4 by age can also be the goals for two hours after meals.** Others just aim for values below 140 mg/dL (< 7.8 mmol/L) two hours after meals. We would recommend that families try to check blood/CGM glucose values two hours after each meal a few times each week. Values obtained two hours after meals can perhaps be flagged by a symbol such as a star.

6. Nighttime

It may be necessary to occasionally check blood/CGM glucose values in the middle of the night (see Chapter 6 on Low Blood Sugar) to make sure the value is not getting too low. This is particularly true if it has been a heavy exercise day. The diabetes care provider may suggest this if very erratic results are noted for the morning blood sugars. The use of CGM can be very helpful in evaluating nighttime values.

A nighttime blood/CGM glucose value is particularly important for people who tend to have reactions (low blood sugars) during the night. More than half of the severe low sugars occur during the nighttime hours. Many families will routinely do a level during the night. Others choose to do a value once or twice weekly. **IT IS IMPORTANT TO CHECK THE LEVELS ON NIGHTS WHEN THERE HAS BEEN EXTRA DAYTIME PHYSICAL ACTIVITY.** The

Figure 2
Blood (CGM) Glucose Level in mg/dL (mmol/L)

VERY HIGH 400-800 (22.2-44.4)		Stomachache Difficulty Breathing
HIGH 200-400 (11.1-22.2)		Low Energy
GOALS 80-200 (4.5-11.1)	Under 5 years	Fine
70-180 (3.9-10.0)	5-11 years	
70-150 (3.9-8.3)	12 years and up	
LOW below 60 (below 3.3)	True-Low	Sweating Hunger Shakiness

NON-DIABETIC NORMAL VALUES FOR CHILDREN*

70-100 (3.9-5.5)	Normal (fasting)*
70-130 (3.9-7.3)	Normal (random)*

*The DirecNet Study Group showed that approximately 95 percent of values for non-diabetic children are in this range. However, occasional values down to 60 mg/dL (3.3 mmol/L) and, for random values, up to 144 mg/dL (8.0 mmol/L) are still normal.

extra activity might be a basketball game in the evening. For a younger child, it might be playing hard outside during the day or on a nice summer evening. The best time to do a check varies with each person. For some, between midnight and 2 a.m. is the best. For others, the early morning hours are the most valuable – perhaps when a parent is getting ready for work. Table 4 also gives suggested values for during the night.

7. With low blood sugar

As noted above, doing a blood sugar when feeling low helps to separate a rapid fall in blood sugar from a "true-low" (< 60 mg/dL [or < 3.3 mmol/L]). A food with sugar must be given for a "true-low" whereas other food may be given (e.g., cheese, peanut butter) for values above 70 mg/dL (> 3.9 mmol/L).

RECORD KEEPING

Examples of daily record sheets are included in this chapter. The pages record either the last one week or the last two weeks of blood sugar values. Many families will fax or email the page to their diabetes care provider if they have concerns. If this is done, make sure the insulin dosages and instructions for return fax or phone contact are included. These sheets may be copied and stored in a notebook to bring along to clinic visits. Keeping accurate records to look for patterns in blood sugar fluctuations is essential. **Patterns of high or low blood/CGM glucose levels will be missed if results are not recorded and/or analyzed at regular intervals.** It is important to note all reactions and possible causes. Some people also circle or highlight all values below 60 mg/dL (< 3.3 mmol/L) or put a star on days of reactions so that these can be easily noted by the diabetes care providers. If times of heavy exercise are recorded, it may be possible to see the effects of exercise on blood/CGM glucose values. Illnesses, stress and menstrual periods may increase the blood sugar and should be noted. It may be helpful to record what was eaten for the bedtime snack and if there was heavy exercise to see if these are related to morning blood/CGM glucose values. Hopefully, occasional determinations will also be done at the time(s) when routine values are not usually done. Also included is a place to record urine or blood ketone checks, as newly diagnosed people must check their ketones frequently. Ketone checks are essential with any illness or anytime the blood/CGM glucose level is above 240 mg/dL (> 13.3 mmol/L) fasting or over 300 mg/dL (> 16.7 mmol/L) during the day.

The insulin dose can be recorded with the units of rapid-acting insulin on top (e.g., 5H or 5NL) and the units of intermediate-acting insulin on the bottom (e.g., 15N).

Fastidious record keeping (or regular viewing of computer downloads) and bringing the results to clinic visits allow the family and diabetes team to work together most effectively to achieve optimal diabetes management. **Complacency and not following values often results in missing patterns of high blood/CGM glucose values and a resultant high HbA1c value (see Chapter 14). We also encourage families who send blood sugar results and who have questions to suggest solutions, which can be discussed with the doctor or nurse.**

DEFINITIONS

Continuous Glucose Monitor (CGM): Medical devices that measure a person's glucose levels every 5-10 minutes. They use a small sensor that is placed under the skin, and results are viewed on a hand-held receiver.

DCCT: Diabetes Control and Complications Trial. This trial was completed in June 1993 and clearly showed that eye, nerve and heart complications of diabetes were related to glucose control.

Glucose: The scientific name for the sugar in the blood or urine.

Insulin reaction (hypoglycemia): Another term for a blood sugar level that is too low. See Chapter 6.

mg/dL and mmol/L: Milligrams of material in 100cc of fluid or millimoles of material in one liter of fluid. Blood sugar (glucose) levels are expressed in mg/dL in the U.S., but they are usually expressed as mmol/L in Europe. It is possible to convert mg/dL to mmol/L by dividing by 18 (or multiplying by 0.0555). The opposite is done to go from mmol/L to mg/dL. A conversion table for glucose values is in the Appendix.

Monitoring: As used in this chapter, keeping track of and following blood sugar levels at home and analyzing them in a record book or with a computer download.

Self blood-glucose monitoring: Checking one's own blood sugar rather than going into a clinic or hospital to have the tests done.

Subcutaneous: Under the skin (but not in a blood vessel).

QUESTIONS AND ANSWERS FROM NEWSNOTES

Q What is the best range for my blood/CGM glucose values?

A This is not an easy question to answer. It depends on the individual person and family as well as the age of the person with diabetes. Most textbooks list a normal fasting level (or when no food is taken for two or more hours) as 70-100 mg/dL (3.9-5.5 mmol/L). It is unrealistic for most people with diabetes to aim for normal non-diabetic fasting sugar levels. *"Understanding Diabetes"* (the Pink Panther book) suggests ranges by ages:

Under five years old:
80-200 mg/dL (4.5-11.1 mmol/L)

5-11 years old:
70-180 mg/dL (3.9-10.0 mmol/L)

12 years old and above:
70-150 mg/dL (3.9-8.3 mmol/L)

However, these are "generally suggested ranges" for fasting or if there is no food intake for at least two hours, and they do not take individuals or families into account. For example, a 10 to 11-year-old who does blood sugar levels regularly, so that the chances of unrecognized lows occurring is unlikely, and who does not have severe insulin reactions (e.g., unconscious episodes), can probably safely aim for a level of 70-150 mg/dL (3.9-8.3 mmol/L). The reason for aiming for the lower level would be so that the HbA1c levels may be lower with a reduced long-term likelihood of complications.

On the other hand, an adult who has severe episodes of unrecognized hypoglycemia might be wiser to try to achieve the middle range of 70-180 mg/dL (3.9-10.0 mmol/L). This might help to reduce the severe insulin reactions.

It is generally wise to discuss the levels of blood/CGM glucose values to aim for with your physician at each clinic visit.

Q Should bedtime blood/CGM glucose values be in the same range as morning values?

A No!

Table 4 in this chapter lists suggested blood/CGM glucose levels for the morning and bedtime. We ask that values be between 130-200 mg/dL (7.3-11.1 mmol/L) at bedtime. The DirectNet study group found that children who had values > 130 mg/dL (> 7.3 mmol/L) at bedtime were less apt to have low values during the night.

With good weather and children playing outside in the evening, it is important to reduce the pre-dinner rapid-acting insulin and to check the blood/CGM glucose value before the bedtime snack. If the value is below the suggested lower limit for the age, an additional snack should be given and the insulin dose further reduced the next day. Levels are also suggested in Table 4 for when it would be wise to check another blood/CGM glucose value during the night. It is only by constant monitoring that some families are able to prevent severe insulin reactions in their children.

Q Do I need to check my child's blood/CGM glucose value every morning at 2:00 a.m.?

A For most children, this is NOT necessary. However, occasional checks during the night are helpful. *Special circumstances that make nighttime checks important are:*

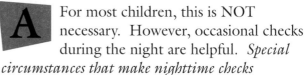 **An illness.** A sick child who may not have eaten well during the day, or who had urine ketones and/or extra (or less) insulin secondary to the illness.

A low pre-bedtime snack blood/CGM glucose: If values are below 80 mg/dL (< 4.5 mmol/L) in a preschooler, below 70 mg/dL (< 3.9 mmol/L) in a 5- to 12-year-old, or below 60 mg/dL (< 3.2 mmol/L) in a person age 12 or above, the blood value should be checked later (when the parents go to bed or during the night) to make sure the value has risen. This is recommended in Table 2 in Chapter 6. It might also be good to give an extra snack (or a larger amount) at bedtime.

🐾 **Frequent low blood/CGM glucose values during the night:** If a child is awakening two or more times during the week with symptoms of low blood sugar, it may be wise to routinely do some middle-of-the-night blood sugars to make sure this is not happening more frequently. The physician caring for the child should also be called.

🐾 **If blood/CGM glucose values are fluctuating without explanation:** A more intensive monitoring schedule for a week or more, including early a.m., can often determine where the insulin dosage needs to be adjusted.

 With all of the good glucose meters and CGMs having memories of glucose values which can be printed out in the clinic, do I still need to write down every blood sugar value?

 This is a difficult question. Unfortunately, we are in a time when families often do not look at values at least once weekly (as we recommend). Thus, they are surprised when they see the download at a clinic visit that many values for a certain time of day are either high or low. FAMILIES MUST DEVELOP A SYSTEM TO LOOK AT VALUES TOGETHER AT REGULAR INTERVALS. They are otherwise not making optimal use of their data. We often ask for weekly faxes or emails if diabetes management is suboptimal and we think the family needs extra help.

Our general rule of thumb is that if more than half of the glucose values at any time of day are above the upper level (see Table 4), an increase in the insulin dose is needed. For example, if an 11-year-old has most morning fasting values above 180 mg/dL (> 10.0

mmol/L), the Lantus insulin should be increased by one unit. Similarly, if the pre-dinner values are all above 180 mg/dL (> 10.0 mmol/L) for a week, the morning intermediate-lasting insulin, or the lunch or afternoon rapid-acting insulin dose should be increased by one or two units. If the values are not being recorded in such a way that values done at the same time of day can be easily compared, it is possible that these trends will be missed. The opposite is also true; if there are more than one or two values in a week below 60 mg/dL (3.24 mmol/L) at any time of the day, the insulin dose working at that time can be reduced. If there is a question whether doses should be changed, the Daily Record Sheet in this chapter can be faxed to the healthcare provider (most schools and work places have fax machines). The faxing of the blood sugars saves valuable doctor/nurse time in having to sit at a phone and write down results.

For the young child or teen who does not want to write values down, it is often acceptable for the parent to push the "M" (memory) button at the end of the day and record the values. This is a way for the parents to stay involved and most teenagers agree to accept this help. The parent is often the family member who does the faxing to the healthcare team as well.

 Are blood/CGM glucose values after meals important?

 Blood/CGM glucose values after meals have previously been largely ignored by children's doctors and families. Yet, the highest values of the day occur in the 1-2 hours after meals. Recent data shows that these high values affect the HbA1c and are thus important in relation to many of the later complications of diabetes. Thus, it is now recommended that people check the blood/CGM glucose values two hours after each of the meals a few times each week.

Q Our family does everything by email now. Is there a way I can get the blood glucose fax sheets from Chapter 7 of the Pink Panther book on my computer?

A Yes, this can now be easily done. Families wanting to use these electronic forms to e-mail to their doctor or nurse can get them from these links:

The Barbara Davis Center home page is at: www.barbaradaviscenter.org. Next, go to Books Online, to Understanding Diabetes. You can then select pages and email them to your doctor and nurse at your Center. The email address at my clinic is:

It is _essential_ for you to give phone numbers and the time to get back to you as it is often best to actively discuss the blood sugar/CGM results and insulin doses.

Please note: depending on the resolution of your monitor, the lines on the sheets may not appear continuous. They will, however, print out accurately.

Appendix
Some Meters with Programs to Allow Downloading at Home

PROGRAM AND COST	VENDOR/ADDRESS PHONE/WEBSITE	METER SUPPORT
OneTouch® Diabetes Management Software: with connecting cable	**LifeScan, Inc.** 1000 Gibraltar Drive Milpitas, CA 95035 800-382-7226 www.lifescan.com	OneTouch Diabetes Management
Precision and FreeStyle Software: CoPilot® System free software is available on the website	**Abbott Diabetes Care** 1360 South Loop Road Alameda, CA 94502 888-522-5226 www.abbottdiabetescare.com	Precision Xtra® FreeStyle Lite® FreeStyle Freedom Lite®
Bayer® WINGLUCOFACTS®: software can be downloaded from website or ordered for $19.95 Connecting cable = $14.95	**Bayer Corp.** 7750 West Morris Street Indianapolis, IN 46231 800-348-8100 www.bayercarediabetes.com	Bayer® Contour® Bayer® ContourUSB® Bayer® Didget® Bayer® BREEZE®
Accu-Chek® 360° Diabetes Management System: software with connecting cable = $44.99	**Roche Diagnostics** 9115 Hague Road P.O. Box 50457 Indianapolis, IN 46250-0457 800-858-8072 www.accu-chek.com	Accu-Chek Aviva, and others

Daily Record Sheet

Name _____

Fax To _____ At _____

Bring these results to your clinic visit

	Breakfast		Lunch		Dinner		Bedtime		Comments: Reactions, exercise, illness, bedtime snack
	Results	Insulin Dose	Results	Insulin Dose	Results	Insulin Dose	Results	Insulin Dose	
Sun Time									
BG/Ket									
Mon Time									
BG/Ket									
Tues Time									
BG/Ket									
Wed Time									
BG/Ket									
Thurs Time									
BG/Ket									
Fri Time									
BG/Ket									
Sat Time									
BG/Ket									

Reminder: 1. Make sure insulin doses are included under the Insulin Dose Heading
2. How to reach you: FAX _____ or Phone _____
    if by phone, best time to reach you:_____ (between 8 a.m.- 5 p.m.)
3. Person to be reached: _____

Concerns (Problem Area)?

_____

_____

_____

_____

_____

Suggested Solution:

_____

_____

_____

_____

_____

The Daily Record Sheet may be photocopied as often as desired.

Chapter 8
Insulin: Types and Activity

TEACHING OBJECTIVES:

1. Describe insulin and what it does in the body.
2. Present the types of insulins to be used and their actions.
3. Discuss the schedule for insulin injections.
4. Identify who and when to call for insulin doses.

LEARNING OBJECTIVES:

Learners (parents, child, relative or self) will be able to:

1. State why the body needs insulin.
2. List the specific types of insulins to be used and their actions (onset, peak and duration).
3. State the schedule for insulin injections (including before or after meals).
4. Identify who and when to call for insulin doses.

INSULIN

Before insulin was discovered in 1921, there was limited treatment for people who had type 1 diabetes. Since then, millions of people all over the world have been helped by insulin.

Insulin is a hormone made in the pancreas, an organ inside the abdomen (see picture in Chapter 2). Special cells called "beta cells" make the insulin. These cells are located in a part of the pancreas called the "islets" (pronounced eye-lets). When a person has type 1 diabetes, there is a loss of the cells which make insulin. Most people with diabetes now use human insulin or insulin analogs. The human insulin does not come from humans, but has the same make-up as human insulin. There are no known advantages of one brand of insulin over another brand. The analog insulins have slight changes that make their activity resemble normal insulin activity.

WHAT DOES INSULIN DO?

Food (carbohydrate) is converted to sugar for the body's energy needs. The insulin allows the sugar to pass from the blood into the cells. There it is burned for energy. The body cannot turn sugar into energy without insulin (see diagram in Chapter 2). Insulin also turns off the making of sugar in the liver (see Chapter 2). If insulin is not available, the sugar builds up in the blood and spills into the urine. The goal of insulin treatment is to use insulin shots to replace what the body's pancreas normally does.

People who have type 1 diabetes can't make enough insulin. These people have to get the needed insulin through injections. **Insulin cannot be taken as a pill, because the stomach acid destroys it.** There are no known vitamins, herbs or other medications which can take the place of insulin injections.

People who have type 2 diabetes still make insulin (although not enough to keep their sugars in a normal range; see Chapter 4). They can take pills to help them make even more insulin or to be more sensitive to their own insulin. However, these pills **are not** insulin, nor are they effective for type 1 diabetes.

TYPES OF INSULIN

Several companies make many different types of insulins.

The three broad classes of insulin are:

1. "rapid-acting" (such as Humalog [H], NovoLog® [NL] and Apidra [AP]) and, although not as rapid-acting, Regular (R) insulin.

2. "intermediate-acting" (such as NPH [N])

3. "long-acting" such as Lantus® (insulin glargine) and Levemir® (insulin detemir)

Insulin action (when it begins working, when it peaks in activity and how long it lasts) may vary from person to person. The action may also vary from one day to the next in the same person. The site of the shot and exercise may influence the insulin action. Increased temperature (bath, shower, hot tub, sauna) may increase blood supply to the skin and cause the insulin to be absorbed more rapidly. Physical activity, or lack of it, can also have an effect. Average times of action for different insulins are shown in Table 1. Commonly used insulins are listed in Table 2.

1. Rapid-Acting Insulins and Regular Insulin

Humalog/NovoLog or Apidra (H, NL or AP) insulins are rapid in **onset** of activity (10-15 minutes). They have a **peak** activity in approximately 95 minutes and effectively last three to four hours. They are usually given to allow the sugar in meals to be used by the body. Figure 1 shows the activities of the rapid-acting insulins given prior to all meals (1-A) or prior to breakfast and dinner (1-B). After the

honeymoon period, the rapid-acting insulins are usually also given to cover snacks. All three rapid-acting insulins are similar in activity. We use the term "rapid-acting insulin" to indicate that the insulin used may be any one of the three (H, NL or AP). Although these rapid-acting insulins have been an advance over Regular insulin in terms of onset of action, they do NOT reach a peak in activity as quickly as desired. This is because the blood (or continuous glucose monitor [CGM]) glucose level peaks in 60 minutes after food is eaten. By taking the H, NL or AP 20 minutes prior to eating, the insulin peak and blood/CGM glucose peak are more closely matched. As a result, the blood/CGM glucose values are not as high after meals (Figure 2). Regular insulin, when used in the past, often needed to be taken 30 to 60 minutes prior to a meal.

Regular insulin begins to act approximately 30-60 minutes after being injected. It has its peak effect two to four hours after the injection and lasts six to nine hours. There is again, considerable variability in these times from person to person.

Humalog/NovoLog/Apidra (H/NL/AP) insulins have several advantages over Regular insulin:

- They start working in 10-15 minutes, rather than in 30-60 minutes as does Regular insulin. They also reach peak activity more rapidly (approximately 95 minutes) than does Regular insulin (approximately 2 to 4 hours).

- Because the rapid-acting insulin does not last as long as Regular insulin, there is less danger of lows several hours after meals or during the night.

- Use of rapid-acting insulin after meals in toddlers who eat varying amounts can help to prevent hypoglycemia as well as food struggles (Chapters 18 and 19). In this case, the higher blood/CGM sugar values are a compromise for safety.

It is important to remember to avoid taking a

warm shower or bath, or getting into a hot tub for one to two hours after taking a rapid-acting or Regular insulin. The warm water increases the blood flow to the skin and causes the insulin to be absorbed faster. This faster rate of absorption could cause a low blood sugar.

2. Intermediate-acting insulins (lasts 10-13 hours)

✔ **NPH (N)** insulin, also referred to as "cloudy" insulin, is made with a protein that allows it to be absorbed in the body more slowly. The letters NPH stand for **N**eutral **P**rotamine **H**agedorn. Protamine is the protein added to the insulin to make it longer-acting. Hagedorn is the name of the man who developed it. Human NPH has its peak activity four to eight hours after the injection in most people. If it is taken in the morning, the peak action usually comes in the afternoon. NPH insulin is often used in the morning for children who are unable to receive a noon injection of H, NL or AP (Figure 1-B). Human NPH insulin lasts an average of 13 hours. The peak in NPH insulin activity and the duration of activity may vary for some people. NPH insulin may be premixed with Regular or H, NL or AP insulin without changing the activities of either insulin. NPH is now called "N" on the bottles.

✔ **Pre-mixed Insulins:** The pre-mixed insulins are used primarily by people who do not wish to draw the insulins from separate vials prior to injecting. They have the disadvantage that the percentage of each insulin is fixed and the individual insulins cannot be varied (for blood sugar, exercise, food, illness, etc.). There are many mixtures available and only a few examples will be given.

- **70/30® and Mixtard®:** Different combinations of pre-mixed NPH and Regular insulin are available. The most frequently used are 70/30 and Mixtard, both of which have 70 percent NPH and 30 percent Regular insulins. The usual times of activity are shown in Table 1.

- **Humalog mix 75/25** (Lilly) is also a combination of a rapid (25 percent) and an intermediate-acting (75 percent) insulin.

- **NovoLog Mix 70/30** (Novo Nordisk) is a mixture of 70% NPH and 30% NovoLog.

3. Long-acting (basal) insulins (last 20-24 hours)

✔ **Lantus™ (Insulin glargine)** insulin became readily available in the U.S. in May, 2001. It is a clear insulin that lasts 24 hours with almost no peak (a basal insulin). Its profile is similar to the basal insulin put out by a normal pancreas. It is often compared with the basal insulin of an insulin pump (Chapter 28).

✔ **Levemir™ (Insulin detemir)** is made by Novo-Nordisk and is also a basal insulin. Its duration is 20 to 24 hours. It may need to be taken twice daily by some people. Levemir was approved by the FDA for use in adults in June, 2005, and for use in children in October, 2005. It is a clear insulin.

Advantages of Lantus/Levemir Insulins:

Their consistency in absorption and activity are more predictable. In contrast, NPH varies in its peak activity even in the same person from one day to the next. Lantus/Levemir insulins have less variability and do not have as great a peak as NPH insulin (unless accidentally injected into the muscle).

- Because they are clear insulins, they do not need to be turned up and down to mix. There is no settling in the vial and insulin concentrations do not vary from one shot to the next.

- Studies have shown a decrease in low blood/CGM glucose values, particularly during the night, when compared with using NPH insulin twice daily. This is due to less of a peak in activity (particularly at night) as well as to more consistent absorption.

Disadvantages of Lantus/Levemir Insulins

- When using Lantus or Levemir, three or more shots per day of rapid-acting insulin may be needed.

- Because they are clear, care must be taken not to confuse them with the rapid-acting insulins, which are also clear.

Basal-Bolus Insulin Therapy (also called Multiple Daily Injections (MDI))

With the rapid-acting insulin analogs (H/NL/AP) and the basal insulins, Lantus or Levemir, it is now possible to more-closely simulate normal physiologic insulin secretion (of a person without diabetes). This can be done using injections or using insulin pumps (see Chapter 28). The pancreas normally (when there is no diabetes) secretes a low-level basal insulin and releases peaks (boluses) of insulin with food or other causes of increased sugar levels. This pattern can be simulated with Lantus/Levemir basal insulin plus a rapid-acting insulin prior to meals, or with an insulin pump. It is then called "basal-bolus" insulin therapy.

The Lantus/Levemir and the Humalog, NovoLog and Apidra insulins are all available in pre-filled pens (see Chapter 9). This makes use much easier for many patients and families.

Two ways we are currently using Lantus/Levemir insulin:

1. Lantus/Levemir can be taken once daily (either consistently in the morning, at dinner or in the evening), with a rapid-acting insulin (H/NL/AP) taken 20 minutes before each meal (see Figure 1-A). The pre-meal insulin is often taken with an insulin pen. An advantage of taking Lantus/Levemir in the morning is that if some of the injection is accidentally given into muscle, there may be a peak in early activity (two to four hours). If this occurs, it is better to have it happen during the daytime. (As discussed in Chapter 9,

intramuscular injections are least apt to occur when using the buttocks.) There is also an increase in peak insulin activity when taking large doses of Lantus/Levemir. The best time to take the basal insulin should be considered jointly between the family and care-providers.

Below are other advantages of taking the long-acting basal insulin in the morning:

a) People usually do not mind a large insulin dose in the morning as much as in the evening.

b) Most high blood/CGM glucose values occur during the day so it is good to have optimal insulin activity during this time.

c) If the activity does diminish at 22-24 hours, it may be best to have this happen in the early morning hours, **especially for very young children or those in the honeymoon phase.**

d) For infants or those who have trouble with shots, Lantus can be given (often in the buttocks) while they are sleeping. Lantus tends to last the full 24 hours more readily than Levemir, which sometimes has to be given twice daily. However, Lantus (initially) may sting more than Levemir.

2. Lantus/Levemir and H/NL/AP are taken separately at dinner, or the basal insulin is taken later in the evening. This may work better for teens who can have elevated hormones in the early morning. A mixture in the same syringe of NPH and H/NL/AP is taken 20 minutes prior to breakfast (see Figure 1-B). This works well for children who are unable to take a noon shot at school. The NPH insulin may also help to cover an afternoon snack. Some people who take a noon shot still do better with a small amount of NPH insulin in the morning.

Some younger children do better getting their Lantus in the morning. Insulin activity can then fall off in the early morning hours of the next day. A separate morning shot of rapid-acting and NPH is then required. A third shot of H/NL/AP prior to dinner is also usually needed.

Lantus/Levemir Dose: the <u>starting</u> dose is often half the total units of intermediate-acting insulin (e.g., NPH) taken per day (a.m. and p.m.).

For example:

If 40 units of NPH insulin was taken in the morning and 20 units at dinner, a total of 60 units was taken per day. We would then start the person on 30 units of Lantus/Levemir insulin.

This dose can then be increased or decreased depending on morning blood/CGM glucose levels. The Lantus/Levemir dose is adjusted based on morning glucose values, no matter when the dose is given.

The goal for the morning and pre-meal blood/CGM glucose values is:

Under 5 years of age:
80-200 mg/dL (4.5-11.1 mmol/L)

5-11 years of age:
70-180 mg/dL (3.9-10.0 mmol/L)

12-18 years
70-150 mg/dL (3.9-8.3 mmol/L)

>18 years:
70-130 mg/dL (3.9-7.3 mmol/L)

It is important to bring morning fasting blood/CGM glucose levels in range. If the day starts with high values, subsequent values are also often high from liver production of sugar (Chapter 2).

Figure 1: Use of Lantus/Levemir Insulin

Two of the most common methods of using Lantus/Levemir insulin:

Figure 1-A. In the first example, Lantus/Levemir is used as the basal insulin (given in the a.m., or at dinner or at bedtime) and a rapid-acting insulin is taken 20 minutes prior to meals and snacks. This is often referred to as basal-bolus insulin therapy, or MDI. This is the method we generally recommend.

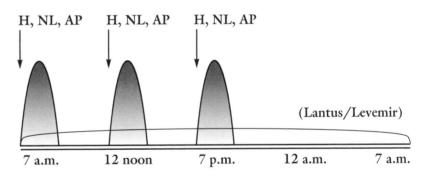

Figure 1-B. In this second example, NPH and a rapid-acting insulin are taken in one syringe in the a.m. A rapid-acting insulin is taken alone at dinner. Lantus/Levemir is taken consistently either in the a.m., at dinner, or at bedtime. Alternatively, the Lantus/Levemir is taken prior to dinner in the same syringe as the rapid-acting insulin (see text).

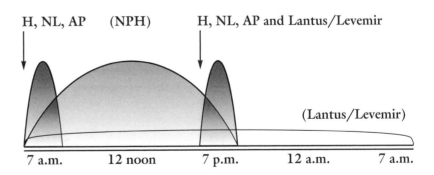

HOW OFTEN IS INSULIN GIVEN?

One Injection Per Day

A few people have optimal blood/CGM glucose values by taking insulin once a day. This is particularly true during the "honeymoon" period that occurs shortly after diagnosis. Lantus/Levemir is usually taken in the morning or, less commonly, at dinner. It has very little "peak" (unless accidentally given into muscle) and lasts about 24 hours (see Table 1). Some people with type 2 diabetes who need insulin may do well with one injection of Lantus/Levemir each day.

People who take one insulin injection per day may do better on two or multiple injections per day if they:

🐾 do not have an optimal level of sugar control

🐾 have frequent low blood/CGM glucose values

🐾 have to take a very large dose in one injection

🐾 have many changes in their daily lives

🐾 come out of the honeymoon phase

Two Injections Per Day

Most people obtain better sugar control using two or more injections of insulin per day. Most doctors now believe it is best to treat all patients with type 1 diabetes with multiple daily injections (MDI) or pump therapy (Chapter 28). When a person receives multiple injections per day, there are multiple small peaks of insulin activity. Each of the small peaks in insulin activity can be adjusted to fit the person's schedule. Figure 1-B shows two injections of insulin per day using a rapid-acting insulin and NPH in the a.m. and Lantus/Levemir combined with a rapid-acting insulin at dinner. In countries in which a basal insulin is not available, it may be necessary to use two injections per day of NPH insulin combined with a rapid-acting insulin (see Figure 2). **There is then a greater risk of low blood/CGM glucose values during the night.** The risk for night-time lows has been shown to

Table 1
Insulin Activities

Type of Insulin	Begins Working	Main Effect	All Gone
RAPID-ACTING and REGULAR			
Humalog/NovoLog/Apidra	20 minutes	90 minutes	3-4 hours
Regular	30-60 minutes	2-4 hours	6-9 hours
INTERMEDIATE-ACTING (lasts 10-20 hours)			
NPH	1-2 hours	3-8 hours	12-15 hours
LONG-ACTING/BASAL			
Lantus (Insulin Glargine)	1-2 hours	2-22 hours	24 hours
Levemir (insulin detemir)	1-2 hours	2-20 hours	20-24 hours
PRE-MIXED INSULINS			
70/30 NPH/Regular	30-60 minutes	3-8 hours	12-15 hours
75/25 NPH/Humalog	20 minutes	90 minutes-8 hours	12-15 hours

Figure 2: Example of Two Injections Per Day Using NPH

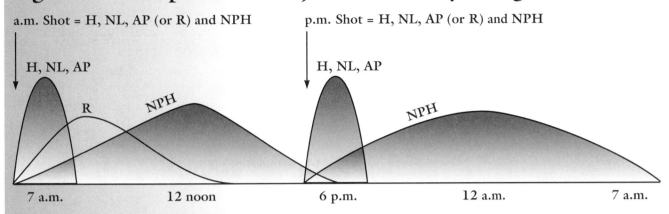

a.m. Shot = H, NL, AP (or R) and NPH   p.m. Shot = H, NL, AP (or R) and NPH

H, NL, AP   R   NPH   H, NL, AP   NPH

7 a.m.   12 noon   6 p.m.   12 a.m.   7 a.m.

Many people receive two injections per day. NPH and a rapid-acting insulin (or Regular) are given prior to breakfast and dinner. When possible, the insulin should be given 20 minutes prior to the meal.

be slightly reduced if the second shot of NPH is taken at bedtime rather than at dinner. This means a third daily shot.

During adolescence, diabetes control may become more difficult for a variety of reasons. Teens usually need more insulin due to insulin resistance. The growth and sex hormones make it more difficult for insulin to work. Blood sugar goals can often be achieved more easily with three or more injections of insulin per day.

Three or More Injections Per Day

Most people now receive three or more shots of insulin each day. The various regimens are usually variations of Figures 1-A, 1-B and 2, depending on the needs of the person. People using Lantus/Levemir as their basal insulin usually take at least four shots per day (including three shots of rapid-acting insulin, see Figure 1-A). Some people refer to three or more injections per day as "multiple daily injections" (MDI).

Figure 3: Example of Three or More Injections Per Day

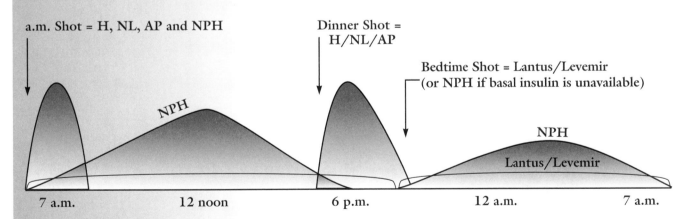

a.m. Shot = H, NL, AP and NPH   Dinner Shot = H/NL/AP

Bedtime Shot = Lantus/Levemir (or NPH if basal insulin is unavailable)

NPH   NPH   Lantus/Levemir

7 a.m.   12 noon   6 p.m.   12 a.m.   7 a.m.

This figure gives an example of three or more injections per day: NPH and H/NL or AP are taken in the a.m.; H/NL or AP is taken prior to dinner; Lantus/Levemir (or NPH) is taken at bedtime. A prelunch shot of H/NL or AP may also be needed.

Four or More Injections Per Day

The example above of Lantus/Levemir insulin given once daily (often by pen) and a rapid-acting insulin given 20 minutes prior to meals and snacks is now the most common insulin regimen used by people willing to take multiple injections. It is the regimen we usually recommend and is referred to above as "basal-bolus" insulin therapy. Children who are not happy with multiple injections may still use this regimen by using an injection portal (e.g., I-Port® or Insuflon®, Chapter 9). Many families give all of the different insulins (including Lantus and Levemir) through the portal.

There are many different insulin regimens and they may need to be individualized to the person with diabetes. Regimens may change with age, hormone levels, food intake, exercise, stress, growth or other factors. The healthcare providers will help to make needed changes between and at the every-three-month clinic visits.

AMOUNT OF INSULIN

Insulin is measured in "units" per cc (ml). All U.S. insulin now contains 100 units per cc (ml). It is called U-100 insulin. Standard insulin syringes hold either 3/10cc (30 units), 1/2 cc (50 units) or 1cc (100 units). The 3/10cc syringes have larger distances between the unit lines and are easier to use if it is necessary to measure small doses. They also have lines for 0.5 unit markings.

Insulin dosage is based on body weight, blood/CGM glucose results, planned exercise and food intake (especially carbohydrate). After the initial diagnosis and treatment, people are usually started on approximately ¼ to ½ unit of insulin per pound (½ to 1 unit per kilogram [kg]) of body weight per day. The dose is then gradually increased as needed up to ½ to ¾ unit per pound body weight (1 to 1.5 unit per kg body weight). After a few weeks to months, many children go into a "honeymoon" or "grace" period when much less insulin is required (see Chapter 2). Frequent telephone contact with the diabetes team is important when the honeymoon starts. The insulin dosage must then be reduced to prevent low blood sugars. We generally recommend continuing the injections during this period. After the honeymoon, most people gradually increase to an average insulin dosage of ½ unit per pound (1.1 units per kg) body weight. During the teenage growth spurt, the growth hormone level is high and blocks insulin activity. The insulin dosage may increase to 0.7 units per pound (1.5 units per kg) body weight. The dosage then goes back down after the period of growth is over. Insulin dosages can and should be adjusted to fit the person's lifestyle and needs.

For example, seasonal changes are common.

🐾 In the winter, when it is cold outside, children may not go out to play after dinner. They may need more H/NL/AP insulin before the evening meal.

Table 2
Insulins Frequently Used

Type	Name	Color of Box or Cap	Manufacturer
Humalog	Humalog	Purple Cap	Lilly
Regular	Humulin-R	White Box With Black Print	" "
NPH	Humulin-N	"	" "
Humalog Mix	75/25	"	" "
Regular	Novolin-R	White Box With Blue Markings	Novo-Nordisk
NPH	Novolin-N	"	" "
Regular (Pen)	Novolin R PenFill	"	" "
NPH (Pen)	Novolin N PenFill	"	" "
NovoLog	NovoLog	Orange cap	" "
Insulin Levemer	Levemir	Green cap	" "
Insulin Glargine	Lantus (clear)	Purple cap, tall thin vial	Sanofi-Aventis
Insulin Glulisine	Apidra	Blue cap, tall thin vial	" "

In the summer, when they go outside to play after dinner, the evening H/NL/AP insulin dose often can be decreased. Chapter 22 deals with how to adjust insulin dosages.

INTENSIVE DIABETES MANAGEMENT

Intensive Diabetes Management involves:

Three or more shots of insulin per day (or use of an insulin pump)

Checking blood sugar levels four or more times per day (or use of a CGM)

Paying attention to food intake

Frequent communication with the healthcare provider

Exercise Daily

The Diabetes Control and Complications Trial (DCCT) used Intensive Diabetes Management to show that sugar control "closer to normal" helped to prevent the complications of type 1 diabetes (Chapter 14). Similar studies have shown this to also be true for type 2 diabetes. Most diabetes doctors now recommend intensive diabetes management for all people with type 1 diabetes (after the honeymoon period). The goal of intensive management is to keep the blood/CGM glucose levels as close to normal as can be done without hypoglycemia. For intensive therapy to be safe, frequent blood/CGM glucose values are needed. Intensive diabetes management is most easily accomplished using Lantus/Levemir insulin (once daily) and a rapid-acting insulin 20 minutes prior to food intake. Insulin pumps provide an alternative and have become safer and more popular in recent years. Chapter 28 discusses insulin pump use.

DEFINITIONS

Analog: A form of insulin with a slightly different make-up that results in different times of onset and duration of activity. Humalog, NovoLog and Apidra are examples of insulin analogs modified to have a rapid onset of activity.

Basal-bolus insulin therapy: Use of a basal (Lantus/Levemir) insulin with injection of a rapid-acting insulin prior to meals, or use of an insulin pump.

Beta cells: The cells in the islets of the pancreas which produce insulin.

cc (cubic centimeter; same as ml or milliliter): A unit of measurement. Five cubic centimeters (cc) equals one teaspoon; 15cc equals one tablespoon; 30cc equals one ounce; 240cc equals one cup.

DCCT: The Diabetes Control and Complications Trial. A very large research trial that showed that better sugar control reduced the likelihood of eye, kidney, nerve, and cardiovascular complications in people over age 13 with type 1 diabetes.

Hormone: A chemical made in certain glands and secreted into the blood for action elsewhere. An example is insulin that is produced by the pancreas and carried by the blood for activity throughout the body.

Insulin pump: A pager-sized device designed to give a preset steady (basal) injection of insulin throughout the day, as well as before-meal supplements (boluses) of insulin which are regulated by the user. Current pumps do not stop injecting insulin when blood sugars are low. See Chapter 28 for more details.

Lantus insulin (insulin glargine): A basal insulin that is flat in activity and lasts 24 hours. It has an acid pH in contrast to other insulins which all have a neutral pH.

Levemir (insulin detemir): A basal insulin that is flat in activity and lasts up to 24 hours. It has a fatty acid attached that binds to plasma albumin resulting in slow release.

QUESTIONS AND ANSWERS FROM NEWSNOTES

Q I sometimes have low sugars in the middle of the night. I take NPH and Regular insulins twice daily. Do you have any suggestions to prevent this?

A You may be helped by changing to "basal-bolus" insulin therapy. There are two main reasons why this might help your number of lows decrease. The first is that the rapid-acting insulins do not last as long as the Regular insulin. The second is that that basal insulins do not peak during the night (especially when given in the morning) as does dinner or evening NPH insulin.

Q What are the main advantages of the insulin analogs, Lantus and Levemir?

A By far the main advantage is in reducing the likelihood of low blood/CGM glucose levels during the night. This is because, when given in the morning, there is no peak in activity during the night as occurs with dinner or bedtime NPH insulin. In addition, the use of a true basal insulin helps to prevent the large "swings" in blood sugars often seen with NPH insulin.

Q Our son is about to go hiking in a very hot part of the U.S. Is there any way to keep his insulin, blood sugar strips and glucagon cool so they don't spoil?

A You can order the FRIO Cool Pouch at www.medicool.com. Hopefully all will fit in their larger pack.

Chapter 9
Drawing Up and Giving Insulin

TEACHING OBJECTIVES:

1. Demonstrate technique for mixing (if applicable) and drawing up insulin.
2. Identify age-appropriate injection sites.
3. Instruct injection technique.
4. Observe family members/self giving insulin injection.

LEARNING OBJECTIVES:

Learners (parents, child, relative or self) will be able to:

1. Complete accurate demonstration for mixing (if applicable) and drawing up insulin.
2. Choose two age-appropriate sites for injections.
3. Demonstrate correct injection technique using saline.
4. Demonstrate correct injection technique using insulin.

WHERE TO INJECT THE INSULIN

Insulin is injected into the fat layer beneath the skin. Proper techniques must be learned so that the insulin is not injected too close to the outer skin (which may cause a lump, pain or a red spot) or too deep into the muscle (which may cause pain and insulin to be absorbed too quickly). If the injections are given in the recommended areas (Figure 1), it is very unlikely that a large artery or vein will be entered. The only problem if this were ever to happen would be that the insulin would last only a matter of minutes rather than hours. Also, it is not true that injecting a bubble of air into someone (even into an artery or vein) would harm them. These are common, but unnecessary worries.

INJECTION SITES

The best places to give insulin (in order) are the following:

- buttocks (seat): slowest absorbing
- abdomen (holding pinch of fat): fastest absorbing
- arms (holding a pinch of fat)
- thighs (holding a pinch of fat)

These are the sites with the most subcutaneous fat (listed in order). Select at least two or three of the usual four areas for injections and skip areas that are not well tolerated. Injections should be moved around within the sites that are used (example: six to nine areas in each buttock site). If there are swollen or lumpy areas, injections should not be given into these sites, as the insulin may be absorbed at a different rate causing high or low blood/CGM glucose values.

Insulin is absorbed more rapidly from the abdomen than from the arm, and more rapidly from the arm than from the thigh or buttock. However, the differences are not great for most people. The buttock should generally be used for injections of Lantus/Levemir insulin to make certain it is given into the fatty tissue. You may also use an area where a large pinch of fat can be held.

Based on studies done in Sweden, it is best to take a pinch of the skin when using most needles. The exceptions may be the buttock area or the central abdomen if there is a sufficient amount of fat tissue and either the BD Ultra-Fine Mini ™ or the new BD Ultra-Fine™ Nano needles are being used.

There is some increase in uptake of rapid-acting insulin when the shot is given in an area that is then exercised. Injecting into an arm or leg which will be used in an activity may increase the likelihood of low blood sugars during exercise, due to the increased blood flow to the area being exercised. Therefore, if you are to play tennis, don't inject into the arm that will be used to swing the racquet. A low blood sugar could result.

Insulin should also not be injected just prior to a bath, shower or hot tub. The warm water will draw more blood to the skin, causing a rapid absorption of the insulin and resulting in a serious low blood sugar. If the water is warm enough to turn your skin pink, then the insulin will be absorbed more quickly. Wait at least 90 minutes after giving rapid-acting insulin to get into hot water.

INSULIN SYRINGES

(See picture diagram of insulin syringes and Table 1)

There are several brands of disposable insulin syringes with varying needle widths (measured in gauges with a larger number for a thinner needle) and varying lengths. The

needles are thin and are sharp for easy insertion. If money is short, the syringes can be reused. If you are mixing insulins in the same syringe, it is not suggested to reuse your needles as this can cause contamination to your rapid-acting insulin. If you must reuse your needle, push the plunger up and down several times to remove as much of the old insulin as possible from the needle. Then store needles in the refrigerator to prevent growth of bacteria. The needle may be dulled as a result of going through the rubber stopper on the insulin vial more than one time. If dulled, then it might cause more tissue damage. There is also the possibility of infection when reusing syringes.

The amount of insulin the syringe will hold varies. There are 3/10cc and 1/2 cc syringes for people using less than 30 or 50 units of insulin per injection, or 1cc syringes for those using more than 50 units per injection (see drawings). The B-D Ultra-Fine II short needles are just 5/16 inch (8mm) in length (compared with the usual ½ inch [12.7mm]

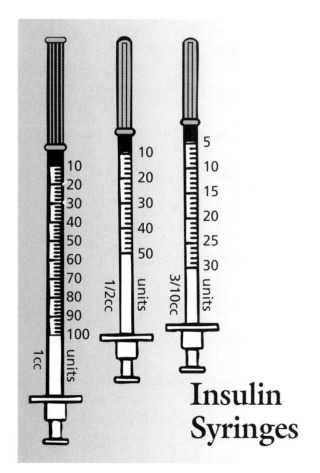

Insulin Syringes

Figure 1
Injection Rotation Chart

length) and at 30 gauge are very thin. There are also 3/10cc syringes with ½ unit markings allowing for smaller doses of insulin to be measured. This syringe can be helpful for young children.

DRAWING UP THE INSULIN

You will be shown how to draw the insulin into the syringe. YOU SHOULD LEARN BY PRACTICE AND FORM GOOD HABITS FROM THE START. When possible, wash your hands first. The picture diagrams show how to draw up insulin and give an injection. Our families often start by doing "air" shots into a doll or mannequin. The next practice step is drawing up sterile salt water (saline) and doing the injection into each other. This helps family members to realize how little pain is caused from the shots. In addition, Table 1 gives a checklist to follow. The nurse will go over the checklist with you at regular intervals.

These are the steps:

🐾 Get everything together: alcohol, insulin and a syringe.

🐾 Wash your hands.

🐾 Push the plunger of the disposable syringe up and down before drawing in the insulin. This will help soften the rubber at the end of the plunger and smooth the plunger action.

🐾 Wipe the top of the insulin bottle(s) with alcohol and allow to air dry.

🐾 Insert the needle through the rubber top of the bottle of rapid-acting (Humalog/NovoLog/Apidra) or Regular insulin with the bottle sitting upright on the table. Turn the bottle (with the needle inserted) upside down. To remove any air bubbles, draw out about five more units of insulin than needed and push quickly back into the bottle. This can be repeated several times as needed until air bubbles are cleared. "Flicking" the syringe barrel with the finger is not recommended as it can cause the needle to bend. After the air bubbles are gone, adjust

the top edge of the rubber plunger to be in line with the exact number of units needed. The needle can then be removed from the vial and held or the cap put on the needle. If also drawing NPH insulin into the syringe, some families leave the needle in the rapid-acting insulin bottle until the NPH insulin is mixed. Others hold the syringe in one hand while mixing the NPH insulin (turning up and down 20 times) with the other hand. NEVER lay the syringe down on the table with the needle touching anything, as this may lead to bacteria collecting on the needle and cause an infection.

The NPH insulin needs to be mixed gently. Do not vigorously shake the NPH insulin as this may break it down and cause the insulin to absorb differently. Some people roll the bottle between the palms of their hands. **The NPH bottle should be turned or rolled gently 20 times to mix thoroughly**. Avoid touching the rubber stopper of the vial if it has already been wiped with alcohol. Clear insulins do not need to be mixed.

🐾 If mixing NPH insulin with a rapid-acting insulin or Regular Insulin, remove the cap from the syringe already containing the rapid-acting insulin. Insert the needle into the bottle of the NPH insulin while the bottle is upside down. This prevents air from the vial getting into the syringe. With the bottle turned upside down, slowly draw the number of units of the NPH insulin needed. The total number of units in the syringe will be the sum of the rapid-acting units plus the NPH units. After mixing the two types of insulin, never re-inject insulin from the syringe back into the intermediate insulin bottle. This will give you an incorrect dose of insulin. If you draw up too much insulin you will need to throw your syringe away and draw up your doses again.

🐾 **Venting the insulin bottles:**

In the past, we instructed families to inject air into the insulin bottles with each dose. This was to prevent a vacuum from

Table 1

Drawing Up Two Insulins Into a Syringe

A. Gather supplies: Insulin, syringe, alcohol wipe for tops of bottles, log book with current tests and insulin dosage (please record each blood sugar result in log book after each test). **Do not confuse the rapid-acting insulin vial with the Lantus/Levemir vial (both are clear).**

B. Technique:

- Know correct insulin dosage

- Wipe tops of insulin bottles with alcohol swab

- Either "vent"* the bottles weekly (smaller doses) or put air into the long-acting (cloudy) insulin with the bottle upright and remove the needle. Put air in the clear insulin and leave the needle in.

- Draw up clear (rapid-acting) insulin, get rid of air bubbles and remove the needle

- Mix the cloudy NPH insulin vial by gently turning the bottle up and down 20 times; this ensures that the insulin gets well mixed

- Slowly draw up the NPH (or Lantus) insulin into the syringe, making sure not to push any insulin already in the syringe back into the vial. For people now mixing Lantus insulin with a rapid-acting insulin, the clear Lantus insulin will become cloudy as it is pulled into the syringe holding the rapid-acting insulin. This does not usually cause problems with needle-plugging.

- If insulin vials have been in the refrigerator, you can warm up the insulin once it is mixed in the syringe by holding the syringe in the closed palm of your hand for 1-2 minutes; it will be less likely to sting if brought to room temperature

- Give insulin injection

   An option now used by some people is to not put air into the bottles, but to just "vent" the bottles to remove any vacuum once weekly (see text).

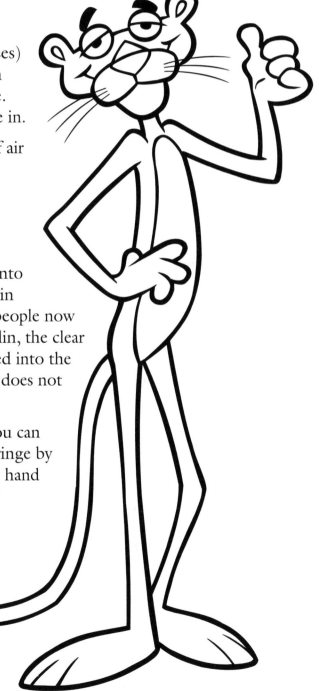

developing, which would pull the insulin drawn out, back into the bottle.

In recent years, most of our families have preferred to "vent" their insulin bottles once a week. This is done by using a new syringe and removing the plunger from the syringe barrel. With the insulin vial sitting upright on the table, insert the needle into the rubber stopper and allow air to equalize in the insulin bottle. This will remove any vacuum, which may be inside the bottle. This will only take a moment. Pick one consistent day of the week to vent the bottles.

Some families may prefer to inject the air when drawing up the insulin. This is particularly true when large doses are being given. The amount of air injected into a bottle equals the number of units of insulin being withdrawn. The air should be added to the **intermediate**-acting insulin bottle first. The rubber stopper of the bottle should first be cleaned with alcohol. With the bottle sitting upright, insert the needle into the bottle and push in the air within the syringe. Remove the needle from the bottle.

Draw air into the syringe again, the amount equal to the dose of the **rapid**-acting insulin. With the rapid-acting bottle upright on a table, insert the needle and push in the air. Leave the needle in the bottle and turn upside down. Follow the steps outlined above to withdraw the insulin doses required.

The people who make insulin recommend changing insulin vials every 30 days if the bottle is kept at room temperature. This is due to the possible growth of bacteria. Blood/CGM glucose values should be watched carefully when the insulin bottle is almost empty or if the 30 days are exceeded. If the values start to be unusually high or low, the last bit of insulin should be discarded. Some people prefer to just routinely discard the insulin when it only fills the neck of the turned bottle. The expiration date on the bottle should always be checked and the insulin discarded if that

date is reached. Unopened, refrigerated insulin is good until the manufacturer's expiration date on the top of the box.

In summary, BE PRECISE ABOUT THE DOSAGE. An overdose can cause an insulin reaction (low blood sugar). If you ever take an incorrect dose, be sure to notify your diabetes care provider. It is wise to have the morning and afternoon dosages posted on the refrigerator or some obvious place to prevent confusion. Children below age 10 do not usually have the fine motor abilities and concern for accuracy to draw up insulin by themselves. Parents should assist them with these tasks (see Chapter 18).

HOW TO INJECT THE INSULIN

(See Table 2 and Figure 2)

🐾 Clean the site of injection with soap and water (or an alcohol swab or hand sanitizer if camping or in a hospital). Alcohol dries and toughens the skin and is not routinely recommended.

🐾 Lift the skin and fat tissue between the thumb and the first finger. **If you are using the BD Ultra-Fine Nano needle and the fat in the area of injection is adequate, the needle can be inserted at a 90° angle without pinching (usually only the buttock [seat area] on younger children).** In other areas, where there is not as much fat, a "gentle pinch" should still be used during the injection. Touch the needle to the skin, holding the syringe at a 90° angle (or less). It is generally best to push the needle all the way into the skin. If the needle is not in far enough, the insulin may not be injected into the fatty layer. If it goes into the layer directly under the skin rather than into the fatty layer, it will sting and may cause a bump or redness and itching. To insure injection into fat, the "gentle pinch" can continue to be held during the injection of the insulin.

Inject the insulin by pushing the plunger down with a **SLOW** and steady push as far as it will go. Some people like to wait a few seconds to let the insulin "spread out" after each five units of insulin is injected. A smooth injection is important. AFTER THE INSULIN IS IN, **WAIT TEN SECONDS BEFORE REMOVING THE NEEDLE.** THIS WILL HELP TO PREVENT INSULIN LEAKAGE FROM THE INJECTION SITE. A loss of one drop of insulin may be equal to two to five units. Loss of insulin is a common reason for variations in the blood/CGM glucose levels. If "leak-back" continues to be a problem move to a new site. Also, two units of air can be drawn into the syringe after removing the needle from the insulin bottle. Then flick the side of the syringe with a finger to make the air rise up under the plunger. The air will then be injected after the insulin and will help to prevent "leak-back."

After the injection, place a finger or dry cotton ball over the site. Press firmly for a few seconds to prevent any bleeding. Gently rub the site to close the needle track. Some bleeding may occur after the needle is pulled out; this is not harmful, although some insulin may be carried out with the blood. Some people put their finger over the site where the needle came out and rub gently. The finger should be clean. (If you are getting pain or bleeding often with shots, you may be depositing the insulin into muscle. You should consider using a different site with more fat tissue.)

The plastic syringes are recommended for one time use only by the manufacturer. The needle becomes dull after one use and may be more painful by the second or third shot. If they are to be reused, after giving the injection, push the plunger up and down to get rid of any insulin left in the needle. Wipe the needle off with an alcohol swab. Put the cap over the needle and store the syringe and needle in the refrigerator until ready for the next use.

Table 2 provides a summary for injecting the insulin.

Table 2
Giving the Insulin

Choose injection site; use a good site rotation plan.

Make sure the site is clean. You may use alcohol if needed.

Relax the chosen area. Deep slow breathing may help with this.

Lift up the skin with a "gentle pinch" (unless using the BD Ultra Fine Nano Needle).

Touch the needle to the skin and gently push it through the skin. Use a 45° angle for the ½ inch or ⅝ inch long needle or a 90° angle is ok for the ⁵⁄₁₆ inch (short or "Nano") needles when giving the injection into the buttocks. If there is not much fat, a "gentle pinch" should still be used even with the short needles.

To insure injection into fat, the "gentle pinch" can continue to be held during the injection.

Push the insulin in slowly and steadily.

Wait five to 10 seconds to let the insulin spread out.

Put a finger or dry cotton over the site after the needle is pulled out. Gently rub a few seconds to close the track.

Put pressure on the site. If bruising or bleeding are common, you may need to consider using areas with more fat tissue for injections.

Observe for a drop of insulin ("leak-back"); note in record book if a drop of insulin is present.

Figure 2
Injecting the Insulin

A. Wash hands

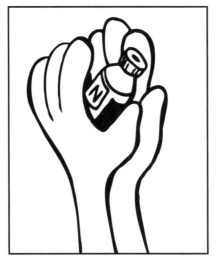

B. Warm and mix insulin

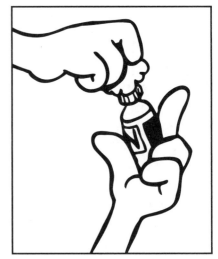

C. Wipe top of insulin bottle with alcohol

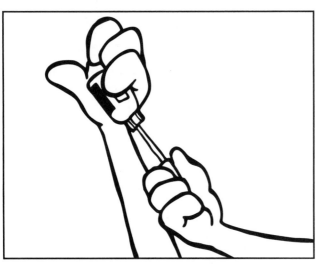

D. Pull out dose of insulin

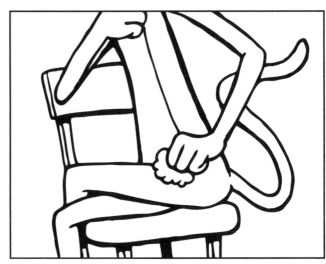

E. Make sure injection site is clean

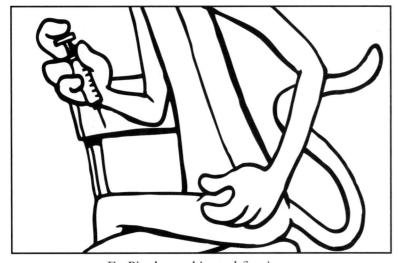

F. Pinch up skin and fat tissue.

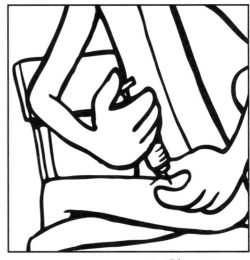

G. Inject insulin at 45° (⅝ inch) or at 90° (short or Nano needles)

WHEN TO INJECT THE INSULIN

Most people now routinely use Humalog/NovoLog/Apidra (rapid-acting) insulin and it is best to give the shot 20 minutes prior to meals if the blood/CGM glucose level is ≥ 80 mg/dL (> 4.5 mmol/L). When the blood sugar is high it is wise to wait even longer after the injection to begin eating (Table 3). The rapid-acting insulins peak in 90 minutes whereas blood/CGM glucose values peak in 60 minutes after food is eaten. It is thus best to get some insulin in 15 to 20 minutes prior to the meal when the blood/CGM glucose value is > 80 mg/dL (> 4.5 mmol/L). For some, it might be easier to remember to wait the one or two left digits of the glucose value (e.g.: 80 = wait 8 minutes; 160 = wait 16 minutes; 320 = wait 32 minutes, etc). An exception is with the toddler or a picky eater who has variable food intake, when it may be better to wait to give the shot until after seeing how much food has been eaten (see Chapters 18 and 19). Higher blood/CGM glucose values after the meals are exchanged for safety. Figure 3 shows the ensuing blood glucose levels when insulin is given 20 minutes prior to the meal versus just before or just after the meal.

With Regular insulin, it is best to take the shot 30 to 60 minutes before eating. This allows the Regular insulin to start working at the time food is eaten. It will prevent the blood/CGM glucose value from going very high in the one or two hours after eating. When the pre-meal blood/CGM glucose level is known, the time can be varied between the shot and eating the meal, as shown in Table 3. It has been our experience that using a time scale such as this can improve blood sugar control and the HbA1c value (Chapter 14).

One of the advantages of an insulin pump is that it is easy to divide the insulin dose without having to give extra shots. Thus, part of the insulin dose (for food most likely to be eaten) can be given 20 minutes prior to the meal. By pushing a few buttons, insulin to cover other food eaten can then be given after the meal (See Chapter 28).

DISPOSING OF NEEDLES

It is never recommended to throw any needles or lancets into the trash; someone may get poked and this can spread harmful germs. It is recommended to dispose of sharps into a red biohazard container. An alternative is to place needles into a very thick plastic container such as a bleach bottle or laundry detergent bottle. Once the bottle is full you may recap it tightly and then tape the cap with strong tape such as duct tape to assure the bottle will not open. This can then be put out with your trash. The BD company provides a **Safe-Clip®** device to clip and store needles. This is a convenient device for traveling. This device holds approximately 1,500 needles, which is about one year's worth of needles.

Figure 3
Blood Glucose Levels Before or After a Meal

Blood glucose levels when insulin was given 20 minutes prior to a meal ("PRE"), at the beginning of the meal ("START"), or after the meal ("POST"). The ADA goal for blood sugars at any time after a meal is to not exceed 180 mg/dL (10 mmol/L).

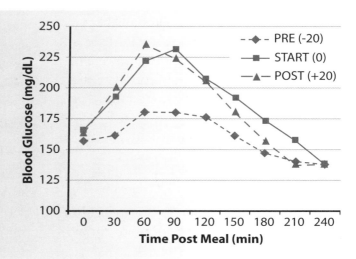

STORAGE

Ideally, insulin should be stored in the refrigerator and warmed to room temperature prior to giving the shot. Most people keep the bottles they are using at room temperature (except in a very hot climate). It will not be as likely to sting or to cause red spots after injection if it is kept at room temperature. After drawing up insulin that has been in the refrigerator, the filled, capped syringe can also be warmed in the closed palm of your hand to avoid stinging. A drawer in the kitchen might be identified for storage of all diabetes supplies. Research has shown that if insulin is stored at room temperature, it loses 1.5 percent of its potency per month (after one month 1cc U-100 insulin would have 98.5 units of insulin rather than 100 units). For most people, this small change would not make a difference (9.85 units rather than 10.0 units). One of the insulin manufacturers wrote: **"Insulin vials currently in use may be kept at room temperature for 30 days, in a cool place and away from sunlight."** Insulin will spoil if it gets above 90° or if it freezes.

Insulin bottles (or pens) should not be exposed to extreme temperature changes, such as being left in a car in the hot summer or the cold winter. If NPH insulin has spoiled, sometimes clumps will then be seen sticking to the sides of the insulin bottle. That bottle and the accompanying bottle of rapid-acting insulin should not be used if this occurs. Unfortunately, the rapid-acting (clear) insulins have only subtle changes and may look cloudy or even slightly yellow. If this is the case the insulin should be thrown away immediately and replaced with new bottles. It may have bacteria (germs) growing in it. We have also suggested throwing away bottles of insulin that have been opened for six weeks or more, even if refrigerated. Families using low dosages of a particular insulin may find it more effective to draw out of 300 unit insulin pen cartridges (for Humalog/NovoLog, Regular, Lantus or NPH insulins). If blood/CGM glucose values rise (for no other reason) after the bottle has been open for 30 days or more, throw away the bottle.

INSULIN PENS

Use of insulin pens has increased greatly in recent years. This is related to people wanting an easy method to take doses of rapid-acting insulins with food intake during the day.

For all pens, the giving of the shot is similar to the giving of a shot with a syringe (Table 2). The same general directions should be followed. The needle must have the paper tab removed and then be screwed onto the pen. This insulin is already present in the pen and does not have to be drawn from a vial. Also, rather then drawing back a plunger in a syringe to determine the insulin dose, the number of units of insulin to be given are dialed in for a pen. With all pens, a two unit "priming-dose" should be entered, the needle pointed upward and the button pushed. This takes care of any "dead-space" without insulin in the needle. Make sure that you see a steady stream of insulin with the priming dose to assure you will receive your total dose of insulin. The desired insulin dose to be given can then be dialed in and given. **The insulin must be injected SLOWLY.** It is important to **count for 10 seconds before removing the needle** from the skin or you may not receive your full dose of insulin. Then, gently rub the injection site with the finger once or twice after the needle is removed. This helps to close the track from the needle and reduce "leak-back." Some care providers do not recommend reuse of pen needles as the needle may become dull and cause tissue damage at the injection site. Using a pen results in increased convenience for the person. In addition, people are more apt to cover the food they are eating with insulin, particularly when away from home.

Pens can be divided into two groups. First are those that are pre-filled disposable pens that are discarded after using. Second are permanent pens that hold cartridges of insulin. The cartridge is replaced in the pen after the insulin is used up (or after one month).

A. Disposable Pens

🐾 Lilly Pre-filled Disposable Pens:

Lilly disposable pens include the Humalog KwikPen™, Humulin NPH, 70/30 NPH/Regular and the Humalog 75/25 KwikPen™. All hold 3 mL (300 units) and are readily available. The pens are simple to use and will take any of the needles described below.

🐾 Novo Nordisk NovoLog and Levemir® FlexPen®:

These Novo Nordisk pre-filled disposable pens hold 3 mL (300 units) of NovoLog or Levemir insulin. NovoFine 30 or 31 gauge needles are used with the pen. The instructions are very similar to the above and are included in the box and on the website (www.novonordiskus.com or www.novologflexpen.com) or talk to your nurse educator.

🐾 Sanofi-Aventis SoloSTAR® Pens

Both Lantus insulin (grey pen) and Apidra insulin (blue pen) are available in 3 mL (300 unit) disposable pens.

With any pre-filled insulin pen, the directions above should be followed in giving the injection.

B. Cartridge Pens

Lilly provides 3 mL Humalog cartridges for use in their HumaPen® MEMOIR™ and HumaPen® LUXURA™ HD insulin delivery devices.

The **NovoPen® 3.0** from Novo Nordisk and the B-D pen offer the use of cartridges of Regular, NPH, 70/30 NPH/Regular or Humalog/NovoLog insulins. The cartridges contain 3.0 mL of insulin (300 units) and are replaced into the pen when the cartridge is empty. The NovoPen 3.0 delivers a dose of two to 70 units. The B-D pen has a maximum dose of 30 units. A colorful pen from Novo Nordisk is called the **Novopen-Junior®** that can deliver ½ unit doses. The minimum dose that can be delivered is 1 unit. It takes the 3 mL insulin cartridges so it can be used with any Novo Nordisk 3.0 insulin cartridge available.

The directions for the NovoPen 3.0 are similar for most pens, and are fairly simple:

1. Remove the cap (the part with the pocket clip) and unscrew the silver bottom to drop the cartridge of insulin down into the holder (metal cap first). Make sure the piston rod is flat (even) at the end of the top of the plunger. Then screw the silver bottom back on tightly.

2. Wipe the rubber stopper with alcohol, remove the paper tab from the needle and screw the needle on the end of the pen (until tight).

3. Turn the dial to one or two units. Pull off both needle caps and, holding the needle upward, push the button on the end to see if insulin comes out. If not, repeat the procedure until insulin appears (to get rid of all air). Do this with each usage of the pen.

4. For giving the shot, starting at "0," turn the dial-a-dose selector to the required dose, lift up the skin (as directed earlier) and insert the needle (assuming adequate fat). As noted earlier, it is not necessary to pinch the fat (particularly when using the abdomen or buttock) if using the BD Mini or the BD Nano needle. The insulin must be injected **SLOWLY**. Press the button on the end down firmly to deliver all insulin. **Wait 10 seconds,** pull the needle out and rub gently. Place the larger plastic cover over the needle and put the cap with the pocket clip back on the pen.

Insulins Readily Available in Pens Include:
Humalog® KwikPen™
Humalog® Mix 75/25® KwikPen™
Humalog® Pen
Humalog® Mix 75/25® Pen™
OptiClik® for Lantus® and Apidra®
Apidra® SoloSTAR®
Lantus® SoloSTAR®
Levemir® FlexPen®
NovoLog® FlexPen®
NovoLog® Mix 70/30 FlexPen®
NovoPen® Junior
NovoPen® 3

C. Pen Needles Currently Available Include:

Name	Length (mm)	Width (gage)*
BD Regular™	12.7	29
BD Short™	8	31
BD Ultra-Fine Mini	5	31
BD Nano™	4	32
Novo Fine™	8	30
Novo Fine™	6	32
Novo Fine Auto Cover™	8	30

*Larger gage = Less width

The BD company has recently introduced their BD Nano™. They cite evidence that there is no difference in glucose levels using these very short needles compared to the longer needles.

INJECTION AIDES

The **I-Port** and the **Insuflon** are plastic cannulas very similar to the insertion tube for the insulin pump. However, instead of connecting to a pump, the end is covered and has a port for giving insulin injections. It can be left under the skin for up to five days (remove sooner if redness develops). EMLA® cream can be applied 30-60 minutes before insertion to diminish pain. All insulins, including Humalog, NovoLog, Apidra, NPH and Lantus may be given through the port.

The best place for insertion is the buttocks, followed by the central abdomen. The skin must be pinched if other sites are used. IV Prep™ (Skin Prep™) can be used to help hold the device in place. These are particularly helpful for people with needle fear and for young children receiving multiple daily injections. School aides will sometimes give injections into the device even though they will not inject insulin into the skin. Glucagon can also be given through the device. The pharmacy of one of our families obtains the Insuflon devices through Amerisource Bergen (1-800-523-4020, item #4509725). It can also be ordered from National Diabetic Pharmacies at 1-800-467-8546 and then hit 48965 or 48964.

Some people have difficulty pushing the needle through the skin. Others would like to inject in a difficult-to-reach area such as the buttocks, but can't. Placing the syringe in an injection device such as the **Inject-Ease®** may help with both of these problems. This is also very useful for people with needle phobia, because it hides the needle from sight and allows for a very consistent shot. After putting the syringe in the device and pushing a button, the needle is automatically pushed through the skin very quickly. It is still necessary to push down on the plunger of the syringe to inject the insulin. The Inject-Ease has a cap for 30, 50 or

Table 3
Pre-Meal Blood Sugar and Time to Wait Before Eating

Blood Sugar Level		Time to Wait Before Eating (Minutes) Type of Insulin	
mg/dL	mmol/L	Regular	Humalog/NovoLog/Apidra
above 200	above 11.1	60	30
151-200	8.4-11.1	45	25
80-150	4.5-8.3	30	20
70-80	3.9-4.5	don't wait (take the shot & start eating)	don't wait (take the shot & start eating)
< 70	< 3.9	eat first (consider reducing the insulin)	eat first (consider reducing the rapid-acting insulin)

100 unit syringes with short needles. If long needles are to be used, a spacer can be added and the cap and the needles then resemble the short needles. Injections are then made at a 90° angle to the skin. It is still important to count before removing the needle and to briefly rub the site to close the needle track and prevent "leak-back."

The **NovoPen 3 Pen Mate®** is a device similar to the Inject-Ease, but for the use with NovoPen 3 or NovoPen Junior®. It can be helpful for people who have needle fear issues. After the top of the pen is screwed into the Pen Mate (with insulin cartridge and needle attached), the insulin dose is dialed in. The side yellow button is then pushed to rapidly insert the needle through the skin. Next, the top button is pushed down to inject the insulin. It may be helpful to have a nurse educator demonstrate use of the Pen Mate.

PROBLEMS THAT MAY ARISE WITH INSULIN INJECTIONS

🐾 Hypertrophy (swelling) of Skin

Swelling of the skin or hypertrophy occurs when too many injections are given in one area over a period of months to years, which causes scarring of the fat tissue. People like to give shots in the same spot because nerve endings (pain) are dulled after a few injections. You can inject insulin into the body anywhere there is enough fat under the skin. Usually there isn't fat over the joints and bones, so these areas are not used. **If swelling or lumpiness in an area does occur, you should not give further injections in that area until the swelling is gone.** This may take several months and varies for different people. **The swelling will alter the uptake of insulin.**

🐾 Skin Dents (atrophy or lipoatrophy)

You may develop "dents" at the injection site. This is different from skin swelling, and is due to a loss of fat in that place. "Denting" is

now rare when human insulin is used. When dents do occur, it is possible to help them go away. To inject into the dented area, pick the skin up at the side of the dent. Slide the needle under the center of the dent. If you inject human insulin four times in a row each week, the dent will gradually go away. This may take several weeks.

🐾 Plugged Needle

Occasionally, a small piece of fat or the insulin will plug the end of the needle during the injection. Sometimes it is possible to pull out the needle a little and then push the needle back into a slightly different place. If you still cannot push down the plunger to finish the injection, you will have to pull the needle completely out of the skin. **NOTE VERY PRECISELY THE UNITS OF INSULIN REMAINING IN THE SYRINGE.** After you fill a new syringe with the total insulin dose as originally drawn, discard the amount of insulin you have already injected. Inject the rest into another site.

🐾 Giving the Wrong Insulin Dose

"To err is human" is very true. Sometimes the dosages of the rapid-acting and the basal insulin are confused. Similarly, an excess of insulin usually results if the morning insulin dose is accidentally given in the evening. This results in a very long night, as someone must awaken every two or three hours, check blood/CGM glucose levels, and if needed, give extra juice and food. Obviously, if the blood/CGM glucose value is low, more frequent checks will be needed. Glucagon may be required and should be kept nearby.

🐾 Bleeding After the Injection

A small capillary blood vessel is probably hit with every injection. Sometimes a drop of blood or a bruise under the skin will be seen after the injection. This will not cause any problem except for the possible loss of some insulin with the blood, but the bruising may be upsetting to some people. As noted earlier in this chapter, place a dry piece of cotton or a clean finger over the injection site and rub gently after removing the needle. This will usually stop any bleeding. Sometimes applying pressure for 30 to 60 seconds will help to reduce bruising. If bruising or blood "leak-back" is happening frequently, you may be injecting into an area with too little fat and depositing the insulin into muscle. This changes the insulin action. Consider giving shots in an area with more fat tissue.

Injecting Insulin Into Muscle

If a person is very thin or very muscular, there may be little fat under the skin. Injections may go into the underlying muscle, causing more rapid absorption of insulin and low blood sugar. There may then be less insulin to act later in the day, resulting in high blood sugar. Injections into the muscle are most likely to occur if the syringe is held at a 90° angle to the body or if the skin is not pinched prior to the injection. This is common when a thin person gives their own shot and reaches over to the other arm and injects. Instead, the fat on the arm can be rolled on the back of a chair or on the knee and then the shot given in the rolled fat. Sometimes extra pain will occur when shots go into muscle, but this is not always the case. Thus, the pain is NOT a good indicator of shots given into muscle. If injecting into muscle is a problem, it may be wise to pull the skin away from the muscle and insert the needle into the "tent" below (while still holding the pinch of skin). Since the entire pinch is not being held, just the upper tip, the insulin should not "leak-back." This technique can be taught by your diabetes nurse. Occasionally, it may be helpful to give an injection in the presence of your diabetes care provider to have your injection technique checked. If the patient is newly diagnosed and has very little body fat, the buttocks may be the safest place for injections.

DEFINITIONS

Atrophy (or Lipoatrophy): Areas of fat loss under the skin, which appear as "dents" in the skin. Although they are believed to be due to a form of insulin allergy, they can occur in areas where insulin has never been injected.

Buttocks: The seat; the part of the body that one sits on.

Hypertrophy: Areas of swelling of the skin, which occur in places where too many shots are being given. Injecting insulin in areas of hypertrophy may cause altered insulin absorption.

Leak-back: The leaking out of a drop of insulin after the insulin injection is completed. This can be a cause of variation in day-to-day blood/CGM glucose levels.

Needle phobia: The intense fear of needles. Working with a social worker or psychologist on "needle desensitization" may help this, as well as use of injection devices.

QUESTIONS AND ANSWERS FROM NEWSNOTES

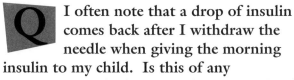

Q I often note that a drop of insulin comes back after I withdraw the needle when giving the morning insulin to my child. Is this of any importance and what can I do to prevent it?

A We are frequently asked this question. We call this "leak-back." Often this leakage is from the pen and is NOT part of the injected insulin.

Some methods to prevent this loss are listed below:

1. Injecting the insulin slowly.

2. Letting go of the lift of skin soon after injecting the insulin so that pressure is not forcing the insulin out from under the skin.

3. Making sure the needle is in the full length and that one does not start to pull the needle out until 10 seconds after the injection is completed.

4. Making sure there is not excessive pressure on the site of injection. For example, if the child is sitting on a chair, he/she should sit on the edge of the chair when injecting in the leg rather than on the back of the chair where the pressure beneath the leg might force the insulin out of the injection site. Having the leg straight rather than bent at the knee may also result in less pressure.

5. Routinely counting for 10 seconds or longer after the insulin is injected before removing the needle.

6. Rubbing the needle track for two or three seconds as the needle is removed to "close off" the track.

7. If nothing else works, consider drawing 2 units of air into the syringe and letting it rise to the top of the insulin so the air is the last to be inserted (see text, Chapter 9).

If these principles are followed, it is unusual for drops of insulin to "leak-back."

Q We notice that when we give the shot to our daughter in the upper outer arm, she frequently has a low blood sugar at school that morning, but is then very high before dinner. Is this possible?

A It sounds like you are injecting the shot into muscle. This is common in the deltoid muscle (upper lateral arm), lateral abdomen and thigh areas as there is not much fat. I would guess that you are also going straight in or are not "pinching" the skin. This results in the insulin being given into muscle. When the insulin does go into muscle, it is absorbed more rapidly so that low blood sugars are common. Then there is not enough insulin left to have its normal effect six to 10 hours later. Sometimes, use of the short needles (Ultra-Fine and/or Nano) and routinely pinching the skin helps to prevent injections into muscle.

Q We just gave our son his afternoon shot and accidentally gave the morning dose rather than the afternoon dose. What should we do?

A We hear this question almost every week. The answer is to eat more at dinner and at the bedtime snack (pizza is particularly effective). In addition, it is wise to set the alarm for every two or three hours, get up, do a blood sugar (or observe CGM value) and give extra juice or food as needed. If the value falls to very low levels (below 70 mg/dL or 3.9 mmol/L), it is necessary to stay up and keep doing the blood sugar levels every 20 or 30 minutes until the value is above 120 mg/dL or 6.7 mmol/L. It is also possible to administer the low dose glucagon as discussed in Chapter 6. Some families find that having the a.m. and p.m. insulin doses taped to the front of the refrigerator can be a helpful reminder. It may also be a good way to communicate or remember recent dosage changes. It is also effective to routinely have a second person check the dose.

Chapter 10
Feelings and Diabetes

TEACHING OBJECTIVES:

1. Reflect with the family typical adjustment feelings associated with diagnosis and encourage expression of feelings.

2. Provide information relating to additional support services.

LEARNING OBJECTIVES:

Learners (parents, child, relative or self) will be able to:

1. List two feelings of adjustment associated with diagnosis.

2. Describe how to access additional support services.

INTRODUCTION

This chapter is about the normal feelings you may experience after learning that you or your child has diabetes. The diagnosis of diabetes is a shock and can be overwhelming. Most people are unprepared for this diagnosis. They struggle with why it has happened to them or to their child. At diagnosis, families must drop everything to focus on their or their loved one's health. They must learn how to provide the necessary care. Learning is often difficult when you are in the middle of an emotional crisis.

The feeling of being **overwhelmed** is common. Families ask: "how are we going to manage this – with work, other children, other responsibilities, or whatever"? This feeling will gradually subside with education, talking with others and "tincture of time." Life will go on! This book aims to help provide education for successful management of diabetes with your diabetes care team.

We expect that people and families will go through many feelings after the diagnosis of diabetes. The emotions felt are common with the onset of any serious medical condition. People frequently wonder what they could have done to prevent this from happening. They think of all the "what ifs?" and try to imagine what they could have done differently. Young adults or parents sometimes blame themselves for eating (or letting their child eat) junk food or for not getting to the doctor right away. Bed wetting is a common problem in children prior to diagnosis and can cause sleep interruptions. Some parents feel guilty they didn't recognize the symptoms or because they were critical of their child. It is very important to talk about these feelings in order to adjust and to help the medical team better understand how they can assist. Most parents feel grief and worry about how this will affect their family and their child's future. Adults diagnosed with diabetes worry about how it will affect their lifestyle, work and future. In our clinic, EVERY newly diagnosed family meets with the clinical social worker, who can be helpful. Some of the feelings that may be experienced are described below.

🐾 **GRIEF.** Talking about the stages of grief can help people understand their own feelings as well as how to help their child through this important process. Adults and children react to the diagnosis and handle grief differently. Typically, adults are upset the most in the first few days after diagnosis. Children who have been feeling quite sick may actually feel happier and have more energy when insulin is started. It is important to remember that they, too, will need to talk over how they feel about having diabetes and what it means to them. Even very young children get upset and will likely show some behavior changes.

🐾 **CONFUSION AND SHOCK** are common feelings for families. Many people describe feeling shocked, scared, upset or even angry that they or their child has been diagnosed with diabetes. They wonder why this has happened, and think: "this can't be real," or "this can't be happening." They worry whether they will be able to give shots without hurting and if they can remember everything that they were taught. Parents experience a stronger sense of anxiety about their child's well-being and worry more about ordinary separations, like going back to school. All of these feelings are very normal and are important to discuss in order to get information and needed reassurance.

Because of the shock, it is often hard for families to focus on what the medical team is saying about diabetes. Sometimes families will ask to have things repeated. The medical team understands and is happy to go over the information several times. Because of the initial shock and sometimes lack of sleep, many clinics teach only survival skills (the "basics") for the first day or two. They then go into more depth at future visits.

🐾 **DENIAL** is often expressed in comments such as: "there must be a mistake in the diagnosis." As a result, people may want to seek second opinions from other doctors. They hope to be told that they or their child doesn't have diabetes. Though initial doubt is a normal reaction, **continued denial may make adjustment much harder.** It can even interfere with medical treatment and education. If denial is very strong, it is important to understand the reason for this feeling. In some cases, there are complicated reasons and even cultural misunderstandings that can interfere with acceptance of the diagnosis.

For a child to accept his or her diabetes, parents need to accept the reality of diabetes and learn what they must do to care for their child. A child takes important cues from their family and will need their involvement, love, support and care. Though an adult with recently diagnosed diabetes will provide their own care, they will also need love, support and involvement from people important in their lives. This will help them to accept the diagnosis of diabetes. Siblings, grandparents, aunts, uncles and spouses (significant others) will all need to work through their feelings about the diagnosis. They can then discover how to be the most helpful. Support from all family members and friends is crucial when coping with diabetes.

🐾 **SADNESS.** It is common, initially, for parents or siblings to cry, be depressed and feel a loss. Some parents fear that their child's life will never be normal again. The child they previously thought of as healthy will now be "different." If their child has had previous medical experiences or has other medical conditions, people may feel it is terribly unfair that their child has yet another challenge. Adults with newly diagnosed diabetes can also have the very same feelings, fears and concerns about themselves.

Sadness is part of grieving and may be experienced off and on during the adjustment process. Sometimes this sadness is affected by previous losses or other traumatic experiences and can be quite difficult for a parent or affected adult. If normal sadness begins to linger too long and is affecting the ability to function, it is a good idea to talk with the psychosocial member of the medical team and get some guidance about what might be helpful during this difficult time.

🐾 **ANGER** is an emotion that is often difficult or uncomfortable to express. Sometimes we feel anger over things we cannot control. No person wants to get diabetes, or to have his or her child get diabetes. This anger may be felt or expressed toward doctors, nurses, God, a spouse, and even friends whose children do not have diabetes. In a sense, anger can be a sign of a family's protection of a member and reflects the difficulty in accepting that a loved one must live with a chronic medical condition. Like sadness, anger can get "stuck" and not get better. When anger persists, it is very important to talk with someone who can help you.

Children can also feel anger about the many changes in their lives—shots, pokes, diet changes, schedules, etc. They often direct it at the parent because they don't yet have the ability to express how they are feeling. Patience and talking will help children work out their feelings.

🐾 **ANXIETY** is a common feeling. Adults with diabetes may worry about how they will manage normal activities with this new diagnosis. Parents worry about their newly diagnosed child's safety and the extra responsibilities of caring for them. Brothers and sisters may worry about seeing shots and about whether they will get diabetes, too. The child with diabetes may worry about whether their friends will treat them differently. Young adults or parents may wonder how diabetes will affect their or their child's future. This anxiety will get better as the family gets practice and experience with care.

Normal everyday types of separations can take on a new meaning. A parent who previously sent their child to day care or school without concern may suddenly worry about whether their child with diabetes will be safe. Although some worry is normal and part of caring for a child, excessive worry can interfere with the child's need for growing independence.

* **A special note about shots:** One of the biggest initial fears for both adults and children is having to give [or get] insulin shots. Nearly *everyone* has fears about shots. This is normal! Fortunately, newer, smaller syringes and good technique can make shots almost painless. But fear often makes one shaky, nervous and tense. Giving or getting a shot when one is shaky, nervous or tense can be *painful*. Health care providers can help review the method used. They can also teach relaxation and breathing techniques to help shots be more comfortable [more about this in Chapter 17]. If pain persists, or the process takes more than a few minutes, then further attention is needed.

🐾 **GUILT** is something that adults and children often feel. When we don't understand why something has happened, it is easy to blame ourselves. A parent with a family history of diabetes may blame him or herself. This idea occurs even when people have been told that autoimmunity (self-allergy), viral infections and other unknown factors are important in causing diabetes. We do not completely understand why someone develops diabetes. There is no proven way at this time to prevent it. Earlier diagnosis would <u>not</u> have prevented the diabetes from happening or change the way it is treated.

Children always seek a reason for why something has happened. When we can't provide clear answers, they sometimes develop their own "theories" about why they got diabetes. Children have told us they thought they got diabetes because they "were naughty," "ate candy" or "were not nice to their brother." It is important to reassure them they did nothing to cause their diabetes. These "theories" can sometimes pop up years later. Keeping an open dialogue with your child will help work through these times.

🐾 ADJUSTING TO DIABETES

The first few weeks after diagnosis may feel like an eternity. The emotional and physical energy needed to manage the many changes resulting from a diagnosis of diabetes can be exhausting. But the good news is that things do get better! As normal household chores, work and school routines are re-established, family members start to settle in with their new diabetes plan. Adults begin to feel more energetic and able to "meet the world" on their terms. Parents are often reassured to see their child feeling better and "back to their old self." Sometimes a child may have great spurts in growth after just a few weeks of care. If weight loss occurred prior to diagnosis, appetite may be increased and the weight regained. Everyone begins to feel more confident in new skills, but may still have many questions. These are very important to review with the health care team.

Adjustment over the long run takes time. Communication about feelings within the family is very important because everyone feels the effects of one member having diabetes. Brothers and sisters may feel jealous that much of a parent's attention is now focused on the child with diabetes. Parents need to be aware of this and avoid making this one child "special." Special treatment will only breed later resentment. Diabetes should not take the fun out of being a family. A child with diabetes is a capable child who wants to be treated like everyone else.

As with any chronic medical condition, there will be times when some of the feelings and frustrations will again feel overwhelming. This may signal that something is not going well and needs attention. Talking with a health care team member, particularly the clinical social worker or psychologist, can be extremely helpful. They can help identify a problem and assist in its resolution.

As individuals and families adjust, everyone usually feels more hopeful. People find strengths that they didn't know they had. Parents may seek out connections with other families who have children with diabetes. They may want to volunteer to raise money for research and care or participate in available clinical research studies. The world of the internet opens up new avenues for information and resources (see websites in back of book). There is a strong worldwide community of families, medical providers and researchers who are very committed to advancing care for people with diabetes and, hopefully, eventually finding a cure. Having hope is a good thing!

DEFINITIONS

Adjustment (adaptation): Gradually learning to live with something (such as the diagnosis of diabetes).

Denial (deny): A refusal to believe something. A person may refuse to believe that he or she has diabetes.

Diagnosis: The process of finding that a person has a disease.

Guilt: A feeling that one caused something to happen.

QUESTIONS AND ANSWERS FROM NEWSNOTES

 Why is the Pink Panther character used in the educational manual, *"Understanding Diabetes"*?

Having a family member develop diabetes is often the most traumatic event that has happened to a family. If a child were pictured to demonstrate a side effect, such as hypoglycemia, it might be harder for a family member to accept than a picture of the Pink Panther having a reaction. Also, a bit of humor at this time of intense emotions can often be a big help.

Chapter 11
Normal Nutrition

H. Peter Chase, MD
Gail Spiegel, MS, RD, CDE
David Maahs, MD, PhD

TYPES OF NUTRIENTS

Families of a newly diagnosed person with diabetes are usually worried about what someone with diabetes should eat. They shouldn't be, as the **ideal diet for someone with diabetes (type 1 or type 2) is really just a healthy diet from which all people would benefit.** This chapter is meant to be a review of normal nutrition, which will help to improve the entire family's nutrition. It will be a good introduction to Chapter 12, Food Management and Diabetes. It will also make some of the words used by the dietitian easier to follow.

Foods provide different nutrients necessary for growth and health. If you know about these nutrients, you can help your family eat the right foods. Learning to read food labels will help you to know what you are buying at the grocery store. The Dietary Guidelines for Americans is available online at: www.healthierus.gov/dietaryguidelines. Table 1 shows the main recommendations.

There are six major nutrient groups:
I.   Protein
II.   Carbohydrate
III. Fat
IV.   Vitamins and minerals
V.   Water
VI.   Fiber

Our bodies need some of all of these nutrients, but in differing amounts.

TEACHING OBJECTIVES:
1. Present basic nutritional components including carbohydrates, protein and fat.
2. Introduce the importance of carbohydrate intake in diabetes management.
3. Present nutritional guidelines for fat/cholesterol intake and desired blood lipid ranges.

LEARNING OBJECTIVES:

Learners (parents, child, relative or self) will be able to:
1. List three major food components and give an example of each.
2. Explain the effect of carbohydrate intake on blood/CGM glucose levels.
3. Describe a dietary method to lower blood cholesterol/lipid levels.

Table 1
Dietary Guidelines:

Fruit and Vegetable Intake
5 to 13 servings per day
(2½-6½ cups/day)

Consume enough fruits and vegetables while staying within energy needs: 1-2½ cups of fruit and 1½-4 cups of vegetables per day for a reference 2,000 calorie intake. Make adjustments for various calorie levels.

Fat Intake
Keep total fat between 20 percent and 35 percent of calories, with most fats coming from sources of polyunsaturated and monounsaturated fats such as fish, nuts and vegetable oils; limit solid fats like butter, margarine, shortening and lard, and foods that contain these.

Salt Intake
Consume less than 1,500 mg of sodium per day (¾ teaspoon of table salt–less for younger children) and include potassium-rich foods such as fruits and vegetables.

Sugar Intake
Choose and prepare foods low in added sugars or caloric sweeteners.

Dairy Intake
(3-4 servings per day)
Consume 3-4 cups per day of fat-free or low-fat milk or equivalent.

Bread, Cereal, Grain Intake
(6-11 servings per day of 3-10 oz.)
Half of one's intake of grains should be in the form of whole grains.

Protein
(2-3 servings per day of 3-7 oz.)
2-3 ounces poultry, fish or lean meat
1½ cup cooked dry beans
1 egg = 1 ounce meat,
4 ounces or ½ cup tofu

Physical Activity
Engage in 30-60 minutes of moderate physical activity on most days of the week.
To help manage weight, engage in about 60 minutes of moderate to vigorous activity on most days of the week, while not exceeding calorie requirements.

I) Protein

Protein is important for muscle and bone growth. However, eating extra protein does **not** cause increased muscle growth. Muscles grow only as a result of proper exercise. Foods high in protein include milk, yogurt, meats, fish, chicken, turkey, egg whites, soy, cheese, cottage cheese, beans and nuts. In addition to fish being a good source of protein, the fish oils (fats) are believed to help prevent heart disease (see "Fat" in this chapter). Protein should provide 15-20 percent of the total caloric intake. Protein from animal sources is a **complete** protein. This means it contains all of the essential building blocks of protein called amino acids.

Adults and teens can receive adequate protein eating only a vegetarian diet, but this is more difficult for growing infants and children. Many people do not realize that protein also is available from non-meat sources. Dried beans, legumes, soy, nuts and seeds are fairly good sources of protein.

Most people eat more protein than they need. In a review of three-day diet records from our clinic, the young men were getting approximately three times, and the young women two times the amount of protein needed. High protein intake usually results in high animal fat intake, which may be unhealthy for the heart. It may also provide an extra stress for some people's kidneys.

It is important to choose low-fat meat and poultry. Low-fat meats may be graded as **lean** or **choice** for lower amounts of fat.

Two examples of reducing the fat content of the diet are:

1. removing the skin from poultry

2. buying meats which do not have a lot of visible fat

II) Carbohydrate ("carbs")

Carbohydrate is the food source we are most concerned about for people with diabetes. This is because it is the main nutrient that is changed to blood sugar. Carbohydrate is important mainly as an energy source for the body. Each gram of carbohydrate supplies four calories.

It used to be believed that sugar, which is a carbohydrate, was rapidly absorbed while starchy carbohydrates were slowly absorbed. This is an easy concept to explain and to believe, but it is **NOT** true. Research has shown that there is no difference in absorption of a sugar as compared with a starchy carbohydrate. This is because the intestine has such high levels of digestive enzymes that starchy carbohydrate is rapidly broken down to sugar. Thus, **"a carbohydrate is a carbohydrate, is a carbohydrate..."**. They all affect blood/CGM glucose levels in a similar way.

Insulin is essential to allow sugar to pass into the cells of the body to be burned for energy. **The balance between all carbohydrate eaten and the insulin dosage is one of the major keys to diabetes management.** These concepts are discussed in detail in the next chapter, Food Management and Diabetes. The Dietary Guidelines for Americans recommends at least 2 cups of fruit and 2½ cups of vegetables per day (for 2,000 calories) and cutting back on foods with added sugar.

Some examples of carbohydrate foods are:

✔ breads (encourage whole wheat grain)

✔ cereals and grains

✔ crackers

✔ fruits

✔ beans (baked, refried, black, kidney, etc.)

✔ vegetables

- starchy (½ cup cooked contains approximately 15g carbohydrate): corn, peas, potatoes and yams

- non-starchy (½ cup cooked contains approximately 5g carbohydrate): green beans, asparagus, broccoli, celery, cabbage, cauliflower and carrots

✔ milk and yogurt (contain protein and may also contain fat)

✔ most desserts

More detailed knowledge about starches and sugars, both of which are carbohydrates, is helpful.

Starch: Starch is a substance made up of hundreds of sugar units. The sugar from starch is now known to be absorbed as quickly as from table sugar (when each is taken alone without other foods). Sources of starch are breads, noodles, pasta, rice, cereals and starchy vegetables such as corn, peas, potatoes and legumes.

Sugar: The World Health Organization (WHO) recommends that all people should limit (processed) sugar intake to less than 10 percent of calories. A diet high in sugars contributes to dental cavities and provides few vitamins and minerals. Often high sugar foods also contain large amounts of fat. A nutritious diet does not contain large amounts of high sugar foods. There are many different kinds of sugar found in foods. Some sugar is often added to foods as a sweetener and may not be noticed unless labels are read. The names for sugars often end in "—ose." Some of the common sugars are listed below.

✔ **Glucose:** Glucose is the name for the main sugar in our body. When we talk about blood and urine sugar, we really mean glucose. Table sugar is half glucose and half fructose. Corn sugar is primarily glucose. Another name for glucose is dextrose.

✔ **Fructose:** Fructose is sometimes called "fruit sugar" as it is the main type of sugar found in fruits. It is sold in pure granulated form and is a part of many food products. Fructose has the same number of calories per gram as table sugar (sucrose). The liquid form is sweeter than table sugar, but the taste is the same in baked products. Generally, only one-half to one-third the amount of fructose needs to be used to have the same degree of sweetness as table sugar.

"High-fructose" corn syrup is different from pure fructose and contains large amounts of sucrose. People with diabetes need to be aware of how much of this is eaten.

✔ **Sucrose or table sugar:** The body breaks down sucrose to glucose and fructose. Foods high in sucrose and glucose include cake, cookies, pie, candy, soft drinks and other desserts.

✔ **Lactose or milk sugar:** Lactose is found in milk and yogurt. Children and adolescents should drink three to four 8 oz glasses of milk per day for calcium and vitamin D.

✔ **Syrups:** Corn syrup, corn syrup solids, high fructose syrups, maple syrup, sorghum syrup and sugar cane syrup are often added to baked goods. They are all primarily glucose and must be consumed carefully by people with diabetes.

III) Fat

Fat is an important energy source and is needed for growth. The dietary guidelines recommend that fat should provide only 20-35 percent of total caloric intake. The types of fats found in fish, nuts and vegetable oils are preferred. A major emphasis in nutrition in the past decade has been the reduction of the total daily fat intake and lower dietary cholesterol intake. Dietary cholesterol intake should be <300 mg/day. People with high LDL cholesterol levels (Table 2) may benefit from lowering dietary cholesterol to < 200 mg/day. Reducing cholesterol and saturated fat intake is discussed as the sixth principle of food management for a person with diabetes in the next chapter. Higher fat and cholesterol intakes may lead to elevated blood fat levels (cholesterol and triglycerides: Table 2) and a higher risk for heart disease. (People may consume as much as 40-50 percent of calories from fat rather than the recommended 20-35 percent.) Fried food eaten in fast-food restaurants is usually very high in fat. Fat has more calories (nine calories per gram) than protein or carbohydrate (four calories per gram). Thus, it is more likely to lead to weight gain and obesity. Most effective long-term

Table 2
Recommended Levels (mg/dL) for Lipids and Lipoproteins

Lipid Type	Desired Level**	
Cholesterol	< 200 mg/dL	< 5.2 mmol/L
LDL Cholesterol*	< 100 mg/dL	< 2.6 mmol/L
HDL Cholesterol*	> 40 mg/dL	> 1.0 mmol/L
Triglyceride*	< 150 mg/dL	< 1.7 mmol/L

* Preferably drawn after fasting overnight. If fasting overnight is not possible, then at least four hours after eating.

** Desired level for a person with diabetes

weight reduction programs emphasize limiting total fat intake.

The main fats in the diet are divided into four types:

✔ **monounsaturated** (high in olive and canola oils)

✔ **polyunsaturated** (most vegetable oils)

✔ **saturated** (mainly animal fats; e.g., meats, cheese, butter)

✔ **trans-fats** (hydrogen has been added back to make them trans-fats)

It is important to eat more of the monounsaturated and polyunsaturated fats than the saturated fats. **Less than 10 percent of total calories eaten per day should be from saturated fat.** Increasing the intake of monounsaturated fats (e.g., olive oil and canola oil) can help prevent heart disease.

There are high amounts of polyunsaturated fat in most vegetable oils (coconut and palm are exceptions). Margarines made from vegetable oils are also polyunsaturated. In general, the softer or more liquid a fat is at room temperature, the less saturated it is. For example, liquid margarine is a better choice than stick margarine, and vegetable oil is better than vegetable shortening. Stick margarine contains more trans-fats. In general, the harder the margarine, the more trans-fats.

The saturated fats include most animal fats such as the fat in meats, cheese, milk, butter and lard. Chicken, turkey and fish are lower in saturated fat than beef or pork, particularly when the skin is removed. Chicken, turkey and fish also contain some polyunsaturated fat.

Blood Lipids (fats)

High levels of the two main blood fats (lipids), **cholesterol** and **triglyceride**, can lead to early aging of the large blood vessels. These vessels carry blood to the heart, legs and other body parts. Other causes of early aging of large blood vessels are diabetes, tobacco use, high blood pressure, lack of exercise and being overweight. As people with diabetes already have one risk factor (by having diabetes), they do not need another. Optimal control of glucose levels will help to keep the blood fat levels in the desired ranges.

In addition to cholesterol levels, the proteins which carry cholesterol in the blood (lipoproteins) are also important. The **LDL cholesterol** (often referred to as the **"bad cholesterol"**) carries the cholesterol into the blood vessel wall. Therefore, this level needs to be low. Some groups are now recommending the value be < 70 rather than < 100 as shown in Table 2. In general, lower is good. The cholesterol build-up in the blood vessel wall may lead to hardening of the arteries

Table 3
Making Food Choices for Fat Content

Food Group (Amount)	Decrease	Instead Choose
Meat, Poultry, & Fish (6-8 oz per day)	Beef, pork, lamb, regular ground beef, fatty cuts, spare ribs, organ meats	Lean beef, pork, lamb (lean cuts), well-trimmed before cooking
	Poultry with skin, fried chicken, fried fish, fried shellfish, regular luncheon meat (e.g., bologna, salami, sausage, frankfurters)	Poultry without skin, fish, shellfish, processed meat – prepared, from lean meat (e.g., sliced turkey from the deli)
Eggs (≤ 2 yolks per week)	Egg yolks: If high blood cholesterol, limit to two per week (includes eggs used in cooking and baking)	Egg whites (two whites can be substituted for whole egg in recipes), cholesterol-free egg substitute
Dairy Products (2-3 servings per day)	Whole milk (fluid, evaporated, condensed), 2% fat milk (low-fat milk), imitation milk, whole milk yogurt, whole milk yogurt beverages, regular cheeses (American, Blue, Brie, Cheddar, Colby, Edam, Monterey Jack, whole-milk Mozzarella, Parmesan, Swiss), cream cheese, Neufchatel cheese	Milk – fat-free, ½%, or 1% fat (fluid, powdered, evaporated) Yogurt – nonfat or low-fat yogurt or yogurt beverages Cheese – low-fat natural or processed cheese
	Cottage cheese (4% fat)	Low-fat or nonfat varieties of cottage cheese
	Ice cream	Frozen dairy dessert – ice milk, frozen yogurt (low-fat or nonfat), nonfat ice cream
	Cream, half & half, whipped cream, nondairy creamer, sour cream	Low-fat coffee creamer, low-fat or nonfat sour cream
Fats and Oils (≤ 6-8 teaspoons per day)	Coconut oil, palm kernel oil, palm oils	Polyunsaturated oils – safflower, sunflower, corn, canola*, olive*, peanut
	Butter, lard, shortening, bacon fat, hard margarine	Margarine – made from unsaturated oils listed above, light or diet margarine, especially soft or liquid forms (e.g., Parkay Squeeze™)

* High in mono-unsaturated fats.

Adapted from Powers, MA; *"Handbook of Diabetes Medical Nutrition Therapy"*, Aspen Publishers, Inc. Gaithersburg, MD, 1996 p. 354.

(atherosclerosis) which makes a heart attack more likely to occur. The **HDL cholesterol ("good cholesterol")** carries the cholesterol out of the blood vessel wall. This level should be high. Desired levels for people with diabetes are shown in Table 2. Since diabetes alone is a risk factor for heart disease, the desired levels shown in Table 2 are lower for people with diabetes than for the general population.

We recommend a low-fat diet that allows no more than 20 to 35 percent of total calories from fat. Cholesterol intake should be < 300 mg/day. We also recommend limiting intake of foods that are high in animal (saturated) fats and trans-fats. Suggestions for changes are shown in Table 3. Reduction of total fat, animal (saturated) fat and cholesterol intake are good nutrition practices whether a person does or doesn't have diabetes. Trans-fatty acids are similar to saturated fatty acids. They both raise blood cholesterol levels. They are found in solid margarines, commercial cookies, crackers and other foods. The dietary guidelines recommend keeping trans-fat intake as low as possible.

Suggestions for good nutrition include eating:

- fish and poultry (with the skin removed)

- cold-water fish (salmon, light tuna), with omega-3 fatty acids, at least twice weekly

- milk with no more than 1 percent fat

- canola, olive, corn, safflower or soy oils should be used for salads and cooking

IV) Vitamins and Minerals

These are important for growth, formation of blood cells, healthy skin, good vision, and strong teeth and bones. Fruits and vegetables are rich in vitamins. Minerals are found in milk, meats and vegetables. Calcium is a mineral that is important for the bones and teeth. People who do not drink milk or eat dairy products may need to take a calcium supplement. Many foods (e.g., cereals, waffles) are now fortified with calcium. Children ages 1–3 years need 500 mg of calcium per day and those who are 4–10 years need 800 mg of calcium per day.

Most people 10-20 years old need 1,300 mg of calcium per day.

Zinc is a mineral that is lost in the urine in proportion to sugar in the urine. Zinc is important for growth. Some children with diabetes may grow better with a zinc supplement.

Sodium is also a mineral, which, in some "salt-sensitive" people, may cause higher blood pressure. It is recommended by the American Heart Association that all people limit their sodium to less than 1,500 mg (approximately ³/₄ tsp) per day (less in young children). If the blood pressure is elevated, this amount should be even lower. Salt in the food we eat (e.g., chips, hamburgers, hot dogs and convenience foods) is often "hidden" but may be a significant source of salt.

Generally, people who eat a well-balanced diet do not need extra vitamins. If a child does not eat a balanced diet (e.g., not liking yellow or green vegetables), a vitamin supplement may be helpful. Also, vitamins and minerals often are recommended in the month following onset of diabetes as the body rebuilds. In general, "mega" doses of nutrients should be avoided, and the vitamins should not contain more than 100 percent of the recommended daily allowance (RDA). The fat-soluble vitamins (A, D, E and K) are stored in the body and excessive doses can be harmful. It is now recognized that vitamin D has immune properties. Low blood levels are quite common due to less time spent outdoors and the use of suntan lotions. Although not proven, some diabetes researchers are wondering if vitamin D could help prevent diabetes. More research is needed to answer this question.

V) Water

Water is the most important nutrient for the survival of humans. It makes up much of the blood, the body fluids and the body's transport system. It serves as a coolant, shock absorber and waste remover. It has many other important functions. Since the body is made-up of about two-thirds water, it is important to drink a lot of it. We recommend at least six 8-oz glasses of liquid per day, including allowed sugar-free drinks, and milk. When a person with diabetes is spilling urine ketones, it is important to drink more water and sugar-free liquids. This helps to replace body fluid loss.

VI) Fiber

Dietary fiber is the part of plants ("roughage" or "bulk") that is not digested and is not absorbed into the body. Foods vary in the amounts and kinds of fiber they contain. Fiber in the diet supplies bulk (without calories) and roughage which helps satisfy the appetite and keep the digestive system running smoothly. In people with type 2 diabetes, increased fiber intake has been helpful in slowing the absorption of sugar. Fiber has not been as helpful in lowering blood/CGM glucose levels in people with type 1 diabetes.

Fiber often is divided into two types. The first is **water-soluble fiber**, such as parts of oats and beans, seeds, citrus fruits and apples. These may help lower the blood cholesterol levels. They also may help reduce the blood/CGM glucose levels after meals in people with type 2 diabetes. The other type, **water-insoluble fiber**, such as parts of wheat bran, most grains, nuts and vegetables, helps prevent constipation and may help other digestive disorders. According to the Dietary Guidelines, the minimum intake of fruits and vegetables is "5-a-Day." The Eat 5-a-Day campaign was developed by The Produce for Better Health Foundation in cooperation with the National Cancer Institute. This includes 2 servings of fruits and 2½ of vegetables. The current recommendation is to eat between 20g and 35g of fiber in the daily diet. They have recently launched a new public health initiative, **Fruits and Veggies - More Matters™**. Their website is: www.fruitsandveggiesmatter.gov.

An example of fiber in breakfast might be: a serving of a cereal with 2.5g or more of fiber, two slices of whole wheat bread (4-6g fiber) and a whole banana (3g fiber). The fiber intake would be 10g or more. Most of us need to increase our fiber intake.

FOOD GROUPS/ FOOD GUIDE PYRAMID

Foods are often divided into groups or exchanges (see Chapter 12). The common divisions include the milk and yogurt, meat, grains and starchy vegetables, non-starchy vegetables, fruit, and fat groups. At least one-half of the servings of grains for the day should be whole grain. The milk and meat groups are important sources of protein, and the milk group is a major source of calcium and vitamin D. Milk also has carbohydrate. Some of the minerals such as iron and zinc are high in the meat groups. Vitamins and fiber are generally highest in the fruit and vegetable groups. Be aware that some foods from each of the food groups should be eaten daily to have a well-balanced diet. The food pyramid (see Figure) is now usually used as a guide to good nutrition (rather than food groups). More information on current recommendations for the food pyramid can be found at: www.mypyramid.gov.

Three-day Food Record

It is sometimes wise to keep a three-day food record. This will show you if you are eating the right foods. Write down all foods and the amounts you eat for three days as shown in the Appendix in this Chapter. The dietitian can then review the record and suggest changes if needed. Chapter 12 emphasizes the use of food records to evaluate carbohydrate counting. While you are doing the recording, you will need to give accurate information. If you feel you need more help with instructions, ask your dietitian.

SWEETENERS
(Sugars and Sugar-substitutes)

Many foods are now available which contain sweeteners that either do not raise the blood/CGM glucose levels or which may cause less of an increase than a similar amount of table sugar. They are divided into the nutritive sweeteners (including table sugar), which do provide calories and carbohydrate, and the non-nutritive sweeteners, which essentially provide no calories or carbohydrate.

The Healthy Eating Pyramid

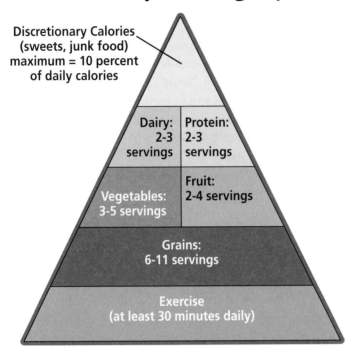

Discretionary Calories (sweets, junk food) maximum = 10 percent of daily calories

Dairy: 2-3 servings

Protein: 2-3 servings

Fruit: 2-4 servings

Vegetables: 3-5 servings

Grains: 6-11 servings

Exercise (at least 30 minutes daily)

What does your plate for a day look like?

Look at the food guide to see if you need to:

- Eat more whole grains (e.g., whole wheat bread, brown rice, beans, potato and pasta)

- Eat more fruits and vegetables

- Eat less protein and fat (particularly red meat)

- In general eat more foods that are low on the pyramid and fewer foods that are higher

- Eat less sweets

The Daily Plate of Food

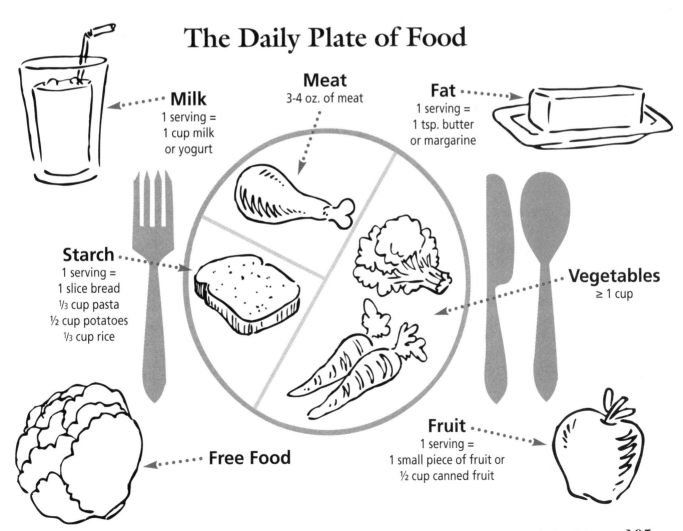

Milk
1 serving =
1 cup milk
or yogurt

Meat
3-4 oz. of meat

Fat
1 serving =
1 tsp. butter
or margarine

Starch
1 serving =
1 slice bread
1/3 cup pasta
1/2 cup potatoes
1/3 cup rice

Vegetables
≥ 1 cup

Free Food

Fruit
1 serving =
1 small piece of fruit or
1/2 cup canned fruit

Nutritive Sweeteners

✔ Sugars

These include all sugars and all sugar-alcohols. Sugars contain 4g of carbohydrate and 16 calories per level teaspoon. The two main sugars used as sweeteners are sucrose (table sugar) and fructose. Both are discussed earlier in this chapter under Carbohydrates, and both cause an increase in blood/CGM glucose levels. High-fructose corn syrup is a combination of both sugars and raises the blood sugar more than pure fructose. **Agave Nectar** is a syrup refined from a cactus-like plant. It has fructose and glucose in it, but is 140-160 times sweeter than table sugar. Foods sweetened with fruit juices, dates or raisins may have the label "no added sugar." This is misleading as there is sugar in these food-additives.

✔ Sugar Alcohols

The sugar alcohols include sorbitol, xylitol, mannitol and others (often ending in "ol"). They provide about 2g of carbohydrate and eight calories per teaspoon. They are more slowly absorbed than sugar, and eating an excessive amount can cause diarrhea. They are often found in "sugar-free" candies and cookies as well as other low carb products.

✔ Erythritol:
Erythritol is a sugar alcohol which is combined with stevia sweeteners like Truvia™ for bulk and sweetness. It contains 0 calories (less than other sugar alcohols) and does not cause diarrhea as some sugar alcohols do.

✔ Xylitol:
Xylitol is a sugar alcohol which is found in products like chewing gum and can also be found in a tabletop sweetener called Ideal™. It can be used for baking.

Non-nutritive Sweeteners

The non-nutritive (or "artificial") sweeteners do not provide any calories or carbohydrate. *The six currently on the market are:*

1. **Saccharin:** Saccharin is 200-700 times sweeter than table sugar. It is found in Sweet'N Low®, other table top sweeteners and in some diet drinks.

2. **Aspartame:** Aspartame is 200 times sweeter than table sugar. It is broken down into aspartic acid, methanol and phenylalanine. (Rare patients with a condition called phenylketonuria cannot metabolize phenylalanine and cannot eat foods with this sweetener.) The products that contain aspartame include: Equal®, NutraSweet®, diet pop, sugar-free JELL-O®, Kool-Aid®, ice cream, Crystal Light® and many others. Use in moderation is generally advised (no more than two diet pops per day!).

3. **Acesulfame-Potassium (Ace-K):** Ace-K is 200 times sweeter than table sugar. It is approved for use as a table-top sweetener and for use in chewing gum, desserts, beverages and other products. It is used in many sugar-free drinks and in other products along with aspartame.

4. **Sucralose:** Sucralose was approved for use in 1998 and is 600 times sweeter than sugar. It is used as a table-top sweetener (Splenda®) and is found in RC Cola®, diet and sugar-free juices, Log Cabin® Sugar-Free Syrup and many other products.

5. **Stevia:** Stevia is a natural sweetener from the herb, Stevia Rebaudiana. It is 300 times sweeter than sugar. Stevia leaf and extracts are available as a sweetener in the dietary supplement aisle. In 2008, the FDA approved Rebaudioside A (Reb A), a part of the stevia leaf, to be added to food and drinks and as a tabletop sweetener. This part of the stevia leaf can be found in tabletop sweeteners, such as Truvia™ and Pura Via™.

6. **Neotame:** Approved by the FDA as a general-purpose sweetener and is 30-40 times sweeter than aspartame.

LABEL READING

Label reading has become easier for people in the U.S. as the law requires labeling of the

Table 4
Reading a Nutrition Label

* The serving size is shown at the top. It is important to observe the serving size. (This is often less than the amount people eat. If you eat two cups rather than one, you would need to double all of the amounts listed.) The total calories and the calories from fat per serving are routinely given and are important.

* The total fat includes all types of fat (saturated, polyunsaturated, monounsaturated and trans-fat). The total fat, saturated fat and cholesterol content are all important in relation to heart disease and it is wise to look for lower fat choices.

* The saturated fats for the entire day should be under 10 percent of the total calories per day. For someone eating 2,000 calories per day, this would mean under 200 calories from saturated fat or under 22g (nine calories per gram). The trans-fat content appears on the label as of 2006.

* †The percent of daily values for fat, carbohydrate and protein are listed on the label based on a 2,000 calorie daily intake. More active people will need more calories, in which case these amounts should be figured based on calories actually eaten.

Nutrition Facts

Serving Size 1.0 Cup (120g)
Servings Per Container   8

Amount Per Serving

Calories 130   Calories From Fat 60

% Daily Value †

Total Fat 6.5g	10%
Saturated Fat 2.5g	12%
Trans-fat	0%
Cholesterol 30mg	10%
Sodium 240mg	10%
Total Carbohydrate 15g	5%
Dietary Fiber 2.5g	10%
Sugars 3g	
Protein 3g	6%

Vitamin A 10%		Vitamin E	5%
Calcium 15%		Iron	5%

†Percent Daily Values are based on a 2,000-calorie diet. Your daily values may be higher or lower depending on your calorie needs:

Calories:	2,000	2,500	3,200
Total Fat (g)	65	80	107
Sat Fat (g)	20	25	36
Cholesterol (mg)	300	300	300
Sodium (mg)	2,400	2,400	2,400
Total Carb (g)	300	375	480
Fiber	25	30	37

Calories per gram:

Fat 9   Carbohydrate 4   Protein 4

Ingredients: Whole wheat, oat bran, raisins, gelatin, malt, flavoring, vitamins, and minerals.

* For those who count carbohydrates, one helping of this cereal has 15g of carbohydrate, which is one carbohydrate count. If one cup of white milk (any type) is added, then one additional carbohydrate count must also be added so that there would be a total of two carb counts. The sugars include those found naturally in the food as well as those added to the food. Both are included in the grams of "Total Carbohydrate."

* The recommended daily amounts for cholesterol stay the same for the 24-hour period for the three caloric intakes.

* The ingredients below are usually included on the label in order of the amount present.

nutrient content of products. Smart buyers can learn a lot about the foods they consider buying by learning to read labels. The information that can be gained from reading a label is discussed in Table 4.

The grams of carbohydrates are listed under "total carbohydrate" on most labels. This value also includes the grams of fiber. Since the body does not completely absorb fiber, half of the grams of fiber can be subtracted from the grams of total carbohydrate to determine the insulin dose if there is more than five grams of fiber. Carbohydrate counting is discussed in detail in the next chapter.

FAST-FOOD RESTAURANTS

It is difficult to eat at fast-food restaurants and not eat foods high in animal fat, calories and salt. Eating at fast-food restaurants often goes against good nutrition principles and may be unhealthy for the heart. In addition, meals are usually low in vitamin-containing fruits and vegetables. Some fast-food restaurants are now trying to provide healthier food choices (salads, fruit, milk [with meals], leaner meat and deep-frying in vegetable oils rather than animal fat). However, eating at fast-food restaurants should be limited.

ALCOHOL

We hesitate to discuss alcohol under normal nutrition. It is, of course, illegal for children and adolescents to use alcohol prior to reaching the legal drinking age in a particular state or country. We do not condone alcohol use for children or adolescents. However, exposure often begins prior to the legal drinking age. Education is important regardless of the age.

Blood sugars may initially be elevated after drinking alcohol. Beer, for example, contains a fair amount of carbohydrate. However, the more dangerous effect of alcohol is the lowering of the blood/CGM glucose levels (as much as 6-12 hours later). The alcohol prevents the other foods stored in the body from being converted to blood sugar.

If alcohol consumption is to occur, some general rules are listed below:

✔ Use alcohol only in moderation. Sip slowly and make one drink last a long time.

✔ Eat (especially carbohydrates) when drinking alcohol. Never drink on an empty stomach.

✔ A low blood sugar is the main worry - and a bedtime snack (solid protein and some carbohydrate) must be taken after drinking in the evening even if the bedtime blood/CGM glucose level is high.

✔ The next morning, get up at the usual time, do a blood sugar, take insulin, eat breakfast and then go back to bed if you feel ill. "Sleeping-in" can result in a bad reaction.

✔ NEVER drink and drive. Ask a friend who has not been drinking to drive, or call someone to come and get you.

A college student, helping to teach our College Workshop course to newly-graduated high school seniors, had a useful recommendation regarding college parties. He noted that if he had a cup in his hand, no one tried to push further drinks. In contrast, if his hands were empty (no glass), he received a lot of pressure. The answer was to hold the same cup all evening and to just have fun!

Appendix
Three-Day Food Record Form

Instructions for completing food record form:

1. Please write down everything you eat or drink for three days. This includes meals and snacks. Often it's easier to remember what you eat if you record your food intake at the time you eat it.

2. Include the amount of food or beverage consumed. Also include the method of preparation (baked, fried, broiled, etc.), as well as any brand names of products (labels can also be enclosed). Use standard measuring cups or spoons. Record meat portions in ounces after cooking. If you do not have a scale, you can estimate ounces. The size of a deck of cards is about equal to three ounces of meat.

3. Be sure to include items added to your food. For example, include salad dressing on salad, margarine or butter on bread.

4. Include any supplements you take (vitamin, mineral or protein powders). Write down the name of the supplement, what it contains and the amount taken. Include a copy of the label, if possible.

5. Please include meal and snack times, blood glucose values, amount and type of insulin, type of food, amount of food, grams of carbohydrate and any activity or exercise. Put a star next to any blood sugar value that is two hours after a meal.

The following is an example of how to complete your food record. Please record what you eat on the forms in this chapter. The forms can then be faxed or mailed to your diabetes care provider. *An example for the start of a day follows:*

Time	Blood Glucose	Insulin	Food (include amounts)	Carbs	Activity
8:00	170	4H/10N	Cheerios—1½ cup	34g	
			Fat free milk—1 cup	12g	
10:00					Jog—20 min.

3-DAY FOOD RECORD
(Copy as needed)

Name:_____

Date: _____

Dietitian: _____

Home Phone: _____

Cell or Work Phone: _____

Best time to be reached:_____

Insulin-to-Carb ratios (if known)

Breakfast:_____

Lunch: _____

Dinner: _____

Snack:_____

Blood Sugar Correction:

_____

Time	Blood Glucose	Insulin	Food	Amount of Food	Carbs	Activity

Fax to: _____

COPY AS NEEDED

DEFINITIONS

Acesulfame-Potassium: An artificial sweetener which does not need insulin to be absorbed by the body.

Artificial sweetener: A very sweet substance (many hundreds of times sweeter than table sugar) used in very small amounts (and thus having almost no calories) to make foods or drinks taste sweet. Six of the non-nutritive sweeteners are described in the text of this chapter.

Aspartame: An artificial sweetener which does not need insulin to be absorbed by the body. It is available as a tablet or powder called Equal or NutraSweet (see text of this chapter).

Calorie: A measurement of the food taken into the body for energy.

Caloric intake: Refers to the energy from foods that are eaten.

Carbohydrate: One of the main energy nutrients. It supplies energy for the body and is further divided into sugars and starches. Carbohydrates are found in all fruits and vegetables, all grain products, dried beans and peas, milk and yogurt. *Carbohydrates include:*

✔ **Starch:** Carbohydrates such as starchy vegetables, pasta, whole grain breads and cereals.

✔ **Sugar:** Carbohydrates such as table sugar, honey, *the four sugars listed below and others:*

1. **Fructose:** The type of sugar found in fruit.

2. **Glucose:** The main type of sugar found in the blood and urine. It is this sugar that is elevated in people with diabetes. Table sugar is half glucose.

3. **Lactose:** The main sugar found in milk. It needs insulin to be used completely.

4. **Sucrose:** Table sugar or "granulated sugar" – the body breaks it down to glucose and fructose. The glucose needs insulin to be used.

Cholesterol: A fat present in foods from animals. It is also made in our body. Our blood cholesterol level results from our own body's production ($\approx$ 85 percent) and from the animal products we eat ($\approx$ 15 percent). A high blood cholesterol level (> 200 mg/dL) results in a greater risk for heart disease.

Cup (c): A measure of volume of eight ounces or 240cc (ml). Two cups equal one pint. Four cups equal one quart.

Dextrose: Another name for glucose.

Fat: One of the energy nutrients. *Total fat includes:*

✔ **Polyunsaturated fat:** Fat found mainly in vegetable oils.

✔ **Monounsaturated fat:** It is high in olive and canola oils. When large amounts (3 Tbsp) are consumed each day, blood cholesterol levels will be lower.

✔ **Saturated fat:** Fat found mainly in animal foods. They may raise blood triglyceride levels and cause LDL (bad) cholesterol levels to rise.

✔ **Trans-fatty acids:** The fat formed when vegetable oils are processed and made more solid. They may raise the LDL (bad) cholesterol and lower the HDL (good) cholesterol.

✔ **Cholesterol and Triglyceride:** Fats present in foods and in our bodies. High cholesterol and triglyceride blood levels for many years are a cause of "clogged" blood vessels and heart attacks.

Fiber: The parts of plants in food that are not absorbed by the body.

Gram (g): A unit of weight in the metric system; 1,000g is equal to 1 kg. There are 448g in one pound and 28g in 1 oz. Carbohydrate, protein and fat in foods are measured as grams. Information can be obtained from label reading.

✔ One gram of carbohydrate provides four calories.

✔ One gram of protein provides four calories.

✔ One gram of fat provides nine calories.

Maltitol: A sugar alcohol that is used in foods to give a sweet taste. It usually does provide calories, but doesn't increase the blood sugar as much as sucrose. Too much can cause diarrhea or an upset stomach.

Ounce (oz): A unit of weight equivalent to 28g. It is also equal to 30cc (or 30 mL) of water.

Protein: One of the energy nutrients. It is found in meat, eggs, fish, milk, yogurt and, in lesser amounts, in vegetables and other non-meat products (e.g., nuts, seeds, beans, etc.).

Registered Dietitian (R.D.): A person trained to help you with your meal planning and nutrition. He/she has a minimum of a four-year college degree in nutrition or a related area, has completed an internship and has passed a national exam.

Saccharin: An artificial sweetener (e.g., Sweet'N Low) which needs no insulin and provides no calories (see text of this chapter).

Sorbitol: A sugar alcohol that is used in foods to give a sweet taste. It does provide calories, but does not increase the blood sugar as much as sucrose (see text of this chapter).

Tablespoon (Tbsp): A measure of 3 tsp or 15cc (15 mL). It is equal to 15g (½ oz) of water. There are 16 tablespoons of sugar (sucrose) in one measuring cup.

Teaspoon (tsp): A measure of 5cc (5 mL). It is also equal to 5g of water.

QUESTIONS AND ANSWERS FROM NEWSNOTES

What is fiber and what is its value in the diet?

Fiber is generally defined as the part of food that is not broken down by the enzymes in the intestine. Some of the physiological effects of fiber are to prolong the time it takes food to leave the stomach, to shorten the transit of food through the rest of the intestine, to reduce fat absorption and to increase stool weight and bulk. Pressure in the colon is generally reduced.

Although fiber sounds like a blessing for the diabetic diet, it has been more useful in type 2 diabetes than in type 1 diabetes. So many things affect the person with type 1 diabetes, particularly insulin dose and exercise, that altering one part of the diet (fiber) and expecting miraculous changes in diabetes control has not been realistic.

Increasing fiber intake should still be a goal for all children and young adults. The high-fiber foods are mainly vegetables, bran or whole grain cereals, whole grain bread and fruits. At a minimum, according to the Dietary Guidelines, for a 2,000 calorie diet, a person should eat 2 cups of fruit and 2½ cups of vegetables per day. If, in addition, whole grain breads are eaten (e.g., "whole wheat" and not just "wheat"), fiber intake will likely be fine.

What does the food label, "low-fat" mean?

"Low-fat" on a label means that the food has 3g of fat or less. It does not say anything about whether the fat is a "good" fat (e.g., polyunsaturated) or a "bad" fat (e.g., saturated fat, trans-fat). It also does not mean that the amount of fat has been reduced in the food. For example, an apple could be labeled "low-fat" as it has less than 3g of fat normally. In contrast, a food labeled as **"reduced fat"** means that one serving of food contains a 25 percent (or more) reduction of fat compared to the usual form of that food. It could still contain a large amount of fat.

Chapter 12
Food Management and Diabetes

H. Peter Chase, MD
Gail Spiegel, MS, RD, CDE
David Maahs, MD, PhD

Food (mainly carbohydrate ["carb"]) is one of the major influences on blood/CGM glucose levels in people with diabetes. As discussed in Chapter 2, the body (particularly the liver) also makes sugar (internal sugar), which adds to the blood sugar. Other sugars (external sugars) come from the food we eat. Recommendations for the use of added sugars for people with diabetes have changed. It has gone from avoidance to allowing sugar within the context of a healthy meal plan. As discussed in Chapter 11, the right amount and types of food are essential for normal growth and health. **TYPE 1 (INSULIN-DEPENDENT) DIABETES CANNOT BE TREATED WITH DIET ALONE.** In contrast, type 2 diabetes can sometimes be treated with diet and exercise alone.

OBJECTIVES OF FOOD MANAGEMENT

No matter which of the food plans are used, the objectives of food management are the same:

- to balance insulin and carb intake in order to keep the blood (or continuous glucose monitor [CGM]) glucose values as close to normal as possible

- to keep the blood fats (cholesterol and triglycerides) and lipoproteins (LDL and HDL) at desired levels

TEACHING OBJECTIVES:

1. Present the principles of food management related to diabetes.

2. Explain the significance of carbohydrates (carbs) in diabetes management.

3. Discuss types of meal planning approaches including carb counting.

LEARNING OBJECTIVES:

Learners (parents, child, relative or self) will be able to:

1. List three objectives of food management.

2. Describe examples of carbohydrate (carb) containing foods and their effect on blood sugar levels.

3. Explain the type of food plan you will be using.

113

- to help prevent high blood pressure
- to improve overall health by maintaining the best possible nutrition
- to help avoid long-term diabetes complications
- to help attain normal growth and development for children and appropriate weight for everyone
- to help prevent severe hypoglycemia

It is amazing how often we hear parents comment, "My child with diabetes is the healthiest in our family BECAUSE HE/SHE EATS THE BEST." Optimal nutrition for a person with diabetes is really just a healthy diet from which **all** people would benefit.

Views on food management for people with diabetes have changed considerably. There was a time when some diabetes care providers believed every family should rigidly be given an ADA exchange food program.

In 1994, the Position Statement of the ADA stated:

> **"Today there is no one 'diabetic' or 'ADA' diet. The recommended food program can only be defined as a dietary prescription based on nutrition assessment and treatment goals. Medical nutrition therapy for people with diabetes should be individualized, with consideration given to usual eating habits and other lifestyle changes."**

This has been the philosophy of the 12 editions of this book over the last 35 years.

The Diabetes and Control Complications Trial (DCCT; Chapter 14) also contributed to our knowledge about food and diabetes. In the DCCT, six main nutrition factors were found that contributed to better sugar control (lower HbA1c levels, Chapter 14).

The six main nutritional factors were:

1. following some sort of a meal plan
2. avoidance of extra snacks
3. avoidance of over-treatment of low blood sugars (hypoglycemia)

4. prompt treatment of high blood sugars when found
5. adjusting insulin levels for meals
6. consistency of night snacks

The DCCT did **NOT** report that one type of meal plan was any more effective than another. However, it is important to have a meal plan.

TYPES OF MEAL PLANNING APPROACHES

Different types of meal planning approaches have been used for people with diabetes for about 4,000 years. They are talked about in an ancient scroll called the "Ebers Papyrus" which was written about 2000 B.C. In 1993 the DCCT showed that people with diabetes who followed a dietary program had better sugar control than those who didn't. There are now many types of food management plans for people with diabetes. All food management plans require people to pay attention to carbs. Over 90 percent of carbs eaten are converted into glucose (sugar) over the next one to two hours. Meats (protein) and fat have very little conversion to sugar. Both meal planning approaches discussed below pay special attention to carbs.

The two approaches used most commonly in our Clinic are:

1. *Consistent (Constant) Carbohydrate (Carb) Meal Plan*

2. *Carbohydrate (Carb) Counting Meal Plan (adjusting insulin for carbs)*

A third approach, the Exchange Meal Plan, is occasionally used for type 2 diabetes. References are given in the back for people wanting more knowledge about this food plan.

The clinic healthcare team caring for the person with newly diagnosed diabetes may prefer one type of meal planning approach over another. It may be unnecessary to read about the other approaches, at least initially. The purpose of all meal plans is to achieve better control of blood/CGM glucose levels. The method that works best for one person may not be the best for someone else.

Any of the meal planning approaches can work. No single approach has been proven better than any other in achieving optimal glucose control. It is up to each family and healthcare team to eventually decide which approach works best for them. Some families will switch from one approach to another or combine parts of each to fit their needs. Many families initially use the consistent carb food plan. They then move to adjusting rapid-acting insulin for carbs to be eaten (carb counting) as they gain confidence, knowledge and carb counting skills. It is important to meet with a registered dietitian to develop a meal plan that meets your lifestyle.

CAREFUL MANAGEMENT OF CARB INTAKE MUST BE PART OF ANY OF THE PROGRAMS. IT IS IMPOSSIBLE TO EAT VARYING AMOUNTS OF CARBS AND KEEP THE BLOOD/CGM GLUCOSE VALUES FROM FLUCTUATING WITHOUT CHANGING THE INSULIN DOSAGE. KNOWING HOW MANY CARBS ARE BEING EATEN IS IMPORTANT IN ANY MEAL PLAN. TABLES 1, 2 AND 3 MAY BE HELPFUL IN PROVIDING GRAMS OF CARBS IN VARIOUS FOODS.

1. Consistent (Constant) Carbohydrate (Carb) Meal Plan

In the consistent carbohydrate meal plan, the amount of insulin (usually two or four shots per day) is kept relatively constant from day-to-day. This is done to match relatively consistent food intake. **The amount of carbs (types can vary) is kept about the same for each meal and each snack from one day to the next.** Insulin dosages vary primarily with different blood/CGM glucose levels. Often families begin by using the consistent carb meal plan. They then move to adjusting insulin for carbs as they gain confidence and carb counting skills.

Labels must be read to know the grams (g) of carbs being eaten (see label reading, Chapter

11). The dietitian may give a range of carbs for each meal. This might be 45 to 60g/meal for a pre-teen. A teenage boy might have a range of 75 to 90g/meal. **CONSISTENCY IS THE KEY.** The consistent carb meal plan is formed around the 10 principles discussed later in this chapter and is then individualized.

The amount of food eaten at a meal or snack may vary with:

✔ expected (or completed) exercise

✔ insulin taken

✔ blood/CGM glucose level

More carbs may be needed (without increasing insulin) for fun activities such as sports, hiking and biking (see Chapter 22 on "thinking scales"). For work-related activities such as ranching and farming, more carbs may also be needed. However, the normal eating pattern of the child and the family should stay the same as much as possible.

Families often ask, "How much carbohydrate is appropriate for me/my child?" They can count carbs even if insulin adjustments are not being made to match the carb intake. This helps to keep the carbs eaten at each meal consistent. The grams of carbohydrate to be eaten at each meal for each age group can be estimated by looking at Table 4. Approximate numbers of calories needed per day can be calculated from the formula in the section on Calculating Calories in this chapter (or ask your dietitian). The formulas are a guide; each person's calorie and carb needs can be different. We recommend consulting with a dietitian to establish a plan that works for you/your child.

2. Carbohydrate (Carb) Counting Meal Plan (adjusting insulin for carbs)

Adjusting insulin for carbs involves counting the grams of carbs that are to be eaten and giving a matching dose of insulin. It allows for greater freedom and flexibility in food choices. It is used with both multiple daily insulin injections or with insulin pump therapy. It is not possible to count carbs without learning to read food labels (Chapter 11). The carb counting meal plan is both similar to and different from the consistent carbohydrate meal plan.

Comparison of the Carb Counting to the Consistent Carbohydrate Meal Plan:

Similarity:
✔ Both emphasize carb intake and keeping protein and fat relatively consistent.

Differences:
✔ It presumes that carb intake (and thus insulin dose) will vary, providing more flexibility and greater safety from hypoglycemia.

✔ It may involve more injections of insulin as extra rapid-acting insulin is taken to cover carbs eaten. Some people take rapid-acting insulin when 15g or more of carbs are consumed, while others cover even lower amounts (5g or 10g) of carbs. This should be discussed with your doctor.

Getting Started (Restarted)

1. Some people prefer to just think of the number of grams of carbs:

When using an **I**nsulin to **C**arb ratio (**I/C** ratio) one usually thinks in grams of carbs. An example of an I/C ratio is 1 to 15 (1/15). This refers to one unit of insulin per 15g of carbs eaten (or to be eaten). Carb counting was greatly aided by the food labeling laws (Chapter 11). They require the grams of total carbs be given on the label of most every food. The method to determine the I/C ratio(s) is discussed below.

2. Others prefer to convert each 15g unit to one carb count (choice):

More detailed quantities of various foods equaling one carb count (e.g., 15g of carb) are given in Table 2. The total grams of carbs to be eaten are divided by 15 to get number of carb counts (15g of carbs equals one carb choice or count). The units of rapid-acting insulin are then adjusted at every meal to match the carb counts (units of 15g of carb). The amount of exercise and the blood/CGM glucose level must also be considered in choosing the insulin dose.

3. Establishing insulin to carbohydrate (I/C) ratios:

If an I/C (insulin to carbohydrate) ratio has not been used previously, it is possible to "guesstimate" the value by dividing the total units of insulin used per day into 500 ("the rule of 500"). For example, if 33 total units of insulin were taken per day, the I/C ratio would be 1 to 15 (500÷33 = 15). This means the person would take one unit of rapid-acting insulin for every 15g of carbs to be eaten. If 50 units were taken per day, the I/C ratio would be 10 (500÷50 = 10). This means one unit of insulin per 10g of carbs to be eaten. These are only estimates and steps must then be taken to more accurately determine the I/C ratio. These are:

We ask families to keep precise food, insulin, blood/CGM glucose and activity records for at least three days. (See the Three-Day Food Record Form in the Appendix of Chapter 11. This page can be copied as desired.) Using a food scale and/or measuring cup may help assure accuracy of carb estimates.

After completing the form (as accurately as possible), fax it to your dietitian for analysis. The dietitian, working with your doctor or nurse, will then make suggestions for **I**nsulin to **C**arb (**I/C**) ratios. The more blood sugars (or CGM tracings) you can do prior to meals and two hours after meals, the better the advice she/he can give. It is also important to include all doses of insulin or oral meds that were taken.

In calculating the I/C ratio, keep in mind that every person is different in his or her need for rapid-acting insulin. The same person may even need different I/C ratios from one time of day to another.

✔ Some people can use one unit of rapid-acting insulin per 15g of carb (one carb choice) for all meals and snacks. This is an **I/C** ratio of 1/15.

✔ Another person might need:

- breakfast – one unit of insulin for each 15g of carb

- lunch – one unit of insulin for every 30g of carb (**I/C** ratio of 1/30 or 1/2 unit per 15g carb)

- dinner – one unit of insulin per 10g of carb (**I/C** ratio of 1/10 or 1.5 units per 15g carb)

✔ Table 4 in Chapter 22 provides an example of using the I/C ratio and correction factor for calculating an insulin dose.

4. Measuring the accuracy of I/C ratios:

The rapid-acting insulin dosages for meals are best adjusted by measuring blood/CGM glucose levels two hours after the meal. When evaluating insulin to determine an **I/C** ratio, it may be helpful to eat a meal with known grams of carbs (e.g., a frozen meal with carbs on the label). The fat content should be less than 20g

as higher fat delays stomach emptying and keeps sugar levels up longer. The meal measurements should be done for each of the three daily meals. It is common for **I/C** ratios to vary at different times of the day for the same person. Most people aim for a blood/CGM glucose level below 140 mg/dL (< 7.8 mmol/L) two hours after each meal. Others use the ranges suggested by age group in Chapters 7 and 22. You may want to discuss this with your doctor.

✔ **If the blood/CGM glucose value is consistently high,** more insulin is needed for the grams of carb in the **I/C** ratio. An example would be to change from 1/15 (1 unit/15g carb to 1/10 [1 unit/10g carb]).

✔ **If the sugar level is below the lower limit** (often 70 mg/dL [3.9 mmol/L]), a lower amount of insulin is needed. An example would be to change from an **I/C** ratio of 1/15 (1 unit/15g carb) to an **I/C** ratio of 1/20 (1 unit/20g carb).

Call your healthcare provider to help you make adjustments.

5. Adding the "correction" factor:

After calculating the dose of insulin for carb content, the final rapid-acting insulin dose must be adjusted considering a "correction" factor for the blood/CGM glucose level at that time. Exercise and many other factors (illness, stress, menses, etc.) affect blood/CGM glucose levels and should also be considered. The method to calculate "correction" factors is discussed in Chapters 22 and 28. In addition, some people subtract one unit if the blood sugar is below 70 mg/dL (3.9 mmol/L).

6. Additional carb counting challenges:

Some degree of math is obviously necessary for carb counting. However, once the best dosages are determined, the process becomes very automatic. Carb counting is most difficult for combination foods such as soups, casseroles and foods with many ingredients. The grams of carbs can be estimated from the amounts of each of the ingredients.

It may be necessary to estimate the grams of carbs when eating out. This could be done on the basis of the grams in the same food prepared at home. Obviously, this does not always work (some cooks add more sugar!). Doing a blood/CGM glucose level two hours after the meal helps to make a better guess the next time.

Refer to the carb counting resources below for help calculating carbs when there are no food labels.

7. Carb counting and insulin pumps:

Most people who use an insulin pump use carb counting to determine the bolus of insulin to be taken with any food intake. The person enters the estimated carbs to be eaten and the pump bolus calculator (using preset information) calculates the insulin dosage. The bolus calculator will calculate the insulin dosage for different I/C ratios that have been entered

for different times of the day. Research has shown that people who use bolus calculators have lower HbA1c values than do non-users.

8. Summary:

Use of carb counting allows people to better observe the relationship between factors affecting the blood/CGM glucose levels and insulin dosage. In some countries, carb counting is done using 10g carb choices. A summary of 15g carb equivalents in foods frequently eaten is given in Tables 1 and 2. In addition, Table 3 gives grams of carbs and carb counts for foods that are high in carbs.

How Many Grams of Carbs?

Table 4 suggests number of grams of carbs for each meal for different age groups. If uncertain how many calories per day are needed, refer to "Calculating Calories" in this chapter or consult a dietitian.

Table 1
One Carbohydrate Choice (Count)*
1 Starch = 1 Fruit = 1 Milk = 15g Carbohydrate = 1 CARB Choice

Food Group	Carbohydrate Content	Portion Sizes
Starch/Grains	15g	1 slice bread 1 6" tortilla ⅓-½ cup cooked pasta ½ small or ¼ large (1 oz) bagel ½ hamburger bun ½ cup peas, corn or mashed potato 1 small potato (3 oz) ⅓ cup rice ⅓ cup cooked dried beans
Fruit	15g	1 piece fruit (small) ½ cup canned fruit ½ cup fruit juice ¼ cup dried fruit 1 cup berries or melon
Milk	12g	1 cup skim, 1%, 2% or whole milk 8 oz plain yogurt

*These are not exact but are close enough for most people.

NOTE: This half-page may be copied and carried in the wallet as needed.

Table 2
Carbohydrate Content of Foods
Amount of Starches/Grains that equal 15g carbohydrate

Food	Serving Size
Bagel	½ small or ¼ large (1 oz)
Beans, cooked, dried, canned	½ cup
Bread, white, whole wheat, rye	1 slice (1 oz)
Corn, cooked	½ cup
Crackers	4-6
English muffin	½
Graham crackers	3 squares
Hamburger bun	½ bun
Popcorn	3 cups
Pasta, cooked	⅓-½ cup
Peas, cooked	½ cup
Potato, baked	1 small (3 oz)
Potato, mashed	½ cup
Rice, cooked	⅓ cup
Roll (dinner, hard)	1 small
Squash, winter	1 cup
Tortilla (6" corn or flour)	1

Fruits
15g carbohydrate

Food	Serving Size
Apple, small	1 (4 oz)
Applesauce, unsweetened	½ cup
Banana	1 small (4 oz) or ½ large
Blueberries	¾ cup
Canned fruit, light or juice packed	½ cup
Cantaloupe, melon	1 cup cubed
Cherries, sweet, fresh	12 (3 oz)
Fruit juice	½ cup (4 oz)
Grapefruit, medium	½
Grapes, small	17
Orange, small	1 (6½ oz)
Pear, large, fresh	½ (4 oz)
Raisins	2 Tbsp
Strawberries	1¼ cup whole berries
Watermelon	1¼ cup cubes

Milk/Yogurt
12g carbohydrate

Food	Serving Size
Milk (skim, 1%, 2%, whole)	1 cup (8 oz)
Yogurt (see "Other Carbohydrates" list)	

Other Carbohydrates

Food	Serving Size	Carbohydrate (g)
Brownie, small unfrosted	1¼" square, 7/8" high	15g
Cake, unfrosted	2" square	15g
Cake, frosted	2" square	30g
Chicken noodle soup	1 cup (8 oz)	15g
Cookie, (sandwich or chocolate chip)	2 cookies	15g
Cookie, medium (homemade)	1 cookie	15g
Cupcake, frosted	1 small	30g
Doughnut, plain cake	1 medium (1.5 oz)	20g
Doughnut, glazed	3¾" (2 oz)	30g
French fries, thin	20-25	30g
Granola bar	1	20-25g
Ice cream (regular, light, fat-free)	½ cup	15-20g
Jam or jelly, regular	1 Tbsp	15g
Macaroni and cheese	1 cup (8 oz)	30-45g
Noodle casserole	1 cup (8 oz)	30g
Pie, fruit, 2 crusts	1/6 pie	45g
Poptart, unfrosted	1	35g
Potato chips	9-13 (¾ oz)	15g
Pizza	1 slice (¼ of 12")	30g
Pudding, regular	½ cup (4 oz)	25g
Syrup, light	2 Tbsp	15g
Syrup, regular	1 Tbsp	15g
Tomato soup (made with water)	1 cup (8 oz)	15g
Tortilla chips	9-13 (¾ oz)	15g
Yogurt, light	1 cup (6-8 oz)	15g

*The carbohydrate amounts listed on this handout are estimates. If the food you are eating has a food label check the Nutrition Facts for the accurate amount of carbohydrate in that product.

Measurement Key

3 tsp = 1 Tbsp	4 ounces = ½ cup
4 Tbsp = ¼ cup	8 ounces = 1 cup
5⅓ Tbsp = ⅓ cup	1 cup = ½ pint

Reference: *Choose Your Foods: Exchange Lists for Diabetes*, 2008.

Table 3
Sugar Content of Some High-Carbohydrate Foods

Food Item	Size Portion	Sugar Content* (teaspoons)	"Carb" Choices	Gram Carb
Beverages				
Cola drinks	12 oz can	10	3	50
Rootbeer	12 oz can	7	2	35
7-Up®*	12 oz can	9	3	45
Grape, orange, apple juice	6 oz can	5	1.5	25
Dairy Products				
Sherbet	1 scoop	9	3	45
Ice cream cone	1 scoop	3½	1	17
Chocolate milk shake	10 oz glass	11	4	55
Milk	8 oz glass	3	1	12
Chocolate milk	8 oz glass	9½	3	52
Fruit yogurt	8 oz cup	9	3	45
Cakes and Cookies				
Angel food cake	4 oz piece	7	2	35
Chocolate cake, plain	4 oz piece	6	2	30
Chocolate cake, w/frosting	4 oz piece	10	3	50
Sugar cookie	1	1½	½	7
Oatmeal cookie	1	2	1	10
Donut, plain	1	4	1	20
Donut, glazed	1	6	2	30
Desserts				
JELL-O	½ cup	4½	1½	22
Apple pie	1 slice	7	2	35
Berry pie	1 slice	10	3	50
Chocolate pudding	1/2 cup	4	1	20
Candies				
Chocolate candy bar	1½ oz	2½	1	12
Chewing gum	1 stick	½	-	2
Fudge	1 oz square	4½	1½	22
Hard candy	1 oz	5	2	25
LIFE-SAVERS®	1	⅓	-	1½
Marshmallow	1 piece	1½	½	7
Chocolate creme	1 piece	2	1	10
Miscellaneous				
Jelly	1 Tbsp	3	1	15
Strawberry jam	1 Tbsp	3	1	15
Brown sugar	1 Tbsp	3	1	15
Honey	1 Tbsp	3	1	15
Chocolate sauce	1 Tbsp	3	1	15
Karo Syrup®	1 Tbsp	3	1	15

*3 tsp = 1 Tbsp = 1 carb choice = 15g of carbs

Carbohydrate Counting Resources:

For those wanting more detailed information on carb counting or on carb quantities in foods, there are now entire books written on these subjects:

1. *"Carbohydrate Counting for Children with Diabetes"*, by Gail Spiegel, MS, RD, CDE and Monica Penkilo, MPH, RD, LD, CDE, Lilly USA, LLC, 2009

2. *"The Complete Book of Food Counts"* (8th Edition), by Corinne Netzer, Bantan Dell, 2009

3. *"The Diabetes Carbohydrate and Fat Gram Guide"* (4th Edition), by Lea Ann Holzmeister, McGraw Hill, 2010

4. *"Nutrition In the Fast Lane"* (condensed version), Lilly USA, LLC, 2010

5. *"Count Your Carbs: Getting Started"* and *"Advanced Carbohydrate Counting"*. The American Diabetes Association and the American Dietetic Association, 2003 (1-800-232-3472 or 1-800-366-1655)

6. *"Complete Guide to Carb Counting"*, 2nd Edition, by H.S. Warshaw and K. Kulkarni, The American Diabetes Association, 2004 (1-800-232-3472)

7. *"Calorie King, Fat and Carbohydrate Counter"*, by Allan Borushek, Family Health Publications, 2010

Websites

www.calorieking.com
www.nutritiondata.com

Exchange Meal Plan Resource:

The ADA booklet, "Choose Your Foods: Exchange Lists for Diabetes, 2008" is available from the American Diabetes Association at 120 South Riverside Plaza, Suite 2000, Chicago, IL 60606-6995. (1-800-342-2383.) www.diabetes.org.

CALCULATING CALORIES

Most children under age 14 years need 1,000 calories per day plus 100 calories for each year of age. For example, a five-year-old would need 1,500 calories:

$$5 \text{ years} \times 100 = 500 \text{ cal/day}$$

$$500 + 1,000 = 1,500 \text{ cal/day}$$

Table 4
Approximate Carb Amounts by Age*

	< 5 years old	5-12 years old	Teens - Adults
Males	30 to 45 grams of carb at each meal	45 to 60 grams of carb at each meal	60 to 75+ grams of carb at each meal
Females	30 to 45 grams of carb at each meal	45 to 60 grams of carb at each meal	45 to 75 grams of carb at each meal

Snacks, if needed, are usually 15 to 30 grams of carb.
Talk to your RD or healthcare professional to help you decide on the amount of carb that is right for your child at each meal and snack.

*Source: Evert, A., Gerken, S. Children with diabetes: birth to adolescence. *On the Cutting Edge.* Summer 2006, Vol. 27, No. 4, 4-8.

TEN PRINCIPLES OF FOOD MANAGEMENT FOR ALL FOOD PLANS

The ten principles listed below are important in all plans and will be briefly reviewed. They would be helpful for any person to follow.

1. **Eat a Well-balanced Meal Plan**

2. **When Possible, Eat Meals and Snacks at the Same Time Each Day (variable depending on food plan being used and current insulin [particularly NPH])**

3. **Use Snacks to Prevent Insulin Reactions (especially if using NPH insulin)**

4. **Balance Carb Intake and Insulin Carefully**

5. **Avoid Over-treating Low Blood Sugars**

6. **Reduce Cholesterol, Saturated and Trans Fat Intake**

7. **Maintain Appropriate Height and Weight**

8. **Increase Fiber Intake**

9. **Avoid Foods High in Salt (Sodium)**

10. **Avoid Excessive Protein Intake**

1. Eat a Well-balanced Meal Plan

A well-balanced meal plan is a step toward good health for everyone in the family. It is particularly important in supporting the growth of children. If you understand normal nutrition (Chapter 11), you can help your family have a well-balanced meal plan. Most people have a period of weight loss prior to being diagnosed with diabetes. Starting insulin treatment allows the body to regain weight. Usually the individual's appetite is ravenous for about one month. The body is returning to its usual growth pattern. The appetite then returns to normal. Most individuals can then self-regulate their caloric intake without a set number of calories being prescribed for each day.

A well-balanced meal plan is currently considered to contain:

✔ 45-55 percent from carbs

✔ 10-20 percent of calories from protein

✔ 20-35 percent from fat

Meals should be balanced and contain:

✔ a rich source of fruits, vegetables and whole grains. This is generally an area children and teens need to increase.

✔ a moderate amount of protein such as low-fat milk, cheese, yogurt, lean meat, poultry, fish, egg white, nuts and seeds.

✔ a limited amount of fat especially butter, egg yolk, animal fat, etc.

An excess of animal fat may result in higher blood fats and a greater risk for heart disease later in life. A high-protein diet is harmful to the kidneys for people who have either early or advanced kidney damage from diabetes. Working with the dietitian will help assure intake of the recommended balance of foods.

2. Eat Meals and Snacks at the Same Time Each Day

For people following a consistent carb meal plan and using relatively constant insulin dosages (particularly if receiving NPH insulin), it is important to eat meals and snacks at the same time each day. Use of an insulin pump or Lantus/Levemir insulin gives more flexibility. This is especially true when used with adjusting insulin for carb intake. Carb counting allows a person to take insulin to match carbs when they are eaten. There can be more flexibility in the timing of meals and snacks as well as in the number of carbs eaten.

3. Use Snacks to Prevent Insulin Reactions

Snacks help to balance the insulin activity. Peaks in insulin activity vary from person to person. You will learn from experience when you need a snack. It may be before lunch, in the late afternoon, at bedtime or for some, only when the blood/CGM glucose level is low. Discuss your need for snacks at your clinic visits. Young children often have a mid- or late-morning snack. Mid- or late-afternoon snacks are eaten by many people with (or without) diabetes. If more than 5g of carbs are eaten in the afternoon snack, and the blood/CGM glucose level is not low, insulin should be taken to cover the snack. This is sometimes easier for those who use an insulin pump or an insulin pen.

Some children with diabetes need a bedtime snack, particularly if they had heavy exercise that day. Some people use a bedtime snack only if their blood/CGM glucose level is below 130 mg/dL (7.3 mmol/L). Once it is decided which snacks are needed, TRY TO BE CONSISTENT. Suggestions for daytime and bedtime snacks are given in Tables 5 and 6.

The type of snack is also important. Fruits are good for a morning or afternoon snack. Proteins with fat, such as cheese or meat, delay absorption. A SOLID SNACK CONTAINING PROTEIN, FAT and CARBS IS BEST FOR BEDTIME. The solids take longer to digest. The fat delays stomach emptying.

4. Balance Carb Intake and Insulin Carefully

It is recommended that about half of the food we eat come from carbs. As insulin must be available to utilize most carbs, it is important to learn to balance your insulin with carb intake. Tables 1, 2 and 3 list the carb contents of different foods. It is known that the rise in blood/CGM glucose levels after eating is dependent upon the total amount of carbs eaten and not the form of carbs.

We know the most important factors are:

A. how much carbohydrate is eaten

B. when the carbs are eaten

C. with what the carbs are eaten

D. having adequate insulin available when the carbs are eaten. Each will be discussed in more detail.

A. How much carbohydrate is eaten

Some meals are much higher in carbs than others.. At breakfast, a meal of eggs, bacon and toast would have fewer carbs than a plate of pancakes. Similarly, a meal of meat, vegetables and salad would have fewer carbs than one of spaghetti and garlic bread or of pizza. More insulin will be required to handle a meal high in carbs compared with one low in carbs.

B. When the carbs are eaten

Large amounts of carbs should not be consumed between meals unless additional insulin is given. An extreme example is using a regular (sugar) pop (40g of carbs) as a morning or afternoon snack.

One boy with diabetes and other problems brought a can of regular sugar pop (10 tsp of sugar, see Table 3) to our clinic with him, freely admitting that he still drank regular pop. We measured his blood sugar before drinking the pop (180 mg/dL or 10.0 mmol/L) and one hour later (450 mg/dL or 25.0 mmol/L). The liquid sugars cause the fastest rise in the blood sugar. That is why we recommend avoiding intake of any sugary drinks!

When extra carbs are eaten, it is best to take extra rapid-acting insulin. The carb contents of some high carb foods are shown in Table 3.

C. With what the carbs are eaten

In a research project, children were fed breakfast on four consecutive Saturday mornings. Four different breakfasts with varying amounts of sugar, protein and fat were evaluated. The blood sugars peaked later and remained higher for a longer time when fat was added (whether extra sugar was added or not).

High fat meals (e.g., pizza, Chinese food, fast-foods) will delay the absorption of carbs and the blood/CGM glucose levels may stay elevated longer. When this is observed, extra rapid-acting insulin can be given the next time. For people using an insulin pump, the use of a "dual-wave" (see Chapter 28) can be very helpful with a meal high in both fat and carbohydrate. DIFFERENT FOODS AFFECT EACH PERSON DIFFERENTLY. EXPERIENCE IS THE BEST TEACHER.

Research on the effects carbs have on blood sugar levels is often studied by giving the carb by itself. Then, blood/CGM glucose levels are measured to see how much the level rises in comparison to the increase in blood sugar caused by a reference food (**"glycemic-index"**). However, the effects of other foods are very important and it is rare that a carb is eaten all by itself. The best way to find out the effect of a given carb is to check the blood sugar, eat the food and/or meal and check the blood/CGM glucose level again in two to three hours.

D. Having adequate insulin activity when the carbs are eaten

Eating extra carbs is possible if extra rapid-acting insulin is added. As discussed in Chapter 8, 9 and elsewhere, if the blood/CGM glucose level is not low, the insulin is ideally taken 20 minutes prior to eating. Measuring the blood/CGM glucose levels two hours after the meal will determine if the insulin dose used and timing were appropriate.

Most adults take extra insulin when snacks are consumed between meals. Diabetes is a high priority. Unfortunately, children do not do as well. A recent research study found that half of afternoon snacks were not covered with insulin.

On special occasions, such as birthday parties, the person with diabetes can consume extra carbs and take extra insulin. Extra sugar **will not make the person ill and will not cause acidosis.** Not taking extra insulin may result in higher than usual blood/CGM glucose levels and more frequent urination as the sugar passes into the urine. The extra activity or excitement at a party may help to balance the extra carb intake.

It is generally acceptable to allow a person to fit in a sweet food on an "as-needed" basis. Allowing this can prevent the sneaking of candy or treats. This can be planned for a time when adequate insulin is available. We encourage the entire family to get used to eating foods without a "sugary" taste. To allow for better nutrition, avoid having sweets (Table 3) such as donuts, cookies, cake, candy, etc. in the home. If they are there, they will be hard to avoid. Most have no nutritional value except adding calories. This will result in better nutrition for the entire family.

There are several alternatives for handling holidays and parties where there are a great number of concentrated sweets. Halloween focuses on candy and is a special problem for young children.

Some suggestions for Halloween trick-or-treating candy:

✔ The child can select a few for his/her regular treats, and give or throw the rest away. If sweets are to be eaten, it is best to eat them when insulin is working. The dose of rapid-acting insulin for that meal can then be increased.

✔ Taking the treats to a sick friend or a child in the hospital is a nice option.

✔ Another option is to "sell" the candy to the parents. The money can then be spent to purchase something the child wants.

It is important not to become upset with a child if he/she does eat extra sweets. The stress of the parent being upset can raise the blood/CGM glucose levels more than the sweets (see Chapter 17 on Family Concerns). Instead, discuss the incident with the child and try to find compromises.

5. Avoid Over-treating Low Blood Sugars

Avoiding the over-treatment of low blood sugars (hypoglycemia) was one of the factors found in the DCCT to relate to better sugar control (a lower HbAlc level). The problem is how to accomplish this. Only a person who has had a truly low blood sugar can know the feeling of being "ravenously hungry" and wanting to eat everything in sight (and so the person does). For many years, people thought "rebounding" to be the cause of the high blood sugar after hypoglycemia. Only in recent years was it realized to be primarily due to excessive eating after the low blood sugar.

Chapter 6 discusses the treatment of hypoglycemia and emphasizes:

A. checking the blood sugar to see how low the value is and repeating this at 10-minute intervals to see if the value is rising

B. drinking one cup of milk (8-10 oz) or ½ cup (4 oz) of juice or of sugar pop (15g carbs)

C. or taking ½ tube of Instant Glucose or four dextrose tablets (e.g., 15g of carb or one "carb" choice). Wait 10 minutes and do the second blood sugar level.

D. if the value has **not** risen, repeat the process using 15g of carb or one "carb" choice every 10 minutes until a rise does occur

E. if the blood sugar is rising after 10 minutes and is above 60 mg/dL (> 3.2 mmol/L)

✔ eat solid food, such as two or three crackers with peanut butter or cheese

✔ if it is close to mealtime, just eat the next meal

Not eating too much, but enough to raise the blood sugar, is tricky. The body may be giving the message to "eat, eat, eat." It can vary from person to person or from one time to another for the same person. Careful monitoring of blood/CGM glucose levels is essential.

6. Reduce Cholesterol, Saturated Fat, and Trans Fat Intake; Reduce Total Fat Intake (see Chapter 11)

Cholesterol and triglyceride are two of the major fats present in our blood.

Cholesterol is found in many foods, but it is particularly high in:

✔ egg yolks

✔ organ meats

✔ large portions of high-fat red meat (e.g., prime rib, hamburger, hotdogs)

Cholesterol is found in animal products only.

*There is **no cholesterol** in:*

✔ fruits	✔ beans
✔ vegetables	✔ nuts
✔ cereals	✔ seeds
✔ grains	

The eating of saturated fat and trans fats (baked goods) in animal products like meat, cheese and whole milk may raise blood cholesterol levels even more than eating high cholesterol foods. This is discussed in more detail in the previous chapter on Normal Nutrition. Blood cholesterol and triglyceride levels can also be high if blood sugar levels are too high.

The blood cholesterol and LDL cholesterol levels should be checked once a year in adults, and starting with puberty in adolescents (see Chapter 23). If your doctor has not checked these levels, you should request that this be done. Suggested levels for people with diabetes are given in Table 2 of Chapter 11. If a high level is found, the dietitian can make suggestions to help lower it. The average American now eats 400-450 mg of cholesterol per day. This should gradually be reduced to about 300 mg per day. Table 3 in Chapter 11 gives suggestions for reducing fat and cholesterol intake. Each egg has about 213 mg of cholesterol. Egg white is a

good source of protein. Some people now just eat the whites, which have no cholesterol.

Triglyceride levels for a given person tend to be variable. They are related to the diabetes control at the time, the amount of exercise in the previous week and other factors. It is necessary to be fasting for accurate triglyceride and lipoprotein (LDL and HDL) determinations. Fasting is sometimes dangerous for people with diabetes (e.g., driving across town with no food intake). We now often draw a "lipid panel" once yearly when it has been at least three to four hours since the last meal (Chapter 11). Total cholesterol, HDL- and LDL-cholesterol can be measured non-fasting.

7. Maintain Appropriate Height and Weight

Normal growth is important for children and teenagers. An important part of clinic visits

Table 5
Healthy Daytime Snacks

Snacks, besides being fun to eat, help prevent low blood sugar levels and provide energy between meals. Typical snacks are usually 1-2 carb choices or 15-30g of carb. Below are some low-fat snack ideas to try.

15g of carb or one carb choice

1 small apple or orange	18 small pretzel twists
2 popcorn cakes	½ small bagel with fat-free cream cheese
8 oz or 1 carton light yogurt	3 cups air popped or low-fat microwave popcorn
1½ graham crackers	4-5 vanilla wafers, 5-6 saltine crackers
½ cup low-fat ice cream	1 fruit juice bar
2 Tbsp raisins	½ cup unsweetened applesauce
½ cup sugar-free pudding	

30g of carb or two carb choices

1 small bagel with fat-free cream cheese	1 oz baked tortilla chips with ¼ cup salsa
1 low-fat granola bar	1 large banana or 2 pieces of fruit (small)
4 oz individual fruit cup and 1 cup skim milk	1 cup Cheerios® with ½ cup skim milk
2 caramel corn cakes	¼ cup dried fruit
15 baked potato chips	1 cereal bar
2 fig cookies and 1 cup skim milk	14 animal crackers and ½ cup skim milk

SPECIAL SUGGESTIONS

🐾 Encourage fresh fruit rather than juice as a routine snack (unless blood sugar is low)

🐾 Sugar-free flavorings (e.g., sugar-free cocoa or milk flavorings) can be added to milk

🐾 If the child is still hungry after the snack, offer water, popsicles made using diet pop or Sugar-Free Kool-Aid® or sticks of sliced fresh carrots or celery placed in a dish with cold water and ice cubes

is to make sure the height and weight are increasing appropriately. Research has shown that if blood/CGM glucose levels are consistently high during the teenage years, final adult height will be less.

About 30 percent of people with type 1 diabetes and 80 percent of people with type 2 diabetes are overweight. **Preventing excessive weight gain by staying active and eating healthy is important. Reducing calories by both a reduction in high fat foods and by portion-control is important for weight loss.** If you have questions about weight management, meet with a registered dietitian.

We discourage the use of quick weight loss diets and diet pills. They do not teach a person to eat correctly. When the fad diet is over, the weight is almost always regained. It is much wiser to work with a registered dietitian to learn healthy eating habits and to develop a plan to gradually reduce weight. It is important for parents to be careful not to be critical or to emphasize a child's weight gain. It can make the problem worse and lead to eating disorders or missed shots. If a parent has concerns, it might be better to express them to the dietitian or to other diabetes team members.

8. Increase Fiber Intake

Fiber is the roughage in our food that is not absorbed into the body. Many of us don't have enough fiber in our diets. Adding fiber may slow the rise in blood/CGM glucose levels. The blood sugar may not be as high two hours after eating an apple (15g of carbs) as it is two hours after drinking ½ cup (four ounces) of apple juice (also 15g of carbs). Extra fiber is good for people, particularly in helping to avoid constipation. Raw fruits, vegetables, legumes, high-fiber cereals and whole grain breads are some of the most effective high-fiber foods.

9. Avoid Foods High in Salt (Sodium)

If a person has borderline high blood pressure, a high salt intake may bring out this tendency. People who eat at fast-food restaurants have a higher salt intake. Those who have early kidney damage seem to be more likely to have an increased blood pressure from high salt intake.

Foods higher in salt are:

✔ many canned soups

✔ frozen vegetables in sauces

✔ fast-foods

✔ many snack foods (especially chips)

The American Heart Association recommends that all people eat under 1,500 mg of sodium (approximately ½ tsp of table salt) each day (less in young children).

Increased blood pressure is an important risk factor for both the eye and the kidney complications of diabetes as well as heart attacks. Therefore, it is important not to eat large amounts of salt. If the blood pressure is elevated even less may be recommended. This can be discussed with the dietitian.

10. Avoid Excessive Protein Intake

It is difficult to avoid an excess of protein when someone has been told not to eat excessive amounts of sugar, animal fat and salt. Many teenagers eat four to six times the quantity of protein needed. This is particularly true for those who frequently eat or snack at fast-food restaurants. Athletes should not consume protein (amino acid) supplements. Only exercise builds muscle - not protein supplements. Extra protein may be harmful when kidney damage is present, as it presents an extra load for the kidneys. It is still unclear whether or not high protein intake contributes to the initial kidney complications of diabetes. The best method to reduce protein intake is to decrease portion size (e.g., smaller meat portions). Meats, eggs and cheese can be eliminated from breakfast and the morning and afternoon snacks. However, we recommend that the bedtime snack include carbs, protein and fat as they may help to keep the blood/CGM glucose values at a reasonable level during the night.

SUMMARY

The key to food management in diabetes is constant thinking and matching insulin to carb intake. The entire family must help with this.

Important points:

✔ In general, carbs from sugar or from starch will raise the blood/CGM glucose levels about the same amount.

✔ A person with diabetes can eat almost any food in moderation if it is worked into the meal plan and the correct amount of insulin is taken at the correct time.

✔ Nutritious carbohydrates (fruits, vegetables, whole grains) should be encouraged whenever possible.

✔ Frequent blood/CGM glucose monitoring (e.g., two hours after eating various foods) is encouraged to determine how a given food affects any individual.

✔ As discussed in other chapters (e.g., Chapter 9), blood/CGM glucose levels are more apt to remain below the desired 180 mg/dL (<10.0 mmol/L) if the Humalog, NovoLog or Apidra are taken 15 to 20 minutes prior to the meal.

✔ Blood sugar monitoring when an insulin reaction occurs is important in avoiding over-treatment of lows. The excessive eating with a hypoglycemic reaction (or just the psychological feeling of hunger) is a major concern in controlling blood/CGM glucose levels.

Remember: Food management for people with diabetes does not mean a restrictive diet, but rather a healthy eating plan that family and friends can also enjoy.

DEFINITIONS

ADA: American Diabetes Association.

"Carb choice": Fifteen-gram equivalent of carbohydrate used to determine the units of rapid-acting insulin to be taken. It is the same as a **"carb count."**

Carbohydrate (carb) counting: A meal plan in which counting the grams of carb to be eaten (and considering the blood sugar level and any planned exercise) is used to adjust the dosage of rapid-acting insulin prior to meals.

Cholesterol: One of the two main blood fats. High levels are related to a greater chance for heart attacks later in life.

Consistent (Constant) carbohydrate diet: A meal plan in which the amount of carb is kept consistent from day-to-day to match a relatively consistent dose of insulin.

DCCT: Diabetes Control and Complications Trial, which ended in June, 1993. It showed that optimal glucose control helped to prevent eye, kidney and nerve complications of diabetes.

Exchange diet: A meal plan in which foods are grouped into one of six food lists having similar nutritional composition. Caloric intake and number of exchanges are set, but foods within a food group can be exchanged with one another.

Glycemic index: A ranking of foods based on the rise in blood sugar when that food is given alone (with no other food).

Tablespoon (Tbsp): A measure of 15cc (15 mL) or three teaspoons. It is equal to 15g (½ oz) of water.

Teaspoon (tsp): A measure of 5cc (5 mL). It is also equal to 5g of water.

Triglyceride: One of the two main blood fats. High levels are believed to be related to a greater risk for heart attacks later in life for people with diabetes.

QUESTIONS AND ANSWERS FROM NEWSNOTES

Q Is there any way to know if the pop received at fast-food restaurants, theaters and other places is truly "sugar-free" or the regular sugar-containing pop?

A This question is asked frequently and the answer is "yes." The Diastix® (the sugar-only part of KetoDiastix), or the distal sugar block on KetoDiastix will change color if there is sugar present. Unfortunately, it is more common for the wrong pop to be served than most people realize, probably in the range of 20 percent of the time (one glass in five). As sugar pop is one of the most concentrated sources of sugar (approximately 10 tsp per can), it usually raises the blood sugar level to the 200-400 mg/dL (11.1-22.2 mmol/L) level. This is especially true if it is consumed without other foods, which slow the absorption of the sugar, or at a time when a rapid-acting insulin is not taken to allow the sugar to enter the cells.

Q How important is a diet in relation to my HbA1c and my blood sugar control?

A The best answer to this comes from the DCCT data (*"Diabetes Care"* 16:1453, 1993). They found that patients in their intensive treatment group (mean HbA1c = 7.1 percent) who followed a meal plan over 90 percent of the time had an average HbA1c level that was 0.9 percent lower than those who followed a meal plan less then 45 percent of the time. As the HbA1c difference in the intensive treatment group was 1.8 percent lower (7.1 percent vs. 8.9 percent), this suggests that half of the difference was related to following a food plan.

Other factors that were important in relation to a lower HbA1c level were:

- doing a prompt correction when a high blood sugar was found
- adjusting the insulin for meal size
- not eating extra snacks
- avoiding over treatment of low blood sugars (hypoglycemia)

Most clinics have a registered dietitian available at the time of clinic visits. The preference in food management at this time is the use of carb counting. Since carbs are the main nutrients that are converted to blood sugar, patients need to learn how to match insulin dosage with carb intake. It would be helpful for all families to meet with a dietitian at least once a year.

Chapter 13
Exercise and Diabetes

TEACHING OBJECTIVES:

1. Discuss the importance of exercise as a critical component of diabetes management.

2. Explain exercise recommendations and precautions for people with type 1 or type 2 diabetes.

LEARNING OBJECTIVES:

Learners (parents, child, relative or self) will be able to:

1. List three reasons why exercise is important.

2. Develop an exercise plan which includes monitoring of blood sugars, use of snacks and medication adjustments.

INTRODUCTION

Many of the people with the best-controlled diabetes are those who exercise regularly. Exercise should be a normal part of life for everyone. The dietary GUIDELINES for Americans recommends 60 minutes of moderate to rigorous physical activity per day to prevent weight gain and a minimum of 30 minutes a day to reduce the risk of chronic disease (e.g., type 2 diabetes). The American Academy of Pediatrics also recommends a minimum of 60 minutes of exercise daily for all. We strongly encourage regular exercise for anyone who has diabetes, even if this means making a special effort to plan daily exercise. Young people from our Clinic have participated in almost every sport: football, baseball, golf, track, swimming, wrestling, dancing, skiing, basketball, soccer, weight lifting, horseback riding, jumping rope, jogging and tennis. In the Figure in Chapter 14, Monitoring Blood Glucose and HbA1c Levels, **EXERCISE** is listed as one of the "Big 4" factors to help attain optimal sugar control. This is true for people with either type 1 or type 2 diabetes.

Many former and present professional athletes have diabetes. Professional baseball players with diabetes include Bill Gullickson (pitcher) and Ron Santo (third base). Gary Hall, Jr. won four medals (two gold) in the 2000 Olympics and the gold medal in the Free Style in the 2004 Olympics. Adam Morrison plays in the NBA: Professional football players include Kenny Duckett (wide receiver), Johnathon Hayes (tight end), Jay Cutler (quarterback) and Jay Leeuwenberg, who was an All-American center for the University of Colorado in the 1990s and then went on to play professional football. At a recent conference Jay spoke about the importance of being "in range" for blood sugars in order to play at his best level in pro football games. He related that he usually did at least 30 blood sugars during a professional football game. In the U.K., Gary

Table 1
Why Exercise Is Important

- 🐾 Exercise lowers blood sugar levels
- 🐾 Exercise helps people feel better
- 🐾 Exercise helps maintain proper body weight
- 🐾 Exercise helps keep the heart rate (pulse) and blood pressure lower
- 🐾 Exercise helps keep blood fat levels normal
- 🐾 Exercise improves insulin sensitivity
- 🐾 Exercise may help maintain normal blood circulation in the feet

Mabbott has type 1 diabetes and is a star football (American soccer) player. Hockey player Bobby Clarke, a former player of the Philadelphia Flyers, developed diabetes at age 15. He won the award for outstanding player in the National Hockey League twice. Nick Boynton, defenseman with the Boston Bruins in 2004, was diagnosed with diabetes at age 19 years. Billy Talbert began playing tennis at age 12, two years after he developed diabetes. He became one of the best tennis players in the world, winning 37 national tournaments and being captain of America's winning Davis Cup Team and a member of the Tennis Hall of Fame. When he was in Denver to instruct youth with diabetes about tennis, we asked Billy why he felt he had no complications after over 40 years with diabetes. He replied, "I have gotten some exercise every day of my life in which it has been possible." These examples are given to show that diabetes does not prevent participation in athletic activities.

WHY EXERCISE IS IMPORTANT

Exercise is important and helps people with or without diabetes in the following ways (Table 1):

🐾 Exercise Lowers Blood/CGM Glucose Levels:

It is not completely understood why blood/CGM glucose values are lower following exercise, but they clearly are (Figure 1). The **immediate effect** is likely due to muscles "burning" extra sugar during the exercise. As a result, values tend to be lower during the period of exercise.

However, there is also a **prolonged effect of exercise** on glucose levels. Following heavy afternoon exercise, blood/CGM glucose values have been shown to be lower throughout the night until the next morning. Figure 1 shows blood sugar (glucose) levels for the same 50 children on a day when they exercised compared to a day without exercise. It may be helpful to think of the exercise as causing

Figure 1
The Effect of Exercise on Blood Sugar Levels

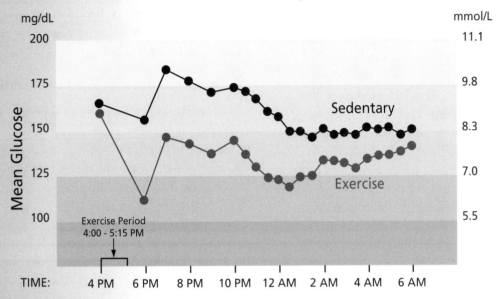

This Figure presents blood glucose (sugar) levels for the same 50 children on a sedentary day (black circles) and an exercise day (red circles). The one hour of exercise at 4 p.m. resulted in lower glucose levels for the next 14 hours (through the night). Insulin doses and food intake were identical for the two days.

(Data complements of the DirecNet Study Group: J Pediatr 147,528, 2005)

increased insulin sensitivity over the next 12 to 16 hours.

As a result of regular exercise, the person is more sensitive to insulin, the insulin can work more efficiently, and a lower daily dose is usually required. Regular exercise (and weight loss) allows some people with type 2 diabetes to stop insulin injections and to change to oral medication. It is now believed many of the beneficial effects of exercise on the risk of heart disease, particularly in type 2 diabetes, are due to improvements with insulin sensitivity. It is important to exercise regularly and vigorously.

The old belief that people should not exercise if they have high blood/CGM glucose levels is wrong. Exercise usually helps lower the sugar levels. IT IS ONLY WHEN KETONES ARE PRESENT THAT PEOPLE SHOULD NOT EXERCISE.

Some families note a temporary rise in glucose levels during exercise. This may be due to eating extra snacks. It can also be due to adrenaline output with the excitement of exercise. Non-aerobic exercise (e.g., sprinting) tends to result in more adrenaline output and higher blood/CGM glucose levels than does aerobic exercise.

Exercise Helps People Feel Better

There is a feeling of "well-being" and pride that comes from being in optimal physical condition. Many people just seem to feel better when they exercise daily. They tend not to tire as easily. Some people even say they are happier.

Teenagers get much of their support from friends. Friends often are made during sports activities. Exercise can give people the opportunity to mix with others. Some people tend to watch TV and eat snacks that raise the blood/CGM glucose levels. Exercise offers a way to prevent this.

❧ Exercise Helps Maintain Proper Body Weight

Exercise is important, not only for people with diabetes, but for everybody. For thousands of years, people had to hunt for food and were very active. In the last 100 years, modern machines have made it possible for people to live with almost no exercise. This lack of activity has led to new health problems such as obesity, type 2 diabetes and heart trouble. THE ONLY WAYS TO PREVENT OBESITY ARE TO EXERCISE AND TO EAT MODERATELY. Exercise helps to burn excess calories and prevent obesity. A recent national study in the U.S. (The Diabetes Prevention Program) showed exercise helped to prevent diabetes in people at high risk for type 2 diabetes. A person who keeps a normal weight is also less likely to have a heart attack later in life.

❧ Exercise Helps Keep the Heart Rate (pulse) and Blood Pressure Lower

The heart is helped by exercise for many reasons. The heart of a person who is in good physical shape can do the same work with fewer heartbeats. An average heart rate (pulse) is 80 beats per minute. Many people who exercise regularly will have values in the 60s. Blood pressure tends to be lower in people who exercise. Thus, the heart doesn't have to pump as hard. Lower blood pressure helps prevent heart attacks as well as the eye and kidney complications of diabetes in later life (see Chapter 23 on complications).

❧ Exercise Helps Keep Blood Fat Levels Normal

We have discussed the importance of reducing cholesterol and saturated (animal) fat in the diet in Chapters 11 and 12. Many people with type 1 and type 2 diabetes have high levels of the blood fats, cholesterol and/or triglycerides. These high blood fat levels can lead to early aging of blood vessels. Exercise and optimal blood sugar control are the best ways to reduce blood triglyceride levels. One study showed that triglyceride levels could be reduced greatly after only four sessions of running 40 minutes a day. Exercise may also help remove cholesterol from blood vessel walls by increasing HDL (high density lipoprotein; see Chapter 11). Lowering the blood fat levels improves the health of blood vessels (including those supplying blood to the heart) and lessens the risk of heart attacks.

❧ Exercise Improves Insulin Sensitivity

The only way humans can increase insulin sensitivity is by exercising. As a result of exercise, the person is more sensitive to insulin, the insulin can work more efficiently, and a lower daily dose is usually required. Regular exercise (and weight loss) allows some people with type 2 diabetes to stop insulin injections and change to oral medication. It is now believed many of the beneficial effects of exercise on the risk of heart disease, particularly in type 2 diabetes, are due to improvements with insulin sensitivity. It is important to exercise regularly and vigorously.

❧ Exercise May Help Maintain Normal Blood Circulation to the Feet Later in Life

Data from the Pittsburgh Diabetes Registry showed that when boys with diabetes played in high school sports, they were more likely to keep normal foot circulation in later years. It is likely that the boys who were active in high school were also more apt to be active in later years.

TYPE 2 DIABETES AND EXERCISE

Although exercise is important for all people, it is **essential** for people with type 2 diabetes. It is also important for those people who are at high risk for type 2 diabetes. The Diabetes Prevention Program (DPP) studied 3,234 people with impaired (not diabetic; see Chapter 4) glucose tolerance tests. They were close to having type 2 diabetes. **The DPP showed that 30 minutes of activity per day, five days per week, combined with a low-fat diet reduced the risk of developing type 2 diabetes by over half (58 percent).**

Why don't people with type 2 diabetes or those at high risk get into exercise programs? *Some reasons might be:*

✔ psychological/stress/can't find the time

✔ started too fast in the past (must start slowly)

✔ too painful in the past (forgot stretching and "working-up" gradually)

✔ lack of motivation (TV, computer games more fun)

✔ not aware of the importance of exercise for good health

Whatever the reason, if the person is unable to achieve a lifestyle modification on his or her own, it may be helpful to join a supervised exercise and/or weight loss program. Counseling could be helpful as well. The cost of NOT modifying the lifestyle is just too great!

Table 2
Calories Per Hour Expended In Common Physical Activities

Moderate Physical Activity for One Hour	Calories Burned Per Hour
Hiking	370
Light gardening/yard work	330
Dancing	330
Golf (walking and carrying clubs)	330
Bicycling (< 10 mph)	290
Walking (3.5 mph)	280
Weight lifting (general light workout)	220
Stretching	180
Vigorous Physical Activity for One Hour:	
Running/jogging (5 mph)	590
Bicycling (> 10 mph)	590
Swimming (slow freestyle laps)	510
Aerobics	480
Walking (4.5 mph)	460
Heavy yard work (chopping wood)	440
Weight lifting (vigorous effort)	440
Basketball (vigorous)	440

Source: Adapted from the 2005 *"DGAC Report"* and the
"Dietary Guidelines for Americans", 2005

GETTING STARTED

Which Kinds of Exercise are Best?

THE BEST EXERCISE IS THE ONE YOU LIKE. Different strokes for different folks! If you hate to jog or swim, but you do it because you are told to, you probably won't exercise regularly. Swimming five days a week in an outdoor pool is fun in the summer, but it may be more difficult to do in the winter. You may need to choose a different exercise, such as jumping rope or riding an exercise bicycle, in the winter. Approximate calories used per hour for different types of exercise are shown in Table 2. Some treadmills and exercise bikes give the "calories-burned."

Only aerobic exercises help heart fitness. Aerobic exercises include most continuous activities (such as jogging, walking, swimming or bicycling) that are done for a period of 30 minutes or longer. Many training programs use machines at health spas that feature continuous aerobic activity rather than short bursts of activity followed by a rest (a non-aerobic activity). When activities such as weight lifting are done in short bursts with rests in between, they are considered strength building, not aerobic.

Boxing is the only activity in which we have asked youth not to participate. The high incidence of eye injuries is not needed by a person who has diabetes (which can also cause eye problems). In addition, the high incidence of brain damage makes boxing dangerous for people with or without diabetes.

When Should I Exercise?

The best time to exercise will vary with your schedule. Think ahead and make changes in insulin doses and snacks to help prevent low blood sugars. Children like to play after school, and most organized sports activities take place at that time. This is the time when most intermediate-acting (e.g.: NPH) insulins are having their main effect so taking extra care to prevent low blood sugar is important. When possible, pick an exercise time, preferably the same time each day, and adjust the snacks and insulin dose to fit the exercise. YOUR DIABETES MANAGEMENT CAN BE ADJUSTED TO SUIT YOUR LIFESTYLE. YOUR LIFESTYLE DOES NOT HAVE TO BE ADJUSTED TO FIT YOUR DIABETES.

When Should I Not Exercise?

If blood or urine ketone levels are elevated, exercise can raise the ketone level even higher. Thus, it is not good to exercise when you have ketones. Remember to check ketones before exercising if you are not feeling well.

How Should I Get Started?

The best way to make exercise a part of everyday living is to begin early in life. Older children may not be as willing to begin a regular exercise program. Exercise should be

part of the normal routine. Many people prefer TV or computer games instead of exercise and the parents may have to encourage exercise. The parents can reward the child with exercise activities such as skating and swimming. It is helpful if the parents can have fun with the child in the activity. Jogging, walking or jumping rope is beneficial for parents too! Whenever a child has a parent's attention and company, the time quickly becomes a reward. A child of any age will often pick up the parents' exercise behaviors. The parents need to be a good example by exercising regularly even if it is not with the child. Exercising with a friend(s) can be fun. Friends can help each other continue the exercise plan.

When beginning a new exercise program, it is always best to START SLOWLY and gradually extend the time and amount of exercise. This will result in fewer sore muscles and a better chance to continue the program. Recommendations for people over 35 years old or who have other risk factors are discussed below under "Age and Exercise."

How Often and How Far?

How often should the person with diabetes exercise? A MINIMUM OF THIRTY MINUTES OF AEROBIC EXERCISE, AT LEAST FIVE TIMES PER WEEK, IS NOW CONSIDERED IDEAL. The more exercise a person gets, the more fat that is "burned." Some people burn more calories with their exercise than others. This is partly related to how hard and how long the person exercises. For example, a person who runs at a rate of seven minutes per mile burns 300 calories in 30 minutes. However, if the person runs at 11 minutes per mile, 200 calories are burned in 30 minutes. If weight loss is one of the goals, it may be necessary to work harder or for a longer period to reach the desired goals.

It is wise to check the pulse immediately (for 10 seconds, and multiply by six) after stopping the activity. If the pulse is more than 160 beats per minute, the exercise has probably been too strenuous.

PREVENTING LOW BLOOD SUGARS (HYPOGLYCEMIA) DURING EXERCISE

Exercise is a known risk-factor for hypoglycemia. It is essential to prevent low blood sugar reactions during and after exercise. The DirecNet Study Group found that children were less apt to have low sugars during heavy exercise if their blood/CGM glucose value prior to the exercise was above 180 mg/dL (10.00 mmol/L). Preventing low sugars can be done in several ways:

✔ **Check blood/CGM glucose values before, during and after the exercise**

The best way to know how any exercise affects a person is to check blood/CGM glucose values before, during (when possible) and after the exercise. The overall effect of activity is usually to lower blood/CGM glucose levels. Once a pattern is detected (e.g., "swimming always makes my blood sugar fall" or "softball doesn't seem to affect my blood sugar"), more accurate insulin and food changes can be made. Sometimes blood/CGM glucose values go up with exercise. This may be because of output of the hormones glucagon and adrenaline (epinephrine), which is a normal response in people with or without diabetes. These hormones cause sugar to be released from the liver. If the blood/CGM glucose value is high, a reduced insulin correction (e.g.: 50%) is sometimes given, knowing that the values will likely decrease. Keeping records is important so when a similar exercise is done at a similar time of the day (with the same insulin peaking) and with a similar starting blood/CGM glucose level, the best plans for insulin changes and food can be made.

Some people become frustrated with the "ups and downs" of blood/CGM glucose values during exercise. It is important to remember, **"DIABETES IS A COMPROMISE."** One must put up with the changes in glucose values in return for the better health of the heart, blood vessels and the entire body.

Table 3
Insulin Dosing Algorithms for *EXERCISE*

Expected Time of Exercise	Infants	Preschool	School Age	Pre-Teen	Adolescents/ College Age
	Birth - 2 yrs.	*3 - 4 yrs.*	*5 - 9 yrs.*	*10 - 12 yrs.*	*13 - 25 yrs.*
Before Breakfast	↓ dinner or p.m. N or Lantus/Levemir by ¼ to ½ unit (evening before)	↓ dinner or p.m. N or Lantus/Levemir by ½ unit (evening before)	↓ dinner or p.m. N or Lantus/Levemir by ½ - 1 unit (evening before)	↓ dinner or p.m. N or Lantus/Levemir by 1 unit (evening before)	↓ dinner or p.m. N or Lantus/Levemir by 1-2 units (evening before)
Mid-Morning	↓ a.m. RAI or R by ¼ to ½ unit	↓ a.m. RAI or R by ½ unit	↓ a.m. RAI or R by ½ - 1 unit	↓ a.m. RAI or R by 1 unit	↓ a.m. RAI or R by 1-2 units
Afternoon	↓ a.m. N or noon RAI or R by ¼ to ½ unit	↓ a.m. N or noon RAI or R by ½ unit	↓ a.m. N or noon RAI or R by ½ - 1 unit	↓ a.m. N or noon RAI or R by 1 unit	↓ a.m. N or noon RAI or R by 1-2 units
Evening	↓ dinner RAI or R by ¼ to ½ unit	↓ dinner RAI or R by ½ unit	↓ dinner RAI or R by ½ - 1 unit	↓ dinner RAI or R by 1 unit	↓ dinner RAI or R by 1-2 units
All Day	↓ all insulins by 10-50%	↓ all insulins by 10-50%	↓ all insulins by 10-50%	↓ all insulins by 10-50%	↓ all insulins by 10-50%

morn. = morning;   ↓ = lower, decrease;   N = NPH

RAI = Rapid-acting insulin (Humalog, NovoLog or Apidra)   R = Regular insulin

✔ Eat before heavy exercise

If you are going to exercise around mealtime, you should eat the meal first. When possible, allow a half-hour for digestion. Liquids such as milk and juices are absorbed most rapidly and generally prevent low blood sugar reactions for the next 30-60 minutes. Solid foods, such as those eaten at mealtime, are digested more slowly and usually provide protection for at least two to three hours. When it is possible to choose the exercise time, try to begin the exercise 30-60 minutes after a meal or snack (and omit or reduce the Humalog/NovoLog/Apidra). Table 4 gives suggestions for snacks for people who take insulin. Although detailed tables are available matching exercise energy spent with food energy to take in, nothing works better than **EXPERIENCE** and **FREQUENT BLOOD SUGARS.**

✔ Reduce insulin dosage before and during the exercise

People who do not have diabetes have very low insulin levels during exercise. To simulate this, it is relatively easy to turn off an insulin pump or to use a (reduced) temporary basal rate during periods of intense exercise. Some people also need to reduce the basal insulin 15, 30 or 60 minutes prior to the exercise. **Experience is the best teacher.**

The DirecNet group found 43% of children to have low blood glucose levels during one-hour of intense exercise when pump basal insulin rates were continued. In contrast, only 16% had low values when the basal insulin rates were discontinued during the same exercise (Figure 2). The ability to quickly alter insulin delivery with exercise is considered by many to be one of the major advantages of insulin pump therapy.

For people using insulin injections the insulin dose is easy to decrease if you know which insulin is having its main effect during the time of exercise. Suggestions for insulin reductions are shown for people of different ages in Table 3.

If extra morning exercise is planned, you can reduce or even leave out the morning rapid-acting insulin or Regular insulin. If late afternoon exercise is planned, you can reduce the morning NPH or noon rapid-acting insulin by 10-50 percent. If the activity is in the evening, the dinner rapid-acting insulin is often reduced. Similarly, Lantus/Levemir insulin at dinner or in the evening may be reduced by a few units with heavy exercise days. People reduce insulin by different amounts. **Experience is the best teacher.**

Figure 2
Percent of Children with Low Blood Sugars (< 70mg/dL [< 3.9 mmol/L]) During Exercise

The same 49 children did the same (60 minute) afternoon exercise on two different days, one with basal insulin continued and one with basal insulin stopped (15). Low blood sugars during the exercise were reduced by almost two-thirds in the group with basal insulin stopped.

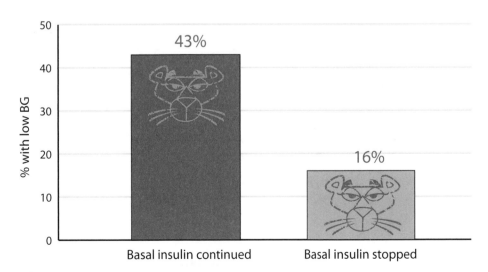

Table 4
Extra Food to Cover Exercise*[†]

Expected length of exercise	Blood sugar level		Examples of foods
	mg/dL	mmol/L	
A. Short (15-30 minutes)[†]	< 80	< 4.5	8 oz of sports drink** or 4-6 oz juice**
	80-150	4.5-8.3	A fresh fruit (or any 15 grams carbohydrate**)
	> 150	> 8.3	None
B. Longer (30-120 minutes)[†]	< 80	< 4.5	8 oz sports drink** or 4 oz juice plus ½ sandwich
	80-150	4.5-8.3	8 oz sports drink or milk plus fresh fruit
	> 150	> 8.3	½ sandwich**
C. Longest (2-4 hours)*[†]	< 80	< 4.5	8 oz sports drink or 4 oz juice, whole sandwich
	80-150	4.5-8.3	Fruit, whole sandwich
	> 150	> 8.3	Whole sandwich

*Remember to also drink water, sports drink or other fluids (one 8 oz glass for **A**, two 8 oz glasses for **B**, and three 8 oz glasses for **C**) before or during the exercise to prevent dehydration. This table is for a moderate degree of exercise (e.g., walking, bicycling leisurely, shooting a basketball or mowing the lawn). If heavier exercise (e.g., jogging, bicycle race, basketball game or digging in the garden) is to be done for the same amount of time, then more food may need to be added. Amounts vary for different people and the best way to learn is to do blood sugars before and after the exercise and keep a record of the blood sugar values (see Table 3).*

**Each of these represent 15 grams of carbohydrate which will last for about 30 minutes of moderate exercise. A sandwich with meat or other protein lasts longer.*

[†] May also need to reduce insulin dosage

✔ **Have extra snacks available before, during and after the exercise**

THE PERSON WITH DIABETES MUST ALWAYS HAVE A SOURCE OF SUGAR AVAILABLE. Parents have sewn pockets in basketball shorts, jogging pants and other clothes to hold three sugar packets, three sugar cubes or three glucose tablets for a possible emergency. Joggers' wallets on shoes work nicely. A sandwich or similar snack should be available nearby, as a sugar packet may last only a few minutes. It is helpful for the coach or instructor to have a tube of instant glucose or some other emergency source of sugar.

It is often difficult to guess the amount of a snack necessary for a particular activity. If the exercise is in the hour after a meal, an extra snack may not be needed. If a person is physically unfit, the blood sugar may drop more rapidly than if the person is physically fit. It is very useful to monitor the blood/CGM glucose values to determine what the correct snack is prior to, during and after the exercise. If the blood/CGM glucose value is low (e.g., below 100 mg/dL or 5.5 mmol/L), a larger snack is needed than when the blood sugar is high. IN FACT, EXERCISING CAN BE A VERY EFFECTIVE WAY TO LOWER A HIGH BLOOD SUGAR (AS LONG AS KETONES ARE NOT PRESENT). Glucose values may actually increase slightly during the first hour of exercise because the body releases the hormones glucagon and adrenaline. Glucose values may then decline. The type of snack can be varied depending on the expected length of the activity. IN GENERAL, THE MORE RAPIDLY ABSORBED CARBOHYDRATES SUCH AS JUICE OR SPORTS DRINKS ARE USED FOR SHORT-TERM ACTIVITIES. More food is added, such as crackers or bread, if the activity is to last longer. THE SNACK THAT KEEPS THE BLOOD SUGAR UP THE LONGEST IS ONE THAT INCLUDES PROTEIN AND FAT ALONG WITH THE CARBOHYDRATE. This might be a cheese or meat sandwich with a glass of juice. It is wise to check the glucose levels after the activity to help decide what to use for a snack the next time. Extra foods taken during the exercise period can help keep blood/CGM glucose values in the normal range (see Table 4). **Experience is the best teacher!**

It is a good idea to keep packets of cheese or peanut butter and crackers in the glove box of the car to eat before or after an activity. This is especially important if the distance is great between home and the activity. ALWAYS CHECK THE BLOOD/CGM GLUCOSE VALUE BEFORE DRIVING.

"DELAYED HYPOGLYCEMIA" refers to low blood/CGM glucose values several hours after the exercise is over. These may occur three to 12 hours after exercise. The 50 youth represented by the lines in Figure 1 had low blood sugar values (<60 mg/dL or <3.3 mmol/L) in 48% of the nights after heavy exercise and in 28% of nights after no exercise. They did not have a reduction in their insulin during the exercise.

In addition to reducing the insulin during the exercise, the injected or pump basal insulin acting during the night may need to be reduced. We have recently shown that use of an 80% temporary basal insulin rate from 9 pm to 3 am can help to prevent delayed hypoglycemia during the night.

Some people with type 2 diabetes may also experience delayed hypoglycemia. The result may be a low blood sugar in the middle of the night. It may happen because extra sugar in the blood goes back into storage in the muscle. Hormone changes with sleep (e.g., lower adrenaline levels) may also be important.

✔ **Change the injection site**

The choice of where you inject the insulin can help prevent low blood sugars. Exercise increases blood flow into the part of the body that is moving. The increased blood flow takes up more insulin. When a person with diabetes exercises, the blood insulin level may increase; whereas insulin levels decrease in non-diabetics during exercise. If you inject insulin into an

Table 5
Suggestions for Exercising Safely

🐾 Eat before heavy exercise

🐾 Try to have the blood sugar above 180 mg/dL (10 mmol/L) before heavy exercise

🐾 Have extra snacks available during exercise; some people use sports drink, 4-8 oz, for every 30 minutes of vigorous exercise

🐾 Always carry sugar

🐾 Reduce the insulin dose (including the basal and/or bolus pump doses)

🐾 Consider the injection site (the abdomen is usually best)

🐾 Check blood (CGM) values before, during and after exercise to learn the best insulin adjustment for the activity

🐾 Wear an ID bracelet or necklace

🐾 Try to exercise with a friend who knows about low blood sugar reactions

🐾 Make sure coaches know about low blood sugars (see letter at end of this chapter)

🐾 Do not exercise if ketones are present

🐾 Drink plenty of water, especially in hot weather

🐾 If delayed hypoglycemia occurs frequently, extra carbohydrates should be taken with the next meal or snack and the insulin dose decreased

🐾 Have fun!! Find an exercise you enjoy and incorporate it into your daily life

arm or leg that you will use heavily during exercise, your body may absorb the insulin too rapidly. If you are going to run, don't inject insulin into the leg. If you are going to play tennis, avoid the tennis arm. The abdomen is a good site for most strenuous exercise days.

✔ **Make sure others know**

It is important that coaches and teammates are aware of the diabetes. A team manager may be a good person to carry extra sugar snacks. It is helpful if the coach can have at least some awareness of the diabetes and know the symptoms and treatment of low blood sugar. A letter is included at the end of this chapter that you are welcome to copy as often as you like to share with coaches. Awareness of diabetes and the care needed to be a successful athlete has improved in part because of "famous" athletes. This chapter and book can help people to better understand the care needed to succeed. Remember that when a low blood sugar occurs during a sporting event, it is important to rest for at least ten minutes to let the blood sugar rise. The coach should be aware of this. Suggestions for exercising safely are summarized in Table 5.

NUTRITIONAL SUPPLEMENTS FOR EXERCISE

We frequently have adolescents ask us, "Can I take a protein supplement and/or should I take amino acids?" The answer to these questions is "No." Taking extra protein or amino acid supplements will NOT build muscles and may be harmful to the kidneys. The only way to build muscles is to do the physical exercise necessary to expand the muscle mass. The foods to eat are described in Chapter 11. Recent scandals about so-called "performance-enhancing" substances have raised awareness of their dangers and illegality.

HYDRATION AND EXERCISE

Proper hydration (drinking fluids) is essential during exercise. Exercising during hot weather requires special attention. Drinking extra fluids should begin an hour or two before starting to exercise. A general rule is to drink 8 oz of fluids for every 30 minutes of vigorous activity. Liquids such as sports drinks and fruit juices help replace water, salts and carbohydrates. Drinking sports drinks at half-hour intervals in conjunction with blood/CGM glucose checks during strenuous exercise works well for many people. Table 4 recommends suggested fluid amounts for different levels of activity.

AGE AND EXERCISE

Adults are advised to discuss plans to begin a new exercise program with their diabetes care provider first. As with everyone, starting slowly and gradually increasing the amount of exercise is important. Proper stretching (five to 10 minutes) **BEFORE, DURING** and **AFTER** the exercise will help prevent cramps and stiffness that may otherwise discourage further exercise.

Having a medical check-up before starting a new exercise program is recommended if you:

✔ are over 35 years of age

✔ have had type 1 diabetes more than 15 years

✔ have had type 2 diabetes more than 10 years

✔ have additional risk factors for a heart attack

✔ have eye or kidney complications

✔ have neuropathy (Chapter 23)

A graded exercise test might also be helpful. The maximum heart rate during exercise should not exceed 220 minus age.

Strenuous activities, including weight lifting and jogging, are discouraged for people who have severe eye changes of diabetes (proliferative retinopathy). This should be discussed with the diabetes eye specialist. Similarly, people with neuropathy should discuss with their diabetes care provider the pros and cons of exercise. When peripheral neuropathy is severe, weight-bearing exercises should be limited. With both severe eye changes and neuropathy, exercises that involve straining, jarring, or that cause increased pressure on the eyes or feet must be avoided. It is sometimes wise to have a "baseline" electrocardiogram (ECG) done prior to beginning a new exercise program. Other tests are then possible if there are any suggestions of abnormalities. People may ask their diabetes care provider to review with them the ADA guidelines for exercise that were published in the January, 2010, Supplement to *"Diabetes Care"*.

SUMMARY

Exercise is important for all people, but especially for a person with diabetes. Exercise can improve the blood lipids, reduce blood pressure and improve cardiovascular fitness. It is very helpful for people with type 2 diabetes to reduce weight. Choose exercises that you enjoy. If possible, the amount of exercise and the time of day should be fairly **CONSISTENT**. You can change the diabetes management to fit the exercise. It is not necessary to change the exercise to fit the diabetes. You can plan the exercise after a meal, reduce the insulin dosage or take extra snacks to help prevent low blood/CGM glucose values. YOU SHOULD CARRY A SOURCE OF SUGAR AT ALL TIMES AND YOU SHOULD ALWAYS HAVE A LONGER-LASTING SNACK AVAILABLE NEARBY. Remember, it is wise to THINK AHEAD about what the day's schedule will bring and plan accordingly.

DEFINITIONS

Abdomen: The area around the belly button. The fatty tissue of the abdomen can be used as an injection site.

Adrenaline (epinephrine): The excitatory hormone. This normally increases early in exercise and may result in an initial rise in the blood sugar.

Aerobic: A continuous exercise usually lasting 25 minutes or longer.

Buttocks (seat): What a person sits on. The fatty tissue of the buttocks can be used as an injection site.

Delayed hypoglycemia: Low blood sugars usually occurs 4-12 hours after heavy physical exercise, often during the night. This often occurs as sugar leaves the blood to replace depleted muscle sugar stores.

DPP: The **D**iabetes **P**revention **P**rogram. A study of 3,234 people who were overweight and had impaired (not diabetic) oral glucose tolerance tests. Exercise and weight loss (see this chapter) reduced the development of diabetes by 58 percent.

Glucagon: A hormone (like insulin) which also is made in the islets of the pancreas. It has the opposite effect of insulin and raises the blood sugar.

QUESTIONS AND ANSWERS FROM NEWSNOTES

Q My daughter just started swimming practices everyday from 3:30-5:30 p.m. Her pre-dinner blood sugars are over 200 mg/dL (11.1 mmol/L) when she gets home. However, she has awakened at 3:00-4:00 a.m. the past two mornings feeling shaky. Is that possible?

A Your daughter has the classic symptoms of "delayed hypoglycemia," which is not uncommon. Her blood sugar is high when she gets home from swimming as she has put out adrenaline (epinephrine), the excitatory hormone, during the exercise. All people, with or without diabetes, normally do this. The adrenaline causes breakdown of stored sugar in the liver (glycogen) to help keep the blood sugar up during the exercise. It is a safety mechanism.

At a later time, the sugar goes back into the muscle – often 4-12 hours later. When this happens, the blood sugar falls and she awakens feeling shaky. This is less likely to happen if the insulin working during the night is decreased. It is often necessary to decrease the dose by as much as two to six units to prevent delayed hypoglycemia. If using an insulin pump, a temporary basal rate of 80% from 9 pm to 3 am will help.

Q Our doctor has told us not to reduce the insulin dose on heavy exercise days, but just to eat more food. We were told on one of the Children's Diabetes Foundation's ski days to also reduce the insulin dose. We are now confused.

A An important part of managing exercise with diabetes is to prevent low blood sugars or "insulin reactions." Planning ahead is very helpful. Some children can just eat more food and will do fine. Many teenage girls are watching their diets, and when told to eat more food, will refuse to do so. Severe reactions can then result. Eating extra food may also offset some of the benefits of exercise. Reduction of insulin dosage is the only way to prevent reactions in such cases. Often a combination of some reduction in insulin dosage and eating extra snacks turns out to be the best solution.

Dear Coach,

This letter is on behalf of _____ who is participating in _____ this year. Although we do not want to single out people with diabetes, there are things that you need to be aware of to help _____'s performance and enjoyment of the sport.

Exercise is very important for children and adolescents with diabetes. The overall effect of exercise is to lower blood sugar. We hope _____ will take the right amount of insulin and eat according to the anticipated activity for the day. However, even when these things are done, there may be times, especially with increased activity, when he/she may have an "insulin reaction" (low blood sugar), a condition requiring immediate attention. The symptoms of an insulin reaction include one or more of the following: shakiness, dizziness, sweating, rapid onset of extreme hunger or tiredness and paleness. Some people complain of double vision and headaches. You may also notice _____'s performance to suddenly become very poor, or his/her overall mood may change to being very crabby or emotional.

If a low blood sugar occurs, a can of fruit juice, 8 oz of Gatorade, or two teaspoons of sugar followed in five to 10 minutes by solid food (fruit, cheese and crackers or a sandwich) will help correct this condition. He/She should rest for a minimum of ten minutes to let the blood sugar return to normal. However, some children will still have a headache and may not feel like continuing. We encourage families to be prepared for insulin reactions at all times by having the proper foods available.

Many people with diabetes will change their insulin dose on days they anticipate a practice or game. The scheduling (or cancellation) of these events ahead of time helps the person (and parents) to be prepared. Again, it is very important for youth with diabetes to be involved in sports. It helps with their sugar control and allows their insulin to work more effectively. A person with diabetes should not be and does not want to be treated differently because of having diabetes.

Please do not hesitate to call if you need more information or have any concerns. Our phone number is _____.

Sincerely,

(You may copy this letter as often as you wish.)

Chapter 14
Monitoring Blood/CGM Glucose and HbA1c Levels

TEACHING OBJECTIVES:

1. Discuss the four factors associated with optimal sugar control.

2. Describe the HbA1c and its relationship to blood/CGM glucose levels.

LEARNING OBJECTIVES:

Learner (parents, child, relative or self) will be able to:

1. List two factors that can affect blood sugar control.

2. Explain the HbA1c, your (your child's) current value and the recommended range.

INTRODUCTION

The term "sugar control" is used in diabetes to describe how close the blood/CGM glucose levels are kept within normal limits. The goal is to have blood/CGM glucose levels that more closely approach the normal sugar levels of someone without diabetes. This generally means at least half (50%) of values in the desired range for age. In this edition we use blood/CGM glucose values to refer to either blood or CGM (continuous glucose monitor) glucose values. A person with constant high blood/CGM glucose levels may have acute side effects such as:

✔ frequent thirst

✔ frequent urination

✔ weight loss (generally a good sign if type 2 diabetes)

✔ episodes of acidosis

It is important to have a reliable method to measure "overall" blood sugar control. This is done using the hemoglobin A1c (HbA1c) result. The glycohemoglobin, glycated hemoglobin or hemoglobin A1 (HbA1c) are names for similar determinations. They all reflect how often the blood sugars have been high every second of the day in the past 90 days. This will be discussed later in this chapter.

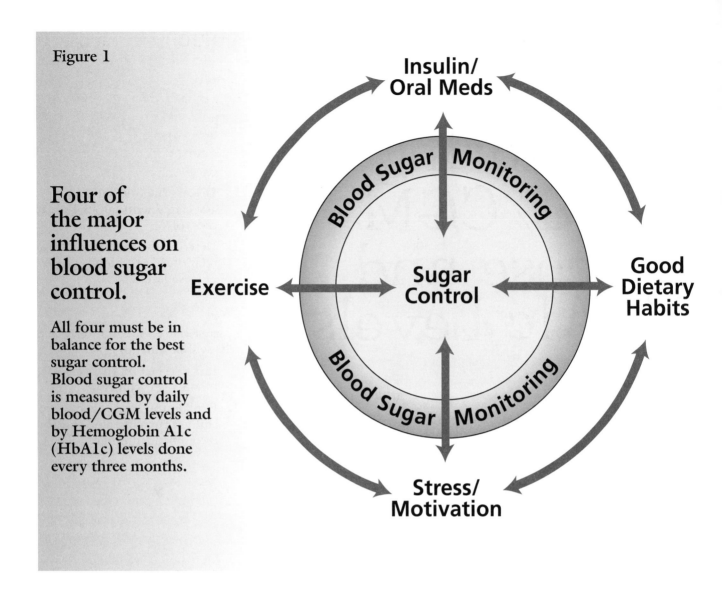

Figure 1

Four of the major influences on blood sugar control.

All four must be in balance for the best sugar control. Blood sugar control is measured by daily blood/CGM levels and by Hemoglobin A1c (HbA1c) levels done every three months.

Insulin/
Oral Meds

Blood Sugar Monitoring

Exercise

Sugar
Control

Good
Dietary
Habits

Blood Sugar Monitoring

Stress/
Motivation

THE DIABETES CONTROL AND COMPLICATIONS TRIAL (DCCT)

The DCCT proved for people with type 1 diabetes that optimal sugar control helped to prevent the eye, kidney and nerve complications of diabetes. People receiving **"intensive management"** (insulin pumps or 3-4 shots of insulin per day along with at least four blood sugar levels per day) had better sugar control (lower HbA1c values) than people receiving **"conventional management"** (1-2 shots of insulin per day with 0-2 blood sugar levels per day). The intensive management group was shown to have a lower chance for the eye, kidney, nerve and cardiovascular (including heart attacks and strokes) complications of diabetes than did the conventional management group. As a result, what was "intensive management" is now the routine treatment for people with type 1 diabetes.

Similar studies done in the U.K. and Japan showed optimal sugar control in people with type 2 diabetes also resulted in a reduction in eye, kidney and nerve complications of diabetes. Some of the studies have also shown a decrease in the risk for heart attacks and strokes with optimal sugar control. However, there is also danger connected with very low HbA1c levels (e.g., <6.5%).

SUGAR CONTROL

Optimal blood/CGM glucose control for people with type 1 or type 2 diabetes is the result of balancing the following four factors (Figure 1):

1. the correct insulin/oral medicine dosage

2. getting regular exercise

3. having good dietary habits

4. positive ways to cope with stress/developing motivation based on realistic goals

Monitoring blood/CGM glucose values assists in maintaining the proper balance between all four factors. Each of these factors is discussed elsewhere in this book in more detail. For people with type 1 diabetes, perhaps the most important of the four is the correct insulin dosage given at the right times. Sugar control will not improve if the insulin dose is incorrect, even if the other three factors are in balance. It will not help to do extra exercise if the person is not receiving the correct insulin dosage. However, any one of the four factors can result in sub-optimal sugar control. For example, if the other three factors are normally in balance, but the person decides to constantly drink sugar pop (10 tsp of sugar per can), sugar control will likely be lost. Similarly, with a lot of stress, the adrenaline (excitatory hormone) levels will be high and will raise the blood/CGM glucose values. Finally, exercise (Chapter 13) is important both for "burning" extra sugar and for making people more sensitive to insulin. Thus, all four of these factors must be in balance to result in the best sugar control possible for any person.

For type 2 patients, optimal sugar control results from a combination of exercise, diet, oral medications (or insulin) and motivation (Figure 1). Little weight will be lost if total food and fat intake are not reduced as an exercise program is initiated. Similarly, following a diet without also exercising is often fruitless. If oral medicines (or insulin) are missed, blood/CGM glucose levels will remain high. If the person

does not have realistic goals that include motivation, they will not succeed. All must be in balance for optimal diabetes control. The regular monitoring of blood/CGM glucose values (Chapter 7) is essential to understand the effects of these four influences.

SIGNS AND SYMPTOMS OF HIGH SUGAR LEVELS

It is not always easy to decide whether a person has optimal sugar control. *Some helpful things that reflect sugar control are the following:*

Control of Symptoms of Diabetes

A person who goes to the bathroom very frequently (including getting up two or more times per night), or who is often thirsty likely has symptoms of high blood and urine sugar. This person usually needs more insulin (or oral medicines), less sugar in the diet and/or more daily exercise.

Occasionally, blurred vision may occur as a symptom of high sugar levels. High sugar levels in the lens of the eye pull water into the lens. This extra fluid makes it difficult for the shape of the lens to change in order to focus for clear vision. The blurred vision usually stops when blood sugar control improves. People should not be fitted for glasses unless blood/CGM glucose levels are stable. If the blurred vision does not improve when blood sugar control improves, the eye doctor should be contacted.

People with diabetes may have numbness, tingling or pain in the feet. This is due to neuropathy (see Chapter 23), which is related to high sugar levels. The sugar and its by-products can collect in the nerves over a period of years. These complaints may be present at the time of diagnosis for people with type 2 diabetes.

Vaginal yeast infections are more common in females with diabetes, particularly if the blood/CGM glucose levels have been high. This may be because yeast grows well in a high-sugar environment. When antibiotics are taken for bacterial infections, yeast also tends to grow as the bacteria disappear. If vaginal itching or burning is noticed, the primary care provider should be contacted.

Normal Physical and Emotional Growth

Children and adolescents who have high blood/CGM glucose levels sometimes have reduced gains in height or weight. One study showed an average growth rate of two inches per year during the adolescent growth spurt when the HbA1c averaged 12.4 percent, but a gain of 3.3 inches per year when the HbA1c averaged 8.4 percent. Research reported from our clinic showed final adult height was more likely to be taller if HbA1c values were lower during adolescence. Following the height and weight every three months is an important part of the diabetes clinic visit.

Some people just don't feel well when they have high blood/CGM glucose levels. They may be constantly tired, have a bad temper or have any of a variety of symptoms. When improved sugar control is achieved, they often are surprised to realize how much better they feel. Feeling tired and poorly over a long time does not allow for normal emotional growth.

Sugar levels that do not produce such severe symptoms may still be too high and result in long-term problems (Chapter 23).

HOW IS SUGAR CONTROL MEASURED?

1. Blood (or CGM) Glucose (Sugar) Measurements

MEASURING BLOOD (OR CGM) GLUCOSE LEVELS IS THE BEST WAY TO MEASURE SUGAR CONTROL ON A DAY-TO-DAY BASIS and is discussed in detail in Chapter 7. All families with someone with diabetes must have a method in the home for measuring blood glucose levels. Studies have shown that checking blood sugars and

using the results are as important for diabetes control as is the method of giving insulin (two shots per day, an insulin pump or more than two shots per day). The blood/CGM glucose levels we consider representative of optimal sugar control vary with the person's age.

Age	Desired Range
	(fasting or ≥ 2 hours after meals)
under 5 years	80-200 mg/dL or (4.5-11.1 mmol/L)
5-11 years	70-180 mg/dL or (3.9-10.0 mmol/L)
12 years and older	70-150 mg/dL or (3.9-8.3 mmol/L)

The aim is to have blood/CGM glucose levels in the desired range for age at least 50 percent of the time. If more than 50 percent of values are consistently above the desired range or if more than 10 percent of values are below these levels, changes need to be made. Blood/CGM glucose levels may also give insight when done two hours after a meal. Families can also use the above age ranges for two or more hours after a meal. Others aim for all two hour values to be below 140 mg/dL (7.8 mmol/L). It is useful to think of half of the HbA1c value related to fasting blood/CGM glucose values and the other half related to blood/CGM levels after meals. The values recommended by the ADA in 2010 (Table 1) are slightly different than the recommended values in this book.

It is important not to be unhappy with blood/CGM glucose results, but instead to always be pleased that the information is available. We do not use the words "good" and "bad" in this book to describe results. Hopefully, all results will be used as information to help attain optimal sugar control. Blood/CGM glucose monitoring was discussed in detail in Chapter 7.

Table 1
ADA*-Recommended HbA1c and Blood Glucose Values
(ADA: 2005*)

	(Hemoglobin A1c) HbA1c Values	Blood Glucose : mg/dL (mmol/L) Fasting/Before Meals	Bedtime/Overnight
Normal (Non-diabetic):	≤ 5.9%	70-102**	70-121**
Desired ranges for someone with diabetes:			
below six years	7.5-8.5%	100-180 (5.5-10.0)	110-200 (6.1-11.1)
6-12 years	< 8.0%	90-180 (5.0-10.0)	100-180 (5.5-10.0)
13-19 years	< 7.5%	90-130 (5.0-7.3)	90-150 (5.0-8.3)
> 19 years	< 7.0%	90-130 (5.0-7.3)	— —

*ADA *"Diabetes Care"* 33 (Suppl 1, S4), 2010
**Data from JDRF CGM Study Group, Diabetes Care 33, 1297, 2010

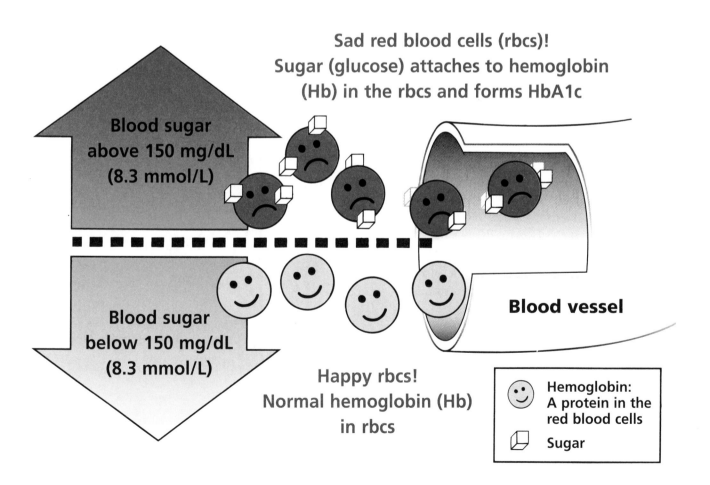

Sad red blood cells (rbcs)!
Sugar (glucose) attaches to hemoglobin (Hb) in the rbcs and forms HbA1c

Blood sugar above 150 mg/dL (8.3 mmol/L)

Blood sugar below 150 mg/dL (8.3 mmol/L)

Blood vessel

Happy rbcs!
Normal hemoglobin (Hb) in rbcs

Hemoglobin: A protein in the red blood cells

Sugar

2. Hemoglobin A1c (HbA1c)

THE HbA1c LEVEL IS THE MOST VALUABLE WAY TO MONITOR BLOOD/CGM GLUCOSE LEVELS OVER TIME. Hemoglobin is the protein in the red blood cells that carries oxygen to the various parts of the body. It was found, by chance, that the hemoglobin molecule has a secondary property that could be used to monitor sugar control. If the blood sugar is high, sugar attaches to the hemoglobin (Figure 2) and remains there for the life of the red blood cell (an average of 2-3 months). The sugar doesn't come off if a low blood sugar occurs. For the purposes of this book, we will call hemoglobin with sugar attached hemoglobin A1c or HbA1c. The HbA1c reflects how often the blood sugars have been high for every second of the past three months (for the past 7,776,000 seconds). No one could do that many blood sugars. **The HbA1c represents the forest while the daily blood/CGM glucose values reflect the trees.** The HbA1c value has been used routinely since the late 1970s and has been called the "answer to a prayer" for people with diabetes and their doctors. Previously there was no way to monitor long-term sugar control. No one really knew if they were in optimal sugar control. The HbA1c solved that problem.

The HbA1c level can be done at the time of the clinic visit and the person does not have to be fasting. Most diabetes clinics now do it by finger-poke and have the result in 10 minutes. THE RESULT IS NOT ALTERED BY ANYTHING THE PERSON DOES ON THE DAY IT IS DRAWN. In contrast the blood sugar level can be affected by eating, exercise habits or emotions. The main disadvantage of the HbA1c is that an illness may make the level go up quickly by as much as one to two points. After the illness, the HbA1c value comes down much more slowly. (It is very "unforgiving.") Table 2 shows an approximate relation between the HbA1c level and the average blood/CGM glucose level over the past three months.

The ADA (American Diabetes Association) recommendations for HbA1c levels for children

Table 2
Approximate HbA1c and Blood Glucose Correlations*

HbA1c %	Blood Glucose (Sugar) Level	
	mg/dL	mmol/L
12	345	19.2
11	310	17.2
10	275	15.3
9	240	13.3
8	205	11.3
7	170	9.5
6	135	7.5

This graph shows the approximate relation between average blood sugar levels and the HbA1c. (The HbA1c does not truly reflect "average" blood sugar as sugar goes onto the molecule when the blood sugar is high but does not come off when the blood sugar is low.)

Taken in part from a production of Partnership to Advance Care and Education (PACE.)

in the U.S. are shown in the Table 1. Most children's diabetes clinics now use a micro-method for doing the HbA1c so it can be done on a finger-stick and not require a venous blood draw. It is also important to be able to get the result back in a few minutes so the health team can discuss the result and future goals with the person/family. The DirecNet research group showed that the DCA 2000 instrument, which fulfills all of these goals, was also very accurate. Other clinics have patients go to the lab in advance to have the result available at the time of the clinic visit.

Half of the HbA1c value reflects the past 30 days. The other half reflects the previous two months. When the result is not in the desired range (e.g., after an illness with high blood sugars), it may be helpful to repeat the value monthly until it is in the desired range.

We encourage different ranges for different ages. We want people 13 years old and above, when complications are more likely to develop, to be in better sugar control than younger children. The pre-teens do not have the same risk for complications, so their values do not have to be as low. Finally, low blood sugars are more dangerous for preschoolers, as the brain continues to grow for the first four years after birth. Low blood sugars are dangerous to a growing brain. The blood sugar values of preschoolers should NOT be kept as low as those of older children. After age 19 years, growth has decreased and life (hopefully) starts to become more consistent so that an even lower HbA1c can be a goal (see Table 1 in this chapter). The ADA recommends that the HbA1c goal for adults be below 7.0 percent. The ADA Standards of Care (see Chapter 21) recommend the HbA1c be done every three months for a person with diabetes. IT IS THE ONLY WAY TO KNOW HOW A PERSON WITH DIABETES IS DOING EVERY SECOND OF THE DAY. We consider it the single best method for measuring long-term diabetes control. **It is currently estimated that for every percentage point reduction in HbA1c levels, there is a 35 percent reduction**

in the likelihood of eye, kidney and nerve damage (Chapter 23). It is thus very important in relation to diabetes complications. The ADA desired ranges shown in Table 1 are achievable and families should continue to strive to reach these goals.

3. Fructosamine (or Glycated Albumin) Level

Fructosamine measures the amount of sugar attached to another serum protein. It reflects the blood/CGM glucose values every second of the day for the past 2-3 weeks (whereas the HbA1c reflects the past three months). It is often helpful to know how someone is doing more recently (in contrast to the past three months). The fructosamine value may also be helpful for someone who is changing treatment (more shots, an insulin pump, etc.).

4. Blood Cholesterol and Triglyceride Level

High blood fat (triglyceride or cholesterol) levels in some people with diabetes are related to suboptimal sugar control. Others may have high blood fat levels from eating poorly or it may be because they inherited a tendency to have high blood fat levels. High blood fat levels are sometimes part of the disease process for people with type 2 diabetes. Triglyceride levels may be high and HDL (the "good") cholesterol levels low. As high blood fat levels can lead to earlier blood vessel aging, this may be a link between high blood sugar levels and later changes in blood vessel walls. We generally recommend that a lipid panel including total cholesterol, triglyceride and LDL and HDL cholesterol levels be measured every one or two years in children and annually in adults. The total cholesterol value should be under 200 mg/dL (5.2 mmol/L). The triglyceride levels vary by age, but fasting levels should be below 130 mg/dL (1.5 mmol/L) for children and young adults. Cholesterol, triglyceride, LDL and HDL cholesterol levels are also discussed in Chapter 11.

DEFINITIONS

ADA: American Diabetes Association

Bacteria: Microscopic (only able to be seen with a microscope) agents that cause infections such as "strep throat."

DCCT: The Diabetes Control and Complications Trial. A very large research trial which showed that better sugar control reduced the likelihood of eye, kidney and nerve problems in people over age 13 years with type 1 diabetes.

Emotions: How one feels psychologically (e.g., happy, sad).

Fructosamine: A method to measure the sugar attached to the albumin in the blood. It reflects how often the blood sugars have been high over the past two or three weeks.

HDL: High **D**ensity **L**ipoprotein **Cholesterol:** This is the "good" cholesterol protein which is believed to carry cholesterol from the blood vessel wall. A higher value is desirable (see desired values in Table 2, Chapter 11).

Hemoglobin A1c (HbA1c): Hemoglobin protein in the red blood cells with sugar attached to it. This is used as a measure of sugar control over the previous three months.

LDL: Low **D**ensity **L**ipoprotein **Cholesterol:** This is the "bad" cholesterol protein, which is believed to carry cholesterol into the blood vessel wall. The aim is to have to have LDL levels below 130 mg/dL (3.35 mmol/L) for the general population or below 100 mg/dL (2.6 mmol/L) for people with diabetes (see Table 2 in Chapter 11).

Lens: The structure in the front of the eye that changes to allow the eye to focus on near or distant objects (see picture in Chapter 23).

"Optimal" diabetes (or blood sugar) control: The lowest reasonable level of HbA1c able to be achieved without significant hypoglycemia or other problems.

Serum: The clear part of the blood when the blood cells are removed.

Symptoms: The complaints of a person; how they are feeling.

Yeast: A fungus that grows more readily when blood sugar levels are high and can cause an infection.

QUESTIONS AND ANSWERS FROM NEWSNOTES

 Does the hemoglobin A1c really give the average blood/CGM glucose value over the past three months?

 No. It reflects how often the blood sugars have been <u>high</u> over the past three months. When the blood sugar is high, the sugar attaches to all body proteins (including the red blood cell hemoglobin) and then stays attached to the hemoglobin (as hemoglobin A1c or HbA1c) until the red blood cell is replaced 2-3 months later. To represent the "average blood sugar," the sugar molecule would also have to detach from the protein when the blood sugar is low. This does not happen. Thus, the value only reflects how often the blood sugar has been high. It is still far superior to any other method to reflect blood sugar control. It should be done on all people with diabetes every three months.

 Our daughter's HbA1c has not reached the desired level. With all the concern from the DCCT on preventing complications, could you please make any suggestions on ways to achieve better control?

We have seven suggestions:

1. This question is often addressed in relation to the idea of doing an afternoon blood sugar after school and judging the afternoon snack and/or insulin supplement on the value at that time. This can be helpful in lowering the HbA1c.

2. The use of rapid-acting insulin, given 20

minutes prior to food intake (especially breakfast), will result in a lower HbA1c value.

3. One of the biggest keys to better control, which was reported in the DCCT, was more frequent blood glucose monitoring, along with making good use of the results. All subjects did a **minimum** of four blood glucose levels each day. An unfortunate trend in recent years has been to not record results as they are all recorded in the meter. When this is not done, trends for high and low values are often missed and insulin adjustments may not be made. The Daily Record Sheet is available (see Chapter 7) to fax or email to your diabetes care provider. This is important if more than half of the values at anytime of day are "above range" for age and you need help with insulin adjustments. Include any notes which might help to explain any unusual blood sugar values. In addition, include your analysis of the values and what insulin adjustments you think need to be made. This will help you to learn dose adjustments. Be sure to include a fax and/or phone number where you can be reached.

4. Strangely enough, preventing low blood sugars is often important in achieving better control. Low blood sugars often result in excessive eating and sending the blood sugar up to 300 or 400 mg/dL (16.7 or 22.2 mmol/L). Although excessive eating is probably the major cause of the subsequent high blood sugars, output of balancing hormones (rebounding) likely plays a secondary role in some people.

5. "Turning off" the liver's production of glucose (sugar) in the early morning is important in relation to keeping liver glucose production "turned off" all day long. If the morning fasting blood sugars are above the recommended range, the dose of Lantus/Levemir or nocturnal pump basal insulin likely needs to be increased.

6. Most recently, the JDRF randomized trial of CGM use showed that if people of any age use a CGM at least six days per week, their HbA1c level will likely decrease.

7. Last but not least, a word must be said about missed insulin shots (boluses). Two meal-time shots (boluses) missed per week over three month results in a half-point elevation in HbA1c.

 Q **Changes in our daughter's insulin dose have confused my wife and me. Initially she was on a low insulin dose which you increased after reviewing her blood sugars and seeing that her HbA1c was high. Her HbA1c level came down, and now her insulin dose is coming back down again. This doesn't make sense to us.**

A This is quite common, and follows an old adage that: **"Good control breeds good control; poor control breeds poor control."** Thus, for someone whose liver is making sugar at a very high rate, it takes very little (stress, infection, etc.) to make even more sugar and it may take a lot of insulin to get the liver's sugar production machinery turned off. This may also be the case for a newly-diagnosed person.

However, once the liver's pathways for making sugar are turned off, it may not take as much insulin to keep them turned off. This may be part of the reason for the "honeymoon" period in the newly diagnosed person. Also, stress and infections will then not have as great an effect.

Chapter 15
Ketones and Acidosis

TOPIC:
Prevent, Detect and Treat Acute Complications (Ketones and Acidosis)

CAUSES OF KETONES AND ACIDOSIS

One "emergency" in diabetes, low blood sugar (hypoglycemia), was discussed in Chapter 6. The other emergency is the build-up of ketones in the blood or urine, which can develop into acidosis (Figure 1). Acidosis is most common with type 1 diabetes, but it can also occur with type 2 diabetes. The measurement of urine or blood ketones is very easy and was discussed in Chapter 5.

When people are referred to our Center, the most common knowledge deficits are:

✔ the dangers/meaning of ketone build-up

✔ when to measure ketones

✔ not having the supplies in their home or on trips to measure for ketones

✔ not knowing what to do when ketones are present

These deficits can result in a serious episode of acidosis.

"Large" urine or blood ketones are usually present for at least four hours before the total body's acidity is increased (acidosis or DKA). Acidosis is very dangerous and people can go into a coma or die from it. It is the cause of 85 percent of hospitalizations of children with known diabetes. The good news is that it is 98 percent preventable if people follow the instructions in this chapter. **Acidosis can be prevented in a person who is known to have diabetes.**

Ketones and acidosis are due to not enough insulin being available to meet the body's needs.

The five main causes for ketone formation are:

1. Illnesses/infections: extra energy may be needed by the

TEACHING OBJECTIVES:

1. Describe causes of ketone production.

2. Present signs and symptoms of having ketones.

3. Discuss treatment plan for preventing or eliminating ketones.

LEARNING OBJECTIVES:

Learner (parents, child, relative or self) will be able to:

1. List two causes of ketones.

2. Describe two symptoms of having ketones.

3. Explain two methods to prevent or eliminate ketones.

157

Figure 1

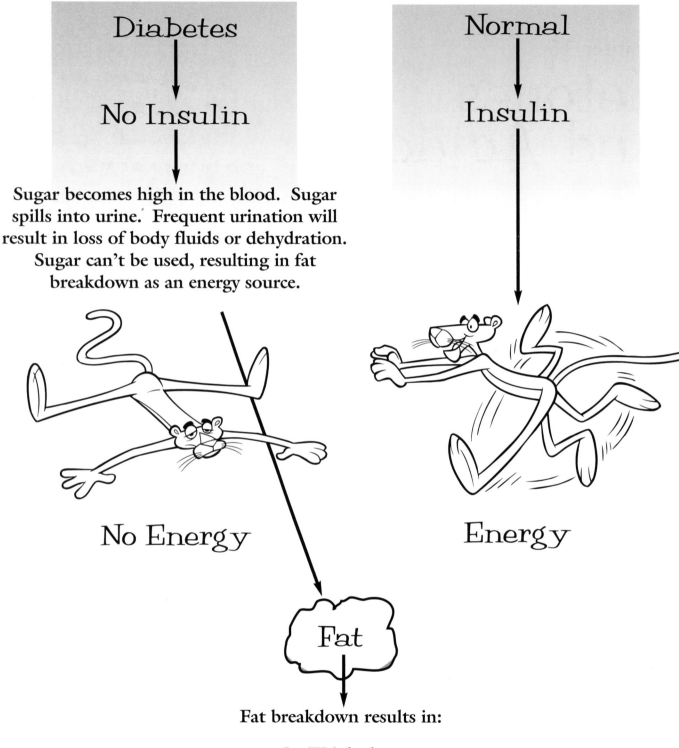

Diabetes

↓

No Insulin

↓

Sugar becomes high in the blood. Sugar spills into urine. Frequent urination will result in loss of body fluids or dehydration. Sugar can't be used, resulting in fat breakdown as an energy source.

No Energy

Normal

↓

Insulin

↓

Energy

Fat

↓

Fat breakdown results in:

1. Weight loss

2. Ketones, which are a breakdown product of fat and appear in the blood and urine

3. Too many ketones in the body = acidosis

Table 1
Main Causes of Acidosis

- Infection
- Missed insulin injections
- Not enough insulin
- Traumatic stress on the body (particularly type 2 diabetes)
- A pump insertion coming out or not functioning (Chapter 28)

Table 2
Main Functions of Insulin

- To allow sugar to pass into cells where it can be used for energy
- To turn off excess production of sugar in the liver
- To turn off fat breakdown

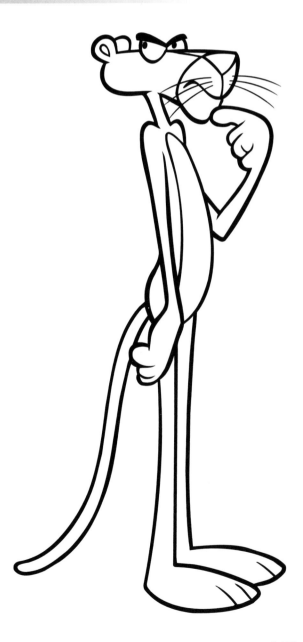

body. This cannot be made unless extra insulin is available to make the extra energy from sugar.

2. *Forgetting to take an insulin shot (bolus) or, for type 2 diabetes, insulin or oral medicine.*

Remember the statement from Chapter 2:

I MUST TAKE MY INSULIN/ORAL MEDICATION EVERY DAY FROM NOW ON. IF I FORGET MY INSULIN/ORAL MEDICATION, MY DIABETES WILL GET OUT OF CONTROL. THERE IS ABSOLUTELY NO WAY I WILL NOT NEED INSULIN/ORAL MEDICATION EVERY DAY FROM NOW ON.

3. *A lack of insulin (see Table 1):* this could happen in a person coming out of the "honeymoon" period who has not had insulin dosages increased.

4. *Traumatic stresses on the body (particularly with type 2 diabetes):* people with type 2 diabetes sometimes get ketones during an illness. However, other body stressors such as surgery or a heart attack may also result in ketone production.

5. *A pump insertion coming out or not functioning (Chapter 28):* As pumps use rapid-acting insulins, there will be no further insulin activity 3-4 hours after an insertion malfunctions.

Three (of the many) functions of insulin are to (see Table 2):

1. allow sugar to pass into cells

2. turn off the body's machinery for making sugar

3. turn off fat breakdown in order to stop ketone production

The blood/CGM glucose levels are usually high with large ketones and acidosis because the second and third functions of insulin are not happening. This is because not enough insulin is available. The stress hormones are also high with illnesses/infections. These hormones act to increase blood sugar and ketone production. The high blood sugar causes sugar to pass into the urine (see Chapter 2) and the person must go to the bathroom a lot (**frequent urination**). The body may lose too much water and become too dry (**dehydration**). The tongue may feel dry and furry. Drinking lots of fluids may help prevent this. The main treatment, however, is taking extra insulin to shut off the body's machinery for making sugar and ketones.

It is not high blood/CGM glucose levels that causes ketones or acidosis. In fact, eating sugar does not cause acidosis. Ketones come from the breakdown of body fat (see picture at the end of this chapter). The third role of insulin (see Table 2) is to shut off fat breakdown. Fat begins to break down because not enough insulin is available and stress hormones are high. The side-product of fat breakdown is ketone production. Ketones are initially passed into the urine (ketonuria). They may start with trace or small levels and gradually build up to moderate and large levels. They also gradually build up in the blood. Once they reach the large level, they may start to build up in the body tissues. They are easier to reverse if treated early. The longer someone has large ketones, the more likely they will build up in the body resulting in acidosis (DKA). Thus, the early detection and reversal by giving extra insulin is critical.

There are several reasons why fat is broken down:

- Not enough insulin is available to help the cells burn the needed sugar.

- The body needs more energy (e.g., for illness/infections) and the fat is broken down to provide this energy.

- The stress hormones; steroids, adrenaline (epinephrine) and glucagon have been released, causing fat breakdown.

- Sugar is not available due to vomiting or not eating, and fat is broken down for the energy needed. Anytime fat is broken down for energy, ketones are formed.

SYMPTOMS OF ACIDOSIS

In any of the above cases, fat is broken down. The ketones are made from the fat. *Acidosis usually comes on slowly, over several hours, and has the following symptoms:*

✔ upset stomach and/or stomach pain

✔ vomiting

✔ sweet (fruity) odor to the breath

✔ thirst and frequent urination (if the blood/CGM glucose level is high)

✔ dry mouth

✔ drowsiness

✔ deep breathing (indicates need to go to emergency room)

✔ if not treated, coma (loss of consciousness)

On occasion, it may be difficult to know if a person is having difficulty with low blood sugar or with acidosis. Measuring the blood sugar and ketones will help identify the correct problem. Table 3 may also be helpful in thinking about the two problems.

Table 3
The Two Emergencies of Diabetes

	Low Blood Sugar (Chapter 6) (Hypoglycemia or Insulin Reaction)	Ketoacidosis (Chapter 15) (Acidosis or DKA)
Due to:	Low blood sugar	Presence of ketones
Time of onset:	Fast – within seconds	Slow – in hours or days
Causes:	Too little food Too much insulin Too much exercise without food Missing or being late for meals/snacks Excitement in young children	Too little insulin Not giving insulin Infections/Illness Traumatic body stress Pump insertions malfunctioning
Blood sugar:	Low (below 60 mg/dL or 3.3 mmol/L)	Usually high (over 240 mg/dL or 13.3 mmol/L)
Ketones:	Usually none in the urine or blood	Usually moderate/large in the urine or blood ketones over 0.6 mmol/L.
SYMPTOMS		**SYMPTOMS**
Mild:	Hunger, shaky, sweaty, nervous	Thirst, frequent urination, sweet breath, small or moderate urine ketones or blood ketones less than 1.0 mmol/L.
Moderate:	Headache, unexpected behavior changes, impaired or double vision, confusion, drowsiness, weakness or difficulty talking.	Dry mouth, nausea, stomach cramps, vomiting, moderate or large urine ketones or blood ketones between 1.0 and 3.0 mmol/L.
Severe:	Loss of consciousness or seizures.	Labored deep breathing, extreme weakness, confusion and eventually unconsciousness (coma): large urine ketones or blood ketones above 3.0 mmol/L.
TREATMENT		**TREATMENT**
Mild:	Give juice or milk. Wait 10 minutes and then give solid food.	Give lots of fluids and Humalog/NovoLog/Apidra **or** Regular insulin every two or three hours.
Moderate:	Give instant glucose or a fast-acting sugar, juice or sugar pop (4 oz). After 10 minutes, give solid food.	Continued contact with healthcare provider. Give lots of fluids. Give Humalog/NovoLog/Apidra or Regular insulin every two or three hours. Give Zofran (a tablet) or Phenergan medication (suppository or topical cream) if vomiting occurs.
Severe:	Give glucagon into muscle or fat. Test blood sugar. If no response, call paramedic (911) or go to E.R.	*Go to the emergency room.* May need intravenous fluids and insulin.

PREVENTION OF ACIDOSIS

Acidosis is the cause of 85 percent of re-admissions to the hospital for someone with known diabetes. Most of these admissions could be prevented if the problem were identified and treated earlier. The simple rules outlined in Table 4 will prevent most cases of acidosis. It is a good idea to review this chapter every year. Families may forget the importance of checking urine or blood ketones during any illness. Some people with diabetes who still make some of their own insulin, or who are in optimal diabetes control, will have the "machinery" (enzymes) for making the ketones remain "turned off." As a result, they may go several years and never have urine or blood ketones with an illness. As they grow older and a few more islet cells are lost, or they outgrow their remaining islets, they may suddenly find ketones present.

The important message is always to remember to check for ketones anytime a person with diabetes is ill. You must also check for ketones anytime the blood/CGM glucose level is above 240 mg/dL (> 13.3 mmol/L) fasting or above 300 mg/dL (> 16.7 mmol/L) during the day.

The prevention of acidosis is based on being able to detect changes early. Knowing when ketones are increasing in the urine or blood, but before the ketones build up to high levels in the body, is important.

Preventing acidosis – the person with diabetes or the family:

✔ must have a method in the home to check urine or blood ketones (see Chapter 5)

✔ must remember to check for urine or blood ketones anytime the person is sick (even with vomiting only one time)

✔ needs to check ketones if the blood/CGM glucose level is high

✔ should call the diabetes care provider immediately (night or day) if moderate or large urine ketones or blood ketones > 1.0 mmol/L are present

✔ needs to give extra rapid-acting insulin (Humalog/NovoLog/Apidra) every two hours or Regular insulin every three hours until the urine or blood ketones have decreased

✔ must drink lots of fluids to wash the ketones out of the body and to prevent dehydration

A low blood sugar can sometimes be present with acidosis, so urine ketones must be checked with every illness, even if the blood/CGM glucose level is not elevated. A summary of the instructions is in Table 4.

Extra Insulin

When ketone production becomes total body acidosis, it is usually because the large amount of ketones has been present for four to 12 hours. This can happen because the urine or blood ketones have not been checked or no extra insulin has been given. Insulin shuts off ketone production. Extra insulin must be given if someone has moderate or large urine ketones or blood ketones above 0.6 mmol/L. The dose of extra insulin varies for different people, and the diabetes care provider can help decide on a safe dose.

General Guidelines When Giving Extra Insulin

The blood/CGM glucose level should always be checked before each insulin injection.

🐾 **For moderate urine ketones or blood ketones between 0.6 and 1.5 mmol/L:**

The extra dose is usually in the range of 5-10 percent of the total daily dose (see Table 5). The extra dose is given as Humalog/NovoLog/Apidra every two hours or Regular insulin every three hours.

🐾 **For large urine ketones or blood ketones above 1.5 mmol/L:**

The dose of extra insulin is usually 10-20 percent of the total daily dose. This extra insulin is given as Humalog/NovoLog/Apidra every two hours or Regular insulin every three hours.

Table 5 outlines a possible treatment schedule.

The extra insulin may seem like a large dose, but ketones block the normal sensitivity of the body to insulin. Although every person is different, dosages in these ranges are usually needed.

- **If the blood/CGM glucose level drops below 150 mg/dL (8.3 mmol/L):**

It may be necessary to sip juice or another sugary drink. This is done to bring the blood sugar back up before giving the next insulin injection.

Remember, the extra insulin and fluids are being given to clear the urine or blood ketones.

Extra Fluids

In addition to taking extra insulin, drinking fluids (e.g., water and fruit juices) is important in the prevention of acidosis. These liquids replace the fluid lost in the urine and help prevent dehydration. The juices also replace some of the salts that are lost in the urine. Orange juice and bananas are particularly good for replacing the potassium that is lost. As discussed in the next chapter, Sick-day Management, medications (Zofran or Phenergan) are used by some providers if vomiting is a problem. The main side effect of Zofran is headaches.

When severe acidosis has been present for many hours, coma (loss of consciousness) can follow. This is dangerous. It is much better to prevent severe acidosis than to have to treat it with IV fluids and a hospital admission. The hospital admission is usually in an intensive care unit, which is scary for everyone. Intravenous lines are usually put in both arms (and sometimes the feet). A constant heart-

Table 4
Prevention of Ketoacidosis

- Remember to check urine or blood ketones with any illness (even an upset stomach or vomiting one time) or anytime the fasting blood sugar is above 240 mg/dL (13.3 mmol/L) or a daytime blood sugar is above 300 mg/dL (16.7 mmol/L).

- Call the diabetes care provider immediately (night or day) if moderate or large urine ketones or blood ketones above 1.0 mmol/L are found.

- Take extra insulin (after checking the blood sugar and urine or blood ketones). Take Humalog/NovoLog/Apidra every two hours, or Regular insulin every three hours, until the urine ketones are small or less or the blood ketones are below 0.6 mmol/L.

- If the blood sugar falls below 150 mg/dL (8.3 mmol/L) and urine or blood ketones are still present, drink juice (preferably orange as it replaces potassium), Pedialyte® or sugared pop (soda) to keep the blood sugar up so that more insulin can be given to turn off the ketone production.

- Drink lots of fluids to help wash out the ketones.

Table 5
Ketone Levels* in Blood or Urine and a Suggested Dose of Rapid-Acting or Regular Insulin

Urine	Blood (mmol/L)	Dose of H/NL/AP every 2 hours or Dose of Regular every 3 hours	
Trace/Small	< 0.6	per "correction" factor for blood sugar	
Moderate - Large	0.6 – 1.5	10% of total daily insulin dose**	
Large - Very Large	> 1.5	20% of total daily insulin dose**	

* The blood and urine ketone results do not agree exactly and the above correlations are estimates. The blood ketone result reflects the ketone level at the exact time the test is done. If the urine has been in the bladder for some time, then the urine ketone result may not tell the current status.

** The total daily insulin dose is the sum of all insulin taken in a 24-hour period (rapid-acting plus intermediate-acting plus long-acting). This is calculated differently per different healthcare providers. Some recommend doubling the dose that would be given by using the person's known glucose correction factor.

monitoring machine is attached to the person. The cost is about $10,000/day in the ICU.

Preventing acidosis is generally possible when the rules in Table 4 are followed. Ketoacidosis in patients with known diabetes rarely occurs in people who attend a clinic regularly. When it does occur, it is usually because the directions in Table 4 were not followed.

DEFINITIONS

Acetone: One of the ketones which builds up in the urine, blood and body during acidosis. It is sometimes used (incorrectly) to refer to all ketones.

Acidosis (diabetic ketoacidosis or DKA): What happens in the body when not enough insulin is available. Blood/CGM glucose levels are usually high at this time. Moderate or large ketones are present in the urine or blood and then build up in the body. The ketones make the body fluids more acidic resulting in total body acidosis.

Beta hydroxybutyrate (ß-OH butyrate): The most important of the three main ketones (along with acetone and acetoacetic acid). It is the ketone that is measured in the blood.

Dehydration: Loss of the body fluids. The tongue and skin are usually very dry and the eyes look sunken. Babies have less than half the usual number of wet diapers.

Ketoacidosis: See Acidosis (diabetic ketoacidosis or DKA) above.

Ketones: Fat breakdown products that initially spill into the urine and later build up in the blood when there is not enough insulin. Many people can smell a sweet odor on the breath. The fat breakdown products cause acidosis (or ketoacidosis).

Potassium: One of the salts (along with sodium) lost in the urine when ketones are spilled in the urine. Orange juice and bananas contain a lot of potassium and are best to give if urine ketones are present.

QUESTIONS AND ANSWERS FROM NEWSNOTES

 Please explain what ketoacidosis (acidosis) is and how it can be prevented.

Acidosis is one of the two emergency problems of diabetes (low blood sugar being the other). It is the main cause of children with known diabetes being admitted to the hospital. It is responsible for 85 percent of hospitalizations. Most of these hospitalizations can be prevented with good family education and with following instructions.

Families can check for ketones at home with urine or blood. If using urine Ketostix, use the foil-wrapped strips. The bottles of strips expire six months after they have been opened. Checking for ketones should be done ANY TIME THE PERSON IS FEELING ILL. Also, check ketones if the blood/CGM glucose level is above 240 mg/dL (> 13.3 mmol/L) fasting or above 300 mg/dL (> 16.7 mmol/L) during the day. If moderate/large urine ketones are found or blood ketones are above 1.0 mmol/L, the healthcare provider should be called immediately. Calling the healthcare provider may be necessary every 2-3 hours for dosages of Humalog/NovoLog/Apidra or Regular insulin. After the ketones have decreased to small amounts or have gone away, the extra injections can be stopped.

On any given day, five to 10 children are being treated for elevated ketones by our staff. This happens especially during the flu season. Fortunately, hospital admissions have gone down dramatically as a result of this treatment and are now infrequent.

The cause of ketone production is the body's need for energy. Sometimes, the body needs extra energy (e.g., during an illness). Because there is not enough insulin or sugar available to use sugar for energy, the fat tissue responds by releasing fats. These fats are then broken down. Some of these fats are made into ketones by the liver. As the ketones build up following the fat breakdown, ketoacidosis eventually results. The most frequent symptoms are a stomachache and, eventually, vomiting. Deep breathing is a late sign and indicates a need to go to an emergency room.

 Why does someone feel sick when the ketones are moderate or large in the urine or > 0.6 mmol/L in the blood?

 There are at least three parts to the answer to this question:

1. The body's acid-base (pH) balance is finely tuned (a bit on the basic side at 7.35-7.45). Acids and bases are difficult to explain. Examples of a base and an acid are: soap is an alkaline (base) material and tomatoes are acidic. Ketones (which are acids) make the body fluids more acidic as they start to build up. As the body becomes more acidic, many of the body's functions can no longer work as they should. If left untreated, death will eventually follow.

2. The second reason a person feels ill is because of a potassium and sodium imbalance. They are important body salts, and are lost with ketones going out in the urine. Potassium is important for the movement of the intestine (moving food through). If too much potassium is lost, this movement decreases or stops. When this happens, an upset stomach and vomiting can occur. We often recommend orange juice (high in potassium) and apple juice in addition to water when someone has urine or blood ketones. Drinking lots of liquids helps to keep good hydration and to flush out the ketones.

3. Poor hydration would be the third reason for feeling ill. Usually, frequent urination due to high blood and urine sugar happens together with urine ketones. This can lead to dehydration. Our bodies are 60 percent

water. If even 10 percent of body weight is lost as water, it is possible to be very sick. Fluids can also be lost in large amounts with the flu (vomiting and diarrhea). If fluid is being lost in large amounts from both the kidneys (frequent urination) **and** from vomiting and/or diarrhea, dehydration can occur even more rapidly. Children under the age of five can become dehydrated in less than four hours. They are more likely to require IV treatment sooner than older children.

Q **What is cerebral edema and how does it relate to diabetic ketoacidosis (DKA)?**

A Cerebral edema refers to swelling of the brain, which is a rare complication of treating DKA. The cause is not fully understood and when it does occur, it is often fatal.

Perhaps we have been lucky in that we have seen only two or three cases of cerebral edema in children under our care who had been previously diagnosed with diabetes. Part of the reason it is so rare relates to the now relative infrequency of DKA. Our families are asked to check urine or blood ketones with every illness or high blood/CGM glucose level. If using a CGM, the alarm can be set to warn the person/family when the value is high. They are asked to call when urine ketones are moderate or large or the blood ketone level is > 1.0 mmol/L. Extra shots of Humalog/NovoLog/ Apidra or Regular insulin are then given to reverse the ketones before DKA occurs. In one period we had only six cases of DKA among 1,200 families in 12 months! Stopping ketone formation early reduces the likelihood of a case of DKA resulting in cerebral edema. It is better to prevent DKA than to deal with its bad effects. Unfortunately, cerebral edema is more common in newly diagnosed children when the ketones have built up over a longer time period.

Q **Our son has had diabetes for over two years. Every time he has gotten sick we have checked for urine ketones. The results have always been negative or trace. Can we stop checking now?**

A **The answer is NO!** This is often the case for someone who still makes some of their own insulin and/or someone who is in excellent sugar control. The machinery (enzymes) for making ketones from fat are so completely turned off that they don't get turned on by the illness. Unfortunately, as your son's insulin production declines or he outgrows his remaining insulin production, he will probably suddenly have ketones with an illness. One never knows when this will occur. Thus, the only answer is to keep checking the urine ketones at least twice each day with each illness.

Chapter 16
Sick-Day and Surgery Management

H. Peter Chase, MD
Georgia Anna Koch, RN, BSN, CDE
David Maahs, MD, PhD

SICK-DAY MANAGEMENT

The purpose of this chapter is to discuss the essential steps to take when a person with diabetes becomes ill or undergoes surgery. In general, the person with well-controlled diabetes can be just as healthy as anyone who does not have diabetes. When a person with diabetes does become ill, more attention and effort needs to be given to their diabetes management. Otherwise there is a significant risk that the illness can become severe and require hospitalization. It is, therefore, extremely important for all persons with diabetes and their families to learn all there is to know about sick-day and surgery management.

WHAT YOU NEED TO KNOW

When you get sick, the first thing you must do is to get the information you need. This will help you decide if you need assistance from health professionals. They will usually want to know this information. Keep your book open to this page to remind you of the things to report when you phone. They are listed in Table 1 and discussed in the following text.

Present Problem: Vomiting, diarrhea, fever, cold, congestion and cough, earache, sore throat, stomachache, labored breathing, chest pain or other concerning discomforts. If vomiting or diarrhea is present, note the number of times and when the episodes happen. It is also important to note if there

TEACHING OBJECTIVES:

1. Discuss the information needed when the person with diabetes becomes ill.

2. Distinguish treatment plans for small, moderate and large ketones.

3. Indicate the appropriate time to call a healthcare provider for assistance with illness or planned surgery.

LEARNING OBJECTIVES:

Learners (parents, child, relative or self) will be able to:

1. List three areas of care that must receive special consideration when the person with diabetes is ill.

2. State treatment plans for small, moderate and large ketones.

3. Identify the appropriate time to call the healthcare provider for assistance with illness or planned surgery.

Table 1
Sick Day Guidelines
When calling a diabetes health provider please give:

1. Name and age of the person with diabetes about whom you are calling

2. About how long the person has had diabetes

3. Name of the diabetes doctor and when last seen

4. Present problem (see below)

5. Blood/CGM glucose results

6. Urine or blood ketone results

7. Injection or pump therapy

8. Time and dose of last insulin given

9. Any noticed weight loss

10. Other types and dosage of medications usually given

11. Phone number of the person calling

12. Phone number of the pharmacy where prescriptions can be called

have been any recent illnesses in other family members or close friends. This will help you decide if this is a similar illness.

Fever does not generally occur with diabetes-related problems. Fever is usually a sign of an infection. However, infections can be present without a fever. It is helpful to take the temperature before calling the diabetes care provider to discuss an illness. If a fever is present, it may be important to call your primary care provider. Sick people usually don't feel like doing much. If you are still active, it is usually a good sign.

Blood/CGM Glucose Values: As noted in the chapter on self blood sugar monitoring, you

must do even more blood sugars than usual on sick-days. Parents, spouses, or friends should know how to accurately measure blood sugars (or observe CGM values) in case you are feeling too sick. **THE BLOOD SUGAR LEVEL MUST ALWAYS BE DONE BEFORE CALLING YOUR DIABETES CARE PROVIDER.**

Ketones: DON'T FORGET, <u>URINE OR BLOOD KETONES MUST ALWAYS BE CHECKED PRIOR TO CALLING,</u> AND AT LEAST TWICE DAILY IF A PERSON DOESN'T FEEL WELL (see Table 2). This is necessary even if the blood sugar is normal! Ketones must always be checked if fasting blood/CGM glucose levels are > 240 mg/dL

(> 13.3 mmol/L). During the day, blood/CGM glucose levels that are above 300 mg/dL (> 16.7 mmol/L) two times in a row indicate a need to check ketones. However, **with an illness, ketones can be present even when the blood/CGM glucose level is lower.** Thus, be prepared to check ketones during an illness even though the blood/CGM glucose level is in range.

As discussed in Chapter 5, to check urine ketones, dip the beige end of the strip into a small amount of urine, shake off the excess urine, and time for **exactly 15 seconds**. Keep small paper cups in the bathroom to collect the urine sample. The urine can be left in the cup so that another person can confirm the results (and to make sure it was actually done). Always use a new strip for double checking results. If you are using the Ketostix in the bottle and not the individually foil-wrapped Ketostix strips (Chapter 5), make certain the bottle has not been opened for longer than six months. The strips in the Ketostix bottle lose their sensitivity six months after opening. Others check the blood ketone level (Chapter 5) using the Precision Xtra meter. **Remember to always check ketones before calling your diabetes care provider for help with sick-day management.**

Signs of low blood sugar or of acidosis: These conditions were discussed in Chapters 6 and 15, respectively. Deep, labored breathing or continual vomiting can be signs of acidosis. It is critical that a person with these symptoms be seen in an emergency room as soon as possible.

Eating and drinking: It is important to know how well the person is taking liquids and/or eating. Use a 1-liter water bottle to help keep track of how much liquid has been consumed. One way to determine if you are becoming dehydrated is to look at your tongue in the mirror. If the tongue is dry (dehydrated), intravenous fluids may need to be given in the emergency room. Be cautious with children five years old and younger as they can become dehydrated in 4-6 hours. If trips to the bathroom occur only 1-2 times per day or if there are half the usual number of diapers, call the healthcare provider immediately.

Insulin dosage: You should know the usual insulin dose and when it was last taken. Were any doses skipped or forgotten? Could the insulin have been in high heat or frozen and thus spoiled? Finally, if you have had a similar illness in the past, it is helpful for the doctor or nurse to know how much extra Humalog/NovoLog/Apidra or Regular insulin was given at that time. Did the dose seem to work? If the morning, noon or evening insulin dose has not yet been given and you have moderate or large ketones, call the diabetes care provider before you give the injection. Extra rapid-acting insulin will probably be needed.

Table 2
Most Important

🐾 **Always check ketones with any illness. Even if the blood sugar is low, check for ketones at least twice daily every day you are sick. Call your healthcare provider if urine ketones are moderate/large or blood ketones are above 1.0 mmol/L.**

🐾 **Always take some insulin. Never skip a dose entirely. Call your diabetes care provider if you don't know how much to take.**

🐾 **It is particularly important to check ketones if you vomit even ONCE! Ketones can cause vomiting. If you vomit more than three times, call your diabetes care provider.**

Fortunately, with use of basal insulin therapy (given as Lantus/Levemir or by pump) many people have their usual number of illnesses (approximately six per year) and do fine. They have less fear of low blood/CGM glucose levels from a peak insulin (NPH) when they can't eat. The basal insulin should be continued during the illness, although the dose may need to be adjusted.

Oral medications: If the person is taking Metformin (Glucophage) and having vomiting, diarrhea, difficulty breathing or any serious illness, **the Metformin must be stopped.** Call the healthcare provider AFTER checking the blood sugar and ketone levels.

Body weight: It is helpful to know the last weight from a clinic visit (within three months) and the present weight (if you have a scale). This will help the doctor choose the right amount of insulin and also know how much weight you may have lost.

CHANGING THE INSULIN DOSAGE FOR ILLNESS

It is important to remember that <u>SOME INSULIN MUST ALWAYS BE GIVEN EACH DAY</u> (Table 2). **You cannot skip taking at least some insulin just because you are sick and/or vomiting. Sometimes the basal insulin (by pump, Lantus or Levemir) is all that is needed.** During illness the body requires more energy to help fight the infection or virus. Hormones in the body other than insulin increase with illnesses and raise the blood/CGM glucose levels. More insulin is needed to allow the body to burn extra sugar for energy when the blood sugar is high. It is usually only the rapid-acting insulin that is increased. If the blood sugar is low, the rapid-acting insulin may instead be reduced or omitted. If using an insulin pump, a temporary basal rate increase or decrease may be helpful. Remember, even if the blood sugar is low during illness, ketones may still be present. Ketones are formed from the breakdown of fat to provide the body with the extra energy it needs during the illness. When this is the case, it is

important to eat carbohydrates to eliminate the formation of ketones. More insulin can be taken once the blood/CGM glucose level is back up.

When **vomiting** is occurring and the blood sugar is low or normal, sips of regular pop, sugar popsicles, honey or other "high-sugar" liquids may help raise the blood/CGM glucose levels. A low dose of glucagon (Chapter 6) may also help. Once the blood sugar is up, insulin is needed to stop ketone production (if ketones are still present). Table 3 gives other suggestions for the management of vomiting.

Supplemental Rapid-Acting (Humalog, NovoLog, Apidra) or Regular Insulin

🐾 If urine ketones are negative or small, or below 0.6 mmol/L in the blood, extra insulin can be based on the blood sugar level alone. Most people have a "correction factor" for high blood/CGM glucose levels already established (Chapter 22). If not, a common formula is to give 1 unit of rapid-acting insulin for every 50 mg/dL (2.8 mmol/L) of blood sugar above 150 mg/dL (8.3 mmol/L).

🐾 If urine ketones are moderate or large, or above 1.0 mmol/L in the blood, and the blood/CGM glucose level is high, then double the dose calculated above.

🐾 Another way to calculate the rapid-acting insulin dose is to give an additional 10 percent of the total daily insulin dose for moderate urine ketones (or for 0.6-1.5 mmol/L blood ketones). For large urine ketones (or > 1.5 mmol/L blood ketones), give an additional 20 percent of the total daily insulin dose.

These dosages are in addition to your usual daily dose. When possible, you should call the diabetes specialist to get help with the dose. **You will need to repeat the giving of rapid-acting insulin every 2 hours if moderate or large urine ketones are still present (or blood ketones above 1.0 mmol/L).** We do not generally give extra insulin for elevated blood or urine ketones *unless* the blood sugar is at least

150 mg/dL (8.3 mmol/L). If the glucose level is lower than that, it may be necessary to first give sips of a high sugar drink, glucose tablets, honey or other high-sugar-containing foods.

GENERAL GUIDELINES: SICK-DAY MANAGEMENT

To review, the body requires more energy during an illness. More insulin allows more sugar to pass into cells, providing more energy to fight infection. **Some insulin is always needed.**

Important things to remember are:

- **Ketones:** Always check for ketones if you feel ill. Always check for ketones if the blood/CGM glucose level is over 240 mg/dL (> 13.3 mmol/L) fasting or over 300 mg/dL (> 16.7 mmol/L) two times in a row during the day.

- **Vomiting:** If you are vomiting and have a low blood sugar, an insulin reaction could occur. At the same time, you may have ketones. Always check for ketones if you are vomiting. Vomiting may be due to an infection, a virus, or due to ketones. Management of vomiting is outlined in Table 3.

- **Insulin:** Keep a bottle of rapid-acting insulin available even if you don't usually use it. You may need to give it during an illness. Be sure it is not outdated.

- **Blood Sugar Levels:** All people with diabetes must have some method of blood sugar monitoring available and be ready to do extra values on sick-days (usually every 2-4 hours). More frequent monitoring of blood sugar and ketones has greatly reduced the need for hospitalizations. The Figure 1 suggests amounts of water versus sugar fluids to give based on the blood/CGM glucose levels.

- **Extra Snacks:** It is important to take in adequate calories on sick-days or the body will start to break down fat for energy. If

this happens, ketones will appear in the urine (see Chapter 15). Sugary soft drinks, popsicles and non-diet JELL-O are good to eat if you do not feel like eating food and your blood sugar is below 180 mg/dL (< 10.0 mmol/L). Much of eating is psychological and we often suggest you eat whatever you feel like eating on sick-days! Also see Table 4.

- **Past Experience:** Base your judgments on past experience. Refer to your record book to see if this illness has occurred before. See what worked in the past, and what didn't.

- **Which Doctor to call:** Call your family doctor for non-diabetes related problems such as sore throats, earaches, fever, rashes, etc. Unless the diabetes specialist also provides general care, only call him/her if the urine ketones are moderate/large or if the blood ketone level is above 1.0 mmol/L. Also call if you need help with an insulin dose, if hypoglycemia is a problem or if you need help with other parts of diabetes management.

Table 3
Management of Vomiting (Negative Ketones)

🐾 Avoid solid foods until the vomiting has stopped.

🐾 If vomiting is frequent, many physicians recommend giving oral Zofran or a Phenergan suppository (or patch) to reduce vomiting and waiting to give fluids for an hour until the medicine is working. For teens or others who do not like suppositories, Phenergan gel can be applied to the skin. The gel requires composition by a Prescription Compounding Center of America (or equivalent). The usual dose for a teen is 50 mg in 1cc. The gel is rubbed into the skin while wearing a rubber glove, and is then covered with plastic wrap. Preteens usually get 25 mg (1/2 cc). The dose can be repeated in four hours. The main side effect of the Phenergan is sleepiness.

🐾 Other physicians will order an oral tablet called Zofran, which dissolves in the mouth. Sometimes the blood sugar can be low (< 60 mg/dL or < 3.3 mmol/L) and the person cannot keep any food down. Glucagon can be mixed (Chapter 6) and given just like insulin – using an insulin syringe. The dose is one unit per year of age up to a maximum of 15 units. If the blood sugar is not higher in 20-30 minutes, the same dose can be repeated.

🐾 Gradually start liquids (sugar pop [soda], juice, Pedialyte, water, etc.) in small amounts. Juices (especially orange) replace the salts that are lost with vomiting or diarrhea. Pedialyte popsicles are also available. Start with a tablespoon of liquid every 10-20 minutes. If the blood sugar is below 100 mg/dL (< 5.5 mmol/L), sugar pop can be given. For the child five years of age and over, sucking on a piece of hard candy often works well. If the blood sugar is above 180 mg/dL (> 10.0 mmol/L), do not give pop with sugar in it. If there is no further vomiting, gradually increase the amount of fluid. If vomiting restarts, it may again be necessary to rest the stomach for another hour and then restart the small amounts of fluids. A repeat suppository or topical Phenergan dose can be given after three or four hours. Dairy products should not be used until the person is able to drink fluids and eat crackers and soup without vomiting.

🐾 After a few hours without vomiting, gradually return to a normal diet. Soups are often good to start with and they provide needed nutrients.

Figure 1
Sick-Day Fluids Based on Blood Sugar (B.S.) Levels

IF: B.S. <150
✔ Check B.S. every 1-2 hours
✔ Check ketones
✔ Give 1-oz fluid per year of age per hour:

¼ WATER

& ¾ SUGAR FLUIDS

NO EXTRA INSULIN

IF: B.S. 150-250
✔ Check B.S. every 2-3 hours
✔ Check ketones
✔ Give 1-oz fluid per year of age per hour:

½ WATER

& ½ SUGAR FLUIDS

MAY NEED EXTRA INSULIN

IF: B.S. >250
✔ Check B.S. every 2 hours
✔ Check ketones
✔ Give 1-oz fluid per year of age per hour:

¾ WATER

& ¼ SUGAR FLUIDS

EXTRA INSULIN USUALLY NEEDED

Table 4

Sick-Day Foods

1. **Liquids (In addition to water – particularly if the blood sugar is below 180 mg/dL [10.0 mmol/L]):**

   🐾 Sugar-containing beverages: regular 7-Up, ginger ale, orange, cola, PEPSI®, etc.[1]

   🐾 Pedialyte or Infalyte® (especially for younger children)

   🐾 Sports drinks: Gatorade®, POWERADE®, etc. (any flavor)

   🐾 Tea with honey or sugar[1]

   🐾 Fruit flavored drinks: regular Kool-Aid, lemonade, Hi-C® [1], etc.

   🐾 Fruit juice: apple, cranberry, grape, grapefruit, orange, pineapple, etc.

   🐾 JELL-O: regular (for infants, liquid JELL-O warmed in a bottle) or diet[1]

   🐾 Popsicles: regular or diet[1]

   🐾 Broth-type soup: bouillon, chicken noodle soup, Cup-a-Soup®

2. **Solids (when ready) – good foods with which to start:**

   🐾 Saltine crackers

   🐾 Banana (or other fruit)

   🐾 Applesauce

   🐾 Bread, toast or tortillas

   🐾 Graham crackers

   🐾 Soup

   🐾 Rice

[1] *Sugar-free may be needed depending on blood sugars (e.g., > 180 mg/dL [> 10.0 mmol/L])*

FLUID REPLACEMENT

If you have difficulty eating or keeping food down and the blood/CGM glucose level is below 180 mg/dL (< 10.0 mmol/L), take sugar-containing liquids (see Table 4). These may include fruit juices, popsicles, slushies, tea with sugar or honey, broth, syrup from canned fruit or even regular pop. Stir the pop to get rid of bubbles and prevent indigestion. If you are vomiting take a small amount (juice glass size or less) of sugar pop after you vomit. If it stays down 15 minutes, some sugar will be absorbed. If there is no vomiting after ½ hour, increase the amount of fluids. If you have ketones and are not vomiting, keep drinking. Children should receive one ounce of fluid per year of age per hour up to age 16 years. Older teens can consume two cups per hour. The liquids help to prevent dehydration and also to "wash out" the ketones. Specific instructions regarding vomiting are given in Table 3.

A LOW DOSE OF GLUCAGON

Sometimes during illness the blood sugar can be low (< 60 mg/dL [< 3.3 mmol/L]) and the person is unable keep any food down. To elevate the blood sugar level, glucagon can be mixed and given just like insulin. Prepare the glucagon as usual and, using an insulin syringe, measure one unit per year of age. The

Table 5
Sick-Day Management: When to Call for Emergency Care

🐾 If you have vomited more than three times and can keep nothing in your stomach, and urine or blood ketones are not elevated, call your primary care physician. If help is needed with an insulin dose, call your diabetes care provider.

🐾 If moderate or large urine ketones or blood ketones (above 1.0 mmol/L) are present, call your diabetes care provider.

🐾 If you have difficulty breathing or have "deep breathing," you need to go to an emergency room. This usually indicates severe acidosis (ketoacidosis; Chapter 15).

🐾 If there is any unusual behavior such as confusion, slurred speech, double vision, inability to move or talk or jerking, someone should give sugar or instant glucose. (Glucagon [Chapter 6] must be given if the person is unconscious or if a convulsion [seizure] occurs.) The healthcare provider should be contacted if a severe reaction occurs. In case of a convulsion or loss of consciousness, it may be necessary to call the paramedics or to go to an emergency room. Have an emergency number posted by the phone.

maximum dose should be no more than 15 units even for adults.

For example:

a five-year-old child would get five units of glucagon

a 10-year-old child would get 10 units of glucagon

If the blood sugar has not risen to at least 90 mg/dL (5.0 mmol/L) in 20-30 minutes, the same dose can be repeated. This treatment has saved many ER visits for our clinic patients.

FOODS FOR SICK-DAYS

Table 4 suggests carbohydrate-containing foods that might be tried during an illness. Eating carbohydrates is important to provide energy and to prevent the body from breaking down fats (and thus making ketones). Drinking liquids is important to prevent dehydration, so liquids are usually tried first. A general rule of thumb is to offer whatever you/your child like(s) best. You may want to have a "sick-day kit" on hand which could include items such as sugar-containing 7-UP, sports drinks, regular and diet JELL-O or pudding, apple juice in small cans, regular Kool-Aid mix, Cup-a-Soup,

Pedialyte and any other items you would like to have available.

EXERCISE

The person with moderate or large urine ketones or blood ketones above 0.6 mmol/L should not exercise. Fat and muscle can be broken down during exercise, further increasing ketone levels.

CONTACTING YOUR DOCTOR OR NURSE

Keep a card with your doctor's and nurse's emergency phone numbers in a place where you can easily find it. Also be sure to have the doctor's emergency phone number for nighttime or weekend calls. Take these cards with you if you are going out of town. It is easier to call your own doctor rather than to go to an emergency room and see a new doctor.

Think ahead! You may want to keep Zofran or Phenergan or other medicines on hand in case of vomiting. Before you call the doctor or nurse, be sure you have the necessary information (see the list at the beginning of the chapter). **Always check the blood sugar and urine or blood**

ketones before calling. Have the number of your pharmacy available in case the doctor needs it. Table 5 tells when to call or get emergency care. Remember to keep sugar pop, popsicles and soups available for illnesses.

CLINIC OR EMERGENCY ROOM VISITS

If you do decide to go to a clinic or emergency room, remember to take your hospital card if you have one, your diabetes records and your insurance information. Take extra clothes in case you must be admitted to the hospital. A relative or friend going with you will need money for food, telephone numbers of people they might need to call, and something to read.

SICK-DAY MEDICATIONS

Our general philosophy is that **if you need a medicine for an illness, take it!** The diabetes health profession will handle the problems related to diabetes. The classic example is asthma. With a bad attack, the person may need medicines which raise the blood sugar. Oral steroids (cortisone) may also be needed which raise the blood sugar. For the short time that these medicines are needed, extra insulin can be taken to help control the blood/CGM glucose levels. Short-term elevations of blood sugar are not what we worry about in relation to the complications of diabetes.

Over-the-counter medications can be purchased with care. Look at the label to see if sugar is added. Tablets are less likely to have sugar (and alcohol) than are liquids. Again, the small amount of sugar in a medicine taken for a short time is okay. *We do not endorse any products and suggest you discuss these with your primary care physician:*

Generic daytime/nighttime cold capsules: Are fine to use in children old enough to swallow the capsules. The capsules are alcohol-free and don't have an after-taste as do liquids.

Nasal sprays (e.g., Afrin®): Can be used for colds and allergies. A nasal spray is less likely to affect the entire body than pills or liquid medicines. If these do not work, or if long-term

---

Table 6
Guidelines for Management Around Surgery

- Always contact your diabetes care provider if surgery is planned – AFTER you find out the time and whether normal food intake will be allowed. You may wish to give the name and phone number of the diabetes care provider to the person doing the surgery.

- Plan to take your own blood sugar and ketone checking equipment.

- Take your own materials to treat low blood sugar (a source of instant glucose and even glucagon).

- Always check the ketones prior to surgery. Then, if they are present at a later time, it will be known that they were negative earlier. If the urine ketones are found to be moderate or large or the blood ketones above 1.0 mmol/L, it may be necessary to cancel the planned procedure. Take the ketone strips with you to the procedure in case vomiting occurs and you need to do a check. It is also wise to check ketones once or twice after the procedure.

- Take your diabetes clinic's phone card so that you may quickly call the diabetes care provider if needed.

- If on basal insulin therapy (Lantus/Levemir or a pump), it is best to continue insulin in this way during the surgery. Often no other insulin is needed.

use is anticipated (as with seasonal allergies), antihistamine tablets or liquids such as Chlor-trimeton® or Triaminic® might be tried next.

Acetaminophen (TYLENOL®) or Ibuprofen: To relieve fever if a flu is going through the community. Do not give aspirin to children or adolescents.

Pepto-Bismol®, Kaopectate® or Imodium AD®: These are fine to use for diarrhea. (Lomotil® should NOT be used in children).

DI-GEL®, MYLANTA®, Gelusil® and Maalox®: These are all sugar-free antacids.

Cough medications: Use a cold air vaporizer if this relieves the cough. During the day, a cough is often protective, keeping material out of the lungs. Thus, we do not give cough medicines. If the vaporizer does not stop the cough at night, use sugar-free cough medicines with less than 15 percent alcohol. Examples: Colrex Expectorant®, CONTAC Jr.®, Hytuss Tablets®, Queltuss Tablets®, Robitussin CF® liquid, Supercitin®, Tolu-Sed®, Tolu-Sed DM®, Tussar-SF®. Remember, a combined cough and fever means the child should be seen by the primary care physician.

Sore Throats: A throat culture to rule out a streptococcal (strep) infection should be considered because strep can lead to rheumatic fever or other problems. Salt water gargles (¼ teaspoon salt in one glass water) may help. Chloraseptic Spray® is sugar-free, as are Cepacol®, Cepastat®, Chloraseptic® mouthwashes or lozenges and N'ICE® lozenges.

FOLLOW THE DIRECTIONS ON THE LABEL FOR ANY MEDICINE YOU USE.

FLU SHOTS

The method of preparing the flu vaccine has improved so that side effects are now less likely. **The American Academy of Pediatrics recommends flu shots for all children with diabetes, and we agree.** Preventing an episode of flu may prevent an episode of ketoacidosis. It is common for the flu (and other illnesses) to raise the HbA1c level by one-half to one point. It is important to get the flu shot early in the fall so it can be working when the flu season begins.

SURGERY MANAGEMENT

Some general guidelines for diabetes management around surgery are outlined in Table 6. The insulin dose may not change if the person is receiving a basal insulin (Lantus/Levemir or an insulin pump). If NPH is taken in the morning for someone also receiving Lantus or Levemir, the NPH (or boluses of rapid-acting insulin) is often omitted. Any change in insulin dose depends on the person, the type of surgery that is scheduled and the time of day the surgery is to be done. If possible, surgery should be scheduled early in the morning. In general, it is best to call your diabetes care provider and discuss insulin changes **after** you find out the time of day the procedure is to be done and whether or not food intake will be limited. Sometimes it is also helpful to have the surgeon or anesthesiologist call the diabetes care provider. This is more likely to be done if the family gives the doctor or dentist a note with the name and phone number of the diabetes specialist. The two of them can then work out the best time for a given person for surgery.

We frequently receive calls from families related to planned dental surgery. Often this can be done under local anesthesia, and sometimes the person can eat regular meals prior to and after the surgery. In this situation it is only necessary to reduce the insulin dose slightly in anticipation of some reduction in food intake due to soreness in the mouth.

If the person is going to have a general anesthetic, eating is usually restricted to prevent vomiting during recovery. Anytime the amount of food intake is to change, the amount of insulin to be given must also be changed. Often the basal insulin (Lantus/Levemir or pump basal dose) is not changed. The peak-insulins (NPH and rapid-acting insulins) are either reduced or omitted with the reduced food intake. Pumps can be very useful, but require a knowledgeable person to supervise. If the person is going to have a general anesthetic in the hospital, some doctors prefer to give all of the insulin by intravenous infusion. Any of these methods work. **The important thing is the close monitoring of blood sugars! By doing this, low blood sugars can be prevented. It is also wise to check the urine or blood ketones before and after the procedure.** These may increase with changes in the insulin dose and with the stress of surgery. Needless to say, your diabetes care provider must always be notified if the urine ketones are moderate or large or the blood ketones are above 1.0 mmol/L following surgery.

Blood sugar monitoring is usually the responsibility of the parent or the patient when procedures are done in the dentist's or doctor's office. If a meter is used for blood sugar monitoring at home, this should be taken along to the dentist's or doctor's office. If the child is being admitted to the hospital, also take the meter along. If the child is to have a general anesthetic, the blood sugar monitoring is the responsibility of the doctor giving the anesthesia or the doctor doing the surgery. Sometimes the doctor orders dextrose, which is glucose (sugar), to be added to the intravenous fluids if the blood sugar is below a certain level (200 mg/dL or 11.1 mmol/L is a safe level to use). This may result in elevated blood sugar levels. Blood sugars are usually measured at regular intervals by the doctor or nurse.

It is also wise to take along urine or blood ketone checking strips. Many doctors or nurses who do not care for people with diabetes on a regular basis may forget the importance of routinely checking for ketones. Also take your diabetes care provider's phone numbers with you. If urine ketones are moderate or large, or the blood ketones are above 1.0 mmol/L, you may wish to call your diabetes care provider.

DEFINITIONS

Anesthetic (anesthesia): A medication (such as ether) used to reduce pain or to allow a person to sleep through an otherwise painful procedure.

Dextrose: The name for glucose (sugar) added to an intravenous (IV) feeding to prevent low blood sugar.

Suppository: A medication inserted into the rectum (bottom), usually because liquid, food or medicine cannot be kept down (as with vomiting).

QUESTIONS AND ANSWERS FROM NEWSNOTES

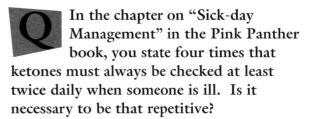

Q In the chapter on "Sick-day Management" in the Pink Panther book, you state four times that ketones must always be checked at least twice daily when someone is ill. Is it necessary to be that repetitive?

A Forgetting to check ketones with an illness is one of the most common errors families make in managing diabetes. As a result, ketones can build up to high levels in the body, which can then be dangerous (and expensive to treat). There is no charge for a few phone calls to a diabetes care provider to receive suggestions for supplemental rapid-acting insulin to combat early ketone formation. In contrast, the charge is greater than $5,000-$10,000 for one or two nights in an intensive care unit as a result of large ketones building up in the body. As pointed out at the end of Chapter 15 on Acidosis (Ketoacidosis), this charge and the related risk from ketoacidosis can be avoided if families will just check for ketones immediately (and at least twice daily) when the person with diabetes is ill. The diabetes care provider must then be called when moderate or large ketones are detected, or the blood ketone level is above 1.0 mmol/L, and every 2-3 hours thereafter until the ketones are below these levels.

Q Should flu shots be given to children with diabetes?

A The American Academy of Pediatrics recommends flu shots for all children with diabetes. Flu is a common cause of ketonuria and of acidosis, so the shots may also help prevent ketoacidosis (and an increase in the HbA1c level). If you do decide to get them for your child, we would prefer that you go to your primary care physician for this purpose. Call first to make sure the doctor's office has the vaccine. If a young child has not previously received the flu vaccine, it may be necessary to get it in two injections, approximately one month apart, and it is best to start during the months of September or October.

Q Should my child receive the chicken pox vaccination?

A Yes, if he or she has not had chicken pox! It is recommended by the American Academy of Pediatrics for all children who have not had prior chicken pox infections, and we support that recommendation. There is an additional factor for children with diabetes who still produce some insulin. Chicken pox is probably one of the many infections that stimulate white blood cells in the pancreas to make toxic particles that cause further islet destruction. This is not proven, but we have heard many times of children being diagnosed with diabetes in the month or two after having chicken pox.

The Varivax is a live vaccine. The main side effects are a mild rash (approximately three percent), and/or a temperature elevation (approximately 15 percent) and/or tenderness at the site (approximately 19 percent). Ninety-nine percent of people are protected as a result of the vaccination.

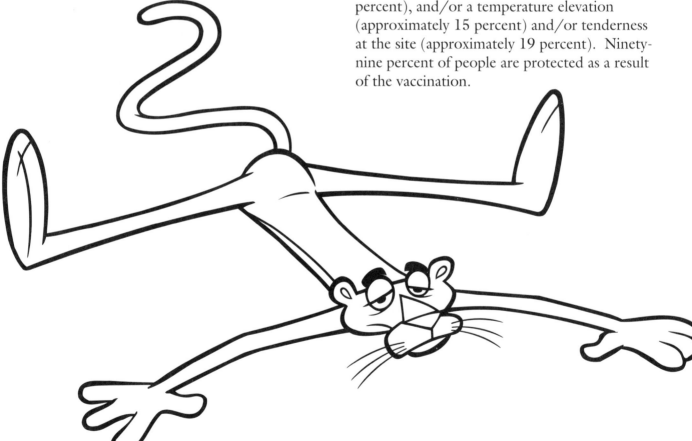

Always remember to check ketones when sick!

Chapter 17
Family Concerns

TEACHING OBJECTIVES:

1. Describe extra stresses which a person/family may experience as a result of diabetes.

2. Provide healthy coping strategies for individual/family stress.

LEARNING OBJECTIVES:

Learners (parents, child, relative or self) will be able to:

1. Identify the stresses experienced by the person/family with diabetes.

2. Describe a healthy coping strategy for an identified stress.

WORKING AS A FAMILY

The challenges a person or a family may have following the initial diagnosis of diabetes include more demands on their time, money and energy. This is due to the daily routine of the diabetes management and the regular clinic visits. Parents and families must decide how to fairly share these new responsibilities. We encourage **both** the mother and father to share the responsibility for the diabetes care of their child. This should include giving the insulin injections. It is important for the parents to support one another. Both parents should also try to attend all clinic visits.

Diabetes affects the entire family. The family must work together to solve problems and manage the diabetes. Research has shown that children and individuals do best with strong family support and involvement.

SINGLE-PARENT/ BLENDED FAMILIES

Approximately one-third of children in the U.S. now live in single-parent families. For children who live in two households, it is important to share vital diabetes information between the households. We emphasize at the first visit that parents in two households must communicate about their child's diabetes care. The adults at this visit are all there because they love the child. This must be the focus.

This information to be shared includes:

✔ blood sugar levels

✔ recent low blood sugars

✔ insulin dosages and recent changes

- ✔ food intake
- ✔ exercise
- ✔ illnesses
- ✔ other items/events which may effect diabetes management

GOOD COMMUNICATION AND COOPERATION ARE ESSENTIAL

Some suggestions for two households are:

- ✔ diabetes supplies can be neatly packed in a carrying case to go with the child between households

- ✔ keep a vial of glucagon and some foil-wrapped urine ketone strips permanently in each household

- ✔ keep a **current** log book with insulin doses and blood sugar results to ensure consistency from household to household

- ✔ remember that the care of the child is the most important thing. Try to put individual differences and conflicts aside and focus on helping the child make a healthy adjustment to life with diabetes.

LEADING A NORMAL LIFE

Diabetes care has changed tremendously over the past 20 years. New insulins, insulin pens, blood glucose meters, insulin pumps and continuous glucose monitors (CGMs) have all been made available. The added flexibility with meal planning and insulin dosing make it easier for children or adults to live normal, healthy and active lives. It is important for them to do so. Though there may be many new worries, it is possible to normalize one's life with diabetes!

For children, leading a normal life means participating in age-appropriate activities with their family and peers. There is no question; diabetes can make fun things like sleepovers and birthday parties a little more stressful. But with a little flexibility and creativity, children with diabetes are able to participate in these activities just like their siblings or friends. When in

doubt about allowing your child to take part in an activity, ask yourself, "Would I let my child participate if he/she did not have diabetes?" If the answer is "yes," it should not change because of the diabetes. If you are uncertain, contact your care provider so they can help you create a plan for the activity.

The issue of discipline and diabetes is also an important aspect of leading a normal life. Whether your child has diabetes or not, there will be times when he/she will test limits and act up. Children with diabetes need limits set like any other child. Sometimes it is hard to tell if your child is being difficult because he/she is "acting like a teenager" (or "a toddler") or because their blood sugar is low. When in doubt, check the blood/CGM glucose values and then deal appropriately with the behavior.

Care providers, parents and children need to strike a balance between optimal diabetes control and an emotionally healthy lifestyle. It is important for all of us to work as a team so that young people with diabetes can grow and develop physically and emotionally.

CONCERNS OF BROTHERS AND SISTERS

When a child first develops diabetes, it is a crisis for the whole family. Often brothers and sisters feel left out. This is because so much attention is given to the child with diabetes.

Some common concerns may be:

- ✔ trouble understanding what diabetes is
- ✔ fearing that their brother or sister will die
- ✔ thinking they caused the diabetes by having an angry thought against the child with diabetes
- ✔ fearing that they will be the next to be diagnosed

Important things for the brothers and/or sisters:

- ✔ to be a part of the beginning education
- ✔ young children will feel less frightened if they can visit the hospital or clinic

✔ asking the children what they think and understand, even if you think everything has been thoroughly explained. *One child used the word "diabetes" very literally. When asked why he was so <u>very</u> sad, he said he thought diabetes meant "die of betes."*

✔ discipline should not be different for their brother or sister with diabetes than it is for them

✔ all children in a family should be treated in a similar way. *One sister said she eats a candy bar in front of her brother with diabetes when he gets away with something. She said, "That's how I get even with him."*

✔ it is important to plan individual time and special activities with all children in a family

Some children with diabetes have the opportunity for group activities such as diabetes camp and ski trips. Many brothers and sisters say, "I wish I had diabetes so I could do special things, too." A family can prevent future stress if siblings understand that these activities need special medical care. Make sure the sibling without diabetes gets their special time too.

FAMILY STRESS

The diagnosis of any serious condition, especially in children and teens, is stressful for the whole family (including the extended family). Getting through the initial shock and grief that comes with the diagnosis is difficult. This can be especially hard if families have had medical or other serious problems to manage. Parents usually have different coping styles around grief. It is normal that some family members find they are less patient or even irritable with one another for a period after the diagnosis. These feelings usually resolve as everyone adjusts and begins to feel more comfortable managing the diabetes.

When grief or conflict <u>does not</u> get better, this can obviously be stressful for parents and for the whole family.

The crisis of diagnosis can bring up many fears and feelings, and:

✔ an individual can become quite anxious or depressed

✔ parents or significant others may feel the strain on the relationship with one another. It is particularly important to seek help to try to be understanding and to get the support that is needed.

✔ children and teens can sense tension between parents and may feel responsible for something they can't help

Talking with the psychosocial member of your diabetes team can be helpful in sorting out these problems.

PROMOTING A HEALTHY DIET

When a child is diagnosed with diabetes, one of the first things that parents often wonder about is how their diet will change. Many people still believe sugar is what causes diabetes and think they will need to have a sugar-restricted diet for their child with diabetes. We now know that eating a healthy diet is important for everyone. Americans already eat more added sugar than is recommended and this contributes to too much weight gain. Diabetes education teaches families about carbohydrates (sugars and starches) and how they affect blood/CGM glucose levels. It is important that everyone in the family try to support one another by selecting healthy foods and snacks.

If possible, foods in the home should not be restricted from the child with diabetes. If too many high carbohydrate, sweet foods and drinks are available in the home, they are hard for anyone to resist, let alone the child with diabetes. Too much of this "junk food" is a major health problem in our country. When parents can, it is important to look at how everyone in the family eats and how they can make healthy changes and limit the amount of "junk food" available.

A healthy diet includes foods from all food groups in appropriate amounts. It is permissible to include some sweets as a part of a healthy diet. Fresh fruit and frozen yogurt are good examples of treats that can provide both nutrition and great taste! With or without diabetes, one should not consume sweets and special treats in excess! When diabetes is part of the picture, the appropriate insulin dose must be given/taken for carbohydrates (including sweets) that are consumed. Trying to avoid all sweet foods may create undue focus on food restriction. Healthy sweet treats may be allowed as a part of a healthy family diet. When in doubt, please consult with the diabetes dietitian.

DEALING WITH STRESS AND EXCITEMENT

Emotions and stress may have a big effect on diabetes control. *Many different life events can cause stress such as:*

✔ family problems

✔ arguments with parents or between parents

✔ parent separation or divorce

✔ death of a relative, friend or pet

✔ a move to a new home or school

Other kinds of stressful situations include special events such as:

✔ athletic competitions

✔ school exams

✔ holidays like birthdays, Christmas or Hanukkah

Most people will have high sugars following stress, though some children can have low sugars because of extra activity. It is important to think ahead and to reduce the insulin dose or give extra food. It is also important to monitor blood/CGM glucose levels more frequently to prevent low blood sugars on days of excitement.

The diagram in Chapter 14 on Diabetes and Blood/CGM Glucose Control shows how the insulin dose, oral medicine dose, diet, exercise and stress must be in balance for optimal sugar control. Sometimes, despite our best efforts, blood/CGM glucose levels just don't behave the way we expect! But it helps to keep working at it.

NEEDLE ANXIETY (FEAR OF SHOTS)

It is now known that needle anxiety of some degree occurs in almost everyone. Both children and adults have worries about shots. In a person with diabetes, it used to be assumed that this anxiety would just go away because they had to have shots every day. We now know that needle anxiety, if strong, doesn't "just go away." There are some things that can be learned to reduce this anxiety if identified as a problem.

First of all, anxiety about shots is normal. When we fear something, we get tense and tend to hold our breath. Our head is filled with thoughts about pain. Parents who have to give these shots can be just as needle anxious as their child. Remember, the syringes that are now used for insulin are much smaller and have shorter needles so that shots are much more comfortable these days. With a few easy techniques, shots can be less stressful. Most diabetes educators have parents or significant others practice injections on each other using saline (sterile saltwater). The practice nearly always reassures them that giving insulin injections to their child is not the trauma they imagine.

Tensing can make shots hurt. So take a couple of deep relaxing breaths ("breathe in through the nose and breathe slowly out the mouth") and try to imagine yourself made of Jell-O. By relaxing the tension, shots can be done more comfortably. Sometimes a little distraction can help refocus the mind from fear to something else. Watching cartoons or listening to some favorite music with headphones can help keep the person from thinking too much about the shot and may aid in relaxation.

Sometimes a person with diabetes doesn't get over their stress about shots. *A few symptoms that might indicate this is going on are:*

✔ persistently high HbA1c

✔ a child wanting to do <u>all</u> their own shots – particularly when they want to do the shot in a room by themselves (some shots will probably be missed)

✔ lack of site rotation (hypertrophy or swelling of the injection site)

✔ missed insulin shots

✔ excuses for wanting to "put off" the shot (stalling)

✔ parental fear or worry about injections or blood draws

The psychosocial member of the team can be very helpful to children or parents with sorting out this problem. Treatment can include behavioral techniques and purposeful distraction. The latter includes TV, music, toys, blowing bubbles and books. Sometimes injection devices help the problem (Inject-Ease, I-Port, Insuflon: Chapter 9) though they do not "cure" it. Behavioral techniques include learning to relax, stickers on a calendar, reward programs, systematic desensitization and biofeedback. As fear of shots, blood or injury decreases, the HbA1c usually improves.

PSYCHOLOGICAL DISORDERS

Families need to be aware of two types of psychological disorders that have been described in people with diabetes. The first is **depression** and the second is **eating disorders**.

Depression: Depression (defined in Definitions at the back of this chapter) is one mood disorder that may be more common in older teens and adults with diabetes than in the general population.

Symptoms include:

✔ change in sleep habits

✔ change in appetite or weight

✔ decline in school or work performance

✔ irritability or sadness

✔ isolation

✔ lack of pleasure in things

✔ decreased energy

If you see such changes, it is wise to seek professional help from your diabetes team or a mental health provider. *Be aware that depression can affect diabetes care in the following ways:*

✔ high blood sugar values/high HbA1c level due to not following treatment plans

✔ irritability around doing blood sugars or getting shots

✔ decreased energy

✔ not caring about daily diabetes tasks

If left untreated, depression can lead to long term poor diabetes control and complications. Treatment of depression and other mood disorders can be very effective these days with a combination of counseling and medications (usually antidepressants). Please ask your primary care physician or diabetes team for recommendations and referrals.

Eating disorders: *The most common types of eating disorders are explained below:*

✔ *Anorexia* usually involves limiting food intake and often engaging in excessive exercise. The goal of these people is to lose weight and maintain unrealistic and unhealthy weight loss. This can become life threatening.

✔ *Bulimia* is defined by excessive intake of food and self-induced vomiting, use of laxatives and/or excessive exercise. This is a very risky form of weight loss or weight maintenance.

Both of these conditions can result in low blood/CGM glucose levels. Many people are not aware of an additional form of eating disorder specific to people who have diabetes.

✔ *Insulin omission.* Some people *miss shots* or *underdose their insulin* to achieve weight control. This is a particularly dangerous form of eating disorder because it leads to chronic poor control and can result in DKA (diabetes ketoacidosis). *The effects of missing insulin doses include the following:*

- The calories consumed go out in the urine rather than into the body. Blood/CGM glucose levels are very high.

- If left untreated, chronic complications (Chapter 23) are more likely.

- Blood/CGM glucose levels sometimes become very erratic. This may mean the person is alternating between restricting food (with low sugars) or binging (with high sugars). It may also mean the person oscillates between taking or not taking the correct insulin dosage.

✔ *Binge eating* is the fourth type of eating disorder. People who binge eat often skip meals during the day and eat excessively at night. It is most frequently associated with type 2 diabetes.

Any of these disorders can be very dangerous for a person with diabetes. They require immediate psychological care from a professional with expertise in this area and who understands diabetes. A healthy body image is important and a healthy body is essential.

CHANGING BEHAVIOR

Sometimes people with diabetes have difficulty with their insulin injections, blood/CGM glucose determinations, the suggested diet, the recommended exercise or other parts of diabetes management. These "problems" can be opportunities to assess what is bothering a child, teenager or adult. At these times it may be very helpful to meet with the clinical social worker or psychologist who specializes in working with people with diabetes. They can help evaluate problems and suggest ways to effect change. Behavioral change takes time, patience and usually requires help from the whole family. A few visits can often be very helpful to the patient and the family.

SCHOOL OR WORK ATTENDANCE

People with diabetes generally shouldn't have more school or work absences for illness. They may have to miss school or work occasionally for routine clinic visits. If a lot of school/work is being missed for diabetes-related reasons, it is very important to review this with the medical team. Working together, the underlying cause can be found. With optimal blood sugar control, there is no reason why people should not participate fully in activities of their choice. However, they may have other concerns that contribute to missing school or work. These concerns should be examined and addressed as soon as possible.

If school or work is missed for a period of time due to illness or hospitalization, the person may be worried about returning. It is not uncommon for the diabetes to remain in suboptimal control when a person is worried about unfinished work, exams, fellow students, teachers, co-workers or other problems.

If a significant amount of school or work has been missed the following can be helpful:

✔ Encouraging the person to return to school or work as soon as possible.

✔ Asking members of the diabetes team to help coordinate matters with the school or work. Sometimes a person may fear how peers or co-workers will treat him/her.

✔ Talking with the school counselor or teacher at school. They can assist in arranging a schedule and homework after a long absence.

✔ Arranging for a nurse educator or parent to talk to the class about diabetes. It allows for the development of good peer support and understanding.

DEFINITIONS

Clinical Social Worker: A person with a Master's degree in social work trained to help individuals or families with stress, emotional or behavioral problems, as well as problems with resources.

Psychologist: A person with a doctorate degree (PhD or PsyD) trained in helping people with behavior, stress or feelings that are causing problems or discomfort.

Psychiatrist: A physician who specializes in psychiatric medicine and may be helpful in diagnosing and prescribing medications for mood disorders and attention problems.

Stressors: Problems or events that make people feel worried, afraid, excited, upset or scared.

Depression: A mood state in which one may show sadness, self-depreciation, a lack of energy, and/or inability to do one's normal work or activity. A lack of interest in enjoyable activities, irritability or withdrawal from friends and family may also be present.

Eating disorder: *The most common types of eating disorders are:*

1. Anorexia: People with a distorted body image who limit their food intake and often exercise in excess to remain very thin.

2. Bulimia: People who eat excessively at times and then vomit (or take medicines such as laxatives) in order to not gain weight.

3. Binge-eating: People who intermittently eat excessively but do not vomit. They may gain excessive weight and develop type 2 diabetes.

4. Insulin omission: In a person with diabetes, skipping insulin shots or lowering doses to maintain or avoid weight gain. This is an extremely dangerous form of weight loss because of the risk of ketoacidosis.

QUESTIONS AND ANSWERS FROM NEWSNOTES

 What are the occupational restrictions for a person with diabetes?

 Restrictions are based on the idea that all people with diabetes are at a greater risk for hypoglycemia. There are studies which show hypoglycemia does result in an increased risk for accidents. In one study, approximately 10 percent of the accident reports in which the accident was due to a medical condition other than alcoholism were due to an insulin reaction (low glucose level).

Our opinion is that restrictions should not be generic and should be individualized. Some people monitor their blood/CGM glucose levels frequently and are careful to eat or make sure they are not low before driving a car. Others are less careful. Everyone pays the price from the latter group.

Currently, legal restrictions include working in the military, commercial truck driving and flying a passenger plane. Some state and local governments may also deny employment in the police or fire fighting forces, but this is changing. Most physicians also recommend that people who have frequent low blood sugars do not work at heights, operate heavy equipment or handle toxic substances. Working rotating shifts can also result in more difficulty with blood sugar control. Generally, if the rotations are on a monthly or greater basis, it is possible to alter the insulin dosage to cope. The use of the insulin pump or of Lantus/Levemir and short-acting insulin can be very effective in providing shift workers the ability to maintain optimal blood sugar control.

Q Are psychological problems more or less common in children and adolescents with diabetes compared with people without diabetes?

A It is a common belief that the presence of any chronic illness increases the likelihood of psychological problems. The presence of pimples or blemishes that make the adolescent feel different from peers can be devastating. We ask youths with diabetes to eat differently than their peers (and not to eat foods generally considered the most tempting), to give two or more insulin shots and to do four or more finger pokes for blood sugar levels (or wear a CGM) every day of their lives. With this, one might expect some psychological problems!

Surprisingly, this is not the case. We have had fewer serious psychological problems (including drug addiction and suicide) than in the general population. Why is this? It is likely related to several factors. One is that "preventive counseling" has been consistently available. The psychosocial member of the team (usually the clinical social worker) can help to identify problems early and offer intervention or referral for treatment. When families come for their three-month clinic visits, the staff is alert for people who might need some extra help. Teenagers may be asked to grade their current stress level from one to 10. An answer of five or above usually means the person is asking for help. A visit to the psychologist or clinical social worker might be helpful. The regular clinic visits and the "preventive counseling" have been major reasons for the low incidence of major psychological problems.

Diabetes often results in the entire family focusing on the holistic health of the individual and family, often in ways that might not otherwise have occurred. These often include eating better, getting more exercise and not using tobacco. Factors such as these may also relate to better mental health.

An added factor in the low incidence of serious problems may be the schedule and seriousness of diabetes care. A number of youths have written in their college applications

that having diabetes required them to "grow up" sooner – to learn at an earlier age when they could have fun or when they had to be serious. Optimal diabetes control and the use of illegal drugs and alcohol do not mix. With the monitoring of diabetes control every three months, any change from optimal control is quickly detected. Preventive counseling can then be done before the problem becomes too serious.

One parent saw some wonderful older kids who were in the clinic when her child was diagnosed. Many were in getting check-ups during their winter break from college. She asked how it could be that these kids seemed to be so much more successful than average. She was told, "It's the extra hugs!" All in all, kids with diabetes are special. We have felt very privileged to work with each of them and their families throughout the years.

Chapter 18
Care of Children at Different Ages

TEACHING OBJECTIVES:

1. Present the importance of long-term family support and involvement in diabetes management.

2. Define age-appropriate skills and tasks.

LEARNING OBJECTIVES:

Learners (parents, child, relative or self) will be able to:

1. Outline family support roles for diabetes management.

2. Identify at least one age-appropriate sign of readiness for learning diabetes skills/tasks.

INTRODUCTION

Daily diabetes care has grown more complex in recent years. In addition to the usual family responsibilities, it is common for families to:

✔ do four or more blood sugars per day (or use a CGM)

✔ give three or more shots each day

✔ use an insulin pump

✔ balance sports and exercise

✔ count carbohydrates or follow other food plans

Optimal sugar control requires the active involvement of parents for many years. The belief that children should be encouraged to do all of their own diabetes care at an early age is misguided. Diabetes is a family disease.

Children of different ages are able to do different tasks and to accept different responsibilities. It is important not to expect more from children than they are able to do. If they are unable to do the tasks, they may develop a sense of failure and poor self-esteem resulting in poor self-care. Family members need to watch for signs that the child needs more assistance, especially during times of high blood/CGM glucose levels.

The ability to do certain tasks may vary from day to day and parents must be available to help as needed. The children should be encouraged to gradually assume care for themselves as they are able. The ability to successfully live independently, both in everyday life and with diabetes care, is the eventual goal for all of our children.

A part of the goal of this chapter is to review "normal" child development and how it relates to diabetes care. Although parts of this chapter may not be important for each reader, individual sections may be helpful. It must be remembered that all children develop at different rates (and our own children are always the most advanced). Table 1 summarizes the non-diabetes- and the diabetes-related responsibilities and traits for different age groups. Table 2 lists average ages of mastery for various diabetes-related skills.

Age alone, as a guideline, does not tell us when an individual child is ready to assume tasks. There is no such thing as a "magic age" when the diabetes suddenly becomes the responsibility of the child or teenager. Be patient! Independence takes a long time. The suggestions below may vary for any given child or family. Diabetes is a **"family disease"** and the family must work together. Family members need to help each other. Sharing tasks will help prevent the diabetes care from becoming the responsibility of just one person.

CHILD UNDER THREE YEARS

Traits and Responsibilities Not Related to Diabetes

This is a time of rapid development of a small, wondrous creature who eats, sleeps, cries, soils diapers and starts to learn about the world.

Motor and brain development are the most rapid of any time in life:

✔ sitting (6-8 months)

✔ crawling (6-12 months)

✔ walking (12-18 months)

✔ language development

These developments open up a whole new world.

Accidents are the infant's major danger. *They must be protected from:*

✔ stairs where they might fall

✔ poisons and medicines they might swallow (from cupboards, garages and purses)

✔ auto accidents

✔ other dangers (including coffee tables with sharp edges)

All infants with or without diabetes need love. Parents and care providers need to cuddle and hold infants frequently throughout the day. This is particularly true after shots and blood sugars, as infants do not understand parents causing pain. Parents must remember that the blood sugars and shots are essential to their infant's life and they must move beyond feelings of guilt (as discussed in Chapter 10). Much of the fussing around blood/CGM glucose measurements and shots is due to the interruption in the child's activity rather than pain. Infants develop trust during this period and combining the diabetes care with love will help to make it a part of normal life. Young adults often look back with appreciation to their parents for the shots and care they gave them when they were young.

🐾 Responsibilities Related to Diabetes

Although babies and toddlers are not able to do any of their own self-care, the following are some special suggestions that may help parents.

✔ **Blood sugar testing:**

- Toes are used more frequently as a site.

- The BD Ultrafine lancets are smaller and may hurt less.

More frequent blood sugar levels (or use of a CGM) is usually needed. This is because the babies and toddlers cannot tell if their blood sugar levels are low.

The parents may learn to recognize a cry, crankiness or body movements that are different than usual and that indicate a need to check a blood sugar level. Teething can be a difficult time when more blood sugars are needed to separate a low blood sugar from normal fussiness. The temptation to let an infant nap longer than usual is offset by the possibility of hypoglycemia.

✔ **Blood/CGM glucose levels:**

- The blood/CGM glucose level to aim for is also higher (80-200 mg/dL [4.5-11.1 mmol/L]; see Chapter 7) as severe lows may be more dangerous to the infant's rapidly developing brain. When the family is ready, they may want to consider use of a CGM. There are obvious advantages to being able to look at the CGM glucose value throughout the day.

- Low glucose levels can be treated with less carbohydrate than for an older child (usually 5-10g due to smaller body size). This amount is found in ¼ cup of milk, orange or apple juice or 2-3 oz of sugar pop (soda), although the amount needed may vary from infant to infant.

- Infants who suck on a bottle of milk or juice frequently during the day or night will tend to have higher blood/CGM glucose levels. Overnight sucking on a bottle can also lead to dental decay.

✔ **Shots:**

- Shots are sometimes given while the infant is sleeping (if he/she tends to get very upset). If the child squirms or awakens at the time of the shot, the dad (or mom) should reassure the child. A statement such as, "It is just daddy (or mommy) giving you your insulin" may be all that is needed.

- The bottom (buttock) is used more frequently as a place to give the shot.

- Insulin pumps have been used in this age group (and in all age groups) with success. If the family is ready to consider pump therapy, the option should be discussed with their diabetes care providers (also see Chapter 26).

Table 1
Age-Related Responsibilities and Traits

	Non-diabetes-related	Diabetes-related
Age below 3 years	• developing gross motor skills • developing speech skills • learning to trust • responding to love	• parents must do all care • acceptance of diabetes care as part of normal life • often give shots (pump boluses) after seeing what is eaten
Age 3-7 years	• imaginative/concrete thinkers • cannot think abstractly • self-centered	• parent does all tasks • gradually learns to cooperate for blood/CGM glucos levels and insulin shots • inconsistent with food choices – may still need to give shots after meals • gradually learns to recognize hypoglycemia • undeveloped concept of time • adult needs to do all insulin pump management
Age 8-12 years	• concrete thinkers • more logical and understanding • more curious • more social • more responsible	• can learn to do own blood sugars (look at CGM values) • at age 10 or 11, can draw up and give shots on occasion, although they still need supervision • can make own food choices; can learn initial carb counting • do not appreciate that doing something now (e.g., optimal diabetes control) helps to prevent later problems (e.g., diabetes complications) • can recognize and treat hypoglycemia • by 11 or 12 years, can be responsible for remembering snacks, but may still need assistance of alarm watches or parent reminders • can do own insulin pump boluses, but needs adult help to remember
Age 13-18 years	• more independent • behavior varies • body image important • away from home more • more responsible • abstract thinking • able to understand the importance of doing something now to prevent problems in the future	• capable of doing the majority of shots or insulin pump management and blood/CGM glucose measurements, but still needs parental involvement and review to make decisions about dosage • knows which foods to eat; can do carbohydrate counting • gradually recognizes the importance of optimal sugar control to prevent later complications • may be more willing to inject multiple shots (or pump boluses) per day

- Eating is often variable and parents can wait to give the shot until they see what is eaten. This is easiest to do when the rapid-acting Humalog/NovoLog/ Apidra insulin is being used. The dose of insulin can then be reduced if intake is low. HbA1c values will be a bit higher as a result of this practice. However, the safety offsets this concern.

  The amount of time taken to eat a meal should be the same for all the children, with or without diabetes. Special treatment can result in eating problems. It is important for the parents to stay in control.

- The amount of rapid-acting insulin is kept low due to body size and due to an apparent increased sensitivity to rapid-acting insulin. With the insulin syringes currently available, it is not usually necessary to dilute insulins. Most parents learn how to judge ½ unit dosages using the 0.3cc (30 unit) insulin syringes. The Precision Sure Dose® 0.3cc syringes have markings for half-unit measurements (Chapter 9). Similarly, the BD Pen Mini® and the NovoPen Junior can deliver half-unit increments.

It is important for parents of infants with diabetes to incorporate the diabetes into their everyday lives. Children learn through imitation. If parents have adjusted to the diabetes and can view their child with the same positive feelings they had prior to the diagnosis of diabetes, it will help the child to grow up feeling positive and psychologically healthy. A summary of non-diabetes and diabetes traits for each age group is shown in Table 1.

AGES 3-7 YEARS

🐾 Traits and Responsibilities Not Related to Diabetes

✔ *They think concretely.*

Concrete thinking means things are either black or white, right or wrong, good or bad. They do not think abstractly. For example,

they are unable to realize that "Having a shot of insulin will help me to stay healthy." Instead, a shot may be considered a punishment for doing something wrong. Parents need to repeat over and over that the child hasn't done anything wrong and to try to describe in the child's language why pokes and shots are important.

✔ *They start to see themselves as separate individuals from their parents.*

Children gradually become very curious in this period. They often want to know how things work. They can annoy parents with the simple words "how" and "why."

✔ *Children of this age are very self-centered.*

They may progress from playing with a toy alone to gradually learning to share a toy or to share the love of their parents. Primary attachments are to parents and family. Interest in other relationships, such as school peers, begins at six to seven years of age.

✔ *Age responsibilities in children 5-7 years old begin to increase dramatically.*

They can help pick up their toys, make their bed or put their dirty clothes in the hamper when guided by the parent. They are capable of fixing simple foods, such as cereal or a sandwich, but still do not understand simple dangers such as putting a knife in a toaster or being careful around boiling water. They must have much parental supervision.

✔ *Children 5-7 years old are learning to read, opening a whole new world.*

They are discovering many new things, asking lots of questions and practicing new skills. They feel more independent and, in some ways, they are. Usually they are cooperative and love to be helpful. However, they still require a good deal of adult supervision.

🐾 Responsibilities Related to Diabetes

✔ *The parents must do all diabetes related tasks.*

Fine motor coordination (the coordination of the fingers when handling small items) is not yet fully developed. They cannot do tasks such as accurately drawing insulin into a syringe. This is also true when a child of this age is using an insulin pump. The adult must always be available to do all of the pump management.

✔ *They can gradually learn to cooperate with their parents* (e.g., sitting still for blood/CGM glucose activities and insulin shots).

✔ *They can help by choosing or cleaning a finger for a blood sugar or by choosing the site for the insulin shot.*

✔ *Children as young as three or four can sometimes recognize low blood sugars.*

They can tell parents when they are hungry. Their complaints may be vague or seem strange to us ("Mommy, my tummy tickles" or "Daddy, I don't feel good.") However, these clues can be very helpful to parents. Helping children verbalize the body sensations of low blood sugars is an important task for family members.

✔ If a shot (e.g., Lantus/Levemir) is going to be given when the child is asleep, this should be discussed between the child and parents. Some children will say "fine." Others want control and will ask to have the shot given when they are awake.

✔ *By age 5-7 years, recognizing low blood sugars is more completely developed, particularly if the parents have encouraged it.*

✔ *Children of ages 4-7 years may have some concept of which foods they can eat.*

They can be taught to ask, "Does it have sugar in it?" or "Do you have a diet pop?" They cannot be expected to always or even very often make the "right" choices over the ones that look or taste good. They will probably choose foods that are similar to what friends or family are eating. They can be expected to have some temper tantrums at being limited in high-sugar food although healthy family eating habits help this.

There is not much concept of time at this age. An adult will need to make sure that a snack is taken at a specific time. Sometimes a watch that beeps at a set time can be used as a reminder for a snack.

✔ *They usually have no objection to wearing a diabetes ID bracelet or necklace.*

It is good to get children into the habit of wearing the ID when they are young. This may help them to do this as they get older. Sources of ID bracelets can be found in Chapter 5.

It is important for parents of children in this age group (as in all age groups) to keep a positive attitude. Remember the blood/CGM glucose data and insulin shots help to keep the child healthy. Playing games around diabetes chores and gradually getting the child to help (even in little ways) may be beneficial. One fun game is to use quarters or stickers to reward the child for guessing the blood sugar number while the meter counts down. Whoever is closest "wins." It will help the child to learn to tell when they are high or low. Hugs and kisses will reassure the child that the parents' love continues. To be able to keep a positive attitude, parents need their own support for their worries and hard work. Friends, family, diabetes support groups or other sources of support can be extremely helpful.

AGES 8-12 YEARS

🐾 Traits and Responsibilities Not Related to Diabetes

✔ *Children of this age continue to think in concrete ways.*

They can gradually think more objectively and understand another person's point of view.

✔ *Fairness and meeting their needs are very important.*

✔ *Children at these ages are more social and peers begin to play a more important role in their lives.*

They usually begin to spend nights at friends' houses. They have more peer activities than do younger children. Becoming involved in some team sports can help them to stay involved as they get older. This is a great age to do classroom education about diabetes. The more peers understand, the less likely they will tease. They can soon become a real support to your child. Peer support is important, especially later during adolescence.

✔ *Children can be helpful by learning to take on increased responsibilities.*

They may help with doing dishes, feeding pets, cleaning their own room and other rooms or taking out the garbage. Special rewards, such as stars on a calendar, may be helpful in encouraging certain activities.

✔ *They are capable of more complex food preparation and can better understand safety and danger issues.*

🐾 Responsibilities Related to Diabetes

✔ *Some children begin to do their own blood sugars at ages 8-10.*

✔ *At about this age some children wish to begin to give some of their own insulin shots.*

The ability to accurately draw up the insulin is a bit slower in developing, but it is usually present at 10 or 11 years of age. The coordination needed between seeing something and using the fingers to successfully do the job (eye-hand coordination, fine motor skills) develops during this age. Use of an insulin pen may help with accuracy. This is an exciting time to watch a child develop. Adult supervision is essential for all of these important tasks.

The child can get "burned out" if:

• they begin any of these tasks at too young an age

• they have too much responsibility without the parent being available to take over when needed

They will be more likely to rebel during the teen years by missing shots or not doing

blood/CGM glucose levels. In addition, they may have difficulty requesting their parents' help when needed if they are expected to perform self-care tasks alone. **Parents must stay involved in diabetes management with this age group!**

✔ *Children of this age sometimes feel that "life isn't fair," particularly as it pertains to diabetes.*

It is helpful to just listen to them if they express such feelings.

✔ *Children may be able to give their own shots when staying at a friend's house.*

As the children are usually very active when staying at a friend's, we often suggest reducing or omitting the dose of rapid-acting insulin and reducing the dose of the evening long-acting insulin by 10-20 percent. The parent can draw up the shot ahead of time and put it in a small box, toothbrush holder or other container and leave it at the friend's home. They may ask the friend's parent to supervise the shot (or pump bolus). It is important to remember to roll a syringe containing NPH insulin between the hands to re-mix it prior to giving the shot.

It is also essential that the friend's parents be informed about hypoglycemia. The handouts in the school or child-sitters sections (Chapters 25 and 26) may be helpful.

✔ *Children of this age can eat lunch at school and make choices to avoid high sugar foods.*

Some will begin to learn to count carbohydrates.

✔ *They can gradually learn to recognize and treat their own hypoglycemic reactions.*

✔ *They are also more aware of time and can learn to be responsible for eating a snack at a set time.*

✔ *Insulin pumps are sometimes considered by the family in this age group.*

It is important for the family to meet with all team members (Chapter 28). This helps to determine who is truly ready to start using the pump.

✔ Sports can be very important at this age.

A child who learns to enjoy athletics is starting a healthy pattern for their life as well as for controlling diabetes.

Parents of the child in this age range must be patient in teaching the child about diabetes and how to do diabetes-related tasks. **The parents must still be very involved in supervision of the diabetes care.** They must also be secure enough to let the child begin to assume some responsibilities on his/her road to becoming an independent person.

Diabetes camp, group ski trips, hikes or other events allow the children to receive invaluable support from each other and to realize that they are not the only person in the world with diabetes.

AGES 13-18 YEARS

🐾 Traits and Responsibilities Not Related to Diabetes

✔ Teens gradually develop independence and a sense of their own identity.

As noted in Chapter 20, Special Challenges of the Teen Years, this age group varies greatly between wanting independence versus needing supervision and guidance. Some rebellious behavior may be demonstrated toward parents as teens grow into separate individuals.

✔ Skills increase greatly in this age group.

Automobiles can be driven legally and power lawn mowers can (hopefully) be used. Teenagers may take jobs to earn their own money. Activities, in general, are greatly increased.

✔ Body image becomes a major concern.

Teenagers worry about how others view them. The slightest pimple may become a catastrophe. Early in this period, friends of the same sex are very important, whereas later, interest in the opposite sex usually begins.

✔ More time is spent with friends.

✔ The older teen is away from the home more and stays out later with friends.

✔ Experimentation with alcohol or illegal drugs at some point may occur.

🐾 Responsibilities Related to Diabetes

✔ Teens gradually take over more of their diabetes care.

Parents still need to be available to assist with giving a shot from time to time. They need to take over the diabetes care for a period of time if the youth seems "burned out." Teens generally do better if they get extra help, particularly with insulin dosage.

As noted in Chapter 20, **A SUPPORTIVE ADULT CAN BE AN ASSET FOR A PERSON WITH DIABETES, REGARDLESS OF AGE.** Even parents of older teens still need to help with making sure adequate diabetes supplies are available (and paying for them) and making sure that clinic appointments are made and kept every three months.

Parents should come to the clinic, although the staff may request to see a teen individually to discuss issues that may be difficult to talk about with parents present.

✔ Many teens dislike the chore of writing blood sugar results in a log book.

If the parents agree to do this at the end of each day (with the teenagers' OK), it is a way for the parents to keep tabs on the diabetes. Having values written down (and faxed to the diabetes care provider if needed) is important in looking at trends and knowing when changes in insulin dosages need to be made. If using a CGM, the family should do a weekly download of the data and discuss the results and any insulin dose changes.

✔ Experimentation with alcohol may upset the diabetes control (see Chapter 11) and can cause severe hypoglycemia.

✔ Experimentation with illegal drugs upsets

Table 2
Average Ages for Diabetes-Related Skills

| Skill | Age of Mastery (in years) | |
	Recommended by the American Diabetes Association	Survey of Care Providers
A. Hypoglycemia		
1. Recognizes and reports	8-10	4-9
2. Able to treat	10-12	6-10
3. Anticipates/prevents	14-16	9-13
B. Blood glucose determinations	8-10	7-11
C. Insulin injection		
1. Gives to self (at least sometimes)	—	8-11
2. Draws two insulins	12-14	8-12
3. Able to adjust doses	14-16	12-16
D. Diet		
1. Identifies appropriate pre-exercise snack	10-12	10-13
2. States role of diet in care	14-16	9-15
3. Able to alter food in relation to blood glucose level	14-16	10-15

Abstracted from a survey done by Drs. T. Wysocki, P. Meinhold, D.J. Cox and W.L. Clarke at Ohio State University and the University of Virginia ("Diabetes Care" 11:65-68, 1990).

schedules and diabetes as well. The use of drugs can result in:

- impaired judgment

- increased appetite and higher blood sugars

- loss of incentive for optimal diabetes management

- eating meals irregularly

✔ *Peer support can help the continuation of:*

- an exercise regimen

- a healthy diet

- a consistent lifestyle

- not using tobacco products (an added risk for diabetic complications). Most people who are going to use tobacco will begin prior to age 20 years. Usually, if the peer group does not smoke or chew, the youth will make a similar choice.

Identification with peers is so important in this age group that their support (or lack of it) may greatly affect the teen's diabetes management.

✔ *A belief in God and church, synagogue or mosque activities may help guide the teen.*

✔ *Continued involvement with parents can provide stability, limits, love and support.*

✔ *Grandparents and other relatives can be a tremendous help at any age (see Chapter 26).*

✔ *There is often a feeling of invincibility or "it can't happen to me."*

Regular clinic visits at this age may help the teen realize that diabetes care and responsibility are important. Teens with diabetes are faced with more difficult tasks and more serious life issues than their peers. Teens with diabetes often seem to mature earlier than teens without diabetes. They learn at an earlier age when they have to be serious in life and when they can have fun.

✔ *Insulin pump use is often considered in this age group (Chapter 28).*

Transition to a pump is more successful if this is the teen's choice. If the parents "push" for an insulin pump, but the teen is not ready, there is a lower chance for success. It is important to have the help of the entire diabetes team when making this decision. Readiness for the pump can be assessed together. This age group is often quicker than parents in learning the use of the pump (a mini-computer). Glucose control can improve ONLY if meal and snack boluses are remembered. This activity can often require adult help.

The parents' role for the teenager is to be available to help when either forward or backward steps toward adult maturity are taken. Providing support, stability, limits and love are essential at this difficult age (as at all ages).

Age alone should not be the primary factor in deciding that a person should assume responsibility for diabetes self-management. Parents who offer continued assistance and who share the responsibilities with the teen will generally have a teen in better diabetes control.

The average ages for mastering tasks as recommended by the American Diabetes Association and by a survey of care providers are shown in Table 2.

DEFINITIONS

Eye-hand coordination: The ability to use the hands to finely adjust what is seen with the eyes. This ability usually develops around the age of 10.

Fine motor control: The ability to carefully move the fingers with precision (e.g., drawing insulin to an exact line on a syringe). This ability usually develops around age 10 or 11.

Self-esteem: How a person feels about himself/herself.

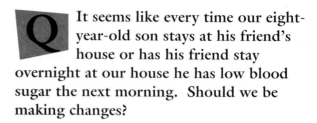

QUESTIONS AND ANSWERS FROM NEWSNOTES

Q It seems like every time our eight-year-old son stays at his friend's house or has his friend stay overnight at our house he has low blood sugar the next morning. Should we be making changes?

A "Overnights" are an important social and developmental step in our society. It is important that children with diabetes be able to participate just like any other child. Overnights are also a step in developing independence and are sometimes the first night spent away from the parents. It is important for the child to be safe in relationship to the diabetes. The children usually run and play a bit harder with their friend on overnights. They also stay up a bit later than normal and use more energy. It is generally wise to reduce the insulin dose, both the rapid-acting (20-50 percent) and the long-acting (10-20 percent) insulins, on these nights.

A bedtime snack is also advisable. Remember the "pizza factor," that pizza tends to keep a blood sugar up better than most other foods. If there is a frozen pizza in the freezer, it may be a good night to use it. It is also wise to awaken the child at a reasonable time in the morning and to get a glass of juice or milk down sooner rather than later.

Do remember that if the child is able to do a shot but is not yet old enough to draw it up, the morning insulins can be pre-drawn. The syringe(s) can be put into a little box or toothbrush holder. If NPH is part of the morning insulin, the syringe containing the NPH (± rapid-acting insulin) can be rolled between the child's hands for mixing. Think about reducing the dose again for the morning shot if it is likely that the two friends will be playing together much of the next day.

Chapter 19
Diabetes Management in the Toddler/ Preschooler

TOPICS:
Psychosocial Adjustment

Goal Setting and Problem Solving

Medications (Insulin)

The age group that is increasing the most at time the of diagnosis is the preschool group (children less than six years old). No one knows why this is happening, although it is probably related to something in the environment. It has been clearly shown that it is NOT due to infant immunizations, and these are important for all infants. Studies are still in progress to evaluate the possible influence of cows milk protein.

Chapter 18, Responsibilities of Children at Different Ages, has special sections dealing with "Children Under Three Years" and "Ages Three to Seven Years". Chapter 18 deals with normal traits for these age groups that are not diabetes-related as well as traits that are related to diabetes. For the younger age group, all diabetes responsibilities fall on the parents or other caregivers. The focus is on helping the parents to incorporate blood sugar testing, shots, etc. as part of the infants' normal life. In contrast, the four and five year old child can gradually learn to cooperate with diabetes-related tasks, even though they cannot yet reliably do the tasks. They may also begin to recognize low blood sugars and tell the parent/care provider.

The major focus of the present chapter will be to discuss insulin management in the preschooler. Parents often ask if there is anything they can do to keep their infant's pancreas working longer. This includes more normal sugar control or dietary supplements. Unfortunately, there are no proven dietary supplements that help. Similarly, a recent study (1) showed that even starting an insulin pump and continuous glucose monitor (CGM) at the time of diagnosis did not preserve insulin production for this age group. What then is the goal of insulin therapy for the preschooler?

TEACHING OBJECTIVES:

1. Present the importance of long-term family support and involvement in the diabetes management.

2. Define age-appropriate skills and tasks.

3. Discuss options for insulin therapy in the young infant.

LEARNING OBJECTIVES:

Learners (parents, child, relative or self) will be able to:

1. Outline family support roles for diabetes management.

2. Identify what is most important in the treatment of a preschooler and what this might involve.

3. Identify the best option for insulin therapy for the child.

THE NUMBER ONE GOAL FOR THE TREATMENT OF THE PRESCHOOLER IS SAFETY. Other goals include convenience for the child as well as the parents. There is no one magic formula for safety or convenience. What works best for one family may not be the answer for another family. However, we will make some suggestions.

BASAL-BOLUS INSULIN THERAPY (See Chapter 8)

A. Basal Insulin

First, when possible, "basal-bolus" insulin therapy should be used. Our early research (2) showed that low blood sugars in preschoolers were less apt to occur using a basal insulin (e.g. Lantus or Levemir or an insulin pump) in comparison to NPH insulin. The evening NPH insulin peaks during the night, increasing the risk of nighttime lows. The brain is still increasing in cell number during the first four years after birth and low blood sugars may be detrimental. We usually suggest giving Lantus or Levemir in the morning in this age group. Then, if the basal insulin does not last for 24 hours, the insulin activity falls off during the early hours of the next morning, reducing the likelihood of early morning lows. Some families give it in the buttocks before the child awakens.

B. Bolus Insulin (Humalog, NovoLog, Apidra)

The rapid acting insulin is usually given after the infant eats in this age group. Appetite can be very variable at this age. It is risky if a shot/bolus has been given and the child does not eat. Giving the shot/bolus after the meal results in slightly higher blood glucose values after meals (in contrast to giving it 20 minutes before meals as in older age groups, see Chapter 9), but results in increased safety. If a very young infant is nursing, start with a low dose (one-half or one unit) and gradually work up if the blood sugars at any time after meals are above 200 mg/dL (>11.1 mmol/L). Weighing the infant before and after nursing is tedious and not necessary.

BLOOD SUGAR AND HbA1c LEVELS (See Chapters 7 and 14)

The usual recommended range for blood sugars in this age group is 100 to 200 mg/dL (5.5-11.1 mmol/L). This is higher than in older aged children due to their inability to recognize hypoglycemia and their increased risk. It is common to have 8 to 12 blood sugar checks per day in this age group. If the child enters a "honeymoon" period (Chapter 2) it is common to see values down to 70 mg/dL (3.9 mmol/L). This is the lower level of normal for all people and is not a concern.

Per the American Diabetes Association, the desired level for the HbA1c in this age group is 7.5 to 8.5%. This is the only age group with a recommended lower limit for the HbA1c. This is for protection against hypoglycemia, as lower HbA1c values are associated with more frequent low blood sugars (other than during the honeymoon period). Achieving lower HbA1c values in this age group may be possible, especially in the honeymoon period, but must be balanced with the primary goal of safety.

INSULIN PUMPS

The first question often asked relates to, "Is pump therapy safe in this age group?" The answer is absolutely **YES**.

The second question often asked is "When should my infant be placed on an insulin pump?". The answer is simple, **"When the parents are ready".** We do not usually start insulin pumps at the time of diagnosis in this age group as we feel the parents have enough to handle. If the family is ready, an insulin pump can be discussed with the diabetes team members at three months or anytime thereafter. Families often worry about other care providers being able to manage the pump. Data from Yale University shows they do just as well as the parents (3). There is initial stress for the parents with pump initiation, but this usually subsides in a few weeks.

A second reason for considering a pump is

temporary basal rates (for low or high blood sugar levels) can be very helpful in management. The toddler who has an active play day often does best with a 50% basal insulin reduction during play and another 20% reduction from 9 PM to 3 AM (just like older children). The latter helps to prevent delayed hypoglycemia (see Chapter 6).

Two controlled studies have not found significant differences in HbA1c values as a result of insulin pump use in young infants (4, 5). Thus, the major reasons for pump use in this age group are safety and convenience.

Parents sometimes wonder if adequate "real estate" is available on their infant to place a pump. Fortunately, even infants have adequate fat in the buttocks, and the upper buttocks (seat) is where the pump catheter is usually inserted. The pump trainer will assist with suggesting sites and methods for cleanliness. Chapter 28 discusses pumps in greater detail, and a Pump/CGM book is also available in the Pink Panther series (see order form in the back of this book).

PSYCHOLOGICAL ASPECTS

A. Preschoolers:
A recent article (6) summarized some of the behavioral issues dealing with insulin pumps in toddlers. They noted that allowing an older preschooler to pick the next infusion site position can make the task easier to accomplish. A reward system (e.g. stickers) for each site change can also be helpful. Pump cases with belts or fanny packs often work better than clipping them on the child's clothing. Picking out his or her own pump case can also encourage the child to feel some ownership of their diabetes. During site changes, a child may choose to use numbing cream such as EMLA or LMX to minimize pain, but this can be left to the child to decide.

B. Parents
Some studies (not all) have reported an improved quality of life for the parents of

for convenience of both the infant and the parents. Multiple small insulin boluses (for corrections or for food—see Chapter 28) can be given. This often results in eight to 12 boluses per day, which would be difficult if giving shots.

Basal insulin per day after the honeymoon is usually lower in preschoolers (0.6 units/kg body weight or 0.27 units/pound body weight). This is in contrast to teenagers who may need approximately 0.9 units/kg (0.45 units/pound) body weight as basal insulin. Basal insulin usually provides about half of the total daily dose and bolus insulin the other half. As discussed in Chapter 28, the use of

preschoolers using insulin pumps. Some observers note that the more meticulous management of diabetes is associated with higher degrees of stress (particularly in the early period of pump use). The use of CGM (see below) may reduce the number of blood sugar checks done per day and may help with hypoglycemia fears. It is amazing that nearly all families of preschool-aged children have chosen to continue pump therapy after participating in research studies.

CONTINUOUS GLUCOSE MONITORING (CGM)

As with insulin pumps, CGMs can be discussed with the diabetes care team **when the family is ready.** The CGM may provide convenience in not having to do so many finger, toe, or heel pokes for blood sugar levels. They may also enhance safety with alarms for high and low glucose levels. Computer connections will become available for parents' bedrooms and baby alarms are currently helpful. The major drawback is once again body "real estate". The diabetes nurse-educator can help to explore if adequate fat is available for both an insulin pump and a CGM. Chapter 29 discusses CGMs in detail and the Pump/CGM book (see above) provides further details.

NEONATAL DIABETES

A final reminder—all children diagnosed under the age of six months should be tested for a genetic alteration (7). They may have a genetic defect that allows treatment with an oral medicine rather than insulin. This genetic defect is rarely found to be the cause of diabetes in anyone diagnosed after age six months.

DEFINITIONS

Neonatal Diabetes: An inherited genetic alteration usually resulting in the onset of diabetes in the first six months after birth (7).

QUESTIONS AND ANSWERS FROM NEWSNOTES

Why is the new chapter on toddlers and preschoolers in the 12th edition of *"Understanding Diabetes"*?

Much had previously been written in Chapter 18 related to toddlers and preschoolers. However, families frequently wanted more information, particularly in relation to insulin treatment. In addition, this is the age group with the highest percent increase in diabetes. Thus, the decision was made to add the new chapter.

Why are references to the medical literature given in this chapter but not in other chapters?

Insulin pump use in infants and the topic of neonatal diabetes are relatively new concepts. Many physicians also use the Pink Panther books for their updated education related to diabetes. One pediatric resident shared with us that four of her five board questions for pediatric boards that were related to diabetes could be answered because she had read *"Understanding Diabetes."* Thus, we have to admit, the references are included in this new chapter primarily for physician education.

REFERENCES
1) Kordonouri O, et al. *Diabetologia.* 53: 2487, 2010.
2) Dixon B, Chase HP. *Pediatric Diabetes.* 6: 150, 2005.
3) Weinzimer SA, et al. *Pediatrics.* 114: 1601, 2004.
4) Wilson DM, et al. *Diabetes Care.* 28:15, 2005.
5) Fox L, et al. *Diabetes Care.* 28: 1277, 2005.
6) Fuld F, et al. *Diabetes Technology and Therapeutics.* 12: 567, 2010.
7) Gloyn AL, et al. *New England Journal of Medicine.* 350: 1838, 2004.

Chapter 20
Special Challenges of the Teen Years

TEACHING OBJECTIVES:

1. Discuss how teenagers typically assume responsibility for diabetes care and the role of their family.

2. Discuss special challenges of teen years, including tobacco use, alcohol, substance abuse, sex, identity issues and lifestyle.

LEARNING OBJECTIVES:

Learners (parents, child, relative or self) will be able to:

1. Support teenagers with diabetes to assume independent care for their diabetes.

2. Develop action plan with diabetes provider(s) to minimize health risks.

A. STRUGGLE FOR INDEPENDENCE

Parents often despair at the thought of their "angelic" child becoming an adolescent. The teen years have been defined as the period in life when one varies between wanting to be a child and wanting to be an adult. These feelings vary from hour-to-hour, day-to-day, week-to-week and year-to-year. The "child" part of the adolescent still wants to be completely dependent on parents and other adults. The emerging "adult" wants to be an entirely independent person. There are many shades between these two extremes that may linger for some time. Daily life has become more complicated and the task of independence is not easy. In the past, we believed that

---

Table 1
Special Challenges for the Teenager

    A. Struggle for independence

    B. Growth and body changes

    C. Identity

    D. Peer relationships, alcohol, drugs, tobacco

    E. Sexuality

    F. Consistency (exercise, eating, emotions and lifestyle)

    G. Driving a car

    H. College

    I. Emotional changes

    J. Transition to an adult diabetes clinic

children with diabetes should assume their own management at a certain age and that they would suddenly become independent. **We now know that independence is not age specific and is a gradual process.** We think of diabetes as a **family condition**. Daily diabetes care has become far more complicated in recent years. It requires a great deal of parent-child partnership to achieve optimal blood sugar control and healthy independence.

The "child vs. adult" struggle can greatly influence diabetes management during the adolescent years. A teenager may want entire responsibility for the diabetes management at one time – faithfully following blood/CGM glucose levels, exercising, watching food and "treat" intake and taking the responsibility for the injections/boluses, (or oral medicines for type 2). At another time, blood/CGM glucose values will not be checked unless the parent is there to help, injections/boluses or oral medicines may be forgotten or "treats" may be consumed in large quantities. Exercise, which is critical for persons with type 1 or type 2 diabetes, may be ignored. Parents can lessen the effects of this variable attitude toward the diabetes care by remaining involved and offering to share these responsibilities with their teenager. Offering to exercise with the teen makes it more fun and challenging for everyone. **We believe that a supportive adult who is readily available, BUT NOT OVERBEARING OR CONSTANTLY NAGGING, can be a help to any person with diabetes, regardless of age. Remember that independence is rarely achieved without occasional conflict.**

Parental partnership (involvement) with the teen can be accomplished in a variety of ways:

✔ drawing up and/or giving injections

✔ keeping a log book or using downloads to record blood sugars and noting trends and problems

✔ helping to fax/email blood/CGM glucose values to the diabetes care team (fax sheets are found in Chapter 7)

✔ helping with weekend dosing when teens may want to sleep in and could use some assistance.

These not only help the teenager, but also help keep the parent "in the loop" and aware of what is going on with management.

Diabetes care is usually NOT the top priority for a teenager. Their main interests may be their peers, schoolwork, sports, a car, a job, etc. (in varying orders of importance for different teens). The parents may need to help in keeping a focus on the care necessary for optimal diabetes control.

If the teenagers' actions (or lack of them) result in possible serious dangers to his/her health, then the parents have no choice but to step back in for a time. This is particularly true when insulin shots/boluses or oral medicines (type 2) are being missed. Hopefully, the next try at taking on more responsibility will be more successful. Remember to take things one step at a time. Just because a young person has had diabetes many years does not mean they have assumed ownership of the care. Sometimes professional counseling is necessary.

The majority of teenagers gradually assume adult independence without too much difficulty. In contrast to the parents' worst fears, they do grow up! In fact, the teenager with diabetes may assume adult responsibilities earlier than other teenagers.

Achieving independence step by step:

The task of how to help children grow to be independent young adults is a challenge for most families. Diabetes complicates that task somewhat. It is normal for parents of children with diabetes to feel anxious about normal separations such as overnights, camp and school trips. Parents worry about injections, low blood/CGM glucose values and whether the schedule and snacks will be remembered. With good preparation and supervision, these separation experiences are an important part of growing up and eventually becoming independent. These experiences are also usually

Julie is a 16-year-old girl who has had diabetes for seven years. She and her family have always prided themselves on Julie's diabetes control. Julie is a talented dancer and hopes to become a professional dancer some day. She dances on Mondays, Wednesdays and Fridays at 5:30 p.m. At a clinic appointment, it is discovered that her diabetes has become out of control with her HbA1c unexpectedly being over 10 percent. In talking with Julie, she admits to missing evening injections sometimes when she goes to dance class. She says she just doesn't have time to get her homework, blood sugar value and injection done and still get something to eat before leaving for dance class.

PLAN:

Julie's parents volunteered to help with the blood sugar and injection on those nights and to make some dinner for her. Julie was relieved to have her parents take over some of the diabetes care, but admitted it was hard to ask for help after being responsible for her own diabetes care for several years.

NOTE: Another possibility is the missed shots were done on purpose in order to keep her "dancer's figure." If so, this is more serious. More discussion on this topic can be found later in this chapter under the topic, "Emotional Changes" and in Chapter 17 under "Eating Disorders."

a lot of fun for kids. It is best to start with brief periods of separation, like staying at a relative's or friend's house overnight.

🐾 Overnights

Staying at a friend's home, even for one night, can be a big step, as can a visit to relatives. This often begins prior to the teen years. We generally suggest a small reduction in insulin dosage (short- and long-acting insulins) for overnights at home or away, since kids are usually up later and tend to burn more energy. This way, the parents do not need to worry quite as much about low blood sugars!

🐾 Summer Camps

Follow these short visits with longer stays at a diabetes camp or other summer camps (often beginning prior to the teen years). Youth learn that they CAN survive without parents and parents learn that their children CAN survive without them! (Re-education for both is important.)

🐾 School and athletic trips

Eventually teens will want to participate in longer school excursions and/or sports trips.

With some insulin adjustments and education of staff, these should be a safe and important part of independence and life experience.

🐾 Clinic Visits

Teenagers can begin seeing diabetes care team members by themselves at diabetes clinic visits. Parents are still needed at these visits to review plans and problems with their teens and the diabetes care team. As noted in Chapter 18, **better diabetes management usually results if parents stay involved in offering continued assistance and sharing responsibilities with the teenager.**

B. GROWTH AND BODY CHANGES

The adolescent growth spurt and the development of adult sexual characteristics result in many body changes, probably more than occur at any other single time in life.

🐾 Growth Hormone

The gain in height is a result of increased hormone levels (growth hormone, testosterone and estrogen). Growth hormone partially blocks insulin activity. Insulin requirements increase dramatically and are usually the highest-per-pound body weight that they will ever be. The insulin requirement usually decreases when growth is completed. If blood sugar control is maintained during puberty, full growth is usually reached. Research from our Center has shown that better growth (to full adult potential) is more likely with optimal sugar control.

🐾 Sex Hormones

Female sexual development includes breast and pubic hair development, widening of the hips and the onset of menstrual cycles. These pubertal changes may be slightly delayed in girls with diabetes. Blood/CGM glucose values may increase during menstruation. Many girls will increase their Lantus/Levemir or pump basal insulin and/or their rapid-acting insulin during this time. Some girls who use an insulin pump will switch to a different basal rate setting to provide more insulin during menses.

Males have enlargement of the testes and penis, and facial and other body hair begins to grow. When body odors become noticeable, for males or females, the use of deodorants is desirable. Acne or pimples ("zits") may develop in either sex, making skin care important. Tetracycline or other treatments are fine to use if acne becomes a problem. Male athletes may be tempted to try steroid drugs to try to make their muscles larger. Use of these drugs can prevent full height attainment and lead to increased blood cholesterol levels and risk for heart attacks later in life. They also may cause aggressive behavior, resulting in problems getting along with others. The drugs reduce insulin sensitivity and cause increased blood sugar levels. Non-prescribed steroid drugs should not be used.

🐾 Thyroid Hormone

The thyroid gland (in the neck) must function properly during this time or growth will not progress normally. As part of the regular diabetes check-up visits, the diabetes care provider will monitor the size and function of the teen's thyroid gland. About half of teenagers with diabetes get some thyroid gland enlargement, although in most cases no treatment is necessary. This is an "autoimmune" disorder, as is diabetes. Antibodies against the thyroid gland can be measured. A simple test called TSH (Thyroid Stimulating Hormone) is usually adequate for screening. Thyroid problems are also discussed in Chapter 24.

🐾 Body Image

Teenagers are often very concerned about "body image" (self-consciousness) and a single pimple can be a disaster. Diabetes does not usually result in visible body alterations. Having diabetes may make teens "feel" different from their peers. Wearing an insulin pump (see Chapter 28 is often visible and a constant reminder of having diabetes. This is a reason why pumps should not be "pushed" on a person until they are ready. The refusal to wear an identification (ID) bracelet or necklace, to wear an insulin pump or to refrain from eating high carb foods may relate to not wanting to feel different from peers. Some teens hide their pumps under baggy clothes. They may choose not to bolus if eating with friends. As they gain confidence and maturity, they will bolus when needed without regard to their peers. Often, peers can be a helpful, supportive part of a teen's diabetes care.

C. IDENTITY

🐾 Who Am I?

Teens are searching for the answer to the question, "Who am I?" It is important to emphasize the positives about who they are at this stage of their lives (e.g., someone who loves a sport, music, mechanics, school plays or other interests), and who secondarily happens to have diabetes. The diabetes should not come first. Reinforcement should be given when a positive attitude toward living with diabetes is demonstrated. Compliments are important. For example, "Good job on managing your blood/CGM glucose measurements even with the stress of finals" (even though the stress and not exercising may have resulted in high values). A sincere offer to record results or give injections during busy times can be helpful for both the teen and the parent.

Additional identity problems may occur in youth living in single-parent or divided-parent households. Approximately 33 percent of youth now live in single-parent homes. Youth may feel a need to help care for a single parent. Their identity may vary between being a care provider and needing to be cared for.

❧ Risk-taking

The "in-the-middle" age range of adolescence (approximately ages 14-17 years) is usually the most difficult time. The teen often sees himself/herself as "invincible." Risk-taking and experimentation tend to occur more frequently.

Some of the experimentation may include:

✔ bright hair colors or styles

✔ unusual clothing

✔ piercings in an unusual place(s)

✔ a tattoo(s)

Some diabetes-related risk behaviors are:

✔ "I don't need to wear my diabetes ID; I've got an ID card in my wallet."

✔ "I'm not going to carry sugar; I can get something at my friend's house if I need it."

✔ making poor food choices without taking the steps to maintain sugar control

✔ not doing blood/CGM glucose levels (particularly prior to driving)

✔ missing shots/boluses

Regular or more frequent clinic visits and measuring HbA1c levels at this time may help the teen. Parents need to let the teen know that they trust their child to act maturely. Patience on the part of the care providers and from the parents is a real virtue.

D. THE PEERS

Peer relationships are very important to teenagers, often more so than relationships with parents. Early in adolescence, close friends are usually of the same sex. In later adolescence this often changes or is "added to" by members of the opposite sex. Being like their peers is very important. Having diabetes and "being different" can be a challenge. Some teenagers are comfortable monitoring blood/CGM glucose levels or giving themselves injections in front of their friends. Others will absolutely refuse to let anyone other than the closest friend know that they have diabetes. The willingness or refusal to wear an ID, as well as doing diabetes tasks in front of friends, may reflect the teen's own degree of acceptance of diabetes.

Much of a teen's identity relates to conforming to their peer group. Peer groups can be important in helping the teen make decisions about the use of drugs, alcohol or tobacco. If the peer group rejects or accepts these, the teen with diabetes will probably do likewise.

Effects of the use of these substances on diabetes are listed below:

✔ **Tobacco use** (smoking or chewing) affects blood vessels in anyone. Tobacco use by a person with diabetes is particularly harmful as it increases the risk of diabetes complications later in life.

✔ As in all people, **chewing tobacco** can lead to dental problems and cancer of the mouth.

✔ **Smoking cigarettes** is associated with an increased likelihood of lung cancer and heart disease.

✔ **Alcohol consumption** can result in delayed severe insulin reactions. (This is discussed in more detail at the end of Chapter 11.)

✔ **Drugs** that alter awareness of time have their greatest effects on diabetes by interfering with consistency in eating and insulin injections. Alterations of judgment can also be very dangerous.

✔ **Chronic drug use** may result in an "I don't care" attitude toward diabetes management with poor health outcomes.

Warning signs which should alert investigation of behaviors:

✔ withdrawal from the usual routines

✔ change in sleeping pattern (sleeping more/less)

✔ changes in friends

✔ not communicating with family members

✔ mood changes and irritability

Participation in an activity group for teenagers with diabetes can be helpful. It may help the teenagers share their feelings with others who also have diabetes. They soon realize that others have many of the same feelings that they do, and they are quite normal in spite of having diabetes!

Teens in an area without such groups might find a useful resource on-line: www.childrenwithdiabetes.com/fsn (the 'fsn' is for Family Support Network) is a useful website for information and support.

Research has shown that the teen with diabetes who involves his/her peers by sharing knowledge about diabetes is more likely to achieve better sugar control. We encourage teens to bring a friend to the clinic visit to continue to learn how they can support their friend with diabetes.

E. SEXUALITY

🐾 **Teenagers with diabetes run the same risk as non-diabetic teens of contracting diseases such as AIDS, herpes, chlamydia and other sexually transmitted diseases (STDs). It is <u>very</u> important to talk with the health care provider about prevention, protection and contraception to reduce the risk of an unplanned pregnancy or STDs.**

🐾 **PREGNANCY in a woman with diabetes (also see Chapter 30) carries added risks for the baby and the mother:**

✔ Attaining a HbA1c level close to the non-diabetic level PRIOR to becoming pregnant will reduce the risk for miscarriage or birth defects in the baby. Advanced planning for pregnancy is essential for a person with diabetes.

🐾 Research has shown that there is no increased risk for teenage girls with diabetes to use birth control pills compared with non-diabetic teenage girls using birth control pills.

🐾 The only sure way to absolutely prevent a sexually transmitted disease or pregnancy is to abstain from sex. If the teen chooses to have sex, a condom should always be used. This will help to prevent sexually transmitted diseases, although there is no guarantee for absolute protection.

🐾 **If a male or female believes they cannot cause or become pregnant due to diabetes, they are absolutely wrong. People with diabetes can cause a pregnancy or become pregnant just like anyone else.**

🐾 The stress of the teen years may be heightened by conflicts about emerging sexuality, and sensitivity to this is important.

F. CONSISTENCY (EXERCISE, EATING, EMOTIONS AND LIFESTYLE)

The word CONSISTENCY is in capital letters throughout Chapter 12, "Food Management and Diabetes." If everything could be the same every day, diabetes management would be much easier. Unfortunately, there is no such thing as consistency in many teenagers' lives. Bedtime may be at 10:00 p.m. on school nights but then at midnight or later on Friday and Saturday nights. Many teens like to sleep late on weekends. If the teen is on Lantus/Levemir insulin or on the pump, this may work well, though we would continue to urge glucose monitoring in the midmorning to make sure the blood/CGM glucose level is not low. Teens who are still on NPH dosing will need to take their insulin on schedule. We suggest an absolute limit of 9:00 a.m. as the time when the NPH insulin must be taken with at least a small snack. The teenager can then go back to sleep for an hour.

Consistent exercise is often a challenge. Seasonal sports, such as football or soccer, call for heavy exercise for a few months, but may be followed by weeks or months of little activity. Erratic exercise will cause blood/CGM glucose levels to vary. The insulin dose and eating plan may need frequent adjustments for changes in activity level. It is wise to have a "back-up" activity such as biking, walking, jogging or aerobics so that there is some exercise every day. Daily exercise is also very effective in controlling weight. Some teens who use an insulin pump use one set of basals for exercise days and another set for days without exercise.

G. DRIVING A CAR

Perhaps no new function in this age group requires more responsibility than the driving of a car. The teen's own life, as well as the lives of friends or total strangers, may be in the balance. The Center's video* on hypoglycemia emphasizes safety while driving. **It is essential to check a blood/CGM glucose level before driving.** This is particularly true after a sports activity or exercising. It has been shown that driving with a low blood sugar results in greater impairment than driving when drunk. **FRIENDS DO NOT LET A FRIEND DRIVE WHEN LOW!**

If a person does feel low while driving, it is essential to pull over and have a snack. They should never assume they can "make it" home or to the nearest convenience store. The person should not resume driving until a repeat blood sugar is shown to be back up. Snacks (a small can of juice, granola bar, etc.) should be kept in the glove compartment.

If an accident does occur as the result of a low blood sugar, most states suspend the driver's license for a year. This points out that teens need to be extra careful not to drive with a low blood sugar.

* The video is available through the Children's Diabetes Foundation (CDF) website shown in the back of this book. The address for CDF is also on the back cover.

H. COLLEGE

Starting college is a challenge for anyone. It is even more so for the person with diabetes. Our Center has offered a "Beyond High School" workshop for the past twenty-five years. Students who have completed one or more years of college are the most helpful in preparing the pre-college students. The Children's Diabetes Foundation website has an educational section about college:

www.childrensdiabetesfdn.org/education.html

Getting all the needed diabetes supplies together in addition to the usual packing is an extra chore.

Other important issues to remember or consider are:

✔ If the college student is to live in a dorm, getting the (meningococcal) meningitis vaccine is important and should be discussed with your primary care physician.

✔ The flu shot is also advised.

✔ Hepatitis shots should be current.

✔ It is important to take emergency phone numbers. Because of health privacy laws, a release for parents to be contacted during illness should be signed and filed with the student health service.

✔ A copy of this book may be helpful with questions about sick days or other diabetes-related problems.

✔ This book or the condensed "First Book" version may also be helpful in educating a roommate about diabetes, especially about hypoglycemia.

✔ A plan for how to discuss the diabetes with new roommates/friends must be made.

✔ A roommate and/or dorm counselor must be able to recognize and treat low blood sugars.

✔ Be aware of the usual high calorie/high fat cafeteria food. Selecting alternatives may help prevent weight gain (often referred to as the "freshman 15").

✔ Doing more frequent blood/CGM glucose levels will help to make the transition safer.

I. EMOTIONAL CHANGES

Much of the above sections of this chapter are about normal changes in adolescence. However, a few other areas still need to be considered. Rapid mood swings are more common during adolescence. Mood swings may change the blood adrenaline level, affecting blood sugars. Adrenaline (epinephrine) causes the blood/CGM glucose levels to rise. In general, normal adolescent mood changes should not affect overall diabetes control significantly. Adolescence is frequently an age when other conditions may emerge. Anxiety and mood disorders like clinical depression are common, though they are often unrecognized conditions. If your teenager shows unusual changes which concern you, please talk with your healthcare team. (Also see Chapter 17 for discussions of depression and eating disorders.)

Such changes to watch for include:

✔ frequent irritability or anger

✔ a drop in grades or school performance

✔ loss of interest in activities that were previously enjoyable

✔ suspected substance abuse

✔ changes in sleep habits (unable to go to sleep or sleeping all the time), loss of appetite

✔ "hanging out" with a different group of friends or dropping friends all together

The above changes may be symptomatic of an underlying mood disorder.

Teenagers' eating habits may be affected by their emotions. Teenagers are notorious for rather unusual eating habits and this poses a challenge for teens with diabetes who might not want to see themselves as "different."

Some teenagers develop mild to severe eating disorders:

✔ Anorexia: not eating

✔ Bulimia: binging on food and self-induced vomiting and/or use of laxatives. With diabetes, skipping insulin shots is a dangerous way to control weight.

Parents should be suspicious of eating disorders if their teen overeats or doesn't exercise and still doesn't gain weight. Weight loss without dieting or exercise should also alert the parents to possible missed insulin injections or boluses. The HbA1c level is usually above nine percent if insulin is being missed (for any reason). Teens tell us that their main reason for missing shots or boluses is just "forgetting."

Stress is a normal part of life (e.g., arguments with friends, worrying about grades or concern about making a team). Learning to deal with stress is an important part of growing up.

Parents and care providers should watch for signs of depression. The teen years can be a time when thoughts emerge about what it means to have a chronic condition for life. Professional counseling can be helpful.

It should be apparent that the saying **"DIABETES IS A COMPROMISE"** fits particularly well with the teenage years. Consistency in areas that would benefit diabetes control sometimes needs to be compromised in helping a teenager to develop normally.

J. TRANSITION TO AN ADULT DIABETES CLINIC

There has been much written in recent years about the importance of transitioning patients, usually between the ages of 18 and 22 years, from a pediatric to an adult diabetes care provider. The Barbara Davis Center is fortunate in that the Young Adult Clinic is just down the hallway from the Pediatric Clinic. We often walk down with the patient/family to introduce them to adult providers and to make certain that the initial appointment is made. It is essential that the parents and clinic staff ascertain that follow-up actually occurs when the transition time arrives.

This transition from pediatric to adult care is particularly necessary from the medical standpoint because most adult diabetes clinics have the ability to follow parameters not evaluated in a pediatric clinic (Doppler blood flow, EKGs, etc.). Many studies have shown that there is a subset of young adults at high risk for severe hypoglycemia, ketoacidosis and the eye and kidney complications of diabetes. Needless to say, focused and timely transition is essential.

More information is available at:
http://ndep.nih.gov/transitions/index.aspx

SUMMARY

The teen years can be stressful for everyone. However, they can also be the happiest years of an individual's life. The teen with diabetes has extra stresses, but with a supportive family, these can be managed. Diabetes is a partnership between the parents and the teenager. It is often important for parents to be patient and to remember that they, too, were once teenagers. Parents must find ways to stay involved in the diabetes management, but not to be overbearing. They must be available to help and to be supportive but still let the teenager gain independence. **The good news is they do grow up!**

DEFINITIONS

Adolescence: The term given to the teenage years.

Adrenaline (epinephrine): The stress hormone made in the adrenal gland in the abdomen. It causes blood sugars to rise.

AIDS: Acquired Immune Deficiency Syndrome. This is a serious condition acquired by sexual contact with an infected person or by sharing needles with an infected person.

Estrogen: Female hormone made in the ovary (located in the abdomen) that causes female body changes.

Growth hormone: A hormone (like insulin) made in the pituitary gland at the base of the brain that is important for growth. It blocks the insulin activity.

Peers: One's group of friends.

Self-consciousness (body image): Concern about how one appears to others.

Sexually transmitted diseases (STDs): Diseases contracted through sexual contact, such as herpes, chlamydia, gonorrhea (clap) or syphilis.

Testosterone: A male hormone made in the testes that causes male body changes.

QUESTIONS AND ANSWERS FROM NEWSNOTES

Q At the last clinic visit, we expected a great HbA1c because my daughter's blood sugar record looked so good. We were shocked to find out that she had not been doing blood sugars and was falsifying her results! Her HbA1c was the highest ever. What should we do?

A Blood sugar measurements can be difficult for some kids, particularly when they see high blood sugars. Unfortunately, they can feel discouraged or feel bad that they will be criticized for their high blood sugars ("what did you eat??"). When kids stop doing blood sugars or falsify numbers, it is important that we find out why they were doing so. Sometimes they worry about disappointing their parents; sometimes high values make them feel like a failure; and sometimes they want to avoid lectures from well-intended adults. There are many reasons why kids do this. If we understand, we are in a better position to help them. Talk with them about how blood sugars are not "good or bad" but helpful information to guide dosing. They may need more involvement by parents for a while to support their efforts to test.

Q Is it true that growth is reduced by poor sugar control?

A Research using longitudinal HbA1c values showed that optimal growth was not reached if long-term HbA1c values were elevated. In addition to the growth rate of the person with diabetes, the final adult height was compared to that of siblings, as well as the expected adult height based on the parents' heights. All were reduced in people with increased HbA1c values. In contrast, growth was not altered in people who kept their HbA1c values in the desired range.

Q Our teenage son has had an elevated HbA1c value (nine percent) over the past year. His physician and his mother and I have warned him about kidney failure and vision problems, but it doesn't seem to do any good. He currently receives Humalog and NPH insulin before breakfast and dinner. What would you suggest?

A First, it has long been known that scare tactics do not work with teenagers. This is particularly true in the mid-teen period (14-17 years) when they are "invincible," which may in itself lead to risky behavior. If you want your son to change, you and his healthcare provider might start with "planting seeds." The use of Lantus/Levemir rather than of NPH in the evening might be helpful. Likewise, use of an Insulin pump could be beneficial. It might be suggested that an extra shot each day, perhaps of Humalog/NovoLog/Apidra using the insulin pen, would help at lunch or with the afternoon snack. At first, he may resist. Continue to offer education but without the scare tactics. Any positive change should be praised and encouraged. Hopefully, this will help him to continue the positive action he has taken. It helps if he is able to feel a benefit (feeling better, less frequent voiding, etc.). If growth picks up with the lower HbA1c value, point this out to him. The lower HbA1c value should also be a plus and give him positive feedback for this. Hopefully, the sum total will be such that he will want to continue with the new behavior. This model for making change has many potential applications, both in diabetes-related change and in other areas.

Chapter 21
Outpatient Management, Education, Support Groups and Standards of Care

TEACHING OBJECTIVES:

1. Indicate the importance and frequency of clinic visits as related to positive diabetes outcomes.

2. Present the minimum standards of care for diabetes management.

LEARNING OBJECTIVES:

Learner (parents, child, relative or self) will be able to:

1. State the anticipated clinic visit schedule, relate its importance as well as necessary items to bring (meter, written materials [especially Pink Panther book], labs, etc.).

2. List three expected tasks in diabetes management.

INTRODUCTION

The majority of new-onset treatment is now done in an outpatient setting. Outpatient care is less traumatic for the person with diabetes and the family. It also saves money compared with the cost of hospital treatment. In addition, it is now relatively rare to hospitalize people with known diabetes in the U.S. to "assess how they are doing." It is possible to have diabetes for decades and never have a diabetes-related hospitalization.

This is a result of many factors, some of which are:

✔ age-appropriate education

✔ good family support

✔ regular clinic visits (every three months)

✔ close communication with the diabetes healthcare providers

✔ fulfilling the diabetes standards of care

211

TELEPHONE/EMAIL MANAGEMENT

Much of diabetes management can be done over the telephone, by fax or by email. Some glucose meters and continuous glucose monitor (CGM) systems have downloads allowing email transmission. The extra equipment needed can be obtained from the meter or CGM company (see website or call phone number on back of device).

The diabetes care team should be called:

✔ prior to the next regularly scheduled injection if a severe hypoglycemic reaction has occurred

✔ if more than two mild reactions occurred within a short time

✔ anytime the urine ketones are moderate or large or blood ketones are above 1.0 mmol/L

People with diabetes should have checkups with the health team about every three months. This is the recommendation of the ADA Standards of Care. Some of these Standards of Care are included in this chapter.

At a clinic visit:

✔ the HbA1c can be done (Chapter 14). It reflects the number of high blood/CGM glucose levels for the past three months.

✔ insulin adjustments can be made

FAX AND EMAIL MESSAGES

Most families have access to a fax machine or email. Blood sugar record sheets can be found in Chapter 7, or for pumpers, in Chapter 28. They hold either one week or two weeks of blood sugar records. The sheets are an ideal size to send through a fax machine.

If the family is using a continuous glucose monitor (CGM), there are also ways to make the data available to the diabetes care provider. The diabetes nurse-educator or the company (number on back of device) may be able to help. The alternative is to take the CGM into the diabetes clinic and ask to have it downloaded. The data can then be given to the diabetes care-provider.

We ask that records be faxed or emailed anytime the family feels they need some help. We prefer faxes or emails to phone calls to report blood sugar values. The fax or email saves time and confusion when trying to listen and write down values while on the phone.

If the parents do not have access to a fax machine or email, most schools (and especially the school nurse) will provide a way to transmit the blood sugars.

Some good reasons for faxing/emailing records are:

✔ if over half of blood sugar values at any time of day are **above** the upper level for age (see Chapter 7) and the person/family needs some suggestions

✔ if there are more than two values **below** 60 mg/dL (3.25 mmol/L) in one week

✔ if the two week or one month average on the blood glucose meter or CGM is > 200 mg/dL (> 11.1 mmol/L)

When families fax/email the records, please remember to:

✔ include the insulin dosages

✔ record the time of any symptomatic low blood sugars (even if it was not possible to do a blood sugar) and include any relevant information relating to why lows occurred

✔ include the sender's fax/email and phone number and when that person can best be reached

✔ include the family's plan on what adjustments to make (We want families to be active in the decision-making process.)

These same forms can be downloaded from Chapter 7 to use when e-mailing records. The text of the book is on the Center's website at: www.barbaradaviscenter.org.

It is only when records are kept that trends can be seen. Faxing/emailing the healthcare

✔ a review of blood/CGM glucose values: looking for patterns of highs and lows

✔ changes in insulin dosage

✔ the HbA1c to be done

✔ growth to be followed

✔ a check for any problems

✔ continued education and introduction of new information/devices

In a clinic, the following people may be seen:

Clinic Nurse, Medical Assistant or Volunteer will:

- measure height and weight

- check the blood pressure

- check a blood sugar

- measure the hemoglobin A1c (HbA1c)

- check for urine ketones and protein

- download blood glucose meters, CGMs and pumps

Diabetes Nurse Educator will:

- continue the diabetes education

- introduce any new information and/or new devices available

- check prescription needs

- review diabetes management

- do the school health plan (if needed)

Doctor, Physician's Assistant (P.A.) or Nurse Practitioner:

- checks to see how the person/family is doing with diabetes care goals

- reviews the blood/CGM glucose values and the HbA1c result

- may change insulin or oral medication doses

- if using an insulin pump, evaluates the pump download

- does a physical examination

- coordinates the recommendations of all team members

provider **when** values are out of the target range is most helpful. Adjustments can then be made immediately. This prevents delaying changes until the next clinic appointment.

CLINIC VISITS

When someone is attending our clinic for the first time, the visit usually takes a half to a whole day. Later visits will be shorter. Snacks should be brought to the appointment. Blood sugar records, meters and CGM devices must **ALWAYS** be brought along for the clinic visit. All meters that we recommend have memories to store the last 100 to 250 blood sugar values and the ability to download the data upon arrival in the clinic. It is important to analyze this data at the time of the clinic visit.

Having a clinic visit every three months allows:

Dietitian:

- reviews food intake and makes suggestions for changes if needed

- provides nutrition education and information about snacks and other food needs

Social Worker or Psychologist:

- assesses personal, family, school or other problems

- provides resource options for the individual or family

- monitors current family issues and their effect on diabetes management

It is also helpful to bring this educational book so that it can be used to review knowledge about diabetes.

EDUCATION, SUPPORT AND WORKING GROUPS

Some families gain extra support from meeting with other families who also have a family member with diabetes.

This meeting can happen at:

✔ the time of the clinic visits

✔ special group meetings

✔ special events: sports, picnics or Halloween parties

Additional education courses are important for families who do not live near a specialized diabetes clinic. These courses are important for people who were diagnosed at a young age and have now reached an age when they are able to understand material they could not understand earlier.

Some of the additional education courses offered at our Center are:

✔ **Transition to Work- and College-Bound Workshop:** Offered as people become independent from their parents. A boost in knowledge at this time can be helpful in preventing later problems.

✔ **Grandparent's Workshop:** A one-day course. It is important that children with diabetes have the same relationships with grandparents as do other children (see Chapter 26). This likely involves staying with the grandparents. The workshop may also be useful for aunts and uncles, babysitters or others who are close to the child.

Grandparents wishing to have a child with diabetes stay with them need to know:

✔ basic knowledge about drawing up insulin and giving shots

✔ how to check blood sugars

✔ how to treat hypoglycemia

✔ the importance of a healthy diet

The grandparents may feel more confident in caring for their grandchild with diabetes as a result of such a course.

STANDARDS OF MEDICAL CARE

Standards of medical care for people with type 1 and type 2 diabetes have been published by the American Diabetes Association (ADA). The standards are for both care providers and the people with diabetes.

These standards can be found in:

"Diabetes Care", Volume 33, Supplement 1, S4-61, Jan, 2010

Knowing these standards will allow people with diabetes to:

✔ assess the quality of medical care they receive

✔ determine their role in their medical treatment

✔ compare their treatment outcomes to standard goals

The person and/or family must assume some of the responsibility for meeting the standards of care outlined below.

For example:

✔ If the family member with diabetes has reached puberty and has had diabetes for at least three years, annual eye and kidney evaluations are needed. The family must set up the eye evaluation with an eye doctor covered by their HMO.

✔ They need to help the family member do two timed overnight urine collections for the important microalbumin screening for the kidneys (directions at end of Chapter 23).

Some of the ADA's recommended standards of care with a few modifications are outlined below.

- Insulin-treated people should have clinic visits every three months.

- A HbA1c level should be done at least every three months. This is done in our clinic using the DCA 2000 instrument. The method was shown by the DirecNet Study Group to be very accurate, and the result is available in six minutes. It is important for the care provider to have the result during the clinic visit so that changes can be made if needed.

- All people with diabetes must be taught a method for blood glucose values.

- A comprehensive physical examination, including sexual maturation in adolescents, should be done **annually** by either the diabetes or primary care physician.

- Parts of the physical exam affected by diabetes (e.g., height, weight, blood pressure, eyes, thyroid, liver size, deep tendon reflexes, injection sites, feet, etc.) should be checked **every three months**.

- People ≥ 10 years of age should have a dilated eye examination by an eye doctor within 3-5 years after the onset of diabetes. Screening for diabetic eye disease is NOT necessary before 10 years of age.

- Laboratory measurements for microalbuminuria (Chapter 23) should be done annually in postpubertal people who have had diabetes for at least three years. People with type 2 diabetes should be checked initially and then annually.

- The occurrence of severe hypoglycemic episodes (episodes requiring the help of others [when not usually required], seizures or loss of consciousness) are serious and require the help of a diabetes specialist in preventing further episodes.

- The stress of illness frequently affects sugar control and necessitates more frequent monitoring of blood sugar and urine or blood ketones by the family. Medical help must be constantly available when moderate or large urine ketones or blood ketones above 1.0 mmol/L are detected.

- In type 1 diabetes a lipid profile, including cholesterol, triglyceride, LDL and HDL should be performed by age 12, and then at least every few years (see Chapters 11 and 23). In type 2 diabetes lipids should be checked at diagnosis and then yearly.

- High blood pressure (hypertension) and borderline elevations in blood pressure contribute to the development and progression of the chronic complications of diabetes. Elevations in blood pressure must be treated aggressively to achieve and maintain blood pressure in the normal range.

FOR PEOPLE WITH DIABETIC COMPLICATIONS

🐾 Known diabetic eye disease requires care by an ophthalmologist experienced in the management of people with diabetes.

🐾 The person with abnormal kidney function requires heightened attention, control of other risk factors (e.g., hypertension and tobacco use) and consultation with a specialist in diabetic kidney disease.

People with cardiovascular risk factors, who have usually had type 1 or type 2 diabetes for many years, should be carefully monitored. Evidence of cardiovascular disease (such as angina, decreased pulses and ECG abnormalities) requires efforts aimed at correction of contributing risk factors (e.g., obesity, use of tobacco, hypertension, sedentary lifestyle, hyperlipidemia and poorly regulated diabetes), in addition to specific treatment of the cardiovascular problem.

DEFINITIONS

ADA: American Diabetes Association.

Physician Assistant: A doctor's assistant who can handle many of the responsibilities of the physician.

Standards of Medical Care:
Recommendations made by an ADA panel for the minimum levels of care for people with diabetes as included and modified in this chapter.

QUESTIONS AND ANSWERS FROM NEWSNOTES

 Why are regular clinic appointments necessary and how often should these be scheduled?

 Clinic appointments should be scheduled approximately every three months. This is the recommended interval in the ADA "Standards of Medical Care". The reasons for this are primarily preventive since this is where the emphasis in healthcare now lies. In the early 1900s the emphasis on healthcare was in the treatment of acute problems. Medicine has now switched to a more preventive based healthcare, particularly relating to chronic diseases.

For people with diabetes, the visits every three months allow continued education and increased motivation for doing day-to-day monitoring of the diabetes. Also, the HbA1c level provides an estimate of blood/CGM glucose levels over the past three months. If regular visits do not occur, diabetes monitoring and knowledge become lax.

In summary, the best management occurs with the family and team working together. Although every three months seems to be an average best time to return to the clinic, there are obviously some situations where more frequent visits are important.

Chapter 22
Adjusting the Insulin Dosage and "Thinking" Scales

TEACHING OBJECTIVES:

1. Discuss when and how to adjust insulin doses.
2. Integrate factors which influence insulin dose into a "thinking" scale.
3. Demonstrate the application of dose adjustment to blood sugar trends.

LEARNING OBJECTIVES:

Learner (parent, child, relative or self) will be able to:

1. Describe when and how to increase or decrease insulin doses.
2. Explain insulin adjustments using blood/CGM glucose records.
3. List two factors which affect blood sugars and describe the appropriate insulin adjustments.

BLOOD/CGM GLUCOSE GOALS (SUGGESTED RANGES)

It is our general goal to have blood/CGM glucose levels in the ranges listed below (also see Chapter 7). These ranges are when no food has been eaten for at least two hours. They apply to fasting in the morning as well as for two hours after any meal or snack.

Under 5 years of age
= 80-200 mg/dL (4.5-11.1 mmol/L)

5-11 years of age
= 70-180 mg/dL (3.9-10.0 mmol/L)

12 years and above
= 70-150 mg/dL (3.9-8.3 mmol/L)

A person who has difficulty recognizing low blood sugars or who has severe insulin reactions may be asked to keep the blood/CGM glucose at a slightly higher level. Families and the diabetes care provider should discuss the desired range. This range should be written down for future reference. It is important to remember that this is a target goal. **If at least 50 percent of the sugar values are in the target range at each time of day, the HbA1c level will usually be in the desired range.** Not all blood/CGM glucose values will be in the target range. The exception to this is during the "honeymoon" period shortly after diagnosis. If more than half of the values are in range and the HbA1c is still high, blood sugars at other times of the day should be done. Chapter 7 gives suggestions for other times – including two hours after meals.

After six to 12 months of dealing with diabetes, many families and older teens begin making some of their own insulin adjustments. The longer people have diabetes the more comfortable they become making adjustments. This should be discussed with the diabetes care provider at a clinic visit. We encourage patients and families to be actively involved in making insulin dose adjustments. When blood/CGM logs are faxed/emailed we ask that families include their plan on how to adjust insulin/CGM glucose. Guidelines for insulin adjustments should be discussed with the care team.

ADJUSTING THE INSULIN DOSAGE

The first step in learning to adjust insulin is to know the times of action of the insulins used. Refer to the figures in Chapter 8 and Table 1 in this chapter to review the times of action of various insulins.

The three rapid-acting insulins are:

1. Humalog

2. NovoLog

3. Apidra

All these have similar activity (Chapter 8). They can be used interchangeably.

Changes in insulin dosage are best considered under four categories:

A. Reducing the Insulin Dose

B. Increasing the Insulin Dose

C. Insulin Adjustments for Food and Correction Factor

D. Insulin Adjustments for People Receiving Lantus/Levemir Insulin

A. REDUCING THE INSULIN DOSE TO PREVENT LOW BLOOD SUGARS: (Tables 1 and 2)

🐾 **Responding to trends in the blood sugar levels**

Reducing a specific insulin dose should be done if:

✔ Frequent (> 2 per week) blood/CGM glucose values below 60 mg/dL (< 3.3 mmol/L), which we consider is the level of true hypoglycemia, or below 70 mg/dL (< 3.9 mmol/L) in a preschooler

✔ Many of the blood sugars/CGM values in a day are below the desired lower limit. The insulin doses should be reduced with the next injection. How much the insulin is reduced depends on the age and size of the person and the dose being given.

We do not know why blood/CGM glucose values will suddenly be low for a day or longer in a person who has been stable. Most often this is due to increased physical activity, eating less food or opening new bottles of insulin. Also, NPH insulin has variable absorption from day-to-day.

When are the low values occurring?

• If the reactions are in the early morning hours, the Lantus/Levemir (given at any time of the day) or evening NPH can be reduced by one or two units.

• If the values are still low the next day, reduce the insulin again.

• If the low values occur before lunch or dinner, the morning NPH insulin can be reduced by one or two units.

Think about what time of the day the reactions are occurring and which insulin is having its main action at that time of day. Reduce the insulin that is working at that time by one or two units.

Table 1
The Four Time Periods of Insulin Activity

Period 1: a.m.	Humalog/NovoLog Apidra/Regular	Works primarily from breakfast (**B**) to lunch (**L**)
Period 2: a.m.	NPH	Works primarily from lunch to dinner (**D**)
Period 3: p.m.	Humalog/NovoLog Apidra/Regular	Works primarily from dinner to bedtime (**BT**)
Period 4: p.m.	NPH (evening) Lantus/Levemir (anytime)	Works primarily from bedtime to the following morning (NPH) or all day (Lantus/Levemir)

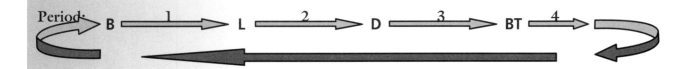

Sometimes the values are high the day after the insulin dose is reduced. This is because the insulin-balancing hormones may require a day or two to adjust. It is important to be patient when a dose is reduced, and **DO NOT GO BACK UP ON THE DOSE** just because blood/CGM glucose values are a bit higher. Wait a few days to let the balancing hormones decline before deciding to go back up on the dose. Remember that even though we suggest waiting a few days to make further changes if the blood/CGM glucose level is high, this is NOT necessary if it is low. **It is OK to make a further reduction the next day if values are still low.**

🐾 Thinking ahead to prevent lows (reactions)

Although discussed in more detail in Chapter 6, families need to **"think ahead" to prevent lows.** Reduce the insulin dosage during days of high excitement and activity or when eating less. **When children stay overnight at a friend's house (or have a friend spend the night)** there is often an increase in activity and less sleep. More energy is expended, and it is wise to reduce the p.m. insulin dose and/or the Lantus/Levemir dose or the pump basal rate.

The following can all lead to low blood sugars:

✔ school trips and field days

✔ family picnics and playing with cousins

✔ long hikes or bike trips

✔ spending the night with a friend

✔ vacations to places like Disneyland® or the beach

✔ deciding to begin a diet

✔ when school is out and the weather is nice, children will play outside after dinner. The evening rapid-acting insulin almost always has to be reduced.

✔ getting cold when playing outside in cold weather (not wearing enough warm clothing)

✔ starting sports or a new exercise program

Temporary reductions in dosage of insulins acting at the time of activity or excitement can help to prevent problems. If there are questions about reducing the insulin dosage, call the diabetes care provider during office phone hours. (Save home calls and pager calls for emergencies.) **Remember it is generally best to err on the safe side.** Alterations in the

Table 2
Insulin Dosing Algorithms for LOW BLOOD SUGARS (B.S.) in mg/dL (mmol/L)

		Infants/Toddlers	School Age	Adolescents	College Age
		Birth - 4 yrs.	*5 - 11 yrs.*	*12 - 18 yrs.*	*19 - 25 yrs.*
Target glucose levels		80-200 (4.5-11.1)	70-180 (3.9-10.0)	70-150 (3.9-8.3)	70-150 (3.9-8.3)
Morning (a.m.) B.S.		B.S. < 80 (4.5) ↓ dinner or bedtime N or Lantus/Levemir ** by ¼ to ½ unit	B.S. < 70 (3.9) ↓ dinner or bedtime N or Lantus/Levemir ** by ½ - 1 unit	B.S. < 70 (3.9) ↓ dinner or bedtime N or Lantus/Levemir ** by 1-2 units	B.S. < 70 (3.9) ↓ dinner or bedtime N or Lantus/Levemir ** by 1-2 units
Noon B.S.		B.S. < 80 (4.5) ↓ a.m. RAI or R by ¼ to ½ unit	B.S. < 70 (3.9) ↓ a.m. RAI or R by ½ - 1 unit	B.S. < 70 (3.9) ↓ a.m. RAI or R by 1-2 units	B.S. < 70 (3.9) ↓ a.m. RAI or R by 1-2 units
Afternoon (dinner) B.S.		B.S. < 80 (4.5) ↓ a.m. N or noon RAI or R by ¼ to ½ unit	B.S. < 70 (3.9) ↓ a.m. N or noon RAI or R by ½ - 1 unit	B.S. < 70 (3.9) ↓ a.m. N or noon RAI or R by 1-2 units	B.S. < 70 (3.9) ↓ a.m. N or noon RAI or R by 1-2 units
Bedtime B.S. (higher goals)		B.S. < 150 (8.3) ↓ dinner RAI or R by ¼ to ½ unit	B.S. < 130 (7.3) ↓ dinner RAI or R by ½ - 1 unit	B.S. < 100 (5.5) ↓ dinner RAI or R by 1-2 units	B.S. < 100 (5.5) ↓ dinner RAI or R by 1-2 units

↓ = lower, decrease; N = NPH; RAI = Rapid-acting insulin (Humalog, NovoLog or Apidra); R = Regular insulin
* Values in parenthesis reprersent mmol/L. ** Decrease Lantus/Levemir given at any time of day.

insulin dose for sick-day and surgery management are discussed in Chapter 16, "Sick-day and Surgery Management."

🐾 Responding to severe insulin reactions

If a severe insulin reaction occurs, it is important to call the diabetes healthcare provider before giving the next scheduled insulin shot. The stores of balancing hormones (e.g., adrenaline) are reduced with a severe reaction and there is a greater risk for more reactions. The insulin dose should be reduced temporarily (often for 2-3 days). It is important to prevent a severe reaction from occurring again. Sometimes it is helpful to schedule a clinic appointment to discuss this.

B. INCREASING THE INSULIN DOSE TO TREAT HIGH BLOOD SUGARS: (Tables 1 and 3)

🐾 Understanding why more insulin is required

An insulin dose may need to be increased:

✔ if the blood/CGM glucose levels have been above the desired range for three or four days in a row and there is not an obvious illness or stress that will soon go away

✔ when children grow, their insulin needs generally increase by one unit for every two pounds (or 1kg) gained. Also, when growth hormone levels increase, insulin activity is blocked.

✔ because in most people their own pancreas gradually makes less insulin

✔ in the winter when many people exercise less and their insulin needs increase

✔ during times of high stress or during menses (menstrual period)

✔ if HbA1c values are high (reflecting blood/CGM glucose levels over the past three months)

✔ during an illness, there may be a temporary need for more insulin (especially if ketones are present). This is discussed in Chapter 16, "Sick-day and Surgery Management."

🐾 Resistance to increasing the insulin dose

Some people resist increasing the insulin dose. When blood/CGM glucose levels have been running high, the person's body becomes accustomed to higher levels. They may feel uncomfortable at glucose levels in the target range. This unpleasant feeling lasts for a short period and will gradually disappear. Also, the most frequent fear of people with diabetes (and their family members) is of low blood sugars. This is particularly true if severe reactions have occurred. People may resist (sometimes subconsciously) increasing the dose and lowering the blood/CGM glucose levels. An increase in the dose may mean a loss of further insulin production in the eyes of some families. This can seem like a time of additional loss.

🐾 Knowing which insulin to increase

It is essential to know the times of action of the insulins and the desired ranges for the blood/CGM glucose levels. The insulins working during the four time periods are shown in Table 1. *When the blood/CGM glucose levels are above the desired range for three to seven days with no obvious cause, the insulin acting in that time period should be increased. Thus:*

✔ if the sugars are high before lunch, increase the morning rapid-acting (Humalog/NovoLog/Apidra) or Regular insulin

✔ if the sugars are high before dinner, increase the morning NPH or the rapid-acting insulin or Regular insulin at lunch. Also, consider if rapid-acting insulin is needed for afternoon snacks!

✔ if the sugars are high before the bedtime snack, increase the dinner rapid-acting or Regular insulin

✔ if the sugars are high before breakfast, increase the dinner (or bedtime) NPH or the Lantus/Levemir insulin given at any time of the day

Table 3
Insulin Dosing Algorithms for HIGH BLOOD SUGARS (B.S.) in mg/dL (mmol/L)

	Infants/Toddlers	School Age	Adolescents	College Age
	Birth - 4 yrs.	5 - 11 yrs.	12 - 18 yrs.	19 - 25 yrs.
Target glucose levels	80-200 (4.5-11.1)	70-180 (3.9-10.0)	70-150 (3.9-8.3)	70-150 (3.9-8.3)
Morning (a.m.) B.S.	B.S. > 200 (11.1) ↑ dinner or bedtime N or Lantus/Levemir ** by ¼ to ½ unit	B.S. > 180 (10.0) ↑ dinner or bedtime N or Lantus/Levemir ** by ½ - 1 unit	B.S. > 150 (8.3) ↑ dinner or bedtime N or Lantus/Levemir ** by 1-2 units	B.S. > 150 (8.3) ↑ dinner or bedtime N or Lantus/Levemir ** by 1-2 units
Noon B.S.	B.S. > 200 (11.1) ↑ a.m. RAI or R by ¼ to ½ unit	B.S. > 180 (10.0) ↑ a.m. RAI or R by ½ - 1 unit	B.S. > 150 (8.3) ↑ a.m. RAI or R by 1-2 units	B.S. > 150 (8.3) ↑ a.m. RAI or R by 1-2 units
Afternoon (dinner) B.S.	B.S. > 200 (11.1) ↑ a.m. N or noon RAI or R by ¼ to ½ unit	B.S. > 180 (10.0) ↑ a.m. N or noon RAI or R by ½ - 1 unit	B.S. > 150 (8.3) ↑ a.m. N or noon RAI or R by 1-2 units	B.S. > 150 (8.3) ↑ a.m. N or noon RAI or R by 1-2 units
Bedtime B.S.	B.S. > 200 (11.1) ↑ dinner RAI or R by ¼ to ½ unit	B.S. > 180 (10.0) ↑ dinner RAI or R by ½ - 1 unit	B.S. > 150 (8.3) ↑ dinner RAI or R by 1-2 units	B.S. > 150 (8.3) ↑ dinner RAI or R by 1-2 units

↑ = raise, increase; N = NPH; RAI = Rapid-acting insulin (Humalog, NovoLog or Apidra); R = Regular insulin
* Values in parenthesis reprressent mmol/L. ** Increase Lantus/Levemir given at any time of day.

The increases are usually by a half unit for a preschooler or by a unit for an older child or adult. The blood/CGM glucose levels will tend to run lower on the first day of increased insulin.

The dose may need to be increased again as the balancing hormones adjust. Extra blood/CGM glucose checks on the first day of an increased dose are often wise. If the blood/CGM glucose levels are still above the desired range after three to seven days, repeat the increase again. **Continue this program until at least half of the blood/CGM glucose levels at the time of day being worked on are in the desired range.** A general rule is to increase the dosage slowly. If you are not sure whether to make further increases in the insulin dose, fax or email the values. Most glucometers will display a 14 and 30-day average - You can also call to discuss changes with your diabetes care provider. Faxing or e-mailing the blood/CGM glucose values allows the diabetes care provider time to review and think about recommendations. It saves the need for copying values over the phone. Sample fax sheets are included in Chapter 7. This reporting should be done during office phone hours. Save home calls and pager calls for emergencies.

C. INSULIN ADJUSTMENTS FOR FOOD AND CORRECTION FACTOR

When choosing a dose of rapid-acting insulin, it is important to think about both the blood/CGM glucose level and the food to be eaten. Many families and care providers choose a **correction factor** which can be added to the food insulin dose to cover high blood/CGM glucose levels. The **correction factor** refers to the units of insulin needed to correct a blood sugar to a given level. The goal is to return the blood sugar level into the desired range. A correction factor is generally used when Humalog/NovoLog/Apidra has not been given within the previous two hours. The most common correction dose is one unit of rapid-acting insulin per 50 mg/dL (2.8 mmol/L) of glucose above 100 mg/dL (5.5 mmol/L). Corrections may be to 150 mg/dL (8.3 mmol/L) during the night. However, every person is different. Pumps with bolus calculators may allow for more precise doses. A preschooler may do better with one unit per 100 mg/dL (5.5 mmol/L) above 200 mg/dL (11.1 mmol/L). The person or family will need to

Table 4
Example of Insulin Adjustments

| Blood Sugar | | Correction Factor* | Carb Choices** | Total Units |
mg/dL	mmol/L	Units of Insulin	(15g carb)	of Insulin
150	8.3	0	1	1
200	11.1	1	2	3
250	13.9	2	3	5
300	16.7	3	4	7
350	19.4	4	5	9

* Assuming a correction factor of one unit of rapid-acting insulin per 50 mg (2.8 mmol/L) above 150 mg/dL (8.3 mmol/L).

** One Carb choice = 15g carbohydrate. In this example, one unit of insulin is given for each 15g carb choice.

find out what works. It is a helpful way to get the blood/CGM glucose levels back on track.

If food is to be eaten at the time of doing the correction (e.g., time for lunch or afternoon snack), the insulin to cover the food should be added to the correction dose. For example, in Table 4, if a person planned to eat 45g of carbohydrate and their I/C ratio (Chapter 12) was 1:15, the dose of rapid-acting insulin would be three units. If their blood/CGM glucose level was 250 mg/dL (13.9 mmol/L), the correction factor would be two units (if their correction was one unit of rapid-acting insulin per 50 mg/dL or glucose above 150 mg/dL). The total dose to be taken would be five units (three units plus two units). If no food were to be eaten, then the dose to be taken would just be the two unit correction factor.

If the correction dose is to be given after an exercise induced high sugar, it should be reduced by half. (Delayed hypoglycemia may follow as adrenaline levels decrease and sugar goes back into muscle – see Chapter 13.) Also, if a correction is to be done at bedtime, many people use half of the usual dose. Prevention of lows during the night is important.

Correction insulin doses are also discussed in Chapter 28 on insulin pumps. Insulin-to-carbohydrate (I/C) ratios are also discussed in Chapter 12 on food management.

D. INSULIN ADJUSTMENTS FOR LANTUS/LEVEMIR INSULIN

In Chapter 8 you can find:

✔ The most common ways we currently use Lantus/Levemir insulin.

✔ A method to determine the starting Lantus/Levemir dose.

✔ An example for Lantus/Levemir given at dinner or in the evening (Figure 1). The dose of Lantus/Levemir is increased or decreased until most of the morning blood/CGM glucose levels are in the desired ranges.

These ranges are:

Under five years of age
= 80-200 mg/dL (4.5-11.1 mmol/L)

5-11 years of age
= 70-180 mg/dL (3.9-10.0 mmol/L)

12 years and above
= 70-150 mg/dL (3.9-8.3 mmol/L)

Most people will adjust up or down by one or two units of Lantus/Levemir insulin (or one-half unit for toddlers) every two or three days until morning values are in the ranges listed above.

If NPH is given at breakfast the amount of NPH is adjusted up or down until the blood/CGM glucose levels at dinnertime are mostly within the ranges listed above. Table 5 provides an algorithm that may be helpful in adjusting insulin dosages.

The H/NL/AP dosages for meals are best adjusted by measuring blood/CGM glucose levels two hours after the meal. The same sugar levels given above can also apply for the desired values two hours after eating. Others routinely aim for a glucose level below 140 mg/dL (7.8 mmol/L) two hours after meals. If the values are not in the desired range two hours after eating, the **I**nsulin to **C**arbohydrate **(I/C)** ratio will need to be changed. If the blood/CGM glucose levels are high, more insulin for carbohydrate in the **I/C** ratio will need to be given. An example would be to change from 1:15 (1 unit/15g carbohydrate) to 1:10 (1 unit/10g carbohydrate). If the blood/CGM glucose level is below the lower limit, less insulin is needed. An example would be to change from a ratio of 1:15 (1 unit/15g carbohydrate) to 1:20 (1 unit/20g carbohydrate; with pumps smaller changes can be made). Call your healthcare provider if you need help.

Snacks are usually not necessary with Lantus/Levemir insulin. However, if the blood/CGM glucose is below 130 mg/dL (7.3 mmol/L) at bedtime, it is usually wise to have a bedtime snack. When the glucose is above this level and the person is having more than 15g of carbohydrate at bedtime, H/NL/AP may be necessary.

Table 5
Algorithm for Adjusting Lantus/Levemir Insulin Regimens

1. **Lantus** dose:

    When using <u>only</u> Lantus/Levemir insulin (*no* NPH), determine the dose based on the pre-breakfast blood sugar (*morning blood sugar goal = 70-180 mg/dL [3.9-10.0 mmol/L]*) *

    If morning blood sugar value is:
    - 60-70 mg/dL (3.3-3.9 mmol/L) = decrease the Lantus/Levemir dose by one unit } daily changes
    - < 60 mg/dL (< 3.3 mmol/L) = decrease the Lantus/Levemir dose by two units } can be made

    - 180-240 mg/dL (10.0-13.3 mmol/L) = increase the Lantus/Levemir dose by one unit } wait 2-3 days
    - > 240 mg/dL (> 13.3 mmol/L) = increase the Lantus/Levemir dose by two units } between changes

2. If using an **a.m. NPH** dose:

    (*afternoon or dinner blood sugar goal = 70-180 mg/dL [3.9-10.0 mmol/L]*) *

    If afternoon blood sugar value is:
    - 60-70 mg/dL (3.3-3.9 mmol/L) = decrease **a.m.** NPH dose by one unit } daily changes
    - < 60 mg/dL (< 3.3 mmol/L) = decrease **a.m.** NPH dose by two units } can be made

    - 180-240 mg/dL (10.0-13.3 mmol/L) = increase **a.m.** NPH dose by one unit } wait 2-3 days
    - > 240 mg/dL (> 13.3 mmol/L) = increase **a.m.** NPH dose by two units } between changes

3. **Humalog, NovoLog** or **Apidra (H/NL/AP)**

    (*two hours after a meal blood sugar goal = 70-180 mg/dL [3.9-10.0 mmol/L]*) *

    If blood sugar value two hours after the meal is:
    - 60-70 mg/dL (3.3-3.9 mmol/L) = decrease the H/NL/AP dose prior to the meal by at least one unit ** } daily changes can be made
    - < 60 mg/dL (< 3.3 mmol/L) = decrease the H/NL/AP dose prior to the meal by at least two units **

    - 180-240 mg/dL (10.0-13.3 mmol/L) = increase the H/NL/AP dose <u>prior</u> to the meal by one unit } wait 2-3 days between changes
    - > 240 mg/dL (> 13.3 mmol/L) = increase the H/NL/AP dose <u>prior</u> to the meal by two units

*For teens and adults, the healthcare provider may wish the blood sugar goal to be 70-150 mg/dL (3.9-8.3 mmol/L) rather than 70-180 mg/dL (3.9-10.0 mmol/L).

**If carb counting, subtract or add these amounts, but it may be necessary to talk with the dietitian to change the I/C ratio.

Call your health care provider if you have questions.

"THINKING" SCALES (AND REPLACING THE TERM "SLIDING" SCALES)

The term "sliding" scale is often used for the system of giving rapid-acting (or Regular) insulin at meals based on the blood sugar value. We prefer to use the term "thinking" scales. They give the person or family ranges of H/NL/AP and/or Regular insulin to "think about." **The blood sugar level SHOULD NEVER be the only factor considered. Food intake and both recent and expected exercise also need to be considered with every shot.** An example would be a five-year-old going out to play with friends after dinner in the summer. Even if the blood sugar was 200 mg/dL (11.1 mmol/L) before dinner, it would be wise to reduce (or omit) the evening dose of rapid-acting insulin. This would also apply if mom (or dad) was making tuna noodle casserole for dinner, and they knew that the five-year-old disliked tuna noodle casserole. **"Sliding" scales that do not account for food and exercise can be dangerous. In contrast, "thinking" scales in which insulin is adjusted based on multiple factors are helpful.** Thinking scales for different aged children are often based on whether they are still quite sensitive to rapid-acting insulin or not as sensitive. Possible scales should be discussed with your diabetes care provider.

Many families adjust Humalog/NovoLog/Apidra and/or Regular (not NPH) insulin dosages with every injection. *They use a thinking scale in which the amount of rapid-acting insulin given is based on:*

1. **the blood/CGM glucose level**

2. **the expected food intake**

3. **both recent and expected exercise**

4. **other factors (e.g., illness)**

The insulin scale can be written down in Table 6. If the blood sugar is low, the amount is decreased. In contrast, the dose is increased for higher blood/CGM glucose levels, if less exercise is expected or if a large meal is to be eaten. Smaller children obviously have lower dosages than larger children. Children in the first year after diagnosis (who make more of their own insulin) are usually more sensitive to rapid-acting insulins and will have lower dosages.

One advantage of thinking scales is that the blood/CGM glucose level must always be measured if the scale is to be used. Sometimes one scale is used for the morning and a different scale for the evening. As indicated in Table 6, it may even be necessary to use one scale for an active day and a different scale for a quiet day.

It is important to remember that thinking scales are not "written in stone." A scale that works fine for a few months may have to be altered if the blood/CGM glucose levels are not in the desired range. Always bring the scale

Table 6

Suggested "Thinking" Scale for Humalog/Novolog/Apidra (H/NL/AP) or Regular (R) Insulin Dosage

Blood Sugar Level	Morning H/NL/AP/R		Afternoon H/NL/AP/R		Dinner H/NL/AP/R	
	Active (or not eating much)	Not active (eating normally)	Active (or not eating much)	Not active (eating normally)	Active (or not eating much)	Not active (eating normally)
_____ =	_____	_____	_____	_____	_____	_____
_____ =	_____	_____	_____	_____	_____	_____
_____ =	_____	_____	_____	_____	_____	_____
_____ =	_____	_____	_____	_____	_____	_____
_____ =	_____	_____	_____	_____	_____	_____
_____ =	_____	_____	_____	_____	_____	_____

NOTE: *This table does not apply to sick-day management (see Chapter 16). Call your diabetes care provider AFTER CHECKING THE BLOOD SUGAR AND KETONES if you have questions. Scales may also be used for rapid-acting insulin dosages given at other times during the day. Copy this table as often as you wish.*

☙COPY AS NEEDED

along to clinic visits so the dose can be reviewed with the diabetes care provider. Also, write down the dose of insulin given in each shot on the blood sugar record sheet (see Chapter 7). This makes it possible for you and the diabetes care provider to more easily review dosages and how the scales being used are working.

While "thinking" scales are an improvement on "sliding" scales, a disadvantage of "thinking" scales is that it can be challenging to determine how to make changes. Using "rules" for carbohydrate counting and for correction factors is preferred. It may be easier to make changes to these "rules" to improve blood sugar control than to make numerous individual changes.

SUMMARY

In summary, it is important for families to consistently look at blood sugar levels. The HbA1c value may be up to one point lower in families who record values and look at patterns. They then need to make insulin adjustments to obtain or maintain optimal diabetes control. **Keeping a blood sugar and insulin dose log (record) will allow the family to see patterns to make the insulin adjustments.** It is most frustrating to the diabetes care team when high blood/CGM glucose values are obtained week after week and no adjustments are made. If a family is uncertain whether changes in insulin need to be made, fax, email or mail the blood sugar values and insulin dosages to the diabetes care provider to get help. Remember to bring your log book to the clinic visit. We have heard every possible excuse ("My dog ate them," "I left it at home"). Needless to say, we don't believe any of them. As a compromise, consider using the log book for 1-2 weeks out of the month. Another helpful time would be if exercise or schedules change. This will help you know when you need assistance with insulin adjustments.

DEFINITIONS

Correction factor: Use of a set amount of insulin to correct the blood sugar into the desired range. The most common example is giving one unit of Humalog/NovoLog/Apidra insulin for every 50 mg/dL (2.8 mmol/L) above 150 mg/dL (8.3 mmol/L) blood sugar level.

Sliding scale: Altering the insulin dose based on the blood sugar levels.

Thinking scale: Altering the insulin dose considering factors **in addition to** blood sugar levels. The other factors might include: food amount, exercise, stress, illness and menses.

QUESTIONS AND ANSWERS FROM NEWSNOTES

 What is meant by "sliding" scales for insulin adjustments and who should use them?

"Sliding" scales generally refer to giving different dosages of Humalog/NovoLog/Apidra or Regular insulin depending on the level of blood sugar. They should not be used for NPH or Lantus/Levemir. We prefer the term **"thinking"** scale to emphasize that the blood/CGM glucose level, food intake and exercise must all be considered before each insulin dose is chosen. On some occasions, illness, stress and menses must also be considered. Although thinking scales can be helpful for some people, most now use carb counting and correction factors to calculate the insulin dosage.

 Do the needs for insulin change with the seasons?

The short answer is "yes." To illustrate this, think of summer camp. Nearly every person going to camp has their routine dose of insulin substantially reduced because of all the extra activity. To a lesser degree this happens in Spring - over a week or two the snow suddenly disappears, the sunshine appears and children are out playing, bicycling, etc. With the increased activity, low blood/CGM glucose levels are more likely. Snacks may have to be adjusted and/or insulin doses may need to be lowered.

In contrast, the opposite happens with going back to school in the fall, especially for those going to new schools. This may be a time of extra stress as well as reduced activity. Activity is decreased with the evening homework. Blood/CGM glucose levels may go up and insulin doses may need to be raised.

A four-year-old diagnosed at age three might do fine with a thinking pre-meal scale of:

| Blood Sugar | | Units of Humalog/NovoLog/Apidra or |
mg/dL	mmol/L	Regular Insulin
< 100	< 5.5	0
100-200	5.5-11.1	1
201-300	11.2-16.7	2
> 300	> 16.7	3

A 16-year-old who developed diabetes at age three might have an entirely different pre-meal scale:

| Blood Sugar | | Units of Humalog/NovoLog/Apidra or |
mg/dL	mmol/L	Regular Insulin
< 70	< 3.9	2
70-150	3.9-8.3	4
151-200	8.4-11.1	6
> 200	> 11.1	8

Chapter 23
Long-Term Complications of Diabetes

INTRODUCTION

In addition to the acute complications of diabetes, hypoglycemia and acidosis, there are also problems known as "long-term" complications. Generally, the long-term complications occur in people who have had diabetes and high blood sugar levels for many years.

About this chapter:

🐾 Many families may prefer to read this chapter when they are ready to deal with the subject.

🐾 Adults and teenagers may be able to understand the material better than pre-teens.

🐾 Many new and difficult words are used in this chapter. They are introduced and defined in the back. If your diabetes care provider uses them you will have a place to find their meaning.

The four most common parts of the body to be affected by high sugar levels are:

1. Eyes (retinopathy)
2. Kidneys (nephropathy)
3. Nerves (neuropathy)
4. Heart and blood vessels

Three other areas that can be affected by high sugar levels are:

5. Joints (finger curvatures)
6. Children born to mothers with poorly controlled diabetes (birth defects)
7. Foot problems

TEACHING OBJECTIVES:

1. Discuss the relationship between glucose control and diabetic complications (eye, kidney, nerve and heart).
2. Summarize the methods to monitor eye and kidney complications.

LEARNING OBJECTIVES:

Learner (parents, child, relative or self) will be able to:

1. Describe the relationship between glucose control and complications.
2. Identify routine methods used to monitor the eyes and kidneys.

229

THE DCCT

The Diabetes Control and Complications Trial (DCCT) has been mentioned previously in this book (Chapter 14). The results of this study became available in 1993 and proved without question that **eye, kidney and nerve problems of type 1 diabetes were decreased in people ages 13-39 years whose blood sugars were kept closer to normal. They also reported that optimal glucose control resulted in a 57 percent reduction in nonfatal heart attacks, strokes and coronary vascular disease.**

For people with type 2 diabetes, studies in the U.K. and Japan showed the risks for eye, kidney and nerve complication were also reduced as a result of better sugar control.

Some important factors which affect the complications:

✔ **optimal blood sugar control:** Although this is one important factor in relation to these complications, **IT IS NOT THE ONLY FACTOR**

✔ **high blood pressure and abnormal blood lipids** are important in relation to eye, kidney and heart complications

✔ **tobacco use** adds to the risk for kidney, eye and heart damage

✔ **increased blood clotting** is also a possible risk factor

✔ **other unknown factors, including genetics**

Some facts about the occurrence of complications:

✔ Most of the long-term complications do not occur in young children.

✔ The years of greatest risk for complications seem to start after puberty. Research has shown that in people with diabetes, the small blood vessels showed no changes before puberty, whether optimal sugar control was present or not.

✔ After puberty, the blood vessels usually remain normal in people with low HbA1c values, but changes are more likely to appear in people with chronic high HbA1c values.

✔ Around the time of puberty, levels of growth hormone, sex hormones and other hormones increase greatly. These hormones cause increased blood sugar levels.

✔ The risk of complications after puberty may increase because of the changes in hormone levels, because of high sugar levels caused by the changes in hormone levels or possibly due to both.

We are continuing to learn more about how the high blood/CGM glucose levels cause the complications.

Sugar does attach:

✔ to the protein (hemoglobin) in the red blood cells to form hemoglobin A1c or HbA1c (see Chapter 14)

✔ to the skin proteins in people who have curvatures of several fingers (see "Finger Curvatures" in this chapter)

✔ to other proteins in the blood vessels and other parts of the body when the blood sugar levels are very high

Once the sugar attaches to any body protein, the protein may not work as well as when sugar is not attached.

Although not yet proven, there is some evidence that the wide fluctuations in blood/CGM glucose levels may also add to the risk for complications. Until people began to use continuous glucose monitors (CGM), it was not realized how much glucose levels fluctuated. These fluctuations usually decrease in people who consistently wear a CGM.

Even though the vascular complications are not usually seen until puberty, it is important to work for optimal blood/CGM glucose control in the pre-pubertal years. There are some side effects of high blood/CGM glucose levels that can occur at any time (see Chapter 14). Also, the habits for the future are formed when the person is young.

COMPLICATIONS IN PEOPLE WITH DIABETES

Complications related, at least in part, to blood sugar control:

1. EYE PROBLEMS

Cataracts

Cataracts are small thickenings in the lens (which is located at the front of the eye; see picture in this chapter)

- The damage to the lens is believed to be caused by sorbitol, a compound made in the lens from glucose.

- Sorbitol damage occurs when blood glucose (sugar) levels have been very high in the body for a long time.

- Sorbitol in foods is changed by the body (liver) and does not cause this damage.

- Damage to the lens can happen at any age.

- Rarely, cataracts can be present at the onset of diabetes if sugar levels have been high for a long time before insulin is started.

- They may show some improvement with optimal sugar control.

- These lens changes are *not* the same as the more severe retinal complications in the back of the eye that are discussed next.

- The eye doctor (ophthalmologist or optometrist) will do a detailed exam for cataracts in the yearly eye exam, starting around the time of puberty.

- If cataracts interfere with vision they can be removed surgically by the eye doctor.

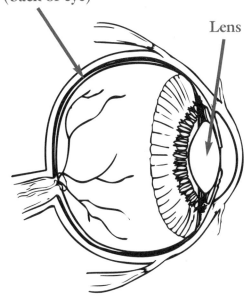

Retina (back of eye)

Lens

Retinal Changes or Retinopathy

The word retinopathy refers to changes of the retina, which is the layer of tissue at the back of the eye (see picture of the eye). This part of the eye has many small blood vessels similar to those found in the kidney.

A. *Retinopathy facts:*

Retinopathy is a change in the small blood vessels found in the back of the eye (retina), which occurs mainly after puberty.

These changes depend on various factors:

▼ the duration of diabetes after puberty

▼ the degree of blood sugar control

The DCCT showed that in people without eye changes from diabetes, lower blood sugars delayed development of retinopathy by 76 percent. The DCCT also showed that, in people with known early eye changes from diabetes, intensive therapy slowed the progression of retinopathy by 54 percent and reduced the incidence of severe retinopathy by 47 percent.

▼ increased blood pressure also results in a greater risk for retinal changes

▼ tobacco use makes these changes progress more rapidly

We do not understand all of the causes of the eye changes of diabetes. There is a small group of people for whom the presence or absence of eye changes seems to not show a relation to sugar control.

B. *Early detection:*

✔ is very important and is one clear argument for having diabetes check-ups every three months.

✔ the diabetes care provider doing the physical exam should be able to detect eye changes and make appropriate referrals to an eye doctor (ophthalmologist) who specializes in diabetic changes (retinal specialist).

✔ **The ADA does not suggest seeing an eye doctor for diabetic reasons before age 10 years. We usually wait until the person with type 1 diabetes has had diabetes three years and is ≥ 10 years old. How long someone has had type 2 diabetes before diagnosis is often not known. For this reason, people with type 2 diabetes should see the eye doctor soon after diagnosis (if ≥ 10 years old).**

✔ Thereafter, if there are no diabetic eye changes, or if the changes are minor, yearly visits to the diabetes eye specialist are adequate.

✔ Minor eye changes include a ballooning of the small retinal blood vessels; these changes are reversible and are called **"microaneurysms."** Some people can have these minor changes for many years and not develop more severe eye disease. Careful blood sugar control is particularly important when any changes are detected. If more severe eye changes occur, then more frequent visits to the diabetes eye specialist are needed.

C. *More severe eye disease:*

✔ "pre-proliferative" and "proliferative" retinopathy:

● Usually involves formation of new (proliferative) and fragile retinal blood vessels, which are at a greater risk for breaking (hemorrhaging).

● The more severe changes are referred for **laser treatment**. This involves the use of a very bright light. It was begun in the 1970s as a way to save vision in people with diabetes who have severe eye changes.

● Laser treatment destroys the fragile (proliferative) new blood vessels and has been very effective in preventing loss of vision.

● The most important factor is to have close follow-up once the more severe changes appear. Laser treatment can then be done at the proper time to prevent loss of vision.

● The biggest danger is a hemorrhage. It could damage the retina or send blood into the vitreous fluid between the lens and retina (vitreous hemorrhage) or cause the retina to separate from the other layers in the back of the eye (retinal detachment).

2. KIDNEY DISEASE OR DIABETIC NEPHROPATHY

A. *The job of the kidneys in the body:*

✔ They normally filter wastes and water from our blood and make urine (Chapter 2).

✔ When blood/CGM glucose levels are high, sugar is passed into the urine. When this happens, the pressures are higher in the kidney filtering system (the glomerulus) and changes in the small blood vessels of the kidney can occur. This increased pressure causes damage to the filtering system so that some proteins start leaking through the filter and appear in the urine.

B. *Kidney disease is one of the most feared of the complications of diabetes and is spoken of as "nephropathy." Nephropathy is more likely to occur in people:*

✔ after puberty

✔ who have had diabetes for a long time

✔ with high HbA1c values

✔ with elevated blood pressure

✔ who smoke or chew tobacco

Outcomes for kidney disease have improved in diabetes in the past few decades. However, it still occurs in about one in three people with type 1 (insulin-dependent) diabetes, and in about one in four people with type 2 (adult onset) diabetes.

C. *Signs of kidney disease may include:*

▼ increased blood pressure

▼ ankle swelling, also known as edema (due to fluid collection)

▼ excessive urine protein spillage

▼ elevation of the waste materials in the blood (increased blood creatinine and urea nitrogen or BUN)

D. *The Microalbumin level:*

● detects diabetic kidney damage at an early stage when it might still be reversible

● is usually done on a timed overnight or on a 24-hour urine sample

● is essential for people who have had type 1 diabetes for three or more years and are at least 10 years of age

● should be done soon after diagnosis for people with type 2 diabetes

● should then be done once yearly so that the interval is not missed when the early damage is still reversible

● is best done by collecting the overnight urine sample (see directions at the end of this chapter)

If there is an increased level of microalbumin in the urine on two separate evaluations:

▼ WITH A LEVEL ABOVE 20 MICROGRAMS (μg) PER MINUTE, IT IS NOW ACCEPTED THAT THERE IS A 95 PERCENT RISK FOR DEVELOPING NEPHROPATHY AND KIDNEY FAILURE IF NOTHING IS DONE.

▼ A "borderline microalbumin level" for timed overnight urine collections is a value between 7.6 μg/minute and 20 μg/minute. This "borderline" range represents a time period when optimal sugar and/or blood pressure control may help to lower the value or keep it from going higher.

▼ Medications are not usually given for a "borderline" level, as it may still be possible to return the value to normal by lowering the HbA1c.

▼ If the urine microalbumin value is between 20 and 300 μg/minute, it is called **"microalbuminuria"** and may still be reversible with lowering of blood/CGM glucose values and blood pressure control and medications (ACE-inhibitor, see part E). There can be spontaneous regression from microalbumin to normal and two (of three) samples above 20 μg/min are required prior to diagnosis.

▼ Smoking cigarettes and chewing tobacco

lead to a greater risk for kidney damage and must be avoided by people with diabetes.

▼ A decrease in protein intake is recommended (to lessen the load on the kidneys) for anyone who has microalbumin levels above 20 μg/minute, but particularly for those who have levels above 300 μg/minute (nephropathy or **macroalbuminuria**).

▼ The DCCT showed that improved glucose control reduced the occurrence of microalbuminuria by 39 percent. Gross kidney damage (nephropathy or albuminuria) was reduced by 54 percent. It must once again be remembered that glucose control is NOT the only cause of diabetic kidney damage.

E. *The past three decades have brought significant advances in the prevention, detection and treatment of diabetic kidney damage.*

✔ It is up to the family and the physician to make sure that the urine collections to detect kidney changes are done at the recommended times.

✔ If the family is unable to collect an overnight urine as described in the back of this chapter, bringing in a portion of the first morning void is second best. This provides a urine sample from when the person slept and it can be analyzed per mg of creatinine. It avoids the 10-15 percent false positives (due to "orthostatic proteinuria") that occur with the "last resort," collecting a random sample in the clinic. For a random or non-timed urine, a concentration of greater than 30 microgram of albumin per milligram of creatinine is considered "microalbuminuria".

✔ If the microalbumin levels are not done, the "window" during which changes may be reversible could be missed.

✔ If the microalbumin levels on the overnight or 24-hour urines are high, medicines may be effective in reversing or slowing the kidney damage.

● The usual medicine that is tried first is an **ACE-inhibitor** (ACE = **A**ngiotensin-**C**onverting **E**nzyme). This medication prevents formation of angiotensin II, which is a very potent constrictor of blood vessels. The result is less pressure buildup in the kidneys. There are several varieties of ACE-inhibitors, all of which are probably effective if given in adequate dosage. Another similar class of medications are called **ARB**s (or **A**ngiotensin **R**eceptor **B**lockers).

● Early kidney damage is detectable and methods to reverse or slow down kidney damage are available. This has now resulted in a decline in the incidence of renal kidney failure from diabetes.

3. NEUROPATHY (NERVE DAMAGE)

Diabetic neuropathy, or "damage to the nerves," is a condition seen after puberty, usually in people who have had very high sugar levels for a long time.

About neuropathy:

✔ It is a complex condition that we still do not completely understand.

✔ The DCCT found that the incidence of neuropathy was 60 percent less in the group with the lower blood sugar levels.

✔ As with cataracts, neuropathy is believed to be related, at least in part, to increased sorbitol levels deposited in the nerves. The sorbitol is made from sugar.

✔ There is also a decrease in another compound (myoinositol) which is important for the nerves.

✔ Some people with type 2 diabetes have neuropathy when they are diagnosed with diabetes.

The neuropathy usually makes itself known with:

▼ numbness, tingling, sharp pains in the lower legs or feet

▼ changes in other parts of the body: e.g., the rate at which food moves through the intestines may change (gastroparesis)

Much research is being done to find new and better medications for the treatment of neuropathy.

4. CORONARY (HEART) AND OTHER LARGER BLOOD VESSELS

The "larger" blood vessels are in contrast to the very small (sometimes microscopic) ones found in our eyes and kidneys. The larger ones include the heart blood vessels that provide blood (and thus nutrition and oxygen) to our heart. When a heart blood vessel is blocked, a "heart attack" can result. Approximately 65 percent of deaths for people with diabetes are due to heart attacks. Heart attacks have many causes, but high risk factors include:

✔ **chronic high HbA1c levels**
✔ **increased blood pressure**
✔ **family history** of relatives who had heart attacks before age 50
✔ **smoking**
✔ **elevated LDL** (low-density lipoprotein) **cholesterol, reduced HDL cholesterol** (high-density lipoprotein), which is the "good" cholesterol
✔ **elevated <u>total</u> blood cholesterol levels**

Some causes of high cholesterol levels:

▼ Until a few years ago, diets that contained 40 percent of calories from fat were routinely recommended. Most dietitians now recommend that no more than 30 percent of calories be from fat sources. High fat intake is known to raise blood cholesterol levels (see Chapters 11 and 12).

▼ Heredity and chronic high HbA1c levels also can be causes of high cholesterol levels.

Recommendations:

● Blood cholesterol levels should be checked at puberty and then every 5 years until adulthood at which point they should be checked annually. Desired levels are given in Table 2 of Chapter 11.

● Medications (the "statins") that block our body's cholesterol synthesis are available for people who have very high cholesterol or LDL levels. The statins have been shown to decrease the risk for heart attacks.

● Blood pressure should be checked at regular clinic visits. Increases in blood pressure should be treated early.

● People with diabetes should not use tobacco!

● Exercise is important to maintain a healthy weight and improve insulin sensitivity.

Sexual Function

✔ Some males with diabetes have problems with penile erections. The cause of this problem is believed to be related in part to microvascular disease. It is also related to autonomic neuropathy. The medicines Viagra®, Levitra® and Cialis® may be helpful to some men with diabetes who have this problem.

5. JOINT CONTRACTURES

Some facts:

✔ Some people cannot touch the knuckles of the second joint in their fifth fingers (little fingers) when their hands are in a "praying" position.

✔ The joints of the other fingers or other joints in the body can also be involved.

✔ When other joints or fingers other than just the fifth finger are involved, there has usually been a period of very high sugar levels and sugar has attached to the proteins in the skin over the joints.

✔ No pain or other problems are usually related to these changes.

✔ Some doctors believe the curvatures of the fifth fingers may be partly inherited.

✔ Parents and siblings of people with diabetes often have curvatures of the fifth fingers even though they don't have diabetes.

6. BIRTH DEFECTS (discussed in more detail in Chapter 30)

This complication is primarily important to a woman who might get pregnant.

Some facts:

✔ IT IS VERY IMPORTANT TO TALK TO YOUR DIABETES PHYSICIAN BEFORE GETTING PREGNANT.

✔ Insulin pumps and intensive diabetes management must be considered PRIOR TO THE PREGNANCY.

✔ If diabetes is not well controlled (e.g., high HbA1c), a pregnant woman with diabetes is more likely to have a baby with one or more birth problems or defects.

✔ The first few months of pregnancy are the most important in preventing defects.

✔ A woman should not stop using birth control or decide to get pregnant until her diabetes is well controlled.

✔ If the HbA1c, blood pressure and kidney microalbumin levels are normal or low prior to the pregnancy, the likelihood of kidney deterioration during pregnancy is minimized.

✔ Diabetic eye changes do sometimes worsen during pregnancy and it is wise to be followed more closely by one's retinal specialist during this time.

7. FOOT PROBLEMS

Some facts:

✔ Foot problems due to poor or decreased blood flow and neuropathy do not occur in children. Some families who are educated by diabetes care providers who care mainly for adults with diabetes will be told that children must "wash their feet daily" or "never go barefoot." Although it is nice to have clean feet for clinic visits, these precautions are NOT necessary for children.

✔ Foot problems usually occur in older adults and may be related to poor circulation or to neuropathy.

✔ There is research suggesting that regular exercise may help to maintain normal foot circulation later in life (see Chapter 13).

✔ It is important for diabetes care providers to do careful examinations of feet in post-pubertal patients.

✔ It is also important for a person to know to call the doctor if a foot sore does not heal well or if there is any sign of an infection (redness, warmth or pus) or ulcer.

✔ Ingrown toenails (an infection) occur with similar frequency in children with or without diabetes.

✔ The ingrown toenails are usually caused by toenails that are cut too short at the corners.

- ✔ The toenails should be cut straight across with a straight nail clipper and the length should be even with the end of the toe. Prevention is much easier than treatment.

- ✔ Ingrown toenails are more of a problem in people with diabetes as infections cause high sugar levels. The high sugar levels, in turn, support the infection.

- ✔ Warts are not more common in people with diabetes. The best way to remove them is with the use of liquid nitrogen.

DEFINITIONS

Blood pressure: The blood pressure consists of a higher (systolic) pressure that reflects the pumping or working pressure of the heart and a lower (diastolic) pressure which reflects the resting pressure of the heart between beats. It is important to have the blood pressure checked regularly.

Blood Urea Nitrogen (BUN): A material in the blood normally cleared by the kidneys. It is elevated in advanced kidney disease as well as with dehydration.

Cataract: A density (clouding) in the lens that **may cause spots, blurred or reduced vision.**

Creatinine: A material in the blood normally cleared by the kidneys. The test to measure its clearance from the blood is called a creatinine clearance test.

DCCT: Diabetes Control and Complications Trial. A very large trial of people ages 13-39 years old, which showed that lower HbA1c values resulted in a lower risk for diabetic eye, kidney, nerve and heart problems. The trial ended in June, 1993.

Edema: Collection of fluid (swelling) under the skin.

Filter: To separate out or remove. The kidneys filter wastes from our blood.

Gastroparesis: Neuropathy involving the stomach and/or intestine.

Glomerulus: Small groups of blood vessels in the kidneys that filter the blood to remove wastes and water to make urine.

Hemorrhage: The breaking of a blood vessel. In the eye, this can occur in the retinal layer or, in more advanced cases, in the fluid (vitreous) in front of the retina (vitreous hemorrhage).

Laser treatment: Using a very bright beam of light to destroy the new (proliferative) blood vessels in the retina, which are at high risk for hemorrhaging and causing a loss of vision.

Lens (see picture of eye in this chapter): The oval structure in the front of the eye that changes shape to allow the eye to focus on near or distant objects.

Microalbumin: A method to measure small amounts of a protein (albumin) in the urine to detect kidney damage from diabetes at a stage in which it might still be reversible.

Microaneurysm: A small dilatation (ballooning) of a blood vessel, which is a minor change that can be reversible. It is caused by diabetes.

Myoinositol: A compound, which is reduced in nerves when sorbitol levels are elevated (in neuropathy).

Nephropathy: A generic name for kidney disease. It is usually used to indicate a more advanced stage of kidney involvement.

Neuropathy: A disease of the nerves. This is believed to happen in people with diabetes due to accumulation of sorbitol (formed from blood glucose), or possibly due to deficiency of another metabolite, myoinositol.

Ophthalmologist: The name for a doctor (MD) who specializes in eye diseases. The ophthalmologist may further specialize in the retinal layer in the back of the eye, which is affected by diabetes. The doctor is then called a "retinal specialist."

Optometrist: An eye doctor who is not an MD (although they are still important care providers). They can also screen for diabetic eye disease.

Podiatrist: A person who is specially trained in the care of the feet. They are not MDs (although they are still important care providers).

Pre-proliferative or proliferative retinopathy: Terms for more advanced stages of eye involvement from diabetes (when a diabetes eye specialist needs to be seen more frequently).

Puberty: The time in a teen's life when adult sexual changes start to occur.

Retina (see picture of eye in this chapter): The layers of small blood vessels and nerves in the back of the eye that are very important for vision.

Retinal detachment: Separation of the retinal layer in the back of the eye from other layers in the eye.

Retinopathy: Changes in the retinal (small blood vessel) layer in the back of the eye from diabetes. These are more likely to occur after puberty in people who have had diabetes for a long time and who have been in poor sugar control.

Vitreous fluid: The fluid between the lens and the retina. When retinal blood vessels break, they can bleed into the vitreous fluid (vitreous hemorrhage).

QUESTIONS AND ANSWERS FROM NEWSNOTES

Q What is the best way to screen for early microvascular (small vessel) disease of the kidneys and the eyes in people with diabetes and when should it be done?

A The microalbumin determination is the best way to currently diagnose early kidney involvement in people with diabetes. This is best done by measuring the microalbumin in a timed overnight urine collections. It is very important to repeat the two overnight urine collections every year. If a person has begun pubertal changes (usually ages 11-13 years) and has had diabetes for at least three years, we recommend doing the two overnight urine collections for microalbumin and having an eye exam by an ophthalmologist once yearly. If we are unable to collect overnight urine, then first morning collection is better than a random sample. Directions for the urine collections are in the back of this chapter.

Q Why is it necessary to reduce my protein intake as I lose protein in my urine? Shouldn't I eat more protein?

A The protein (albumin, microalbumin) loss in the urine is most likely due to kidney damage from diabetes. This is a result of HbA1c levels being too high, the blood pressure being too high (hypertension) or as a result of using tobacco. There are probably other causes as well that we do not yet understand. When someone gets kidney damage from any cause (diabetes, hypertension, nephritis, lupus, etc.), it generally helps to slow down the process by eating less protein. The protein seems to be an extra load for the kidney to handle, and reducing the protein will make less work for the damaged kidneys. It is wise to meet with the dietitian and kidney specialist at this stage to discuss what the correct amount of protein should be.

What level of glucose control is necessary to prevent the eye and kidney complications of diabetes?

 A study reported in the *"Journal of the American Medical Association"* in 1989 showed that longitudinal HbA1c values were definitely related to the eye and kidney complications. No person who had kept their HbA1c levels below 6.8 percent for the DCA 2000 method (normal to 6.0 percent) had evidence of eye changes. Likewise, no person who had kept their HbA1c below 7.4 percent had kidney changes, and only two of 230 had serious eye changes. This is in contrast to people who had a mean HbA1c above 9.3 percent, where 41 percent of the people had more severe eye changes and 28 percent had evidence of kidney damage.

The extra effort to stay in optimal blood sugar control may indeed save much work later in life in dealing with diabetes complications, such as eye and kidney.

 Is cigarette smoking bad for someone with diabetes?

Yes. It is linked to lung cancer, high blood pressure and heart attacks in ALL people and is thus a poor choice for everyone. In addition, data from our Center has shown that smoking results in about a three-fold greater likelihood of diabetic kidney complications. Smoking also causes diabetic eye disease to progress more rapidly. The mechanism by which smoking does this is unknown, but as people who chew tobacco seem to have the same consequences, it may be from the absorption of nicotine into the body. HbA1c levels are often high in smokers with diabetes. Therefore, these effects had to be removed before a conclusion about smoking could be reached. Smoking results in higher HbA1c levels by increasing levels of other hormones, such as adrenaline, which raise the blood sugar. The heart rate and blood pressure also increase and this may be related to the increased eye and kidney problems.

 How common is kidney disease in association with diabetes, and can it be prevented?

 Kidney problems occur in up to 30 percent of people with type 1 diabetes, although uncommon before the person reaches age 30 or 40 years. There are things that we can do now to help reduce the likelihood of kidney problems. These include: optimal sugar control, keeping the blood pressure normal, prompt treatment of bladder and kidney infections and not smoking. It is very important to get the urine microalbumins checked yearly for people who have had type 1 diabetes for three or more years who have reached puberty.

 Are contact lenses OK for a person with diabetes to use?

 Yes, people with diabetes can wear contact lenses, but there are some extra precautions. The contact lens fits over the superficial layer of the eye called the cornea. The cornea needs a constant supply of oxygen and tears to keep it healthy. Thus, the contact lens must fit properly so that the cornea is not injured and the tears are able to continue to flow. It is even more important for people with diabetes to follow the instructions for care and cleaning of the contact lenses than it is for other people. The corneas of people with diabetes are sometimes less sensitive to pain or irritation, so people may be less likely to feel discomfort when their contacts are causing problems. Infections may also not clear as quickly if they do occur. Thus, use the solutions and disinfectants exactly as your eye doctor recommends. Don't get lazy in cleaning or try to cut corners. Don't leave the contacts in any longer than recommended. Don't mix cleaning solutions.

MICROALBUMINS

Doctor: _____ Your Name: _____

A. INSTRUCTIONS FOR DOING THE OVERNIGHT URINE COLLECTIONS

COLLECTION #1   DATE: _____

1. Empty your bladder at bedtime and discard this sample.   **TIME:** _____

2. Save **EVERY DROP** of urine during the night.

3. Save **EVERY DROP** of the first morning sample.   **TIME:** _____
   ALL urine from collection #1 should be placed in the same container.

4. Measure the volume of the urine sample.   **TOTAL VOLUME:** _____

COLLECTION #2   DATE: _____

1. Empty your bladder at bedtime and discard this sample.   **TIME:** _____

2. Save **EVERY DROP** of urine during the night.

3. Save **EVERY DROP** of the first morning sample.   **TIME:** _____
   ALL urine from collection #2 should be placed in the same container.

4. Measure the volume of the urine sample.   **TOTAL VOLUME:** _____

B. IMPORTANT INFORMATION ABOUT YOUR COLLECTIONS

1. Label each container with your name and #1 or #2.

2. You may use any CLEAN container you have at home that will not leak to collect the sample. We do not provide containers.

3. Store urine aliquots in refrigerator until your visit (samples are good for one week if kept cold).

4. **DO NOT** mix collections #1 and #2 together in the same container.

5. **DO NOT** drink caffeinated or alcoholic beverages or use tobacco after 10 p.m. the evening of the collections.

6. **DO NOT** exercise strenuously for the four hours prior to bedtime.

7. **DO NOT** collect specimens during a menstrual period.

8. Failure to follow directions exactly may cause incorrect results.

9. If you have any questions, please call your healthcare provider.

C. DIRECTIONS FOR MEASURING THE VOLUME

1. Have a measuring cup or (better) a cylinder - preferably marked in cc (ml). One cup is 240cc. Urine is sterile and it is ok to use cooking measuring cups (just wash prior to next use for cooking).

2. Measure the total cc of each overnight sample and put the amounts in the blanks for step 4 for collections #1 and #2.

3. Put a sample of each urine collection in a clean tube. The rest may be discarded. Any clean red top tube from a doctor's office, clinic or hospital lab will work. Label which sample (#1 or #2) it is, put your name on the tube, and put the tube in a cup in the refrigerator until you get to your clinic. Bring this sheet with the times and total volumes with you.

Chapter 24
Associated Autoimmune Conditions of Type 1 Diabetes

TEACHING OBJECTIVES:

Present associated autoimmune diseases (e.g., thyroid and celiac).

LEARNING OBJECTIVES:

Learner (parents, child, relative or self) will be able to:

List one symptom associated with each autoimmune disease.

H. Peter Chase, MD
Loise A. Gilmer, MS, RD CDE
Darcy Owen, MS, RD, CDE
David Maahs, MD, PhD

INTRODUCTION

Other autoimmune (self-allergy) diseases are also associated with type 1 diabetes. This is due to the inheritance of genes increasing the risk for autoimmunity. Some examples of autoimmune diseases seen more frequently in people with type 1 diabetes are discussed below:

Thyroid Disorders

Some facts:

✔ Some thyroid enlargement occurs in about half of people with type 1 diabetes, although only about one in 20 ever needs treatment. The reason for this is believed to be a similar "self-allergy" (autoimmune) type of reaction that causes both diabetes and the related thyroid enlargement.

✔ People who get diabetes often have an antibody (allergic reaction) in their blood against their pancreas (specifically, the islet cells in the pancreas, as discussed in Chapter 3). Likewise, people with diabetes who get thyroid problems usually have an antibody (allergic reaction) in their blood against the thyroid gland.

✔ Thyroid antibody tests can be done, although doctors frequently only measure thyroid function.

✔ It is important for the diabetes care provider to always check the size of the thyroid gland at the time of clinic visits.

✔ If the thyroid is not producing enough thyroid hormone, body growth may be slowed.

✔ The person may feel tired all the time.

✔ If the gland is enlarged, specialized blood tests should be done (particularly a TSH level, as this is almost always the first test to become abnormal). If the TSH level is abnormal, it is wise to repeat the TSH level and to also evaluate other thyroid parameters.

✔ If the thyroid tests are abnormal, a thyroid tablet can then be taken once daily. Thyroid problems are not serious unless unrecognized or untreated. The treatment is excellent, easy, inexpensive, and involves taking pills (not shots).

✔ Sometimes the tablets can be discontinued (under a doctor's supervision) when the person is finished growing.

✔ Thyroid problems are common even in people who do not have diabetes (about one in 50 adults).

✔ Rarely, people with diabetes can also have an overactive thyroid gland that produces excess thyroid hormone (hyperthyroidism).

Adrenal Disorders (autoimmune adrenal insufficiency, Addison's Disease)

Some facts:

✔ Autoimmunity against the adrenal gland can also occur.

✔ It is quite rare (about one in 500 people with type 1 diabetes), but it is important to diagnose and treat, as it can result in death if untreated. Cortisol, the hormone the body

is unable to produce in Addison's Disease, is especially important during stress. If Addison's disease develops, additional teaching will be required. President Kennedy is an example of a famous person who had autoimmune adrenal insufficiency.

Some early signs for someone with diabetes may be:

✔ An increased frequency of severe low blood sugars

✔ Episodes of feeling weak or faint (with normal blood sugars - but sometimes low blood pressure)

✔ Two electrolytes in the blood, sodium (Na+) and potassium (K+), may be low and high, respectively.

✔ Later, darker skin coloring over the back of the hands (or knuckles or elbows) may occur.

✔ Initial screening may be for an antibody against the adrenal gland.

✔ Eventually, morning ACTH and cortisol (cortisone) blood levels (and eventually an ACTH stimulation test) should be obtained.

✔ The treatment (as with thyroid disease) is with tablets. Treatment includes training the person (or family) to increase the tablets during periods of stress (as with an infection or with surgery).

Celiac Disease

Celiac disease (also known as gluten sensitivity, gluten-enteropathy or celiac sprue) is an inherited disorder in which the small intestine is damaged by an autoimmune reaction to gluten, a protein found in grains like wheat, rye and barley. The damage to the small intestine causes nutrients to be malabsorbed.

Some facts:

✔ The risk for celiac disease is carried on one of the genes (DR types, DR3) that is also related to being at high risk for type 1 diabetes (see Chapter 3).

✔ Approximately one in 20 people with

Table 1
Grain, Seeds, Beans, Flours, and Cereals List for Celiac Disease

ALLOWED	Use with Caution	NOT ALLOWED
Amaranth	*Oats	Barley
Arrowroot		Bran
Buckwheat		Bulgur
Corn		Couscous
Flax		Durum
Hominy		Einkorn
Legume flours (bean, chickpea, garbanzo)		Emmer
		Farina
Millet		Farro
Montina™ (Indian rice grass)		Graham
Nut flours (almond, hazelnut, pecan)		Kamut
		Rye
Potato flour		Semolina
Potato starch		Spelt
Quinoa		Triticale
Rice		Wheat
Sorghum		Wheat germ
Soy and other beans		White flour
Tapioca		Whole wheat
Teff		

*Oats cannot be guaranteed to be gluten free. Contamination can happen when oats are grown on the same field or processed in the same building as gluten containing grains.

(Table adapted from The Children's Hospital General Clinical Research Center's "Introduction to the Gluten-Free (GF) Diet" packet, Denver CO)

diabetes also has celiac disease.

✔ As other family members who do not have diabetes may also have the DR3 genetic type, they are also more likely to have celiac disease (even though they do not have diabetes).

✔ It can be diagnosed using a blood antibody test (transglutaminase and/or anti-endomysial antibodies). At present, an intestinal biopsy is often also done to confirm the diagnosis.

Symptoms may include:

- Stomach pain

- Gas

- Diarrhea or constipation

- Decreased height or weight gain in children

- Iron deficiency anemia

- Irritability

- Dental enamel defects

- Osteoporosis

The symptoms, the abnormal blood tests and the intestinal biopsy changes may return to normal within a few months after treatment is begun.

Treatment:

✔ The only acceptable treatment for celiac disease is strict adherence to a 100% gluten-free diet for life.

✔ Remove all wheat, rye, and barley products

REFERENCE LIST FOR CELIAC DISEASE

Celiac Associations in the United States

Celiac Disease Foundation
818-990-2354
13251 Ventura Blvd. #1
Studio City, CA 91604
www.celiac.org

Celiac Sprue Association/USA, Inc.
402-558-0600
877-CSA-4-CSA (Toll Free)
P.O. Box 31700
Omaha, NE 68131-0700
www.csaceliacs.org

Gluten Intolerance Group of North America
206-246-6652
15110 10th Ave. SW, Ste. A
Seattle, WA 98166
www.gluten.net

Websites and Support Groups:

www.celiac.com is an excellent site for safe/forbidden food additive lists, mainstream GF food products by brand name, GF recipes, discussion of controversial grains, etc.—just a good reference overall

www.glutenfreediet.ca Shelley Case's (Expert Celiac RD) website with free patient education handouts, information on celiac disease and the gluten free diet

www.clanthompson.com Gluten free food lists for purchase (printed and software products), "Ask the Expert," and other resources for people with celiac disease

www.celiachealth.org Children's Digestive Health and Nutrition Foundation
Can download: Gluten-Free Diet Guide for Families

www.glutenfreedrugs.com Lists gluten free drugs and vitamins and is maintained and run by clinical pharmacists

www.zeer.com Lets you search a database of over 30,000 foods for gluten free products, reads labels for you and gives you the gluten free status of each product

www.triumphdining.com Guide for eating out and grocery shopping

www.glutenfreemom.com Website with good information for parents of kids with celiac disease

Books:

Living Gluten-Free for Dummies by Danna Korn, For Dummies, 2010. www.amazon.com

Gluten-Free Diet: A Comprehensive Resource Guide by Shelly Case, Case Nutrition Consulting, 2010. www.glutenfreediet.ca

The Gluten-Free Gourmet Bakes Bread by Bette Hagman, Henry Holt, 2000. www.celiac.com

The Gluten-Free Gourmet Cooks Fast and Healthy by Bette Hagman, Henry Holt, 2000. www.amazon.com or www.celiac.com

Kids with Celiac Disease: A Family Guide to Raising Happy, Healthy, Gluten-Free Children by Danna Korn, Woodbine House, 2001. www.woodbinehouse.com

Incredible Edible Gluten-Free Food for Kids by Sheri L. Sanderson, Woodbine House, 2002. www.woodbinehouse.com

The Gluten Free Kid: A Celiac Disease Survival Guide by Melissa London, Woodbine House, 2005. www.woodbinehouse.com

Wheat-Free, Gluten-Free Cookbook for Kids and Busy Adults by Connie Sarros, McGraw Hill, 2010. www.amazon.com or www.celiac.com

Pocket Dictionary: Acceptability of Foods and Food Ingredients for the Gluten-Free Diet Canadian Celiac Association. www.celiac.ca

Magazines:

Gluten-Free Living: The Resource for People with Gluten Intolerance. A newsletter available by contacting Gluten-Free Living, P.O. Box 105, Hasting-on-Hudson, NY 10706.

Living Without: A Lifestyle Guide for People with Allergies and Food Sensitivities. www.livingwithout.com

from the diet and any ingredient that contains these grains. Oats and oat products may also be removed from the diet initially.

✔ Many foods are naturally gluten-free and are allowed on the diet, such as rice, corn, potatoes, fruits, vegetables, meats and dairy products. (see Table 1 for grains that are allowed).

The National Institutes of Health Consensus Development Conference in 2004 came up with some elements needed in the management of Celiac disease:

C   Consultation with a skilled dietitian.

E   Education about the disease.

L   Lifelong adherence to a gluten-free diet.

I   Identification and treatment of nutrition deficiencies.

A   Access to an advocacy group.

C   Continuous long term follow up by a multidisciplinary team.

(NIH Consensus Statement on Celiac Disease. NIH Consens State Sci Statements. 2004 Jun 28-30 (1) 1-22.)

Skin Problems

Some facts:

✔ Yellow fatty deposits (**necrobiosis**) can collect in the skin over the front of the lower legs. No one knows what causes these fat deposits, although they are most likely due to autoimmunity.

✔ A rare condition called **dermatitis herpetiformis** is also related to a sensitivity to the protein, gluten (see celiac disease). It is characterized by blisters on the elbows, buttocks and knees. Like celiac disease, it responds to a gluten-free diet.

SUMMARY

In summary, much is now known about autoimmune problems associated with diabetes. Screening and treatment are now available for most conditions.

DEFINITIONS

Adrenal gland: A hormone-producing gland located above each kidney, which has the function of making cortisol, salt-retaining hormones and other hormones.

Autoimmunity (self-allergy): As defined in Chapter 3, this involves forming an allergic reaction against one's own tissues. This happens in type 1 diabetes and can happen in thyroid disorders and, more rarely, with the adrenal gland.

Celiac disease (Sprue, Gluten-enteropathy): Is an inherited disorder in which the small intestine is damaged by an autoimmune reaction to gluten, a protein found in grains like wheat, rye and barley.

Gluten: The protein found in wheat that people are allergic to if they have celiac disease.

Necrobiosis: The name for yellow fatty deposits that can occur over the lower legs in people with diabetes.

Thyroid: A hormone-producing gland in the lower front of the neck on each side of the windpipe (trachea). The hormone is called thyroid hormone.

QUESTIONS AND ANSWERS FROM NEWSNOTES

Q Are thyroid problems more common in children with diabetes, and if so, why?

A Yes, thyroid problems are more common in children with diabetes. They are caused by an "autoimmune" or allergic-type reaction that is very similar to the allergic-type reaction that is believed to be important in causing diabetes. Thus, most people with new-onset diabetes have islet cell antibodies (an allergic reaction against the islet cells that make the insulin) at the time of diagnosis of type 1 (but not type 2) diabetes. Likewise, many of the people with diabetes who develop thyroid problems have an antibody in their blood against the thyroid gland. The pancreas and the thyroid are endocrine glands that make insulin and thyroid hormone, respectively. Thus, the two glands have much in common. Some physicians recommend thyroid blood tests yearly or every other year in children with diabetes. The practice in our clinic is to do the tests more frequently if the thyroid gland is large or if there is a special indication, such as a fall-off in height. Fortunately, when low thyroid function is detected, it can be treated with a tablet. Also, the pills can sometimes be discontinued after growth is complete.

Q My doctor has found my child to have high transglutaminase antibodies that are associated with celiac disease. Does my child need to have an intestinal biopsy before considering a gluten free diet?

A *From Dr. George Eisenbarth:*
Children with type 1 diabetes are at higher risk for celiac disease, an illness in which gluten in the diet from a number of sources (e.g. wheat) causes the body's immune system to attack the inner wall of the intestine. When children have severe celiac disease associated with weight loss and diarrhea, avoiding gluten usually makes the symptoms go away and allows the child to grow normally. Nowadays we screen for celiac disease with a simple blood test for an antibody that appears in the blood, termed transglutaminase. If high levels of the antibody are found, we recommend a biopsy to confirm the diagnosis, as celiac disease is a life-long diagnosis and no single test is diagnostic. The biopsy is usually done with anesthesia so the child is not conscious for the procedure. A tube with a camera is swallowed and at the first part of the small intestine several pieces of the intestine are taken through the swallowed tube, each about the size of a pencil tip. The biopsy is then analyzed by the doctors under a microscope to confirm a diagnosis of celiac disease and determine the amount of intestinal damage, if any.

Many children do not have symptoms of celiac disease even though they have antibodies in the blood. High levels of antibodies usually indicate that there is damage to the intestine, and in general we recommend biopsy only when the antibody levels are high, unless there are also celiac disease symptoms. In many children without symptoms with high levels of the antibody there is severe damage to the intestine. It is remarkable, but even with severe damage, with a gluten free diet the intestine can grow back and be normal as long as gluten is avoided. In general with a diagnosis of celiac disease we recommend life-long avoidance of gluten. It is very important to have a firm diagnosis for people with symptoms or high levels of antibodies, and thus the recommendation for confirmation through a biopsy.

Chapter 25

The School or Work and Diabetes

Susie Owen, RN, CDE
H. Peter Chase, MD
David Maahs, MD, PhD

INTRODUCTION

The first and main job of parents in relation to school is to educate those who will be working with the child at school about diabetes. Parents want to feel that their child is in safe hands while at school (often the place where the majority of the child's waking hours are spent). Parents also want to make sure their child is not treated differently because of having diabetes. Permission is granted to copy the next few pages as often as wished. It is wise for the parent to phone the school nurse, teacher or principal to discuss the best way to inform all of the necessary people. The week before classes start is usually the best time. A checklist is provided in Table 1 to remind parents of their responsibilities.

Some parents buy or borrow a copy of the videos (see Resources at the end of this chapter) on diabetes and the school or on hypoglycemia to lend to the nurse, health aide, teachers and others likely to be involved with their child. It can be a good starting place for a discussion about hypoglycemia, the most likely emergency to occur at school.

It is essential for the family and school nurse to educate the following people:

✔ teacher(s); including gym, art and music

✔ health aide

TOPICS:
Monitoring (checking blood sugars/ketones, giving insulin)
Prevent, Detect and Treat Acute Complications
Psychosocial Adjustment

TEACHING OBJECTIVES:

1. Assess who will educate school/work personnel about diabetes.
2. Identify supplies needed to prevent acute complications at school/work.
3. Develop a "health action plan" for school/work.

LEARNING OBJECTIVES:

Learner (parents, child, relative or self) will be able to:

1. Define who will educate school/work personnel about diabetes.
2. List all supplies needed at school/work to prevent acute complications.
3. Design a health action plan for school/work with healthcare provider(s).

Table 1
School Diabetes Management and Supply Checklist for Parents

_____ Discuss specific care of your child with the teachers, school nurse, bus driver, coaches and other staff who will be involved.

_____ Complete the individualized school health care plan with the help of school staff and your diabetes care staff (see Tables 3 and 4 in this chapter).

_____ Make sure your child understands the details of who will help him/her with testing, shots and treatment of high or low blood sugars at school and where supplies will be kept. Supplies should be kept in a place where they are always available if needed (not in a locker).

_____ Make arrangements for the school to send home blood sugar records weekly.

_____ Keep current phone numbers where you can be reached. Collect equipment for school: meter, strips and finger-poker, lancets, insulin, insulin syringes or pen, biohazard container, log book or a copy of testing record form, extra insulin pump supplies, ketone testing strips, photo for substitute teacher's folder.

_____ Food and drinks; parents need to check intermittently to make sure supplies are not used up:

▼ juice cans or boxes (approximately 15g of carb each)

▼ glucose tablets

▼ instant glucose or cake-decorating gel

▼ snacks, such as Fruit Roll-Ups, dried fruit, raisins, crackers (± peanut butter or cheese), granola bars or other snacks

▼ quarters to buy sugar pop (soda) if needed

_____ box with the child's name to store these food and drink items

- ✔ bus driver
- ✔ lunchroom workers
- ✔ playground aides
- ✔ others involved with their child at school

Sometimes the school nurse or the teacher will help educate other staff. It is also important that when a substitute teacher is at school, the substitute knows that a child in the classroom has diabetes. A copy of your child's school care plan should be placed in the "substitute" folder and in the teacher's attendance book. Attach a recent photo of your child to the plan. **It is important NOT to leave it up to the child to inform and educate the school.** They may be self-conscious or embarrassed and not get the job done.

A second job of parents is to keep an adequate supply of items at school for the treatment of low blood sugars. Suggested items are listed in Table 1.

The supplies should be kept in a container in the classroom, teacher's, principal's or nurse's office. The container should be clearly labeled with the child's name and a set of instructions with contact phone numbers. They should be readily available to the child at all times. They shouldn't be locked in the young person's locker. The child may not remember their own locker combination if hypoglycemic.

There is often a special anxiety about a young child starting preschool.

This anxiety is due to a young child who:

- ✔ may not yet be able to recognize low blood sugars

- ✔ may not be mature enough to help remember snacks. The teacher will need to remind the child or the child may wear a watch with a preset alarm.

- ✔ might not have been away from the care of the parents for any significant period of time prior to starting preschool

Separation may be difficult for the parents and the child. And yet, preschool may be

important for the child in learning social and other skills. It is important to allow participation just as one would if the child did not have diabetes. The information at the end of this chapter may also be given to the preschool teacher.

SCHOOL HEALTH PLAN

Schools in most states now require a School Health Plan. Table 2 represents orders from the physician to the school nurse. The school nurse can then incorporate this information into the Individualized Health Plan (Table 3). Both would be appropriate for all children and schools. In addition, a School Health Plan specific for students using an insulin pump and other tables related to pump supplies needed at school, pump insulin dosages, etc., are included in Chapter 13 of the book, *"Understanding Insulin Pumps and Continuous Glucose Monitors"*. Also note that there is a letter for sports coaches at the end of Chapter 13. Any of these letters or tables may be copied as often as desired. Finally, directions for accessing a "504" health care plan online are included in the legal portion of this chapter. This is often reserved for use when other means have failed.

A checklist for the school nurse to follow in developing the Individualized Health Care Plan (IHP) is shown in Table 4.

BLOOD SUGARS IN THE SCHOOL

All children must have at school:

- ✔ a blood sugar (glucose) meter; it should NOT be kept in the child's locker

- ✔ strips for the meter

- ✔ a lancing device (finger poker) and lancets

At a minimum, a blood sugar must be done whenever the child is feeling low. Many physicians and parents ask that a blood sugar be done routinely prior to lunch or snacks. Often children carry their own meter in their backpack. Other children are now wearing a

Table 2
Healthcare Provider Order for Student with Diabetes

Student: _____ D.O.B.: _____ School _____ Grade _____

Doctor _____ Phone _____ Diabetes Educator _____ Phone _____

Monitor Blood Glucose: ☐ Before Lunch ☐ After Lunch ☐ Before PE ☐ After PE ☐ Before Snack
☐ Before leaving to get on bus/going home ☐ As needed for signs/symptoms of low or high blood glucose

Blood glucose at which parent should be notified   Low **<** _____ mg/dL and High **>** _____ mg/dL

Target range for blood glucose **>** _____ mg/dL to **<** _____ mg/dL

Hypoglycemia Student should not be sent to the office unaccompanied if symptomatic or BS less than 70 mg/dL

- Blood glucose below _____ mg/dL and/or symptomatic: Treat with 10 to 15 gram carbohydrate snack.

- Mild symptoms: Treat with juice, glucose tabs, etc. until above: _____ mg/dL, then snack or lunch.

- Moderate symptoms, if unable to drink juice: Administer glucose gel. Repeat until above: _____ mg/dL, then snack or lunch.

- Severe symptoms, which may include seizures, unconsciousness, unable or unwilling to take gel or juice:
  Administer Glucagon _____ mg (_____ cc) subQ or IM if trained staff available and call 911.

Hyperglycemia

☐ Check urine ketones if blood glucose is over 300 mg/dL or with symptoms of illness/vomiting. If ketones present, call parents, provide water and student should not exercise. Student may need insulin via injection.

☐ Use insulin orders (see below) when blood glucose is _____ mg/dL.

☐ Recommend student be released from school when ketones are moderate/large or symptoms of illness in order to be treated and monitored more closely by parent/guardian.

Medication

Student is on ☐ oral diabetes medication(s)   Dose: _____ mg/dL   **Times to be given** _____

Student is on ☐ insulin. Type: _____   Dose: _____ mg/dL   **Times to be given** _____

Blood Glucose Correction and Insulin Dosage using (Rapid Acting) Insulin: _____ units/_____ mg **>**_____ mg/dL

or: Blood Glucose Range _____mg/dL (_____ mmol/L)   Administer _____ units

Blood Glucose Range _____mg/dL (_____ mmol/L)   Administer _____ units

Blood Glucose Range _____mg/dL (_____ mmol/L)   Administer _____ units and check ketones

Blood Glucose Range _____mg/dL (_____ mmol/L)   Administer _____ units and check ketones

Carbohydrate counting _____ unit(s) of insulin per _____ grams of carbohydrate with lunch.

☐ Parent/guardian authorized to increase or decrease correction within the following range: +/– 2 units of insulin

☐ Parent/guardian authorized to increase or decrease insulin to carbohydrate ratio within the following range: 1 unit per prescribed grams of carbohydrates +/– 5 grams of carbohydrates.

Student's Self Care (ability level to be determined by school nurse and parent with input from healthcare provider)

Totally independent management..........................☐ **Yes** ☐ **No**	Self injects with trained staff supervision ....☐ **Yes** ☐ **No**	
(If independent, complete self-management agreement)	Injections to be done by trained staff.......................☐ **Yes** ☐ **No**	
Needs verification of blood glucose by staff..........☐ **Yes** ☐ **No**	Self treats mild hypoglycemia ....☐ **Yes** ☐ **No**	
Assist/testing to be done by trained staff..............☐ **Yes** ☐ **No**	Monitors own snacks and meals...............................☐ **Yes** ☐ **No**	
Administers insulin independently ....☐ **Yes** ☐ **No**	Independently counts carbohydrates........................☐ **Yes** ☐ **No**	
Self injects with verification of dose ....☐ **Yes** ☐ **No**	Monitors and interprets urine/blood ketones..........☐ **Yes** ☐ **No**	

SIGNATURES
My signature below provides authorization for the above written orders and exchange of health information to assist the school nurse in developing an Individualized Health Plan. I understand that all procedures will be implemented in accordance with state laws and regulations and may be performed by unlicensed designated school personnel under the training and supervision provided by the school nurse. This order is for a maximum of one year.

Physician_____ Date _____

Parent _____ Date _____

School Nurse _____ Date _____

Table 3
Individualized Health Plan (IHP): DIABETES Page 1

Student: _____ D.O.B.: _____ Home Phone: _____

Mother: _____ Work Phone: _____ Cell Phone: _____

Father: _____ Work Phone: _____ Cell Phone: _____

Guardian: _____ Phone: _____

School Nurse: _____ Phone: _____

School: _____ Grade: _____ Teacher: _____

Physician: _____ Phone: _____ Fax: _____

Diabetes Educator: _____ Phone: _____ 504 Plan on file ☐ Yes ☐ No

Hospital of Choice: _____ Date of Diagnosis: _____

Health Concern: Diabetes ☐ Type 1 or ☐ Type 2

Target Blood Glucose Range: _____ to _____

Required blood glucose testing at school:

☐ Trained personnel must perform blood glucose test.

☐ Trained personnel must supervise blood glucose test.

☐ Student can perform testing independently.

☐ Student can carry supplies and test where needed.

Times to test blood glucose:

☐ Before meals   ☐ Before P.E.   ☐ Other _____

☐ After meals   ☐ After P.E.

☐ Before snack   ☐ Before getting on bus/going home.

☐ As needed for signs/symptoms of low/high blood glucose.

Call parent if blood glucose values are below _____ or above _____.

Medications to be given during school hours:

Student is on ☐ oral diabetes medication(s)   Dose: _____ **Times to be given** _____

Student is on ☐ insulin. Type: _____   Dose: _____ **Times to be given** _____

Blood Glucose Correction and Insulin Dosage using (Rapid Acting) Insulin: _____

Blood Glucose Range _____ mg/dL (_____ mmol/L) Administer _____ units

Blood Glucose Range _____ mg/dL (_____ mmol/L) Administer _____ units

Blood Glucose Range _____ mg/dL (_____ mmol/L) Administer _____ units

Blood Glucose Range _____ mg/dL (_____ mmol/L) Administer _____ units and check ketones

Blood Glucose Range _____ mg/dL (_____ mmol/L) Administer _____ units and check ketones

Blood Glucose Range _____ mg/dL (_____ mmol/L) Administer _____ units and check ketones

Blood Glucose Range _____ mg/dL (_____ mmol/L) Administer _____ units and check ketones

Insulin to Carbohydrate Ratio _____ unit(s) for every _____ grams of carbohydrate (or to be) eaten

☐ Student independently administers insulin.   ☐ Student self injects with supervision by trained school personnel.

☐ Student self injects with verification of dosage by trained school personnel.

☐ Injections should be done by trained school personnel.

☐ Parent/guardian authorized to increase or decrease sliding scale +/– 2 units of insulin.

☐ Parent/guardian authorized to increase or decrease insulin to carbohydrate count within the following range: 1 unit per prescribed grams of carbohydrates +/– 5 grams of carbohydrates.

Diet: Lunch time: _____ Scheduled P.E. Time: _____ Recess Time: _____

Snack time(s): _____ a.m. _____ p.m. Location where snacks are kept: _____

Location eaten: _____

Table 3 (continued)
Individualized Health Plan (IHP): DIABETES Page 2

TREATMENT PLAN: Low Blood Glucose (Hypoglycemia) – Below 70 mg/dL (< 3.9 mmol/L)

Causes:
- Too much insulin.
- Too few carbohydrates consumed for the amount of insulin given.
- Too much exercise.
- High excitement.

If you see this:	*Do this:* ACTION PLAN

Signs of Mild Low Blood Glucose **(STUDENT IS ALERT)**
➢ Headache
➢ Sweating, pale
➢ Shakiness, dizziness
➢ Tired, falling asleep in class
➢ Inability to concentrate
➢ Poor coordination
➢ Other
	1. Have responsible person accompany student to health office or check blood glucose in the classroom.
	2. Check blood glucose.
	3. If less than 70 mg/dL (< 3.9 mmol/L), give one of the following sources of glucose:
	  • 2-4 glucose tablets
	  • 6-9 Sweetarts® candies
	  • 2-4 oz. orange or other 100% juice
	  • 4-6 oz. sugar soda (<u>not sugar-free</u>)
	4. After 15 minutes, check blood glucose again.
	5. Repeat if necessary until blood glucose is > 70 mg/dL

Signs of Moderate Low Blood Glucose **(STUDENT IS NOT ALERT)**
➢ Severe confusion
➢ Disorientation
➢ Not able to or unwilling to swallow
➢ May be combative
	1. Check blood glucose.
	2. Keeping head elevated, give one of the following forms of glucose:
	  • 1 tube Cake Mate® gel applied between cheek and gum.
	  • ½ - 1 tube instant glucose applied between cheek and gum.
	3. After 15 minutes, check blood glucose again.
	4. Re-treat until blood glucose is > 70 mg/dL (> 3.9 mmol/L).
	5. Notify parent/guardian.

Signs of Severe Low Blood Glucose ➢ Not able or unwilling to swallow ➢ Unconsciousness ➢ Seizure ➢ **GIVE NOTHING BY MOUTH!**	1. Place student on side. 2. If personnel are authorized to use Glucagon, give prescribed dose: _____ mg(s) (Intramuscular or subcutaneous) 3. Call 911, then parent and physician, notify school nurse. 4. Remain with student until help arrives.

Table 3 (continued)

Individualized Health Plan (IHP): DIABETES Page 3

Student: _____ D.O.B.: _____

HIGH BLOOD GLUCOSE:

☐ Student needs to be treated when blood glucose is above _____ mg/dL.

☐ Call parent or guardian when blood glucose is greater than _____ mg/dL.

☐ **Symptoms** could include (check all that apply): ☐ extreme thirst ☐ headache ☐ abdominal pain ☐ nausea ☐ increased urination

Treatment of High Blood Glucose:

✔ Drink 6-16 oz. sugar-free fluids (caffeine free) <u>every hour</u>.   ✔ Be allowed to carry water bottle.   ✔ Use rest room as often as needed.

☐ Use prescribed sliding scale insulin orders when blood glucose is over _____ mg/dL if no insulin given in past two hours. Recheck blood glucose in two hours.

☐ Check urine ketones or blood ketones, if glucose is greater than **300 mg/dL (> 16.7 mmol/L) 2x** or when ill/and or vomiting.

- If urine ketones are **moderate to large** or if blood ketones are greater than 0.6 mmol/L, **call parent immediately!**
- Recommend child be released from school when ketones are large in order to be treated and monitored more closely by parent/guardian.

✔ If student exhibits nausea, vomiting, stomacheache or is lethargic, contact parent; student should be released from school.

✔ Student can return to class if none of the above physical symptoms are present.

Field trip information and special events:

1. Notify parent and school nurse in advance so proper training can be accomplished.
2. Adult staff must be trained and responsible for student's needs on field trip.
3. Extra snacks, blood glucose monitor, copy of health plan, glucose gel or other emergency supplies must accompany student on field trip.
4. Adult(s) accompanying student on a field trip will be notified of student's health accommodations on a need to know basis.

SUPPLIES	NEEDED	NOT NEEDED
Blood glucose meter and blood glucose strips	☐	☐
Lancets with lancing device	☐	☐
Blood ketone strips (if using the Precision meter)	☐	☐
Urine ketone strips	☐	☐
Insulin syringes	☐	☐
Antibacterial skin cleanser or alcohol wipes	☐	☐
Bottle of refrigerated rapid acting insulin — Type: _____	☐	☐
Glucose tabs, Cake Mate® gel, juice, or other source of glucose	☐	☐
Carbohydrate snack	☐	☐
Glucogen Emergency Kit®	☐	☐
Sharps container	☐	☐

As parent/guardian of the above named student, I give my permission to the school nurse and other designated staff to perform and carry out the diabetes tasks as outlined in this Individualized Health Plan (IHP) and for my child's healthcare provider to share information with the school nurse for the completion of this plan. I understand that the information contained in this plan will be shared with school staff on a need-to-know basis. It is the responsibility of the parent/guardian to notify the school nurse whenever there is any change in the student's health status or care. I also give the school permission to contact my child's health care provider. Parents/Guardian and student are responsible for maintaining necessary supplies, snacks, blood glucose monitor, medications and equipment.

Parent/Guardian_____ Date_____

School Nurse_____ Date_____

Table 4
Individualized Health Care Plan Check List for the School Nurse

STUDENT: _____ D.O.B.: _____

STUDENT #: _____ SCHOOL: _____ DATE: _____

> 1. Enter completion date and initial each step listed below.
> 2. File completed checklist in the student's health file.

Date and Initial

_____ 1. Health Care Plan developed with _____ and _____
　　　　　　　　　　　　　　　　　　　　　　　　parent or guardian　　　　area nurse consultant

_____ 2. Physician signature needed: _____ is not needed: _____

_____ 3. Send home original Health Care Plan and memo from nurse consultant:

　　　　　　　with student: _____ by mail: _____ by email: _____ for parent signature

_____ 4. School staff information and copy of Health Care Plan to the following:

Clinic aide	_____	Secretaries	_____	Classroom teacher(s)	_____
Admin.	_____	P.E.	_____	Art	_____
Music	_____	Cafeteria	_____	Transportation	_____

　　　　　　　Others: _____

　　　　　　　　　　　　　　　　　　　　　　List Names

_____ 5. Copies of signed plan in　　　_____ Clinic Health Care Plan Book

　　　　　　　　　　　　　　　　　　　　_____ Substitute Folder

　　　　　　　　　　　　　　　　　　　　_____ With student information/emergency page

_____ 6. Original plan with signatures in health file

_____ 7. Classroom presentation requested: __ No __ Yes __ Who requested: _____

_____ 8. Inservice: ___ No ___ Yes Who requested: _____

_____ 9. Training/delegation needed: ___ No ___ Yes ___

　　　　　　　Procedure: #1_____

　　　　　　　Staff: Name: _____ Position: _____ Date: _____

　　　　　　　Staff: Name: _____ Position: _____ Date: _____

　　　　　　　Staff: Name: _____ Position: _____ Date: _____

　　　　　　　Procedure: #2_____

　　　　　　　Staff: Name: _____ Position: _____ Date: _____

　　　　　　　Staff: Name: _____ Position: _____ Date: _____

　　　　　　　Staff: Name: _____ Position: _____ Date: _____

> ## ALL HEALTH CARE PLANS ARE CONFIDENTIAL
> (Information to be shared on a need-to-know basis only!)

continuous glucose monitor (CGM) which gives the current glucose level (Chapter 29). As a result, blood sugar measurements may not be needed as frequently. This should then be noted in the School Health Plan.

We prefer that the child be allowed to check the blood sugar in the classroom. Less school is missed when this is allowed. If done in the classroom, an adult may need to look at the result. The adult can determine if a low blood sugar has occurred. A disadvantage of doing the blood sugar in the classroom is that the teacher may have many other responsibilities and may not have time to supervise a young child. Another disadvantage is that the teacher may be very busy and unable to deal with possible problems. Also, the hands cannot be washed first if there isn't a sink. A trace of sugar on the finger can cause a high reading. If alcohol is used to clean the finger, be sure to let it dry completely before lancing.

It should be noted, if the child feels low and no blood sugar equipment is available, **TREAT the low with a source of carbohydrate. ALSO A REMINDER THAT A PERSON WHO HAS A POSSIBLE LOW SUGAR MUST NEVER BE ALLOWED TO LEAVE THE CLASSROOM ALONE.**

INSULIN IN THE SCHOOL

If insulin is to be given at school, the parent and the child's physician must sign a school medication form (see example). It must specify when the insulin is to be given and the dose. This "physician order" is usually mandatory in order for the nurse to deliver a dose of insulin at school. Individual state laws often dictate how this dose can be delivered. In some states, only a school nurse, the child or the child's parent/guardian may administer the insulin. In other states, the nurse or principal may delegate this task to a layperson(s) in the school setting. If a child is drawing up the insulin and giving their own dose, it is recommended to have an adult check the amount. On other occasions the parent may need to come in and give the injection. If a layperson will be responsible for

the injection, it's important that there be at least two people trained (in the event one is absent). These delegates should be recertified routinely and their names should be recorded in the child's care plan. Insulin pens are often a great tool for injections at school. They are very convenient, more accurate and leave less room for error when drawing up the dose at school. Unfortunately insurance may not cover their cost.

GLUCAGON IN THE SCHOOL

As discussed in Chapter 6, glucagon is a hormone with the opposite effect of insulin. It raises the blood sugar, but it is not sugar. Glucagon is used for emergencies when a person becomes unconscious, has a seizure or is unable to safely drink a liquid carbohydrate due to low blood sugar. Glucagon is safe to give and results in a rapid rise in blood sugar. The use of glucagon in the school can be found on the second page of the Individualized Health Plan (IHP) under "Severe Low Blood Glucose" - Table 3. Unfortunately, the glucagon must be mixed with a liquid before it can be injected. It can be injected under the skin into the subcutaneous fat just like insulin or deeper into muscle. It works just as well either way. Some physicians, schools and families work out a way that the glucagon can be given at the school in case of an emergency. (The physician must give orders for dose and when to give it.) If the family lives in a rural area, where emergency personnel are not immediately available (we have heard of responses taking as long as 40 minutes), glucagon must be kept in the school. It may have to be administered by a lay person, but most parents are lay people, and they administer glucagon. At least two people should be trained. The school nurse must arrange for routine recertification of these skills for the school staff members assigned to do this task. The instructions from Chapter 6 should be taped to the box. A helpful website giving instructions for glucagon use is: www.humalog.com/humalog-diabetes-and-insulin/glucagon-tutorial.jsp?WT.srch=1 (click on "Resources and Education" to get the tutorial) which can also be accessed from www.barbaradaviscenter.org. Our video on hypoglycemia (see Resources at the end of this chapter) also teaches how to give glucagon. You can also access a video and written directions for training online at the American Diabetes Association's website (www.diabetes.org/living-with-diabetes/parents-and-kids/diabetes-care-at-school/school-staff-trainings/diabetes-care-tasks.html).

LOW BLOOD SUGAR ("Insulin Reaction" or "Hypoglycemia")

See the Individualized Health Plan: Table 3, page 2 for the specific care for a given child.

This is the only emergency likely to occur at school. The severity of the low blood sugar is not determined by the glucose value but rather by symptoms.

A. *Onset:* SUDDEN and, if not treated promptly, can be an emergency.

B. *Signs:* Variable, but may be **any** of the following:

- hungry
- sweating, shaking
- pale or flushed face
- headaches
- weak, irritable or confused
- speech and coordination changes
- eyes appear glassy, dilated or "big" pupils
- personality changes such as crying or stubbornness
- inattention, drowsiness or sleepiness at unusual times
- if not treated, loss of consciousness and/or seizure

C. *Most likely times to occur:* Before lunch or after gym class.

D. *Causes:* Too much insulin, extra exercise, a missed snack or less food at a meal than is usually eaten. Field days or field trips with extra exercise and excitement may result in reactions. The parents should be aware of all field days or trips so that the insulin dose can be reduced and/or extra snacks can be provided.

E. **IF YOUR CHILD IS SENT TO THE OFFICE, THEY MUST ALWAYS HAVE SOMEONE ACCOMPANY HIM/HER.** The child may become confused and not make it to the office if he/she is alone.

F. *Treatment:* This depends on the severity of the reaction:

1. *Mild Reaction* (also see Table 4: Emergency Response Plan)

Symptoms: Hunger, shaking, personality changes, drowsiness, headache, paleness, confusion or sweating.

Blood sugar: If equipment is available to do a blood sugar, this is ideal to do even if treatment has been taken. We prefer this to be done by the student (if old enough) in the classroom so that extra energy is not spent going elsewhere. However, we realize that for some schools this is not possible. It takes up to 20 minutes for the blood sugar to rise after the carbs have been given. Doing the blood sugar will help to tell if the value was truly low and how low. A rapid fall in blood sugar, even though the value is in a normal range, may cause symptoms of being low and require a solid food snack to stop the symptoms.

Treatment: Give three or four glucose tablets, or 4-6 oz or ½ cup of juice, or any sugar-containing food or drink. Liquids are absorbed in the stomach more rapidly than are solid foods. Do not give solid foods until the blood sugar has returned to normal. Avoid use of high fat foods until the blood/CGM glucose is back up. The higher the fat content the slower the food will be absorbed. **INSULIN REACTIONS TREATED WITH LIQUIDS**

INITIALLY SHOULD BE FOLLOWED IN 10-15 MINUTES WITH MORE SUBSTANTIAL FOOD (e.g., cheese and crackers or ½ sandwich, etc.).

2. *Moderate Reaction*

   <u>Symptoms:</u> Combative behavior, disorientation, lethargy.

   <u>Blood sugar:</u> Do the same as in a Mild Reaction (see above).

   <u>Treatment:</u> Always check for the risk of choking **before** treating. Elevate the child's head. Give instant glucose or cake-decorating gel immediately, and then give sugar or juice when the person is more alert. After the person is feeling better (10-15 minutes), give solid food as above.

3. *Severe Reaction*

   <u>Symptoms:</u> Seizure or unconsciousness

   <u>Treatment:</u>
   i) Give glucagon (see IHP for dose)
   ii) Call 911

HIGH BLOOD SUGAR/KETONES (see Individualized Health Plan [IHP] – Table 3)

People with diabetes may have high blood sugars (or high CGM glucose values) and spill extra sugar into the urine on some occasions. These occasions include periods of stress, illness, overeating and/or lack of exercise. High sugars are generally NOT an emergency (unless accompanied by vomiting). When the blood sugar is above 300 mg/dL (16.7 mmol/L), urine or blood ketones also need to be checked. When the sugar is high, the child will have to drink more and urinate more frequently. **It is essential to make bathroom privileges readily available.** If the teacher notes that the child is going to the bathroom frequently over a period of several days, a parent should be notified. The diabetes care provider can then adjust the insulin dose.

The student may also occasionally need to check ketones at school. This may be because ketones were present earlier at home, because the blood sugar is above 300 mg/dL (> 16.7 mmol/L) or because the child is not feeling well. The parents should be notified if moderate or large urine ketones (or a blood ketone level > 0.6 mmol/L) are present, as extra insulin will be needed. When a child has moderate or large ketones, or a blood ketone level > 1.0 mmol/L, we recommend that the child be treated by adults who can provide constant supervision, usually at home.

CLASS PARTIES

If the class is having a special snack, the child with diabetes should also be given a snack. Parents should be notified ahead of time so that they can decide whether the child may eat the same snack as the other students, or they may want to provide an alternate food.

If an alternate snack is not available, the student should be given the same snack as the other children. A plan on whether to give an extra dose of insulin for the snack can be

Table 5
LOW BLOOD SUGAR (Hypoglycemia) MANAGEMENT
(for Classroom Teachers, Bus Drivers and other Support Staff)

Student: _____ School: _____

Teacher: _____ Grade: _____

Insulin administered at school by: ☐ Pump ☐ Pen ☐ Syringe ☐ None

Causes of Hypoglycemia
- Too much insulin
- Missed food
- Delayed food
- Extra exercise
- Excitement

Onset
- Sudden

PHOTO HERE

IF SYMPTOMS — TAKE ACTION
- Check blood glucose if possible. Treat if below 70 mg/dL (< 3.9 mmol/L).
- Always treat if in doubt or if blood sugar is unavailable.
- Never leave unattended.
- Always send to clinic accompanied by responsible person.
- If away from school, call parent to inform of situation and need for intervention.

MILD (alert)
- Hunger
- Irritable
- Anxious
- Crying
- Personality Change
- Tired, drowsy
- Shaky
- Dizzy
- Sweating
- Pale
- Spacey

MODERATE (not alert)
- Confusion
- Slurred speech
- Poor coordination
- Behavior changes

SEVERE
- Seizure
- Loss of consciousness
- Unable to swallow
- Combative

MILD
- Treat = provide sugar source
  → 3-4 Glucose tablets OR
  → 4-6 Ounces juice OR
  → 4-6 Ounces regular soda OR
  → Glucose gel/icing
- Wait 10-15 minutes
- Repeat if symptoms persist or blood glucose under 70 mg/dL (< 3.9 mmol/L)
- Provide solid snack after blood sugar back up

MODERATE
- Treat = provide sugar source
  → Glucose gel/icing
- Wait 10-15 minutes
- Repeat if symptoms persist or blood glucose under 70 mg/dL (3.9 mmol/L)
- Provide solid snack after blood sugar back up
- Contact parent/guardian

SEVERE
- Call 911
- Position on side
- Disconnect pump if present

For Seizure or if unconscious, give:
- Glucogen – if ordered
- Contact parent/guardian

worked out with the family.

BUS TRAVEL

It is important for the child with diabetes to take some food with him/her on the bus. If the child feels low, he/she must be allowed to eat the food. At times, bus rides take longer than usual due to bad weather or delays, and the child needs to have a snack available and permission from the bus driver to eat it if necessary. **Table 5 provides a flow-chart on hypoglycemia for bus drivers and other support staff.**

SUBSTITUTE TEACHERS

Ask to have a copy of the School Health Plan (Table 3) placed in the substitute teacher's folder and the attendance register so that a substitute would know:

1. which child in the class has diabetes (attach a photo)

2. when he/she usually eats a snack

3. symptoms and treatment of an insulin reaction

4. where the treatment supplies are kept

GYM (PHYSICAL EDUCATION) TEACHERS AND COACHES

It is particularly important for the gym teacher or coach to also have a copy of the School Health Plan. Low blood sugars may occur during exercise and a source of instant sugar should be close. Often a snack is recommended before gym. The child should get the snack early enough to help them be on time. Exercise is even more important for children with diabetes than for other children. They should not be excluded from gym or sports activities. If the child is wearing an insulin pump and disconnects during PE, provision must be made for the pump to be

stored in a safe place.

AFTER SCHOOL DETENTION

Children with diabetes should not be singled out or treated differently from the rest of the class. However, if required to remain after school (at noon or in the afternoon) for a longer time than usual, the child should have access to equipment for blood sugar determinations and snacks as needed. Most parents will have packets of cheese and crackers, peanut butter and crackers or some such snack for the teacher to keep in the drawer. This is a common time of the day for the morning or afternoon insulins to be peaking. If a snack is not taken, an insulin reaction is likely to occur.

SPECIAL DAYS (FIELD TRIPS, FIELD DAYS)

Field trips or field days usually involve extra excitement and exercise. Both of these can result in an increased chance of low blood sugars. The parents should ask to be notified beforehand so that they can reduce the dose of insulin. They may also wish to send extra snacks (granola bars, fruit roll ups, etc). Table 3 (the IHP) provides extra information related to field trips. It is important for parents to be aware that in the public school system, the child's diabetes should never be a cause for the school to exclude him or her from any school sanctioned activity, whether during or after regular school hours. This includes overnight field trips and band or sporting activities away from the school. If the child would be allowed to participate without diabetes, the school must accommodate the needs of the child with diabetes.

INSULIN PUMPS IN THE SCHOOL

More and more children are now using insulin pumps. The pumps allow sugar control to be more like that of a person who does not

Table 6
Insulin Pumps in the School Setting

_____ is a student in your school who has diabetes and is wearing an insulin pump. An insulin pump is a device that provides small amounts of fast-acting insulin (**basal**) every few minutes through a small catheter under the skin. The student then takes an additional amount of insulin doses (**boluses**) through the pump for meals and snacks. We would like to emphasize that problems and complications with insulin pumps are seldom seen. For the most part, you will not be aware that the student is using the pump, although you may hear an occasional quiet beep when insulin is taken for a meal or a snack. The following information may assist you in helping the student wearing an insulin pump.

Low and High Blood Sugars

These occur with the students receiving insulin pump therapy just as they do with children receiving insulin shots. They are handled similarly, and this is outlined in the Individualized Health Plan (IHP): Table 3, page 2. If a severe low did occur in a person using a pump, it is important for the school personnel to know how to disconnect the plastic tube from the pump to the person's insertion under the skin.

High blood sugars with moderate to large urine or blood ketones (levels > 0.6) **will** necessitate administration of an injection of rapid-acting insulin with a syringe. The student may need to perform a change of infusion set at school. Provision must be made for this in the child's school care plan. See the IHP – Table 3, page 3.

Basal and Bolus Insulin Pump Dosages

Insulin pumps give a constant basal dose of insulin that is set by the doctor and family. The school personnel will not be involved with the basal settings. A bolus insulin dose is ideally given approximately 15 minutes before food intake. It may require assistance from the school staff to help to calculate the bolus dose. **Some children need help from the school staff in remembering to administer their bolus dose, particularly prior to lunch.** Missing bolus dosages of insulin is the main reason for poor diabetes control (high blood sugars) in people who use pumps.

Calculating the Bolus Dose

This is usually done by counting grams of carbohydrate (carbs) and giving a unit of insulin for a certain number of grams of carbs. The latest "smart pumps" allow the entry of the number of grams of carbs into the pump which then calculates the appropriate insulin dose based on pre-programmed ratios.

In addition, a correction insulin bolus to bring the blood sugar into the desired range is often added to the above food dose. This is based on sensitivity (how much one unit of insulin lowers blood sugar) and the desired target sugar level. Both of these parameters are pre-programmed into the pump. An entry of a current blood sugar value into the pump will trigger the pump to automatically calculate the appropriate dose of insulin based on what parameters were pre-programmed. The wearer must then activate the pump to deliver these dosages.

Exercise

During times of vigorous exercise, the student may need to disconnect the pump. For this, the student needs to place the pump in a safe place where it will not be damaged. During prolonged exercise, many students reconnect the pump periodically and take insulin. Some students wear their pump during exercise and use a special case to protect it.

Alarms

Pumps are programmed to alarm under various circumstances, e.g., low battery, no insulin delivery, out of insulin, etc. This is discussed in detail in Chapter 28. There is also a 1-800 number on the back of all pumps to call for assistance.

There is an entire chapter (Chapter 28) in this book about insulin pumps. There is also an entire book, *"Understanding Insulin Pumps and Continuous Glucose Monitors"* (see "Ordering Materials" in the back of this book) for those wanting more information.

have diabetes. Table 6 lists some of the special issues of insulin pump use in the school. If more information is desired, Chapter 28 deals with insulin pumps.

In addition, a School Health Plan specific for students using an insulin pump and also other tables related to pump supplies needed at school, pump insulin dosages, etc. are included in Chapter 13 of the book, *"Understanding Insulin Pumps and Continuous Glucose Monitors"* (see ordering materials in the back of this book).

CONTINUOUS GLUCOSE MONITORS (CGM) IN THE SCHOOL

More and more children are now wearing CGMs to know their glucose levels every few minutes rather than just a few times during the day. Table 7 summarizes some of the key features of CGMs. In addition, the book, *"Understanding Insulin Pumps and Continuous Glucose Monitors"* goes into much more detail about CGMs (see "Ordering Materials" in the back of this book.

MEDICAL RELEASE

It is important for the parent or legal guardian to give the school written permission to contact the child's health care provider. This may be necessary in the event of an emergency. Without this "medical release" in place, the doctor or care provider may not discuss or give advice pertaining to the child's care. This permission is included in the last paragraph of the Individualized Health Plan – Table 3.

LEGAL RIGHTS

Section 504 of the Rehabilitation Act of 1973 prohibits recipients of federal funds from discriminating against people on the basis of a disability (including diabetes). A formal contractual health care plan outlining all accommodations necessary to care for the child with diabetes during school is known as a "504" plan. Putting this plan together usually involves meetings between the parents, child, school staff (nurse, teachers, principal, special education facilitator) and diabetes health care providers. The child is not only protected from

Table 7
Continuous Glucose Monitoring (CGM) in the School

A continuous glucose monitor reads glucose (sugar) levels from a sensor in the interstitial fluid (under the skin). It usually reads within 20% of a finger stick blood sugar value. It can be programmed to alert (vibrate or alarm) for high and low glucose levels. CGM is meant to provide adiitional glucose information. It is not approved for use in making treatment decisions.

Always be sure hands are clean and check a blood sugar via finger stick before performing treatment.

Alarm Settings

CGM will alert if interstitial glucose is less than _____ or above _____. If CGM alerts for low or high glucose levels, check finger stick blood sugar and treat according to doctor's care plan.

Arrows

Some continuous monitors show arrows on the screen to indicate the speed at which the glucose levels are changing. Arrows on the face of the monitor may point straight down, indicating a rapidly falling glucose level. Treatment should then be as in 1b below. The arrows may also point straight up, which means a rapid increase in glucose level. Treatment should be as in 3 below. A horizontal or 45° arrow (or one arrow in contrast to two arrows) may mean that the glucose level is not changing as rapidly.

When to Use CGM Information

1. **Lows or Pending Lows**
   a) **CGM screen shows < 70 mg/dL (< 3.9 mmol/L) with or without arrow(s):** Check finger stick blood sugar and if low proceed with doctor's care plan for treatment and food. Repeat blood sugar every fifteen minutes until level is above 70 mg/dL (3.9 mmol/L).
   b) **CGM screen shows < 100 mg/dL (< 5.5 mmol/L) with downward arrow(s):** Check finger stick blood sugar. If blood sugar is between 70 and 100 mg/dL (3.9-5.5 mmol/L) give 5-10 grams of carbohydrate (to prevent blood sugar from going lower). If < 70 mg/dL (< 3.9 mmol/L) proceed with doctor's care plan for treatment and food.

2 **Glucose levels in good range**
   a) **CGM screen shows < 80-200 mg/dL (4.5-11.1 mmol/L):** Check blood sugar as usual per care plan or if symptomatic.

3. **Highs or Pending Highs**
   a) **CGM screen shows > 200 mg/dL (> 11.1 mmol/L) with upward arrows or > 250 mg/dL (> 13.9 mmol/L):** Check finger stick blood sugar and follow doctor's care plan for treatment of high blood sugar. Recheck blood sugar in 2 hours. If still high, call parent. Check ketones and, if positive, give correction insulin dose with a standard syringe or an insulin pen.

For those wanting more information, Chapter 28 in this book is on CGM. Also, an entire book is available — see Ordering Materials in the back of this book.

discrimination by this law during the school day but on any school-sanctioned activity as well. In our experience, the parents and school staff are usually able to agree on a School Health Care Plan (Table 3). Formalizing the care through a 504 plan is then not necessary. However, in the rare case where it is necessary, additional resources are provided below. A child with diabetes has the right to a free and appropriate public education including accommodations to manage their diabetes at school. The child may also need special accommodations under the "Individuals with Disabilities Act" (IDEA). This law protects children who may be experiencing learning difficulties due to their disability. In the case of diabetes this may arise as a result of reoccurring hypo- or hyper-glycemia impacting the ability to learn or think clearly on exams. If the child must leave the classroom frequently to do blood sugars, snack or inject and misses lesson time this may also impact their ability to learn. Accommodations for any of these cases must be made to assist the child to learn. This may, for example, mean making provision for the child to do blood sugars in the classroom so as not to miss teaching time. It may also provide for the child to check a blood sugar level before exams in order to bring sugar levels to the appropriate target prior to sitting for an exam. The plan outlining what provisions must be made to assist the child to learn is called an IEP (individualized education plan). It will be put together through the school's special education program in conjunction with the parents, child and health care providers. You can review these rights on the ADA website, www.diabetes.org. The ADA also has a brochure called "Safe at School".

ADDITIONAL READING

"Understanding Insulin Pumps and Continuous Glucose Monitors", **Chase HP and Messer L, 2nd Ed, June, 2010. Children's Diabetes Foundation. Available at 1-800-695-2873 or www.ChildrensDiabetesFdn.org.**

Additional resources for parents who wish to formalize the health care plan through a Section 504 are listed here:

1. The Law, Schools and Your Child with Diabetes at: www.childrenwithdiabetes.com/ d_0q_000.htm (please note the underscore)

   This website allows access to: www.diabetes.org/safeatschool, from the American Diabetes Association, discusses the legal obligations of school systems under Section 504 of the Rehabilitation Act of 1973 and the Education for All Handicapped Children Act of 1975, amended in 1991.

   The National Information Center for Children and Youth with Disabilities (NICHCY) is a U.S. Government-sponsored clearinghouse that provides information about disabilities, including information about obtaining assistance at school.

2. The *US Department of Education* website (www.ed.gov) includes:

   The *Individuals with Disabilities Education Act*, with detailed information about IDEA.

   IDEA: The Law contains links to downloadable versions of the law.

3. *"Helping the Student With Diabetes Succeed (A Guide for School Personnel)"*. This is a 76 page primer that can be downloaded from: www.ndep.nih.gov.

4. *"How to Write an IEP"*, a book designed to help parents who have children with disabilities succeed in school.

5. www.childrenwithdiabetes.com/504

6. www.niddk.nih.gov and search for schools.

7. http://www.ndep.NIH.gov/media/Youth_ NDEPSchoolGuide.pdf

QUESTIONS AND ANSWERS FROM NEWSNOTES

Q My son recently had a cold and small urine ketones when he woke up. He felt good enough to go to school and wanted to go. Was I wrong in letting him do this?

A As long as he felt well enough and wanted to go, I think it was good that you let him do so. At least he wanted to go and must like school! You might have sent one of the large plastic drinking cups with a straw so that he would remember to drink fluids to help wash away the ketones. Probably a special note to the teacher explaining the situation and the possible need for extra bathroom privileges would be wise. Finally, it would be important for a parent (or the child, if old enough) or the school nurse to be certain the urine (or blood) ketones were checked again at lunchtime to make sure they went away and did not increase to the moderate or large level. Children with moderate or large urine ketones or blood ketones ≥ 1.0 mmol/L need to stay home with adult supervision until the ketones have gone down.

Q We have had difficulty with our child getting the care we request at school of late. What are our legal options?

A The Individual Disabilities Education Act (IDEA) provides an opportunity for the school to obtain extra funds for an aide to help with an <u>individualized education program</u> (IEP). Diabetes is listed as one of the covered health conditions, but in order to obtain the assistance the student's diabetes must adversely affect educational performance so that the student requires special education and/or related services. An example is a student who has trouble concentrating because of recurring high or low blood sugars that adversely affect the student's educational performance. Examples of supplementary aides that might be requested could be: help with administering insulin or glucagon, providing assistance in doing blood sugar checks and help in choosing snacks. The school must apply for the grant through the Office of Special Education Programs (OSEP) in the Office of Special Education and Rehabilitation Services (OSERS) in the U.S. Department of Education.

RESOURCES

1. *"Managing and Preventing Diabetic Hypoglycemia"*. This video, made in 2001, is available from the Children's Diabetes Foundation. Call for prices at 303-863-1200 or 1-800-695-2873. Credit cards may be taken by phone. Their address is: Children's Diabetes Foundation at Denver, 777 Grant Street, Suite 302, Denver, CO 80203.

2. www.diabetes.org/safeatschool

3. *"Diabetes Care Tasks @ School: What Key Personnel Need to Know"*. 13 PowerPoint Presentations online at www.diabetes.org/living-with-diabetes/parents-and-kids/diabetes-care-at-school/school-staff-trainings/diabetes-care-tasks.html

4. *"Living With Diabetes: Tips for Teachers"* is a 19-minute video tape available from Maxishare. Call for prices. Their address is: Maxishare, P.O. Box 2041, Milwaukee, WI 53201. Phone: 1-800-444-7747, Fax: 414-266-3443. A customer service representative for Maxishare can be contacted at 414-266-3428. Hospitals can pay for this video with purchase orders and individuals can pre-pay with a check or credit card. Some clinics have copies of these videos that can be loaned to parents to take to their school.

5. *"Partners for Success: School Nurses & the Care of Children with Diabetes at School"*. www.albany.edu/sph.coned/partners.htm, School of Public Health, University at Albany, State University of New York.

6. Diabetes Management in School and Child Care RN Instructor Guide. www. coloradokidswithdiabetes.org/index.php/Training-and-Delegation/download-document/-500

Off to school!

Chapter 26
Child-Sitters, Grandparents and Diabetes

INTRODUCTION

Cut out these pages and/or make copies of them to have available for child-sitters or grandparents. The time required to instruct a sitter or grandparent will depend on how long he/she will be with your child. A person helping for a few hours will generally do fine after you teach him/her the basics in this handout. A person staying with a child for a longer time or day-sitting for many weeks, will require more time to learn to give shots and to gain other knowledge. You are welcome to bring the sitter or grandparent along to diabetes clinic visits. In some cities, child-care courses are offered to teach people diabetes-related skills.

Our Center offers a one-day course several times each year for grandparents and other caregivers of children with diabetes. It is important for grandparents to have a normal relationship with their grandchildren. This includes having the children for a day or, when parents are away, caring for them for a longer period. This requires having some knowledge and skills in many areas of diabetes management. Certainly recognizing low blood sugars and knowing how to treat them is essential. Checking blood/CGM glucose levels (Chapter 7) and, if the child is going to spend more than the day, knowing how to draw and give insulin (Chapter 9) is also essential. Grandparents do not usually need to know how to manage illness or how to adjust insulin doses. They should be in contact with the parents or health care team if the child is ill or has high blood/CGM glucose levels for other reasons. Grandparents who take the time to learn about diabetes are showing love and support for their children and their grandchildren. Aunts, uncles, godparents and others close to the child are encouraged and welcome to attend if they will have the opportunity to care for the child.

TEACHING OBJECTIVES:

1. Present the signs, symptoms and treatment of hypoglycemia to caregivers.

2. Instruct caregivers about essential information for the care of the child (e.g., meals and activity).

3. Teach the skills needed for the care of the child (injections, blood sugar and ketone checking, etc.).

4. Encourage the utilization of child-sitters and grandparents for the occasional relief of parental and child stress.

LEARNING OBJECTIVES:

Learner (parents, child, relative or self) will be able to:

1. Describe three signs and symptoms of hypoglycemia with the appropriate treatment.

2. Define two factors important in the management of diabetes.

3. Demonstrate the necessary skills for the care of the child.

4. Formulate a "stress relief" plan for the family.

Information for the Sitter or Grandparent

Our child, _____, has diabetes.

Children with diabetes are generally normal and healthy. In a child who has diabetes, sugar cannot be used by the body because the pancreas no longer makes the hormone insulin. Because of this, daily insulin injections are needed. Diabetes is not contagious. Caring for a child with diabetes is not very difficult, but it does require a small amount of extra knowledge.

Low Blood Sugar

The only emergency that could come on quickly is **LOW BLOOD SUGAR** (otherwise known as "hypoglycemia" or an "insulin reaction"). This can occur if the child gets more exercise than usual or does not eat as much as usual. *The warning signs of low blood sugar vary but include any of the following:* (They are discussed in greater detail in Chapter 6.)

1. Hunger
2. Paleness, sweating, shaking
3. Eyes appear glassy, dilated or "big" pupils
4. Pale or flushed face
5. Personality changes such as crying or stubbornness
6. Headaches
7. Inattention, drowsiness, sleepiness at an unusual time
8. Weakness, irritability, confusion
9. Speech and coordination changes
10. If not treated, loss of consciousness and/or seizure

The signs our child usually has are: _____

_____

_____

BLOOD SUGAR: It is ideal to check the blood sugar if this is possible. It takes approximately 10-20 minutes for the blood sugar to increase after taking liquids with sugar. Thus, the blood sugar can even be done after taking sugar. If it is not convenient to check the blood sugar, go ahead with treatment anyway.

TREATMENT: Give SUGAR (preferably in a liquid form) to help the blood sugar rise.

You may give any of the following:

1. One-half cup of soft drink that contains sugar – **NOT a diet pop**

2. Three or four glucose tablets, sugar packets or cubes or a teaspoon of honey

3. One-half cup of fruit juice

4. LIFE-SAVERS candy (FIVE or SIX pieces) if over three years of age

5. One-half tube of Insta-Glucose or cake decorating gel (see below)

We usually treat reactions with: _____

If the child is having an insulin reaction and he/she refuses to eat or has difficulty eating, give Insta-Glucose, cake decorating gel (½ tube) or other sugar (honey or syrup). Put the Insta-Glucose, a little bit at a time, between the cheeks (lips) and the gums and tell the child to swallow. If he/she can't swallow, lay the child down and turn the head to the side so the sugar or glucose doesn't cause choking. You can help the sugar solution absorb by massaging the child's cheek.

If a low blood sugar (insulin reaction) or other problems occur, please call (in order):

1. Parent: _____ at: _____

2. Physician: _____ at: _____

3. Other person: _____ at: _____

🐾 Meals and Snacks

The child must have meals and snacks on time. The schedule is as follows:

	Time	Food to Give	Insulin to Give*
Breakfast	_____	_____	_____
Snack	_____	_____	_____
Lunch	_____	_____	_____
Snack	_____	_____	_____
Supper	_____	_____	_____
Snack	_____	_____	_____

* Can be drawn ahead of time by the parent.

Sometimes young children will not eat meals and snacks at exactly the time suggested. If this happens, DON'T PANIC! Set the food within the child's reach (in front of the TV set often works) and leave him/her alone. If the food hasn't been eaten in 10 minutes, give a friendly reminder. Allow about 30 minutes for meals.

🐾 Blood Sugars

It may be necessary to check the blood sugar (Chapter 7) or ketones (Chapter 5).

The test supplies we use are: _____

The supplies are kept: _____

Please record the results of any blood or urine tests in the log book.

Time:_____Result: _____

🐾 Side Trips

Please be sure that if the child is away from home, with you or with friends, extra snacks and a source of sugar are taken along.

🐾 Other Concerns: *Concerns that we have are:*

_____

_____

_____

_____

_____

_____

If there are any questions or if our child does not feel good or vomits, please call us or the other people listed above.

Thank you.

QUESTIONS AND ANSWERS FROM NEWSNOTES

 What is the Grandparents' Workshop and why does the Center have this?

 The Center has the Grandparents' Workshop (usually two to four times per year based on need) so that grandparents can care for grandchildren and grandchildren can stay with grandparents. Both are very important to each other! I recently had a family tell me that when their five-year-old was diagnosed with diabetes, one set of grandparents jumped in and learned about diabetes including how to check blood sugars, give insulin shots and the whole "ball of wax." The other set of grandparents was scared of the diabetes and never learned any of the needed diabetes skills. Needless to say, the first set of grandparents gained a grandchild while the second set lost one; the grandchild lost the opportunity for a close relationship with the second set of grandparents.

For most grandparents, attending the one-day workshop and possibly reading the Center's detailed educational book, or the shorter more basic book, results in enough skills to be able to have the child spend a night or a week with them like any other grandchild. Perhaps even more important, attending the workshop helps lessen the fears of diabetes, particularly involving hypoglycemia and giving shots.

The child must not feel different or punished because of having diabetes. If siblings get to stay with the grandparents, the child with diabetes must have the same opportunity. It is also a chance for the child (and parents) to break inter-dependencies.

Finally, all parents need a break and an occasional vacation without the children. Grandparents are often the best possible solution and can sometimes be the only option. The chance to get to know one's grandparents better and to have memories of staying with them is something that is valued for many years to come.

Chapter 27
Vacations and Camp

TEACHING OBJECTIVES:

1. Explain the benefits of camps and vacations.

2. Discuss the value of developing independent knowledge and skills.

LEARNING OBJECTIVES:

Learner (parents, child, relative or self) will be able to:

1. List three benefits of attending camps or having vacations.

2. Identify one area of additional knowledge and/or one skill and/or one more area of personal growth needed for the person with diabetes.

VACATIONS

Diabetes should not interfere with vacations, which are a normal part of life. Some extra "planning ahead" should help prevent problems related to the diabetes.

Planning may include:

✔ discussing your vacation at your clinic visit before leaving

✔ sharing with the healthcare team if your travel will be out of the country

The information should include:

✔ both departure and arrival times – going and returning

✔ the number of hours traveling

✔ a review of sick-day management and the need to have a way to check for ketones

✔ buying Kaopectate and Imodium AD if going to areas where the risk for diarrhea is high

✔ taking along your doctor's/nurse's phone numbers

✔ remembering to plan for security measures (see below)

SECURITY MEASURES

The official security measures since 9/11/01 for flying in the U.S. (often now not required):

1. Passengers may board with syringes or insulin pumps only if they can show a vial of insulin with a professional pre-printed label which clearly shows the medication. Since the prescription label is on the outside of the box of the vial of insulin, the FAA recommends that passengers come with their vial of insulin in its original labeled box.

2. For passengers who have diabetes and must check their blood sugar levels but do not take insulin, bringing their lancets is all right as long as the lancets are capped. The lancets must be with the glucose meter that has the manufacturer's name on the meter (e.g., One Touch meters say "One Touch", Accucheck meters say "Accucheck", etc.).

3. People who are traveling with a glucagon kit should keep it in its original pre-printed labeled container.

4. Travel letters help explain the need for carrying on diabetic supplies (see letter in this Chapter).

5. Insulin pump (and CGM) companies recommend that a pump or CGM not be taken through X-ray (including total body scanners). They state that the electronic components of the pump/CGM may be altered. We suggest explaining to airport security and having them manually check it.

FOOD

Concerns regarding food should include:

✔ Meals (often best to carry-on)

✔ Have a good supply of snacks (e.g., cheese or peanut butter crackers, granola bars, etc.)

✔ Have sources of sugar always available (glucose tablets, fruit roll-ups or whatever works best)

EXERCISE

Concerns regarding exercise include:

✔ If traveling in a car, plan regular stops to get some exercise.

✔ When traveling in a car, **MORE** insulin will probably be needed due to less physical activity.

✔ On active days (e.g., at beach or at Disney World) **LESS** insulin will probably be needed (THINK AHEAD!).

✔ The best way to know the effects of

increased or less activity is to do more frequent blood/CGM glucose checks.

INSULIN

A few points to remember:

✔ Pack enough insulin to last the entire trip. Supplies may not be available at your vacation area.

✔ If going on a plane, carry <u>insulin, glucose strips and glucagon</u> on board in case you need these. If put in checked luggage, they can freeze and spoil or be lost if luggage doesn't arrive.

✔ If going by car, keep all three items listed above in plastic bags in a cooler so they do not get too hot and spoil.

✔ If using an insulin pump, see the list of supplies to take in the Q and A section in the back of Chapter 28.

Make a **check list** ahead of time of things to take. Double check this list at the last minute. If using an insulin pump, take Lantus/Levemir insulin and syringes in case the pump breaks down and you need to return to shots. If going overseas, some companies will provide a second pump to take along. It is helpful to know the dosages you were on before starting the pump. Remember you can always take the rapid-acting insulin (Humalog/NovoLog/Apidra) from the pump every three to four hours until you can get other insulins.

Some "Generic Reminders" are:

✔ **ALWAYS** carry a form of **sugar** with you to treat reactions.

✔ Have enough **snacks** available.

✔ Always wear a diabetes **identification tag**.

✔ Get the name of a **doctor** or emergency room/urgent care in your vacation area so you can call him/her if necessary. Take your own doctor's and nurse's phone number, too. He/she knows your case best, and it may be comforting to make a long distance phone call when help is needed.

✔ Visit your doctor **two weeks before** you leave so you have time to work out any problems. Discuss your plans at your visit. Remember to take his/her list of suggestions with you.

✔ If you expect to be **more active** on the vacation (hiking, camping, skiing, etc.), you may need to reduce the insulin dose. Discuss this with your doctor or nurse.

✔ For <u>international travel</u>, remember to check far enough ahead of time to see if you need special immunizations. State health departments can usually give this information.

✔ If <u>international travel</u> is planned, it is wise to carry a letter from the doctor explaining why insulin syringes and other supplies are being taken through customs. As stated earlier, it may be necessary to have prescription labels on the insulin and any other supplies to be carried on board. Check to see if your health insurance covers you in other countries, or if you need supplemental insurance.

✔ The most important advice is to **HAVE FUN!**

CAMP

Children with diabetes are very dependent on their parents for:

✔ blood/CGM glucose levels

✔ injections

✔ proper nutrition

✔ help with preventing and treating potentially dangerous low blood sugars

These are in addition to their non-diabetic needs. The diabetes care for their child can become one of the main functions in life for a parent. As a result, children with diabetes may become too dependent on their parents.

Advantages of Attending Diabetes Camp

- Diabetes camp often offers the first chance to alter these dependent relationships.

- Most diabetes camps have doctors and nurses at the camp so the parents can feel their children will be safe.

- Camp food is monitored and the amounts calculated by a dietitian. This helps to have the correct content and amounts available for the increased activity.

- Adequate snacks are routinely available and provided.

- It is often a major help for children to meet other friends who take shots and do tests just like they do. Diabetes is "the norm" at camp.

- It is also a chance for a child to realize that he/she is not the only person in the world who has diabetes.

- Children who are old enough and who do not give their own shots or do their own blood sugar levels may try doing these tasks at camp.

- The children also understand that with proper planning, they can do the same hiking, overnights and other activities that other children do.

- Other youth with insulin pumps and CGMs will be at camp. This may stimulate an interest in these devices.

- Older teens with diabetes may serve as junior counselors and find that they must take care of themselves in order to set a good example for younger campers.

It is important for parents not to be upset if they receive the "typical" camp letter from their child asking the parents to come and get them immediately. This type of letter is not unusual and should not cause concern. Most campers are having a wonderful time. If you are overly concerned, call the camp coordinator for support. Whatever you do, don't upset the child by trying to call them at camp, and don't suddenly appear at camp ready to take the child home.

Most diabetes camps also have some educational programs. *These may be:*

✔ "rap-sessions"

✔ problem-solving sessions

✔ games to help learning (e.g., carb-counting "guesstimates")

The **major** goal of the camp, however, should be to **have fun** and to make new friends. It is not unusual to develop pen pals who can't wait until the next camp when they can meet again.

Insulin doses are generally decreased due to increased activity and to avoid hypoglycemia as much as possible.

Scholarship programs are offered at most diabetes camps. If finances are a problem, a request for financial help should be made. Sometimes children can earn part of their own expenses.

After having been at a diabetes camp, the child may decide to try other camps. When this happens, the parents will need to:

✔ discuss insulin dose changes with their diabetes care provider

✔ be in touch with the nurse at the other camp

✔ provide all of the diabetes supplies needed for the camping period

✔ give telephone numbers for emergencies

✔ work out an emergency treatment plan as in the school chapter (Chapter 25)

✔ work out a way to have the blood sugars faxed/phoned/e-mailed to the family or healthcare provider

Attending a diabetes camp or another camp is often the first step toward independence for the child with diabetes. Encouraging camp attendance can result in a healthy parent-child relationship.

Updated camp information for camps throughout the world can be found at: www.childrenwithdiabetes.com/camps

---

Date: _____

Re: _____

DOB: _____

To Whom It May Concern:

_____ *is a patient at the* _____.
_____ *has type 1 diabetes and requires daily insulin injections to remain healthy.*
To manage diabetes _____ *must carry medical supplies, including insulin, syringes, blood glucose and ketone checking strips, lancets, a glucose meter, glucagon emergency kit, as well as an emergency food supply and water.*

Please call _____ *should any emergencies arise.*

Sincerely,

_____
Physician

QUESTIONS AND ANSWERS FROM NEWSNOTES

  Should my child go to diabetes camp?

We are often asked this question. The lower age limit for the Colorado camp is eight years, although not all eight-year-olds are mature enough to be away from home. Some camps take children at even younger ages. This question was directed to me specifically as it relates to a 10-year-old and I replied without hesitation, "Yes, your child should go to camp."

Camp offers many benefits:

✔ fun (our major emphasis!)

✔ getting to know and live in a cabin with other children the same age who also have diabetes

✔ a great help for children to learn that they are not the only persons their age in the world with diabetes

✔ ten others in the cabin also have to take shots and do blood sugars

✔ the first chance to break the child-parent inter-dependencies which can develop when diabetes is diagnosed at a young age

✔ a good time for parents to also have a break!

 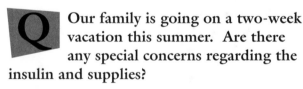 **Our family is going on a two-week vacation this summer. Are there any special concerns regarding the insulin and supplies?**

The means of travel and the type of vacation are important. *If you are traveling by plane:*

✔ Make sure the insulin is carried with you and not in the luggage. Freezing or pressure changes in the baggage compartments may change the insulin, blood sugar strips and glucagon. Besides, you need access to these supplies for any emergencies. If your luggage is lost, all of your supplies would be as well.

✔ You may need a pharmacy label on the insulin and any other supplies you will be carrying on board.

✔ Have two vials of each insulin in case one is broken (many foreign countries do not have all of the insulin types [particularly Lantus/Levemir]).

✔ Do not forget that meals on airplanes are never served on time, so extra snacks are essential.

✔ If time changes during travel to foreign countries are known, sharing these with your nurse or physician is important so the insulin dose can be adjusted.

For long trips in a car:

✔ Tips for avoiding high blood sugars, which result in frequent urination:

  ● stopping for regular exercise at two-hour intervals

  ● eating less

  ● taking extra Humalog/NovoLog/ Apidra and/or Regular insulin

✔ Remember that insulin does lose activity at temperatures above 90°. Insulin, glucagon and blood sugar strips must always be kept in the thermos or cooler with ice. The strips should be brought to room temperature before use.

✔ Do not forget to take your ketone strips and a card with your doctor's phone number(s).

It is often better to call your doctor or nurse long-distance when you have questions than to get advice from someone who may be unfamiliar with your diabetes. Routines are often broken during vacations. Sleeping late or eating snacks or meals late can result in insulin reactions. Be aware of possible inconsistencies and try to prevent problems. Thinking ahead can help prevent problems and result in more fun!

We are going to the East Coast on vacation this summer. Will times for giving shots need to be adjusted?

 No. A change of one or two hours does not usually make a difference; simply adjust to their time zone.

This is not the case when traveling to Europe, the Far East or even Hawaii. *When greater time changes happen, call your diabetes care provider with the:*

✔ time of leaving home and/or the U.S.

✔ number of hours you will be traveling

✔ time of planned arrival, including a.m. or p.m.

✔ scheduled meals on planes

✔ same information for your return trip

Your diabetes care provider can then help you with the insulin adjustments.

 Our son is about to go hiking in a very hot part of the U.S. Is there any way to keep his insulin, blood sugar strips and glucagon cool so they don't spoil?

 You can order the FRIO Cool Pouch at www.medicool.com. Hopefully all will fit in their larger pack.

Swimming is good and fun.

Chapter 28
Insulin Pumps

H. Peter Chase, MD
Susie Owen, RN, CDE
David Maahs, MD, PhD

INTRODUCTION

This chapter is somewhat complex and does not need to be read until the family is ready to consider insulin pump therapy. The chapter is not meant to teach everything one needs to know about insulin pumps. There is a separate book in the Pink Panther series, *"Understanding Insulin Pumps and Continuous Glucose Monitoring (CGM),"* which goes into more detail. Also see Other Materials Available in the back of the book. The use of CGM (Chapter 29) will be referred to frequently as these two technologies are now often used together. An insulin pump is a microcomputer (the size of a pager) that constantly provides insulin. When an insulin pump is used, insulin is first put into a special syringe which is then placed within the pump case or injected into a pod. A small plastic tube called a cannula is then inserted under the skin with a needle. After insertion, the needle is removed, leaving just the plastic tube in place. Insulin is infused through the small plastic tube under the skin (most commonly placed in the abdomen or buttock). Tape may be placed over the cannula set to keep it in place for up to three days.

Pump management involves a high level of diabetes care. It requires a commitment by the entire family to help with the daily management. No matter what age a person begins pump therapy he/she will need assistance to ensure safety and a positive outcome. Pump management needs to begin during a time when the person with diabetes is ready and when the family can focus on developing new knowledge and skills.

It is important to realize that the current insulin pumps do not vary the insulin dose based on the blood or CGM glucose levels. The pump is programmed to give a pre-set amount of insulin at regular intervals (called the **"basal"** rate). The basal rates do not automatically change as blood sugars change. In addition, each time the person eats or if the blood sugar is elevated, buttons on the pump must be pushed to give a **"bolus"** insulin dose. The bolus calculators (explained below) help to calculate the amount of insulin the person should give. **However, there is not a "closed-loop" pump at this time that measures blood or CGM glucose levels and turns off the basal insulin if the glucose level is low or gives more insulin if the glucose level is high.** This will likely become possible at some time in the future (see Chapter 31 on Research).

Extra visits and training sessions are generally required to begin treatment with an insulin pump. A nurse educator, social worker, dietitian and physician may spend time with the person and family in a routine clinic visit deciding as a team if a pump is the right choice. If it is decided to proceed, the family may then attend educational sessions to learn the basics of pump therapy. This is often the time when the brand of pump is selected. Once the family has the pump they will attend instructional sessions on the use of their specific pump. Although different centers do it differently, we use a total of three pump training classes: a saline class, an insulin class, and an advanced pump-training class. The pump trainer and physician spend 3-4 hours at the time of starting saline in the pump and then another 2-3 hours at the time of starting insulin in the pump. The "Advanced Pump Training" class occurs about one month after starting the pump.

There is not a "best age" to begin using an insulin pump. The time is right when the person with diabetes and their family are ready and willing. It must not be the parents who want and are pushing for the pump. (The situation is obviously different for young children.) The ability to count carbohydrates and to reliably calculate and give an insulin dose is an obvious need. Younger children who cannot count carbohydrates or reliably give a

bolus insulin dose must be considered on an individual basis. The availability of a parent becomes a major factor when putting younger children on a pump. A willingness to check blood sugars frequently (or use a CGM) is very important. No matter at what age a person begins pump treatment, assistance will be needed when the person is ill or shows a lack of consistent follow-through with daily tasks.

POSSIBLE ADVANTAGES OF INSULIN PUMPS

Some of the possible advantages of insulin pumps include:

✔ improved HbA1c levels

✔ reduced hypoglycemia events

✔ increased flexibility and freedom of insulin management

✔ improved glucose control after meals

✔ increased safety around management of hypoglycemia and exercise

The advantages (and disadvantages) are discussed in more detail in the book, *"Understanding Insulin Pumps and Continuous Glucose Monitors (CGM)."*

POSSIBLE DISADVANTAGES OF INSULIN PUMPS

Some of the possible disadvantages of insulin pumps include:

✔ forgetting to give insulin boluses prior to food intake

✔ psychological factors

✔ expense

✔ weight gain

✔ skin infections

✔ spoiling of insulin in the reservoir with heat or cold

✔ limitations in "real-estate" for site insertions

STARTING THE PUMP: CLINIC VISITS AND PUMP TRAININGS

❂ Pre-pump Visits

Insulin pumps are not for everyone. The person with diabetes (not just other family members) must be ready for the insulin pump, want the pump and be fully committed to using the pump. The visits and training described below may vary at different centers.

1. Initial Pre-pump (Routine Clinic) Visit

✔ The person with diabetes and the family meet with the physician, nurse, dietitian and social worker to discuss the basics and possible advantages and disadvantages of pump therapy.

✔ We request at least four or five blood sugars be done per day (or use of a CGM) and recorded and faxed/emailed to us weekly (often for one month). This gives us an idea of the commitment of the person and the family, as well as their reliability. The proof of blood sugar checking may also be required by the insurance company.

✔ If the person is not already counting carbohydrates (carbs), the dietitian will give instructions in this area. We usually ask that potential pump users or their parents be able to count carbohydrates. We also ask that they bring or send completed blood/CGM glucose levels food records and insulin dose records, to the dietitian. These are then used to help adjust insulin-to-carb ratios.

✔ A DVD/CD on the pump and other information is sent home with the family for review or is available online from the pump company. Either the user or an adult must be able to reliably give bolus dosages, and must be able to deal in tenths of units of insulin.

✔ For children, a "dummy" pump may be taped on to see how the child tolerates it.

✔ Further instruction with the dietitian about carb counting is usually necessary.

✔ The social worker is available to discuss concerns about using or beginning to use the pump.

In summary people who are ready for a pump:

- are willing to share with others that they have diabetes

- want the pump themselves and are not being pressured by others

- are willing to do frequent blood sugar monitoring or to wear a CGM

- are either doing carb counting (Chapter 12), are willing to learn, or have a parent who can do it for them

- are willing to use all possible injection sites

2. Pump Preparation Class(es)

Much of the basic information in this chapter is presented in this class(es). Families are shown (either at this time or at another arranged time) the different brands of pumps to help them make their selection. Families are asked to review this chapter together at home.

3. Saline-Start Training Class (some clinics do not use the saline-start visit)

The person (and family) is trained to wear the pump, program the pump and to do infusion set changes.

✔ We recommend that the instructional video/DVD be viewed at least two times to become familiar with all of the basic pump functions before the saline training.

✔ The family must bring the pump, case, batteries and supplies for two or three insertions and reservoirs (in case needed) to this class.

✔ Only sterile saline (salt water) is initially used in the pump. They learn whether they are able to do the required every-two-or-three-day infusion set changes. It is important to practice using the pump between the saline and the insulin trainings to become comfortable with how it works. The usual syringe insulin injections continue while wearing the pump with saline.

✔ All technical aspects of the pump are taught at the saline start.

✔ The learning objectives from the beginning of this chapter are reviewed with the family(ies) to make sure they are learning the essentials.

✔ *The person/family should bring significant others who:*

  ● may help with future pump programming and/or problems

  ● may assist with blood/CGM glucose values (particularly in the middle of the night)

4. **Insulin-Start Visit (See Table 1)**

a. The morning of the visit:

✔ We ask that NO NPH OR LANTUS/LEVEMIR INSULIN be taken on the morning when insulin is started in the pump. The normal dose of rapid-acting insulin can be taken to cover breakfast prior to coming to the visit. If Lantus/Levemir insulin is usually taken at dinner or in the evening, the person will be asked to just take NPH insulin (or multiple shots of rapid-acting insulin) the night before starting the pump. If Lantus/Levemir was accidentally taken on the prior evening, the starting of the pump basal insulin can be withheld using a temporary basal rate of zero for 12 hours. Individual instructions are outlined in Table 1.

✔ *The person/family should bring significant others who:*

● must be available to help with possible hypoglycemia or hyperglycemia

● should review glucagon administration

● will be assisting in the day-to-day maintenance of the pump and infusion sites

The support of the significant other(s) helps with success in pump use.

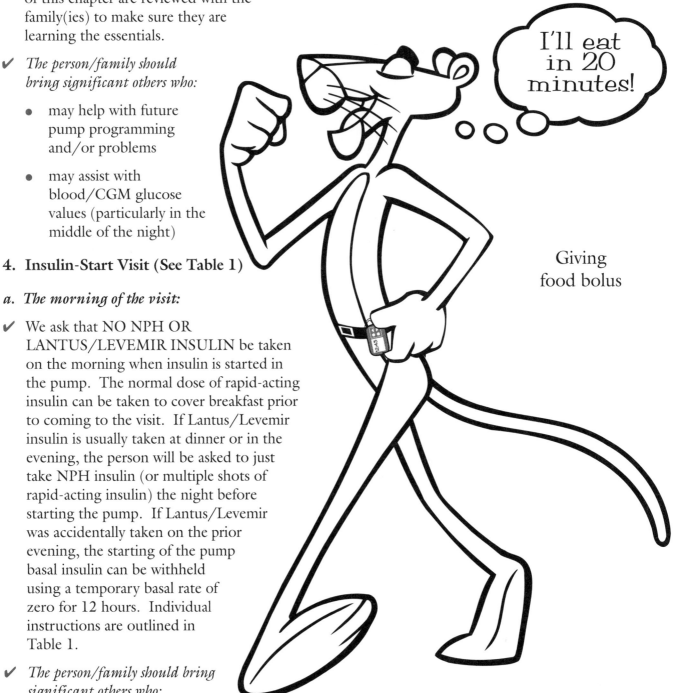

I'll eat in 20 minutes!

Giving food bolus

Table 1
Pre-Insulin Pump Start Instructions

Name: _____ Saline Start Date: _____ Insulin Start Date: _____

The following instructions should be <u>discussed</u> at the <u>saline pump start</u>:

IF YOU ARE CURRENTLY ON <u>N</u> (NPH), or <u>Lantus/Levemir</u> at dinner or in the evening, your physician recommends the following for the night before your insulin pump start (physician to check all that apply):

☐ Switch your evening dose of Lantus or Levemir to N (NPH) and take _____ units of NPH (N) at _____ p.m.* (If on Lantus or Levemir, usually about 40 percent of the Lantus dose is given as NPH.)

☐ Do not take any long-acting insulin the evening before your pump start. Instead, supplement with _____ units of rapid-acting insulin every _____ hours through the evening and night.

* If needed, get a prescription from your physician for Humulin or Novolin N (NPH).

If you are currently taking **Lantus or Levemir** in the **morning,** you may take it the morning of the day <u>before</u> your pump start. (**Do not take it the morning of your insulin pump start!**)

<u>The night before the insulin pump start:</u>

- Give the usual insulin dose at dinner of rapid-acting insulin and follow the directions prescribed above for your other insulin. Eat a regular meal.

- Get all of your supplies (see below) organized to take to the clinic.

- Watch the pump instructional video/DVD or use the interactive computer software one more time.

- Read Chapter 28 on pumps in "Understanding Diabetes" once again (or the pump sections of the book, *"Understanding Insulin Pumps and Continuous Glucose Monitors"*).

<u>The morning of the insulin pump start:</u>

DO NOT give any N (NPH) or Lantus/Levemir <u>this a.m.</u>

- Give the usual Humalog/NovoLog/Apidra dose with breakfast. Do not take any other insulins.

- Bring your pump and pump supplies, Humalog/NovoLog/Apidra insulin, blood sugar testing equipment, snacks and written materials with you to the clinic.

If you have any questions, please contact your healthcare provider.

_____ _____ _____
Physician   Phone   Date

_____ _____ _____
Nurse   Phone   Date

Remember, you <u>must</u> call or <u>fax or email blood sugar records in daily</u> for the first 1-2 weeks after your pump start (see Table 4)! Discuss this with your physician or nurse at your insulin start.

Table 2
Insulin Doses

Name _____ *Date_____

(*For insulin start)

Starting Basal Rate(s)

	Start Time	Units per Hour		Start Time	Units per Hour
1.	_____	_____	7.	_____	_____
2.	_____	_____	8.	_____	_____
3.	_____	_____	9.	_____	_____
4.	_____	_____	10.	_____	_____
5.	_____	_____	11.	_____	_____
6.	_____	_____	12.	_____	_____
			Total	_____	

Carb Counting

Starting Bolus Dosages

	Time	Insulin/Carb Ratios		Time	Insulin/Carb Ratios
1.	_____	_____	3.	_____	_____
2.	_____	_____	4.	_____	_____

Insulin Sensitivity Ratio

	Time	1 unit lowers BG by:		Time	1 unit lowers BG by:
1.	_____	_____ mg/dL	3.	_____	_____ mg/dL
2.	_____	_____ mg/dL	4.	_____	_____ mg/dL

Target Blood Glucose Levels

	Time	Target BG		Time	Target BG
1.	_____	_____	3.	_____	_____
2.	_____	_____	4.	_____	_____

Duration of Insulin Action: _____ Hours

If you have any questions, please contact your healthcare provider:

MD: _____ Phone: _____

RN: _____ Phone: _____

Remember, you must call or fax blood sugar records in daily for the first 1-2 weeks after your pump start (see Table 4). Discuss this with your MD or RN at your insulin start.

Table 3
Pump Infusion Set Options

Your doctor and your insulin pump trainer can help you choose the infusion set that will work the best for you. The variety has increased greatly and many new options are appearing on the market every few months. Some of the most widely used infusion sets are listed below:

	Cannula Lengths	Tube Lengths	Inserter or "Sertable"
Medtronic Mini-Med Paradigm Pumps			
Paradigm Quick-Set	6 or 9mm	23" and 43"	yes
Paradigm Silhouette	13 or 17mm	18", 23", 33" and 43"	yes
Mio	6 or 9mm	18", 23" and 32"	yes
Sure-T	6mm	18", 23" and 32"	no
Animas			
Inset (90° insert)	6 or 9mm	23" and 43"	yes
Inset (30° insert)	6 or 9mm	13" and 23"	yes
Comfort	13 or 17mm	23" and 43"	no
Contact D	6mm	23" or 43"	no

*All but the Paradigm infusion sets have a luer lock end that will work with all "non-Paradigm" pumps.

b. The process:

✔ The physician sets the initial basal insulin doses (see Table 2 in this chapter).

✔ The dietitian again reviews carb counting (Chapter 12) and the food records.

✔ The nurse educator or pump trainer finishes the technical training for the insulin pump and teaches how to trouble shoot and maintain infusion sites and pump.

✔ It is important to review how to reduce the basal doses using the **"Temporary Basal Rate."** The percent entered into the pump is the percent of the usual basal dose to be delivered. For example, if the usual basal rate is to 1.0 units per hour, and 70 percent is entered, 0.7 units per hour will be given. The time to use the temporary basal rate must also be entered.

✔ The social worker is available to discuss concerns or fears.

INSULIN DELIVERY

 **Insulin Infusion Sets**

We do not recommend one infusion set over another. Every person is different and the favored set varies from person-to-person. Some of the sets most frequently used at present are shown in Table 3. However, new sets are becoming available all the time. For people who have difficulty with needles, it is fine to use EMLA® or L▪M▪X-4® cream. These are topical anesthetic creams that need to be applied 30 to 60 minutes before doing the insertion. The table indicates sets which have an automatic "inserter." These devices push the needle and plastic tube through the skin, usually with the push of a button. The person does not have to use their own strength to push the needle in. The needle is then removed, leaving the tube in the fatty layer under the skin. There are also sets in which the metal needle stays in. These are most helpful when a person has frequent problems with "kinking" of the plastic tube.

For most people, the tape holds the cannula in without difficulty. However, if needed there are several tips to making infusion sets stick better. The first is to start with clean skin (shaved if necessary). Many people then apply Skin Prep™ or IV Prep™ to make the skin sticky (let it dry). Some then place a dressing (Tegaderm™, IV-3000™) directly on the skin and insert the infusion set through the dressing. A second dressing can be placed on top of the infusion set to sandwich it in place. If this is done, a hole must be cut in the top dressing so the set can be connected. Some people prefer to just tape the set in place with medical tape (Transpore™, Hypafix™) or standard waterproof athletic tape (e.g.: Kinesio Tape™). If the tape is irritating the skin, a wipe-on skin barrier such as Cavilon™ may help. Also, Tincture of Benzoin, Mastisol® or Skin Bond® can be applied to the skin before the tape or set and will work like glue. A medical adhesive remover (Uni-Solve®, Detachol) may then be needed to remove the set and tape. More information about adhesive issues can be found in *Understanding Insulin Pumps and Continuous Glucose Monitors (CGM)*.

When possible, it is best to do the set change in the morning. This is because the person may be more sensitive to insulin in the new (non-swollen) site. If the set were changed at night, this might lead to overnight hypoglycemia. Doing the set change in the morning also gives time to make sure the set is working well before going to bed. Many times with the typical busy family schedule, set changes are not possible until later in the day. The second best time to change the infusion set is after school and activities, but before dinner. Then if the set is not working properly, the family will know before bedtime. If it is necessary to do a set change in the evening or night it is essential that the blood/CGM glucose value be checked 2-3 hours later, both to make sure the infusion set is working and to make certain the value is not low. Many families use a temporary basal setting (approximately 70 percent) for the next 4-6 hours if the glucose value is not high prior to a nighttime set change. It is generally recommended that set changes be done every two to three days. If blood/CGM glucose values tend to routinely run high on the third day or if the weather has been hot, it may be necessary to do the set change after two days.

❧ Methods of Delivery

The pump delivers insulin in three ways:

1. Basal Dosages

Basal dosages are programmed into the pump with the direction of the healthcare provider and remain the same day-after-day unless purposely changed. Table 2 can be used to direct initial insulin pump doses. A major goal in the first week is to calculate and fine-tune the optimal basal dosages.

The basal rate:

✔ reflects the units of insulin per hour that would be needed to maintain stable blood/CGM glucose values if the person were not eating meals

✔ is similar to the small amount of insulin released by the pancreas every few minutes to turn off sugar production by the liver and to prevent fat breakdown

✔ usually consists of 40 to 50 percent of the total daily pump insulin dose

Dosing

In starting insulin in the pump, the instructions in Table 1 should be followed. The insulin dose for the pump is calculated by different doctors in different ways. Sometimes the total insulin dose taken by shots in a day (rapid and long-acting insulin) is added and 70-100 percent of this total is used.

Approximately half of the pump insulin is given as the basal insulin and half as boluses. If the person is on Lantus/Levemir insulin, the total basal insulin per 24 hours is about the same as the previous dose of Lantus/Levemir. Many doctors divide the day into parts (e.g., in three hour time periods; see Table 2) and initially reduce the doses during the night and give a bit extra after meals. (The latter is because most people do not bolus adequately to cover meals.)

Basal doses vary:

✔ The number of basal dosages to be used varies between doctors. Some start with one or two basal rates and others with 8-12 basal rates.

✔ Many teenagers and young adults need more insulin in the early morning hours to cover the body's normal increase in growth hormone (the "dawn phenomenon")

✔ ALL people are different, and the use of different basal doses allows for individual fine-tuning

✔ Once the basal rates are regulated, they tend to stay quite consistent

Some reasons to change basal rates are:

● puberty (physiologic increase in insulin resistance)

● large changes in body weight

● change of time zones (just change time on pump)

● injuries or illness

● some medications (e.g., steroids)

● temporary reductions for exercise

● temporary increases for menses

✔ At a later date, basal rates can be checked by having the person not eat a meal. If the basal rate is correctly set, the person will not have a low (< 70 mg/dL [< 3.9 mmol/L]) or high (> 200 mg/dL [> 11.1 mmol/L]) sugar despite not having eaten. Skipping the bedtime snack, fasting overnight and having a late breakfast while measuring the blood sugars every 2-3 hours (or using CGM) is often the first basal test to do.

2. Bolus Dosages for Food:

✔ Approximately 50-60 percent of the daily pump insulin doses are given as boluses before meals and snacks. At least a part of the bolus (for the correction and for food which definitely be eaten) should be given 20 minutes prior to the first bite. (Carbs cause blood/CGM glucose values to peak in 60 minutes whereas Humalog/Novolog/Apidra peak in 95 minutes.) People can then give an additional bolus if they decide to eat more.

✔ Everyone is different and boluses can be chosen to fit individual eating habits.

✔ The dietitian is an important member of the pump team and will need to review and reinforce carb counting. Changes are often suggested in Insulin/Carb (**I/C**) ratios for different meals after reviewing food records, insulin dosages taken and blood (or CGM) glucose levels two to four hours after meals.

✔ Many families attend carb counting classes (if not yet counting carbs) prior to starting insulin pump therapy. However, dosages sometimes change after starting the pump. Good record keeping in the period after beginning the pump is essential.

✔ The only way to know if an insulin dose for food was correct is to do a blood (or CGM) glucose level before and two hours and four hours after the meal. The ADA now recommends that the peak blood/CGM glucose levels be less than 180 mg/dL (< 10.0 mmol/L) at any time following a meal. Many care providers recommend the two-hour value after meals be below 140 mg/dL (< 7.8 mmol/L). To test the I/C ratio, start with the blood sugar in the target range and eat a low-fat (< 20 gm) microwavable meal with known carbs. (Excess fat delays stomach emptying and prolongs sugar elevations.) Blood glucose (or CGM) values must be monitored as described above. Most people use different insulin to carb (I/C) ratios for different meals and times of the day. Thus, blood/CGM glucose measurements should be made after each meal. A "less aggressive" I/C ratio is often used at night, thus lessening the chance for nighttime hypoglycemia.

✔ The "rule of 500" is sometimes used to help calculate I/C ratios. The total insulin per day (e.g., 50 units) is divided into 500. For this example (500 ÷ 50 = 10), one unit of insulin would cover 10g of carbohydrate. The I/C ratio would be 1 to 10.

✔ The bolus calculator can be programmed with I/C ratios for different times of the day. Then, when the grams of carbs to be eaten are entered in the pump, the units of insulin to take appears on the screen. The person must activate the suggested insulin dose in order to have it be delivered. This is particularly helpful for people who have different I/C ratios at different times of the day. It is also helpful for people who are not adept at math.

3. Bolus Dosages for "Corrections"

Extra (unscheduled) insulin boluses are important to use if the blood/CGM glucose level is high. Remember that larger dosages will be required if ketones are present (and should be given by syringe or pen). The healthcare team should be contacted if moderate or large urine ketones or blood ketones > 1.0 mmol/L are found. There are several ways to determine correction boluses. The best way is by entering the blood sugar value into the pump and letting it calculate the dose based on the correction factor for that time of day (as previously entered into the pump). Any "insulin on board" from the previous bolus is automatically subtracted by the bolus calculator built into the pump.

✔ If a person is using the correction factor of one unit for every 50 mg/dL the glucose is above 150 mg/dL, then 50 mg/dL is the sensitivity factor that says one unit will reduce the blood sugar 50 mg/dL and the 150 mg/dL is the target blood sugar. If the blood sugar level was 300 mg/dL, three units of insulin would be the bolus amount used to bring the blood sugar to 150 mg/dL. (This was determined by subtracting 150 from 300 = 150 and then dividing by 50 = 3 units of insulin.) Most teens and adults correct to 100 mg/dL (5.5 mmol/L) during the daytime hours (e.g., 7 a.m. to 7 p.m.). Younger children often use a target of 120 or 130 mg/dL

(6.7 or 7.3 mmol/L).

✔ For people using mmol/L for glucose values, one unit of insulin for every 2.8 mmol/L above 8.3 mmol/L could be used. For a level of 16.7 mmol/L with a desire to reach 8.3 mmol/L, divide 2.8 into 8.4 (16.7 minus 8.3) and give three units of insulin.

✔ The above calculation and a new bolus can be repeated after two to three hours if the blood sugar/CGM value is still high.

✔ Some people use one target blood/CGM glucose level for the day (e.g., correct to a glucose level of 100 mg/dL [5.5 mmol/L]) and a second, less aggressive target for during the night (e.g., 150 mg/dL [8.3 mmol/L]). It is helpful for the less aggressive target blood sugar to begin two to three hours before bedtime to lessen the chance that the person will have to treat a blood sugar that has dropped below 100 mg/dL (< 5.5 mmol/L) at bedtime.

✔ The bolus calculator may suggest a reduced dose when the blood/CGM glucose value is under the target value and some food is being eaten. If the value is below 70 mg/dL (3.9 mmol/L) the pump may not suggest taking any insulin. These adjustments are based on the glucose level, the sensitivity factor, and the target blood sugar level.

✔ If a blood/CGM glucose value during the day is high (> 300 mg/dL [16.7 mmol/L]), an extra unit of insulin may be added to the bolus. If moderate or large urine ketones or a blood ketone level > 1.0 mmol/L is present, some people double the recommended correction insulin dose. The bolus calculator does not take ketones into account.

BLOOD/CGM VALUES

More frequent blood/CGM glucose values are required in the first week or two of insulin pump therapy to help set the basal and bolus insulin dosages. The levels to aim for are the same as those shown for different ages in Chapter 7.

At a minimum:

✔ levels should be determined prior to each meal

✔ before bedtime

✔ two hours after eating each meal

✔ once during the night: start at 12 midnight the first night and then test one hour later (e.g.: 1 a.m.) the second night and one hour later in each succeeding night for one week

✔ two hours after a correction dose

This amounts to at least eight or ten blood/CGM glucose values per day. This number may be reduced in the second week to four or five per day. It is obvious that parents or a significant other are extremely helpful at this time. The minimum will eventually be four values daily with occasional checks during the night. However, when striving for safe "tight" control, more than four blood/CGM glucose values a day are needed. The form we like for reporting (faxing or e-mailing) blood sugar results is shown in Table 4 and may be copied as often as desired. It can also be found on our website (www.barbaradaviscenter.org) for use in e-mailing results. Many meters (and CGMs) can now be downloaded and emailed to the care-provider.

The person (or family member) faxes/emails blood/CGM glucose results daily for the first week, then weekly for several weeks and then every two to four weeks. Good communication at this time is essential.

✔ Sick-day management, site care and hypoglycemia are reviewed.

ADVANCED PUMP TRAINING

Approximately one month after the insulin pump start, families complete their training with Advanced Pump Training. *The following activities and topics are covered:*

✔ Any problems the person/family is having with the pump.

✔ Programming and application of the advanced features.

✔ How to use the pump to adjust for exercise and how to evaluate the effectiveness of the exercise adjustment. A second set of basal doses may be programmed into the pump to use on heavy exercise days.

✔ If the Sof-Set® or Quick-Set™ is primarily being used, the Silhouette Infusion Set® may be demonstrated. The Silhouette set often stays in place better with heavy exercise.

✔ Trouble shooting is reviewed for pump and blood/CGM glucose issues.

✔ A food record may be brought to this visit to fine tune the insulin-to-carbohydrate (I/C) ratios with the dietitian. Other methods of preventing high blood/CGM glucose values after meals such as giving the bolus 20 minutes prior to the meal are discussed. Special bolus features are introduced called the "square" or "extended" wave, or a "dual" wave. These allow a bolus to be given over a period of time (square and extended boluses) or with a portion of bolus given in the usual fashion and a portion as a square wave (dual wave). These special features are helpful for meals such as pizza or spaghetti, which are high in carbs and fat and may cause prolonged sugar elevation for some people.

✔ An HbA1c level is checked.

Table 4 Weekly Insulin Pump Management Record

Name _____ Week of _____

Day & Date	12M	1A	2A	3A	4A	5A	6A	7A	8A	9A	10A	11A	12N	1P	2P	3P	4P	5P	6P	7P	8P	9P	10P	11P	Notes
BG																									
Carbs																									
Basal*																									
Food (Bolus)																									
Correction (Bolus)																									
BG																									
Carbs																									
Basal*																									
Food (Bolus)																									
Correction (Bolus)																									
BG																									
Carbs																									
Basal*																									
Food (Bolus)																									
Correction (Bolus)																									
BG																									
Carbs																									
Basal*																									
Food (Bolus)																									
Correction (Bolus)																									
BG																									
Carbs																									
Basal*																									
Food (Bolus)																									
Correction (Bolus)																									
BG																									
Carbs																									
Basal*																									
Food (Bolus)																									
Correction (Bolus)																									

*Basal dosages are only reentered if a change has been made.

Time	I/C Ratio

Target Range:
Correction:

This table may be copied as often as desired.

Table 5
Keys to Avoiding Lows

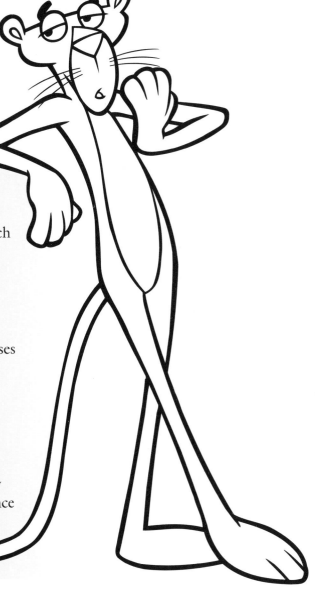

- Always do AT LEAST four blood sugar/CGM values daily (and occasional checks during the night)

- Estimate grams of fat to be eaten and give insulin bolus 20 minutes prior to eating (so insulin is not peaking after blood sugar [CGM] value is down)

- Test before, during and after exercise

- Recognize the symptoms of lows and treat promptly

- Think ahead regarding variations in daily schedule which could result in low blood sugars

- If the blood sugar (CGM) level is below 70 mg/dL (3.9 mmol/L) and it is time for a food bolus dose, subtract one unit from the bolus amount

- Reduce bedtime boluses for the bedtime snack or boluses during the night by half (the reduction may vary for different people)

- Use a temporary (or alternate) basal pattern for heavy exercise and/or during the night after days of heavy exercise

- Try not to do routine set changes after dinner. The new area may be more sensitive to insulin increasing the chance of hypoglycemia. More frequent blood glucose/CGM values after a set change are essential.

HYPOGLYCEMIA

The causes of hypoglycemia are discussed in Chapter 6 and are similar for people using insulin pumps to those of people using insulin injections. *These include:*

✔ too few blood/CGM glucose values

✔ incorrect insulin (bolus) doses or timing of insulin

✔ wrong adjustments for exercise

Some keys to avoiding lows are listed in Table 5.

If low, treat as described below and then check the blood/CGM glucose value 15 minutes later to make sure the value is back up (particularly at night). Also think about what was different the previous day (extra exercise, bolus insulin, less food, etc.). This will allow planning ahead to prevent the low with a similar occurrence in the future. If you have questions, call your doctor or nurse.

Treatment of Hypoglycemia

If hypoglycemia is suspected, the person with diabetes should be treated as described in Chapter

6. If the blood sugar is below 60 mg/dL (< 3.3 mmol/L), we prefer 15g of "quick-acting" carbohydrate first (four ounces of juice or sugar pop or four glucose tablets). If it is still below 60 mg/dL (< 3.3 mmol/L) after 10-15 minutes, repeat this treatment. When it is above 60 mg/dL (> 3.3 mmol/L), give solid food.

If the glucose value is below 50 mg/dL (< 2.8 mmol/L) or if the person is "out of it" or unconscious, the pump should be placed on "suspend" or disconnected for a period of at least 30 minutes. Others will set a temporary basal of 0.0 units per hour for the next hour so that the pump will restart without the person having to remember. A parent, teacher or significant other must know how to do this, as the person with the low blood sugar may be confused. It must be remembered that insulin already infused will not yet have peaked, so giving the sugar is essential. Instant Glucose (or cake decorating gel) and glucagon (Chapter 6) must be readily available (as for all people with diabetes).

HIGH BLOOD/CGM GLUCOSE VALUES

🐾 Non-Pump Related Causes

Some of the causes of high blood sugars for pump users are the same as for people taking their insulin by shots:

✔ extra food intake without an extra bolus

✔ lack of exercise

✔ forgetting insulin or giving just before or after meals

✔ illnesses/infections

✔ hormones (stress, menses [many young ladies use a second basal setting which is 0.1 or 0.2 u/hr higher during menses])

✔ over-eating with low blood sugars

✔ spoiled insulin

In addition, causes of high blood/CGM glucose values related to the pump include:

✔ the reservoir being out of insulin

✔ a clogged, kinked or leaking infusion set

✔ an infusion set which has come out

If the blood/CGM glucose level has not responded to a correction bolus with the pump or if the value is extremely high or if there are ketones present, the infusion set must be changed and a correction dose given using an insulin syringe. If moderate or large urine ketones or a blood ketone level > 1.0 mmol/L is present, the correction insulin dose is often doubled. If a syringe correction has been given and the blood sugar does not respond, the insulin used could be spoiled.

In order to prevent running out of insulin, the pump reservoir should be filled every 2-3 days as the set is changed. Table 6 summarizes some possible pump problems. **Remember that all pumps have a 1-800 number on the back to call for help 24 hours a day.**

Table 6
Possible Pump Problems

Problem	Pump Alarm
🐾 Empty insulin reservoir (syringe)	Yes
🐾 Low pump reservoir	Yes
🐾 Clogged infusion set	Yes
🐾 Partially blocked infusion set	No
🐾 Leaky infusion set	No
🐾 Weak or dead battery	Yes
🐾 Low battery	Yes
🐾 Pump malfunction	Yes
🐾 Cannula has come out	No
🐾 Spoiled Insulin	No

EXERCISE
(See Chapter 13 for further discussion)

There are several options for altering the insulin dose with exercise. Experience is usually the best teacher to see what works. **Doing more frequent blood sugar (or evaluating CGM) values to determine the effects of the exercise and the changes in insulin dosage is MOST helpful!** Many athletes find pumps are easier to use than injections when exercising. This is because a temporary basal rate can be selected when a time to exercise is suddenly chosen. In contrast, it is not possible to negate insulin activity from a previous basal insulin (Lantus or Levemir) injection.

✔ If the exercise is mild to moderate (walking, golf, dancing, etc.), reducing the basal dosages by half (50 percent reduction) during the exercise may be sufficient. Some people start the reduction 30 to 60 minutes before the exercise and continue it for 30 minutes or longer after the exercise is over. Every person is different and will need to find what works best. Use of a **"temporary basal"** can be very helpful and many pumpers use it on a daily basis.

✔ During intense exercise (jogging, football, basketball, etc.), most people just disconnect from the pump. Some disconnect 30 to 60 minutes before the start of the exercise.

There are then several options for insulin adjustments:

Estimate the amount of insulin to be missed while disconnected from the pump and take part of the dose before the exercise (particularly if the blood sugar is high) and the rest of the dose after the exercise. A temporary basal rate after an exercise of long duration and/or high intensity (e.g.: an 80% basal from 9 p.m. to 3 a.m.) may lower the incidence of delayed hypoglycemia. This is particularly helpful during the night for some people.

Correction boluses given after exercise are frequently reduced by half. This helps to prevent hypoglycemia.

In general, if the pump is to be disconnected for two hours or more, more frequent blood/CGM glucose values must be done (at least each hour). If the value is rising, it is easy to reconnect, take a small bolus and again disconnect.

✔ If it is to be an all-day exercise (e.g., a long hike or all day skiing), it may work best to reduce the basal and the bolus rates (perhaps by half) or possibly to not give any bolus doses. People must determine what works best for them.

✔ With exercise, it is important to remember to stay hydrated and to take extra snacks (see Chapter 13). Drinking water or sports drinks works for some people. The carbohydrates from the sports drinks will provide extra calories and energy. Often a bolus is not given or is reduced to cover the carbohydrate intake. Snacks such as granola bars provide extra carbohydrates and calories. Make sure that coaches or others around at the time know that the person has diabetes and wears an insulin pump.

SCHOOL

If the person using the pump is in school, the school nurse should have some knowledge of the pump. You may wish to copy the pump table in Chapter 25 on Schools (or this entire chapter) for the school nurse. You have our permission to make copies as desired.

SUMMARY

Insulin pumps have advantages and disadvantages. It is up to each person and family, working with their healthcare team, to decide if a pump would be appropriate.

DEFINITIONS

Basal dose: A pre-set hourly rate of insulin (for 24 hours) as programmed into an insulin pump.

Bolus dose: An amount of insulin taken prior to a meal or to correct a high blood sugar as entered at any time of the day by the person wearing the insulin pump.

Carbohydrate (carb) ratio (see Chapter 12): The number of units of insulin to be taken for a certain number of grams of carbohydrate eaten (e.g., one unit for 15g of carbohydrate).

Closed-loop pump: An insulin pump (not currently available) which would increase insulin given for high blood sugars or decrease insulin given for low blood sugars.

Correction bolus dose: A bolus of insulin used to correct a high blood sugar down to the desired level.

Insulin "on board": A term referring to insulin still remaining active from previous boluses. It is automatically subtracted by the bolus calculator (see smart pump, below).

Insulin pump: A microcomputer with a syringe of insulin within the pager-sized device that can infuse a basal insulin dose at a pre-set hourly rate. Bolus insulin dosages can also be entered and given at any time by the person wearing the pump.

Smart pump: An insulin pump with a bolus calculator. This is now an outdated term, as all pumps now have bolus calculators. It will recommend units of insulin to give when the number of grams of carbs to be eaten is entered. It also recommends a correction insulin dose when the blood sugar level is entered or transmitted to the pump from the glucose meter. (The I/C ratios and correction factors must have been pre-entered into the pump by the user.) Any insulin still acting ("insulin on board") from previous boluses will be automatically subtracted.

ADDITIONAL READING

1. *"Understanding Insulin Pumps and Continuous Glucose Monitors"*, Chase HP and Messer L, 2nd Ed, June, 2010. Children's Diabetes Foundation. Available at 1-800-695-2873 or www.ChildrensDiabetesFdn.org.

Websites for four commonly used insulin pumps are:

Animas® Ping™
www.animascorp.com

Medtronic MiniMed Paradigm® Revel™
www.minimed.com

Insulet OmniPod®
www.myomnipod.com

Roche ACCU-CHEK® Spirit
www.disetronic-usa.com

QUESTIONS AND ANSWERS FROM NEWSNOTES

Q **What do you currently recommend for airport screening for people wearing an insulin pump?**

A The TSA offers the option of requesting a visual inspection of your medical supplies rather than putting them through an X-ray. This must be requested before the screening process begins. Your medical supplies should be ready in a separate bag when you approach the security officer.

Walking through the metal detector is not usually a problem. It is better to leave the pump on the person and not put it on the conveyer belt. If a body scan is requested we recommend taking the pump off and handing it to the person doing the screening and getting them to manually check it. Information provided by the pump companies suggests that electronic components of the pump can potentially be damaged if exposed to ionizing radiation such as x-rays or CT scanner. Again, remember to take your travel letter with you.

Q **My son is going on a trip without other family members. He uses an insulin pump. Could you remind us of supplies he should be taking along?**

A In case of pump malfunction, we generally recommend he take extra syringes and bottles of the long-acting insulin he was on prior to starting the pump. You should also look back in your records to send the dosages as well. It is also important to have him pack his diabetes supplies in his carry-on luggage.

A summary of important items to include are:

1. 24-hour clinic phone number
2. a supply of rapid-acting insulin
3. long-acting insulin
4. insulin syringes
5. extra pump batteries
6. glucose meter/strips/lancets
7. extra meter battery
8. extra infusion sets and inserter (if used)
9. extra pump syringe (reservoir)
10. alcohol pads
11. dressing, tape
12. glucose tablets/instant glucose
13. urine or blood ketone testing strips
14. glucagon emergency kit

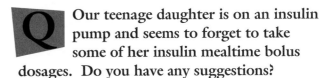

Q **Our teenage daughter is on an insulin pump and seems to forget to take some of her insulin mealtime bolus dosages. Do you have any suggestions?**

A Missing bolus dosages with food is unfortunately fairly common. It is probably the number one cause of elevated HbA1c levels (> 8 %) for people who receive pump or injection insulin therapy.

When teens show signs of forgetting insulin, the parents must again get more involved. They may need to actually observe the breakfast and dinner boluses. Perhaps a friend or teacher can be found to make sure the noon bolus is taken.

Some pumps and meters have alarms to help remind youth to bolus.

One family found a watch with five separate alarms. It could be set as a reminder for bolus dosages. Cell phones and text messaging are other options.

Q **I know pump supplies can be ordered through the pump companies. Are there other good sources?**

A Yes, some families order through 50/50. Half of the profits then goes to support diabetes research.

Chapter 29
Continuous Glucose Monitoring (CGM)

H. Peter Chase, MD
Laurel Messer, RN, MPH
David Maahs, MD, PhD

One of the major advances in the treatment of diabetes in recent years has been in the development of continuous glucose monitors (CGM). These devices give readings of subcutaneous (not blood) glucose levels every one to ten minutes. This compares with finger-stick blood sugar (glucose) readings which are usually done only four or five times each day. The subcutaneous CGM glucose values are approximately 10 minutes behind the blood sugar values, as the sugar must pass through the blood vessel wall into the subcutaneous space, and then the CGM system must determine the value. This delay is of almost no clinical significance with the frequency of CGM readings.

The purpose of this chapter is to present an overview of CGM. An entire book, *"Understanding Insulin Pumps and Continuous Glucose Monitors (CGM)"* is available for people wanting detailed information (see Ordering Materials in the back of this book). It is important to emphasize that, as with insulin pumps, the CGM technology is not for everyone. Some essential points to consider are:

✔ In order for CGM to be successful, the person (except for the very young) must want to use CGM, not just the parent or significant other.

TOPICS:
Monitoring Diabetes (following CGM glucose levels)

TEACHING OBJECTIVES:

1. Present CGM glucose concepts (rationale, times, frequency and desired ranges for the individual).
2. Provide instruction for the CGM of choice.
3. Discuss how to trouble shoot problems with their CGM.
4. Introduce the concept of following CGM glucose levels and observing trends.

LEARNING OBJECTIVES:

Learners (parents, child, relative or self) will be able to:

1. Describe rationale for monitoring CGM glucose levels.
2. Demonstrate use of real-time and retrospective CGM data.
3. Choose and apply a method for following CGM results and recognizing trends.
4. Locate and state the 1-800 number listed on the CGM to call for problems.

✔ Blood sugar levels must still be done approximately twice daily to calibrate the CGM (see below). They must also be done anytime an insulin dose is to be administered, when a low blood sugar is suspected, or if the CGM value is in question.

✔ CGM values will not always match the blood sugar values.

✔ People who wear the CGM at least six days per week are the most likely to have an improved HbA1c value.

THE COMPONENTS OF A CONTINUOUS GLUCOSE MONITOR (CGM)

The CGMs currently available in the US all have three basic parts:

1. **Sensor:** As with the insulin pump, a small plastic probe is inserted (with the push of a button) under the skin. The sensor reads subcutaneous (not blood) glucose levels for the next five to seven days (it is often possible to make them last even longer).

2. **Transmitter:** The transmitter attaches to the sensor and sends the glucose reading to the receiver.

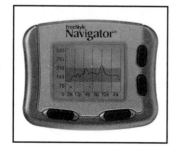

3. **Receiver or Monitor:** The receiver receives the subcutaneous glucose readings from the transmitter and converts the signal to a mg/dL value like we are used to dealing with for blood sugars. It is a mini computer that records and displays much information. The MiniMed Paradigm system has the receiver built into an insulin pump, with the glucose values displayed on the face of the pump. **However,** the CGM **DOES NOT** control insulin output by the pump. Other CGMs are entirely separate from a pump.

INITIATING CGM THERAPY

As with initiation of insulin pump therapy, various clinics will have different protocols. The criteria for deciding who is ready to begin CGM therapy are similar to those discussed in Chapter 16 for starting an insulin pump and include:

✔ interest on the part of the person as well as family members (with young children being an exception)

✔ willingness to wear the sensor (ideally with a commitment to wear it at least six days per week)

✔ a stable diabetes care and support system

✔ willingness to evaluate and use a new system/new information

✔ adequate financial resources – which may or may not include health insurance coverage. Most CGM systems cost ~$1000 USD and each sensor (lasting 5-7 days) costs $35 to $60 USD.

✔ adequate body fat – although everyone has adequate fat on the buttocks, this is sometimes a concern for parents of young children already using an insulin pump.

A course (slides) we offer for people interested in CGM is available (free) on our website at www.barbaradaviscenter.org.

CALIBRATION OF CGMS

A CGM is calibrated by entering a fingerstick blood sugar value into the receiver. With the Navigator CGM the blood glucose meter is built into the receiver; with the MiniMed system the blood glucose value from the meter can be transmitted into the receiver. Depending on the

CGM, this occurs 1-3 times each day. A difficult issue with CGM involves calibrating the system so that the CGM values are as accurate as possible and are matching the blood sugar values. Everyone wants their CGM values to match their blood sugar readings. This is most likely to happen if the calibration (entry of the blood sugar value) can be done at a time when blood sugars are relatively stable (e.g., before breakfast, late afternoon). If the person has just eaten and the blood sugar is rising, or if the blood sugar is rapidly falling, the difference between the blood sugar value and the CGM value will be further apart. As a result, the CGM values will not match as well until another calibration is performed later in the day.

SENSOR PLACEMENT AND ADHESION

Placement: Each CGM company has suggestions for where to place their sensors. In general, they can be worn on the back of the arm, the abdomen, hips, or buttocks. The selected area must have enough skin/fat to be able to pinch up a little bit with two fingers. Sensors tend to stick best when inserted while the patient is standing up straight or lying down. This is to make sure that the skin and tissue are relaxed. It is best to avoid areas where the body bends or that are against the pants line. If the skin is hairy, a scissors or a razor can be used to trim the hair short. Finally, it is important to rotate sites so that the skin has time to breathe without tape on it. Using the same site repeatedly can lead to skin irritation and adhesion issues.

Skin preparation: Perhaps the most important tip to ensure a successful sensor insertion is to start with clean and dry skin. Although this sounds simple and obvious, sensors easily fall off skin that is oily, wet, or prone to sweating.

Adhesive use: There are many different adhesive wipes, tapes, and bandages that can help sensors to stick to skin. It is quite common for a person to use an adhesive wipe to treat the skin under the sensor, then place the sensor on the skin, and finally reinforce it with additional tape (Table 1). Many CGM companies recommend that a sensor not be inserted through an adhesive layer, so a small circle can be drawn on the skin to mark where the sensor is to be inserted. Then adhesive can be applied all around that adhesive-free circle. Every person is different, and what works for one person may not work for others. Some people may need all the help they can get to keep the sets in place, while others may only need reinforcements during particular activities or at specific times of the year. All people need to know the problem is not unique to one product and there are ways that can help improve the adhesion properties of each set. It may be helpful to review Table 1 with a diabetes nurse educator.

Table 1
Adhesive wipes, tapes, and bandages for CGM sensors

Adhesive wipes (from least sticky to most sticky) to be used underneath sensor tape

	IV Prep™ (Smith & Nephew)	Contains alcohol so may not need to wipe with alcohol first
	Bard wipes® (Bard)	Offers greater protection of skin
	Skin Prep™ (Smith & Nephew)	Offers protection of skin and some additional stickiness. Can be removed with Unisolve (Smith & Nephew)
	Skin Tac™ (Torbot)	Our most commonly used product because of higher degree of stickiness. Can be removed with Tac-Away (Torbot)
	Mastisol® (Ferndale)	Most sticky product listed here. Can cause some skin irritation, so only use if other products don't work. Can be removed with Detachol (Ferndale)

Adhesive Tapes: To use in addition to the sensor tape

Overbandages	*IV3000*™ (Smith & Nephew)	✔ Can place directly over the sensor and transmitter ✔ Can be cut into strips and then placed around the sensor/transmitter like a picture frame (Best for Navigator and DexCom). This helps to reinforce the sensor tape and prevent water from getting into tape creases.
	Tegaderm™ (3M)	✔ If skin is sensitive to the sensor tape, can be used under the sensor mount. *Note that a sensor cannot be inserted through tape, so a hole must be cut for the sensor to insert through.*
Medical tapes	*Transpore*™ (3M)	Use medical grade tapes with the "picture frame" technique described above.
	Hypafix™ (Smith & Nephew)	
	Silk Tape	
	Kinesio Sports Tape	

Bandages and additional support

	Coban™ (3M)	Wrap bandages are helpful for securing sensors to the arm. We suggest using this technique for people involved in sports or high levels of activity. The bandage can be wrapped around the arm with the sensor/transmitter, and comes in bright colors (which appeals to many children). It is important to unwrap these bandages when not needed and at night in order to give the skin a chance to breathe. A professional football player wore an ACE bandage over the sensor on his arm during practices!
	Co-Flex® (Andover)	
	ACE® *bandage*	

CGM DATA

There are two types of data that can be obtained from CGM usage. This chapter will not go into great detail on how to make insulin adjustments from the data. This is done in the 2nd edition of the book, *"Understanding Insulin Pumps and Continuous Glucose Monitors"* (see Ordering Materials in the back of this book).

The two types of information received from CGM are:

A. **Real Time CGM data:** These are the values displayed immediately as the current CGM glucose value is determined.

B. **Retrospective CGM data:** this is the glucose data previously collected and downloaded from the receiver to a computer program to help the user analyze glucose data over various periods (e.g., the past week or month).

Both Real Time and Retrospective data are important for the user and family. The person using the CGM can glance at the receiver throughout the day and see glucose values and trends (see below). We strongly encourage users/families to download Retrospective data at least weekly. Patterns of high or low glucose levels that occur at consistent times throughout the week can then be recognized. An insulin dose should generally not be changed unless a pattern is seen on two or more days in the week.

A. REAL-TIME CGM DATA

Different people use different aspects of the Real Time CGM data, and three examples will be presented here.

1. **Current CGM glucose values:** Knowing this value – for the user, or for the parent of a young child in the middle of the night – can be VERY reassuring. A system will soon be available from MiniMed (the MySentry System) in which the parents can see the values or hear alarms for high or low glucose values via a remote monitor in their bedroom.

2. **Real Time Trend Graphs:** Trend graphs show the line of previous glucose values over recent hours. For example, when a blood sugar value of 240 mg/dL (13.3 mmol/L) was detected, the person did not know if the values were climbing, falling or staying the same. Trend graphs (Figure 1) now enlighten the wearer and make appropriate treatment possible.

3. **Trend Arrows:** The trend arrows help to show how rapidly the change in glucose levels is occurring. A CGM value of 70 mg/dL (4.9 mmol/L) with trend arrows indicating a rapid rate of fall is more urgent than if a horizontal arrow is indicating a steady glucose level. Table 2 shows the meaning of the trend arrows for the three commonly used CGMs in the U.S.

Figure 1
Real –Time DexCom® SEVEN PLUS Trend Graphs

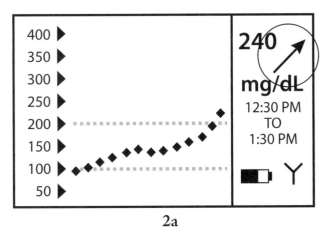

2a

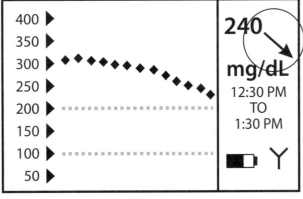

2b

Table 2
Trend arrows for the three CGM devices

Symbol on CGM	What it means	What to do with insulin
Medtronic*: ↑↑ Navigator®: ↑ (Abbott) SEVEN PLUS: ↑ or ↑↑ (DexCom)	RAPID RISE (Glucose rising >2 mg/dL [>0.11 mmol/L] per minute)	Increase dose by 20% (and possibly more if illness or ketones)
Medtronic: ↑ Navigator: ↗ (Abbott) SEVEN PLUS: ↗ (DexCom)	MODERATE RISE (Glucose rising 1-2 mg/dL [0.06-0.11 mmol/L] per minute)	Increase dose by 10% (and possibly more if illness or ketones)
Medtronic: none Navigator: → (Abbott) SEVEN PLUS: → (DexCom)	STABLE (Glucose level changing <1 mg/dL [<0.06 mmol/L] per minute)	No change in dose of rapid-acting insulin (unless illness or ketones are present)
Medtronic: ↓ Navigator: ↘ (Abbott) SEVEN PLUS: ↘ (DexCom)	MODERATE FALL (Glucose falling 1-2 mg/dL [0.06-0.11 mmol/L] per minute)	Decrease dose by 10% (and possibly more if post-exercise)
Medtronic: ↓↓ Navigator: ↓ (Abbott) SEVEN PLUS: ↓ or ↓↓ (DexCom)	RAPID FALL (Glucose falling >2 mg/dL [>0.11 mmol/L] per minute)	Decrease dose by 20% (and possibly more if post-exercise)

* Medtronic refers to the Guardian® or the Paradigm® REAL-Time systems.

B. RETROSPECTIVE CGM DATA

Retrospective CGM data comes from downloading the data in the receiver to a computer which then provides further insight into glucose data. We recommend that the retrospective data be evaluated by the person/family at least once weekly. Three examples of the use of Retrospective data will be presented here.

1. **Trend Graph Reports:** These reports give the CGM glucose values for each day as a continuous line for that day. Several days can be reported on the same graph with each day coded by a different colored line (see Figure 2). By comparing multiple days, it can be rather easy to detect a pattern of high or low glucose levels at specific times of day. Missed insulin boluses for meals are also often detectable.

2. **Pie Charts:** The pie charts show the percentage of glucose values that are high, in-range, or low for different periods of the day. Pie charts give rapidly-interpretable data for people who like visual presentations.

3. **Tables:** Tables can give much information. Data can include average glucose values and high and low values for different periods of the day. Standard deviations can be helpful in evaluating fluctuations of glucose levels.

Figure 2
Retrospective trend graph report

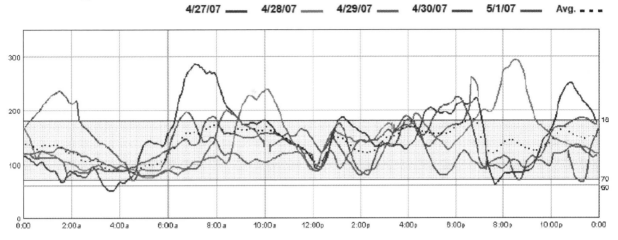

In summary, CGM provides a patient/family with a wealth of information about diabetes control that is not possible with blood sugar checking alone. The use of CGM can enhance both safety and collection of information. Different people/families will learn to use and favor different aspects of CGM. Although it should not be initiated until the person and family are ready for it, CGM often becomes the users' "best friend."

DEFINITIONS

Calibration: The entry of a blood sugar level into the CGM system to allow the subcutaneous glucose level to be adjusted to match the blood glucose level.

Continuous Glucose Monitor (CGM): A system consisting of a sensor, transmitter and receiver which determines subcutaneous glucose levels every 1 to 5 minutes.

Real Time Glucose Data: Information on the CGM receiver that indicates current glucose levels, direction of glucose change, and if glucose levels are currently too high or too low.

Retrospective Glucose Data: CGM data reviewed from past time periods. This can either be shown on the receiver or from a computer download of the CGM information.

QUESTIONS AND ANSWERS FROM NEWSNOTES

 We have been doing weekly downloads of our daughter's CGM tracings. She is frequently high after meals. Do you have suggestions?

The easiest change to make is to give her injections/boluses of rapid-acting insulin (Humalog, NovoLog or Apidra) 15 to 20 minutes prior to the meal. The rapid-acting insulins peak in 90-95 minutes whereas blood sugars from food peak in 60 minutes. A closer matching of the peaks helps to keep all glucose levels after meals below 180 mg/dL (<10 mmol/L) which is the current goal.

The Barbara Davis Center puts on a conference every other year to help with education of doctors, nurses, dieticians and psych-social staff from around the U.S. regarding childhood type 1 diabetes. A panel of four youth (names changed) currently using continuous glucose monitors (CGM) answered some questions from the audience:

 How long have you used the Continuous Glucose Monitor (CGM)?

 Charles (age 12): "I have been on it almost 3 ½ years."

Don (age 16): "I have used it about nine months."

Ken (age 7): "1½ years."

Nancy (age 13): "I have used it for a year."

Q **Do you wear your CGM 24/7?**

A Don and Nancy: "Yes." (Though Don noted he would occasionally takes a day or two off.)

Ken: "I mostly wear it when I have been having periods of high or low sugars."

Charles: "I wear it most of the time, but occasionally will take a week break."

Q **Do you have trouble with the sensors staying in?**

A Charles: "I use Mastisol with the Navigator and it stays on OK (even with ice hockey)."

Don: "I put Skin Tac beneath it and then put an IV-3000 cover over it and it stays in OK."

Nancy: "I use the MiniMed sensor with IV3000 over it. I swim with it and have even gone off the high dive and it has usually stayed in. I use an IV Prep before inserting and that is kind of sticky."

Ken: "I use the MiniMed sensor too and I usually put IV3000 over it."

Q **Can you or your parents hear the alarms for low sugar levels at night?**

A Charles: "I don't hear them, but my mom has a baby monitor and can hear the alarms at night."

Ken: "My parents have a monitor so they can hear the alarms in their bedroom."

Don: "I can usually hear them."

Nancy: "I sometimes hear them and will clear the alarm, but I don't remember what it was for in the morning."

Q **How do you deal with the alarms when you are at school?**

A Don: "I put it on vibrate, but it still makes some noise."

Nancy: "I put it on vibrate at school and it works great."

Ken: "Early on I got lots of alarms and I would go to the office and miss class."

Q **Do you like your CGM?**

A Don: "I didn't initially, but now I wouldn't be without it."

Nancy: "I really like it."

Ken: "Yes."

Charles: "No, but my parents do."

Q **Any other comments, youth or parents?**

A Charles's mom: "It has helped me to be able to sleep during the night."

Nancy: "It has helped keep my HbA1c in the sixes."

Don: "It helped me to see the highs after meals and taught me to give my food boluses 15 minutes before meals."

Ken's mom: "With Ken being younger and not having much fat, it has been a problem to find room on his bottom for both the pump and sensor. Real estate and alarms have been our two biggest issues."

Q **What do you like best about CGM?**

A Don: "Being able to go anywhere, anytime and know my number."

Charles: "When I am going out to play I know when I am low or high."

Nancy: "I can glance at it throughout the day to see if I'm in the target range."

Q **What do you like least about CGM?**

A Don: "The alarms are annoying and repetitive."

Charles: "Having to carry the receiver when I am out playing."

Nancy: "Sometimes it alarms for no reason. And sometimes when we start a new one it doesn't work."

Chapter 30
Pregnancy and Diabetes

H. Peter Chase, MD
Mary Voelmle, MS, FNP
David Maahs, MD, PhD

INTRODUCTION

This book has been used primarily by families of children with diabetes. Because of the increased readership recently by people of all ages, this brief chapter on pregnancy is included.

For a woman with diabetes, the best blood sugar control possible is most important before and during pregnancy. Normal or near-normal blood sugars reduces the risk of miscarriage and birth defects. Unfortunately, many women with (or without) diabetes do not plan their pregnancies. When possible, it is recommended that a continuous glucose monitor blood/CGM be used consistently during pregnancy.

High blood/CGM glucose levels can:

✔ increase the rate of birth defects (heart, spine, lip, etc.) during the first trimester

✔ result in the birth of large babies

✔ increase the risk for injury during delivery because of a baby's size

✔ increase the risk of developing high blood pressure, swelling of feet and protein leakage in urine (pre-eclampsia)

Proper planning for pregnancy will result in better HbA1c values before the beginning of pregnancy. Pregnancy should be delayed until the HbA1c is < 6.5 percent and folic acid has been taken for three months (see Section C).

TOPICS:
Preconception Care, Management During Pregnancy and Gestational Management

Monitoring

Prevent, Detect and Treat Acute Complications

Prevent, Detect and Treat Chronic Complications Through Risk Reduction

TEACHING OBJECTIVES:

1. Present the importance of preconception planning.

2. Define the aspects of intensive diabetes management.

3. Discuss the monitoring necessary to prevent complications.

LEARNING OBJECTIVES:

Learner (parents, significant other, relative or self) will be able to:

1. State the most important consideration when planning a pregnancy.

2. Name the four aspects of intensive diabetes management.

3. List the additional eye/kidney evaluations, clinic visits and monitoring required during pregnancy.

1. GLUCOSE (SUGAR) CONTROL

Intensive diabetes management is essential during pregnancy. *As discussed in Chapter 8, this involves:*

A. insulin pump therapy or multiple daily injections (MDI)

B. frequent blood/CGM monitoring

C. close attention to nutrition

D. frequent contact with the healthcare team

Although all four of these have been discussed in earlier chapters, some details related to pregnancy follow.

A. Insulin Pump Therapy or Multiple Daily Injections (MDI)

The two methods now usually used to normalize blood/CGM glucose levels are:

✔ the **insulin pump** (discussed in detail in Chapter 28). Early use of the pump is often recommended to improve sugar control during pregnancy. It is recommended that this be initiated before pregnancy.

✔ **multiple daily injections (MDI** – discussed under "Intensive Diabetes Management" in Chapter 8)

Most commonly, NPH (N) insulin is used for the intermediate-acting insulin in MDI. Three or four doses per day (in addition to Humalog or NovoLog) are often used (e.g., breakfast, lunch, bedtime).

Either method of intensive diabetes management (insulin pump or MDI) is capable of achieving near-normal glucose levels. Standard diabetes care (two shots a day, etc.) rarely achieves a normal or near-normal HbA1c and thus should not be a choice during pregnancy.

Lantus/Levemir Insulins

Hardly any insulin has been properly and prospectively studied during pregnancy. The safety of Lantus/Levemir use during pregnancy has not been established. However, isolated reports of using either during pregnancy with successful outcomes have been reported. Thus many physicians now allow patients to continue using Lantus or Levemir insulins during pregnancy.

Humalog/NovoLog/Apidra

There are a number of reports on the safety of rapid-acting insulins and most doctors now allow their use. Normalizing blood/CGM glucose levels after meals is very important. Higher blood/CGM glucose levels after meals have been associated with "big babies" and adverse outcomes. Numerous studies have shown Humalog/NovoLog or Apidra to be more effective for this purpose than Regular insulin. Humalog/NovoLog or Aprida should ideally be taken 20 minutes prior to the time when food is eaten. Use of a pen (Chapter 9) is a convenient way to do this for people choosing MDI.

B. Blood/CGM Glucose Measurements

Some suggestions:

✔ Blood/CGM glucose and HbA1c goals are given in Table 1.

✔ It is best to do 8 to 10 blood sugars per day as outlined in Table 1 (or use a CGM).

✔ The use of CGM is addressed in Chapter 29.

✔ HbA1c values between 5.0 and 5.8 percent, result in no increase risk of congenital anomalies in the baby.

✔ The values one and two hours after meals (Table 1) are important for optimal glucose control. Higher blood/CGM glucose levels after meals have been associated with big babies and adverse outcomes.

✔ Stay in close contact with the healthcare providers (see "D" in this Section). During pregnancy this should be at least weekly. (Tables for faxing or emailing are included in Chapters 7 and 28.)

✔ Checking blood/CGM glucose levels will allow the person to adjust their insulin dosages for different times during the pregnancy.

Table 1
Target Values for Plasma Blood Sugars and HbA1c Before and During Pregnancy*

Blood Sugars

	mg/dL	mmol/L
Fasting and premeal	60–99	3.3–5.4
1 hour after meal	< 129	< 7.3
2 hours after meal	< 129	< 7.3
2:00 a.m. - 6:00 a.m.	60–99	3.3–5.4
Meter average	100–130	5.5–7.3
HbA1c (%)	**< 6.0%**	

* Per ADA Consensus Statement: *Diabetes Care*, 31:1060, 2008

C. Nutrition

Nutrition is important during pregnancy and lactation. Carbohydrate counting and the other methods of food management are discussed in Chapter 12.

Special goals:

✔ Provide adequate calories for maternal and fetal weight gain. (This usually involves an additional 300 calories a day during the 2nd and 3rd trimesters and during lactation.) A 25 to 35 pound weight gain is optimal with pregnancy although this depends on the pre-pregnancy weight.

✔ Provide adequate vitamins and minerals (including iron and calcium). All women wanting to become pregnant should be certain they are taking 800 µg/day of folic acid (preferably for at least three months prior to pregnancy). This helps to prevent birth defects.

✔ Alcohol must be avoided to prevent fetal alcohol syndrome and serious congenital defects.

✔ Not smoking is important in reducing the risk for a premature or low-birth weight infant.

✔ The carbohydrate content of meals should be < 33% of calories.

✔ Regular meals and snacks are important to prevent hypoglycemia. The evening snack is important to prevent lows during the night and ketone formation.

D. Frequent Contact with the Healthcare Team

✔ The blood/CGM glucose values should be emailed weekly.

✔ Clinic visits will vary but are usually at least monthly.

✔ Care from a care-provider with knowledge in the areas of diabetes as well as of pregnancy is essential.

✔ Frequent contact with the eye doctor or kidney specialist may also be important (see Section 3).

2. PREVENTING ACUTE COMPLICATIONS

Low Blood Sugar

✔ Frequent blood/CGM glucose checking will help to prevent severe hypoglycemia.

✔ It is well recognized that severe insulin reactions occur more frequently with tight control (Chapter 6), especially at night with sleep.

✔ There has not been evidence that low blood sugars are damaging to the fetus.

✔ They are not pleasant for the mom, however, and should be avoided if possible.

🐾 Ketones

✔ Frequent blood/CGM glucose checking will also help to prevent ketone formation and acidosis (Chapter 15).

✔ Acidosis has been related to miscarriage and is important to avoid.

Ketones should be checked:

- anytime a fasting blood/CGM glucose is above 240 mg/dL (13.3 mmol/L)

- if a random sugar is above 300 mg/dL (16.7 mmol/L)

- every morning during pregnancy (see methods in Chapter 5)

3. PREVENTING CHRONIC COMPLICATIONS

A. Kidney (Renal) Damage

✔ Kidney damage does not usually worsen as a result of pregnancy in women who do not already have kidney damage. (This is in contrast to the movie, *"Steel Magnolias".*)

4 Women planning a pregnancy can do a urine microalbumin screening (and a blood creatinine) prior to pregnancy and after each trimester.

4 If the person **does** have some kidney damage already present, it can get worse.

The following are then suggested:

- Urine microalbumin and blood creatinine levels should be done every month.

- ACE-inhibitors (see Chapter 23) must be stopped (possible cause of birth defects) in any woman considering pregnancy. Use of other medications should also be evaluated.

- If blood pressure increases, other medicines should be used.

- During pregnancies, clinic visits every 2-4 weeks may be advised.

B. Eye (Retinal) Complications

✔ Women who have had diabetes < 5 years or who do not have eye (retinal) damage already present do not usually get eye damage due to pregnancy. They do need their eyes examined prior to the pregnancy and every three months.

✔ If a person already has moderate eye (retinal) damage from diabetes, this may worsen during pregnancy.

✔ If control (HbA1c) has not been optimal and improves dramatically, there is more risk for eye (retinal) changes. These women must be followed closely. The time interval for visits recommended by a retinal specialist is based on the amount of eye changes.

4. BIRTH

✔ Large babies (macrosomia) are a result of higher blood sugar levels in the mother.

✔ Glucose freely crosses the placenta to the baby resulting in increased insulin output from the fetal islet cells.

✔ Due to islet cell hyperplasia (increased size), babies after birth are at a higher risk of developing hypoglycemia (low sugar) and low calcium levels.

✔ Over 50 percent of deliveries are vaginal but many times large babies require a cesarean (C-) section.

5. GESTATIONAL DIABETES

Gestational diabetes is diabetes which occurs as a result of insulin resistance resulting from hormones from the placenta. After diagnosis, the care becomes similar to the care for the person who had diabetes prior to pregnancy.

Facts:

✔ Regular aerobic exercise and diet may help to lower blood sugars before and after meals.

✔ Insulin treatment may be necessary.

✔ Most women revert to normal glucose metabolism after pregnancy.

✔ Thirty to 50 percent of women will again have gestational diabetes with subsequent pregnancies.

✔ There is an increased risk of developing type 2 diabetes later in life.

DEFINITIONS

ACE-inhibitor: A blood pressure medicine often used to treat people with early diabetic kidney disease (Chapter 23). It must be discontinued if pregnancy is being considered.

Birth defects: Abnormalities in the newborn baby such as heart malformations, spinal cord abnormalities or lip or palate defects. These are more common if glucose control for the mother was suboptimal in the first trimester.

Folic acid: One of the B-vitamins that, when deficient in the pregnant mother, is related to birth defects in the baby.

Gestational diabetes: High glucose levels noted during pregnancy (most frequently in the last trimester). It is treated with diet, exercise and sometimes insulin. It usually reverses after pregnancy is over.

Intensive diabetes management: Diabetes treatment directed toward the goal of having blood sugar and HbA1c levels as close to normal as safely possible.

Microgram (µg): A common unit of weight in the metric system. It refers to one thousandth (0.001) of 1g.

Chapter 31
Research and Diabetes

TOPICS:

Research: A Cure

Prevention

Improved Monitoring

Delay of Complications

INTRODUCTION

Banting and Best received the Nobel prize for their discovery of insulin in 1921. It was believed that a "cure" for diabetes had been found. Before the discovery of insulin, people with the more severe form (now called type 1) lived only about one year. Insulin was not a "cure," but did save lives. Continued developments in the past three decades have resulted in great improvements in diabetes control and in lifestyle. These advances will likely continue in future decades.

Four Common Research Questions

The four questions about research asked most often are listed below:

1. When will there be a cure?

2. Will there be a "bionic" pancreas?

3. Can diabetes be prevented (type 1 or type 2)?

4. Are there advances in preventing diabetic complications?

There has been wonderful progress in diabetes research over the last ten years. The next ten years will likely show even more progress.

TEACHING OBJECTIVES:

1. Discuss current research related to type 1 and type 2 diabetes.

2. Present available research opportunities to families.

LEARNING OBJECTIVES:

Learner (parents, child, relative or self) will be able to:

1. List one current research study related to the individual's type of diabetes.

2. Name one research opportunity specific to the family.

1. WHEN WILL THERE BE A CURE?

The following research shows promise:

🐾 Islet Transplantation

In 2001, successful islet cell (the cells that make insulin) transplants were done in Edmonton, Alberta, Canada by Drs. A.M.J. Shapiro, E.A. Ryan, R.V. Rajotte and team.

All patients had "hard to manage" diabetes. Most were having severe insulin reactions (unconscious episodes or seizures) as a result of not recognizing lows ("hypoglycemic unawareness"). For this reason they were willing to take the three potent immunosuppressant medicines needed after receiving the transplant.

The most recent report on the "Edmonton Protocol" involved islet transplants in 325 adult recipients at many centers, sponsored by NIDDK and JDRF. Three years after their first islet transplant (most had two transplants), 23% were insulin injection-free, and 29%, although back on insulin injections, were still producing some insulin. However, the results have been somewhat variable, and some centers have discontinued their programs due to patient complications. In addition, it has now been reported that the three initial immunosuppressant medicines used in the "Edmonton-Protocol" were causing kidney damage. Thus, current research is focusing on the use of other anti-rejection medicines.

Dr. Bernhard Hering (University of MN) and his team have reported success for eight patients using just one donor pancreas per patient. Their method of preparing the islets differs from the Canadian group. They are also using a new anti-CD3 antibody to help prevent rejection. Five of their patients remained off insulin for more than one year.

However:

✔ there are not enough human-donor islets

✔ the medicines used to prevent rejection still cause side effects

✔ the medicines must be taken for the person's lifetime

✔ the medicines are costly

This procedure is currently used only in adults with diabetes that is hard to control. These people often have severe low blood sugars due to "hypoglycemic unawareness." With the advent of continuous glucose monitoring (CGM), it has been our experience that hypoglycemic unawareness can often be reversed.

The main goals for the future for islet transplantation involve:

✔ getting islets from an easier source (such as pig islets)

✔ continued evaluation of new medicines to prevent rejection

✔ investigating new medicines to allow "tolerance" of the new islets so that potent immunosuppressant medicines do not have to be taken indefinitely

✔ protecting the transplanted islets from the immune system so diabetes does not reoccur
A group in New Zealand, under the direction of Dr. Robert Elliott, is using islets from one-week-old pigs for transplantation. The islets are covered with alginate (from seaweed) to prevent white blood cells from getting into the islets and destroying them. No immunosuppressant medicines are being used. Although this research is still in a preliminary stage, it does offer hope.

🐾 Whole Pancreas Transplantation

Type 1 diabetes can be cured by a whole pancreas transplant. It is important to remember that in people with type 1 diabetes, the immune system will also attack the transplanted tissue. The medications needed are the same as those given after any organ is transplanted (e.g., kidney, liver, heart). The medicines have improved but still have harmful side effects. Some of these are:

✔ infections

✔ low white blood cell counts

✔ an increased risk for cancer

If a kidney transplant is needed due to kidney failure so that the immunosuppressant medicines are needed anyway, a pancreas transplant may also be done. This may be done at the time of the kidney transplant or at a later time. Approximately 80 percent of the whole pancreas transplants are still functioning after one year.

🐾 Stem-Cell Transplants

Families frequently ask about hope from stem-cell transplants. Unfortunately, this is taking longer to develop than initially anticipated. It is not likely to result in a "cure" for humans in the near future.

In summary, the most important goal at this time is to keep in optimal diabetes control. This will help prevent complications. Then, if a cure becomes possible, the person will be able to benefit from this miracle.

2. WILL THERE BE A "BIONIC" PANCREAS?

The "bionic" pancreas refers to a combination of a continuous glucose monitor (CGM) sending glucose data to a mini-computer, which then instructs an insulin pump to give more or less insulin based on the glucose values. These systems are already being studied in hospital settings. It will be some years, however, before complete "bionic" pancreas systems are approved for routine day-to-day use. This is due to many reasons, including difficulties with CGM accuracy at low glucose levels; the need to further develop computer algorithms (mathematical formulas) for insulin delivery; the need for a more rapid-acting insulin; and the Food and Drug Administration's (FDA) need to approve such devices.

In the meantime, it is likely that parts of the bionic pancreas will become available in the next few years. Because severe hypoglycemia is dangerous, the ability to stop an insulin infusion from an insulin pump with a low CGM glucose level, or even better, with a pending low CGM

glucose level, may be the first part of the partial bionic pancreas that is approved. In children, 75% of severe lows occur during sleep. Warning alarms during sleep are not heard 71% of the time. Thus, decreasing basal insulin or turning a pump off with actual or pending hypoglycemia during the night could be extremely valuable. It is known that the pump can be turned off for up to two hours without danger of ketone formation. Better warning alarms will also be valuable and are being developed.

3. CAN DIABETES BE PREVENTED?

🐾 Prevention of Type 1 Diabetes

It is now possible in many people to predict that diabetes will occur. This is done by measuring the following antibodies in the blood (see Chapter 3):

✔ insulin autoantibody (IAA)

✔ GAD-antibody

✔ ICA512 antibody

✔ ZnT8 (Zinc transport antibody)

✔ fluorescent ICA antibody

Type 1 Diabetes/TrialNet (T1D/TrialNet)

The National Institutes of Health (NIH), with assistance from the Juvenile Diabetes Research Foundation (JDRF) and the American Diabetes Association (ADA), have wisely decided to support research aimed at preventing diabetes. The assumption is that if you can recognize who is at risk years before disease onset (which is now possible), there must be some way to prevent the disease. A consortium of 18 centers in the U.S. and Canada and five centers in Europe and Australia are working together to identify people at high risk. Families having a first- or second-degree relative who started insulin treatment prior to age 40 years can receive free screening for the above antibodies.

Some exciting initial data suggested that

diabetes can be delayed by six to nine years in relatives with high levels of insulin autoantibodies (IAA) as a result of daily ingestion of oral insulin capsules. Similarly, data from Sweden showed that two injections (using an insulin syringe) of the GAD antigen might help to preserve insulin production in newly diagnosed subjects. Families must agree to participate in this research if they wish to be able to prevent diabetes in future generations.

The phone number to call to be screened is:

1-800-425-8361. More information is available on the website: www.diabetestrialnet.org.

The T1D/TrialNet consortium is also doing studies in people with recently-diagnosed diabetes to attempt to halt the destruction of the insulin-producing islet cells. It is now known that if a person continues to make some of their own insulin, the course of the diabetes will be easier and the eye and kidney complications, severe low blood sugars (Chapter 6), and ketoacidosis (Chapter 15) will all be less likely. Several immunosuppressive agents have already been found to have a protective effect, and these studies are continuing. The above number can be called for more information (or go to the website above).

A third approach is to try to prevent the initial autoimmune reaction against the islets from occurring (true prevention). As the group in which type 1 diabetes is increasing the most is children under age five years, studies starting early in life are important. The number above (or the website) can be contacted for more information.

🐾 **Prevention of Type 2 Diabetes**

The Diabetes Prevention Program (DPP) is discussed in Chapters 4 and 13. The DPP studied 3,234 people with impaired oral glucose tolerance tests. Although not yet diabetic, this group was close to having type 2 diabetes. The results of the DPP were released in 2002 (N Engl J Med 346:393-403, 2002).

Results:

✔ 30 minutes of activity five days per week with a low-fat diet and weight-loss **reduced the risk for developing type 2 diabetes by 58 percent**

✔ taking metformin (Glucophage) also reduced the chance of getting type 2 diabetes by 31 percent

People with a strong family history of type 2 diabetes now have a clear way to lessen their risk of getting this disease.

4. ARE THERE ADVANCES IN PREVENTING DIABETIC COMPLICATIONS?

The good news!

The life span for people with type 1 diabetes continues to improve.

✔ *The main reasons for this improvement are:*

- **improvement in overall glucose control**

- **lessened risk of developing diabetic kidney disease**

- **kidney disease diagnosed at an earlier stage**

- **treatment with ACE-inhibitors or other high blood pressure medicines**

- **treatment with lipid-lowering medicines (including statins)**

The bad news!

Families often do not bring in the two overnight urines for the kidney-microalbumin screening to detect kidney damage. The healthcare providers cannot always remember to ask people to do this.

If you or your child has had diabetes for:

✔ at least three years
and

✔ has reached puberty (usually 11-13 years of age)

The two overnight urines should be

collected every 12 months. Families must help by making sure this is done yearly. Directions for the collections can be found at the end of Chapter 23.

In summary, the life span and quality of life for people with diabetes keeps getting better! Reducing the risk of kidney disease is a major reason.

There is less kidney disease because …

✔ glucose control is better

✔ blood pressure control is better

✔ fewer people with diabetes are smoking

✔ with use of the **microalbumin determinations,** kidney damage is found earlier

✔ early kidney damage can be reversed before it becomes permanent

Another risk associated with type 1 or type 2 diabetes is cardiovascular disease (particularly heart attacks and stroke). Optimal sugar control, not smoking, regular exercise and control of blood pressure and blood lipids are all important in the prevention of cardiovascular disease.

DEFINITIONS

ADA: American Diabetes Association. This non-profit organization is involved with promoting care, education and research for type 1 and type 2 diabetes.

Bionic pancreas: A man-made device that would turn insulin off or on based on glucose levels. This type of device is currently in the research phase.

FDA: Food and Drug Administration.

JDRF: Juvenile Diabetes Research Foundation International. This non-profit organization helps to fund research on type 1 diabetes.

QUESTIONS AND ANSWERS FROM NEWSNOTES

  When is a cure coming?

I am asked this question almost daily in clinic. I do not know the answer other than to say that progress is being made.

 Which do you think will come first, a safe cure or the ability to prevent type 1 diabetes?

 A cure is, of course, already possible if one is willing to take the medicines that may be risky. If enough people are willing to enter studies such as Type 1 Diabetes/TrialNet, I would guess we will be able to prevent the onset of some cases of type 1 diabetes before we can easily and safely cure those who already have it.

Table 1

Type 1 Diabetes/TrialNet

People can call 1-800-425-8361 to find out the nearest place to go to obtain the free ICA screening test.

1. **Screening (Phase 1):** Islet cell antibody (ICA) tests

   The five antibodies that can be used in screening (see Chapter 3) are:
   - GAD antibody
   - ICA512
   - IAA (insulin autoantibody)
   - ZnT8 antibody
   - Fluorescent ICA (if one or more of the antibodies listed above are present)

   ✔ If one antibody is found, a second sample will need to be drawn to confirm the result. If the antibody is present in the second sample, then the person can enter Phase 2.

   ✔ If more than one antibody is present, a second sample can be drawn for confirmation OR the person can go directly into Phase 2.

2. **Phase 2:** The following tests are done:
   - Oral glucose tolerance test (OGTT) - to make sure diabetes isn't present
   - Islet cell antibody test (as described above)
   - HLA (looking for the 0602 protective gene)
   - HbA1c

   In a few cases an additional test, the intravenous glucose tolerance test (IVGTT), will be required:

   With all of the test results, the person can be provided with a risk level related to the devlopment of diabetes (within the next five years).

   The risk levels are: less than 25 percent, 25-50 percent and greater than 50 percent.

3. **Phase 3:** The Phase 2 tests (minus the HLA) are repeated every six months

4. **Oral Insulin Trial**

   Oral insulin was studied in the initial Diabetes Prevention Trial – Type 1 (DPT-1). Because a subgroup showed a favorable effect in delaying the onset of diabetes, a second study is now being done. The oral insulin trial is a double-blinded study in which the participants will receive either 7.5 mg of insulin or a placebo once daily and will not know which they are taking. The insulin taken by mouth does not have any low-blood sugar effect, as it is broken down into smaller particles by the stomach acid.

   The participants in this trial have a 25-50 percent chance of developing diabetes in the next five years. In order to enter this study, the Phase 2 test results must show:
   - a positive ICA test (x2)
   - a positive IAA (insulin autoantibody) test (x2)
   - normal insulin production on one IVGTT
   - no protective genes (HLA-DQ 0602)
   - a normal oral glucose tolerance test (OGTT)
   - a mixed meal test (MMT) is done shortly after entering the trial

Some day,
A CURE!

WEBSITES

Barbara Davis Center for Childhood Diabetes
University of Colorado Denver
Anschutz Medical Campus
Mail Stop A140
P.O. Box 6511
Aurora, CO 80045
303-724-2323 · Fax 303-724-6779
www.barbaradaviscenter.org

Children's Diabetes Foundation at Denver
www.childrensdiabetesfdn.org

Children With Diabetes
www.childrenwithdiabetes.com

Juvenile Diabetes Research Foundation
www.jdrf.org

American Diabetes Association
www.diabetes.org

Appendix I:
Glucose Conversion Between mg/dL and mmol/L

Parts of the world use one system, and other parts use the other system. This will allow the book to now be used by both. An easy way to make the conversion from mg/dL to mmol/L is to divide by 18. To convert mmol/L to mg/dL, multiply by 18. The table below may also help.

mg/dL	mmol/L	mg/dL	mmol/L	mg/dL	mmol/L	mg/dL	mmol/L
10 =	.6	125 =	7.0	240 =	13.3	355 =	19.7
15 =	.8	130 =	7.3	245 =	13.6	360 =	20.0
20 =	1.1	135 =	7.5	250 =	13.9	365 =	20.3
25 =	1.4	140 =	7.8	255 =	14.2	370 =	20.6
30 =	1.7	145 =	8.0	260 =	14.5	375 =	20.8
35 =	2.0	150 =	8.3	265 =	14.7	380 =	21.1
40 =	2.3	155 =	8.5	270 =	15.0	385 =	21.4
45 =	2.5	160 =	8.9	275 =	15.3	390 =	21.7
50 =	2.8	165 =	9.2	280 =	15.6	395 =	21.9
55 =	3.0	170 =	9.5	285 =	15.8	400 =	22.2
60 =	3.3	175 =	9.8	290 =	16.1	425 =	23.6
65 =	3.6	180 =	10.0	295 =	16.4	450 =	25.0
70 =	3.9	185 =	10.3	300 =	16.7	475 =	26.4
75 =	4.2	190 =	10.5	305 =	16.9	500 =	27.8
80 =	4.5	195 =	10.8	310 =	17.2	525 =	29.2
85 =	4.7	200 =	11.1	315 =	17.5	550 =	30.5
90 =	5.0	205 =	11.3	320 =	17.8	575 =	31.9
95 =	5.3	210 =	11.6	325 =	18.0	600 =	33.3
100 =	5.5	215 =	11.9	330 =	18.3	625 =	34.7
105 =	5.8	220 =	12.2	335 =	18.6	650 =	36.1
110 =	6.1	225 =	12.5	340 =	18.9	675 =	37.5
115 =	6.4	230 =	12.8	345 =	19.2	700 =	38.9
120 =	6.7	235 =	13.0	350 =	19.4		

Appendix II:
Shopping List and Approximate Cost of Diabetes Supplies

Supplies	Cost in Dollars
Equipment for Injections	
Regular	50.00
NPH	50.00
NovoLog	110.00
Humalog	110.00
Lantus or Levemir	100.00
Alcohol Sponges (Box of 100)	2.50
BD Lo Dose Insulin Syringes (Box of 100)	30.00
Or	
Monoject 1cc Insulin Syringes (Box of 100)	30.00
NovoLog Pen	45.00-50.00 each
Humalog Pen	45.00-50.00 each
Lantus/Levemir Pen	40.00-50.00 each
Equipment for Urine Testing	
Ketodiastix #100	22.00
Ketodiastix #50	10.00
Ketostix #100	20.00
Ketostix #50	12.00
Ketostix #20 (foil wrapped)	7.00
Chemstrip uGK #100	13.00
Chemstrip K #25	20.00
Equipment for Blood Glucose Testing	
Finger stick device	10.00-25.00
Lancets (Box of 200)	11.00
One Touch Strips #100	100.00
Freestyle Lite #100	110.00
Precision Xtra Strips	50.00
Blood Glucose Monitor (with memory)	70.00-140.00
Chemstrip BG #50	35.00
Miscellaneous Supplies	
Insta-Glucose	4.00
BD Glucose Tablets	2.50
Identification bracelet or necklace	2.50-20.00
Glucagon	150.00

Index

DISCLOSURES

Dr. Maahs received funds in the past year from
Abbott Diabetes Care, Eli Lilly, USA, LLT, and
Merck & Co., Inc.

ORDERING MATERIALS

Additional copies of *Understanding Diabetes*
as well as other diabetes informational material may be ordered by using this form,
by calling the Children's Diabetes Foundation at 303-863-1200 or 800-695-2873,
or by visiting our website at www.ChildrensDiabetesFoundation.org

---

Children's Diabetes Foundation
777 Grant Street • Suite 302 • Denver, CO 80203

Name_____

Address_____

City, State, ZIP_____

Phone_____Email_____

Quantity	Item	Price	Total
	Understanding Diabetes – "The Pink Panther Book" 12th Edition	$20.00	
	Understanding Insulin Pumps and Continuous Glucose Monitors – Second Edition	$18.00	
	A First Book for Understanding Diabetes Presents the essentials from *Understanding Diabetes* in synopsis-fashion.	$10.00	
	Un Primer Libro Para Entender La Diabetes Spanish version of *A First Book for Understanding Diabetes*	$10.00	
	VIDEO: Managing Diabetic Hypoglycemia Offers people with diabetes of all ages and backgrounds practical suggestions for how they can manage and prevent low blood sugar during a busy, productive day.	$20.00	
	Colorado residents add 7.72% sales tax	TAX	
	Shipping: $3.00 per order		
		TOTAL	

☐ Please include me on the Children's Diabetes Foundation mailing list.
☐ Check enclosed payable to: The Guild-CDF at Denver
☐ VISA   ☐ MasterCard   ☐ Discover

Card # _____ Exp. Date _____

Signature _____

All orders must be paid in full before delivery.
Books are mailed USPS or Ground UPS. Allow one to three weeks for delivery.

Canadian and Foreign Purchasers:
Please include sufficient funds to equal U.S. currency exchange rates.

For quantity order pricing and additional information call 303-863-1200 or 800-695-2873
or visit our website at: www.ChildrensDiabetesFoundation.org

NOTES

NOTES